A READER ON PR

M000317242

Every Sunday all over the world people rise up and cl[...] [...]eak in the [...] of God [...] astonishing thing to do and an astonishing claim to make. It is small wonder that the sermon has been the focus of debate, discussion and investigation. It has been dismissed as irrelevant in today's culture and has become the butt of numerous jokes and caricatures. Yet the claim persists that these human words in some way can become God's message to these hearers.

This collection of twenty-nine articles by international experts in the area of homiletics coincides with the revival of interest in preaching over the last twenty-five years. It is practical without being merely tips for preachers; and it offers the necessary theoretical discussion for anyone who wants to take the art of preaching seriously. No important issue has been omitted and, taken as a whole, the book constitutes a first class introduction to the principles, processes, context and theology of preaching.

Contributors include: Walter Brueggemann, David Buttrick, Fred Craddock, Edward Farley, John Killinger, Richard Lischer, Thomas Long, Elaine Lawless, Jolyon Mitchell, Cheryl Sanders and Thomas Troeger.

Explorations in Practical, Pastoral and Empirical Theology

Series Editors: Professor Leslie J. Francis, University of Wales, Bangor, UK
and Professor Jeff Astley, Director of the North of England Institute for Christian Education,
Durham, UK

Theological reflection on the church's practice is now recognized as a significant element in theological studies in the academy and seminary. Ashgate's series in practical, pastoral and empirical theology seeks to foster this resurgence of interest and encourage new developments in practical and applied aspects of theology worldwide. This timely series draws together a wide range of disciplinary approaches and empirical studies to embrace contemporary developments including: the expansion of research in empirical theology, psychological theology, ministry studies, public theology, Christian education and faith development; key issues of contemporary society such as health, ethics and the environment; and more traditional areas of concern such as pastoral care and counselling.

A Reader on Preaching

Making Connections

edited by

DAVID DAY
Formerly Principal
St John's College with Cranmer Hall
Durham, UK

JEFF ASTLEY
Director
North of England Institute for Christian Education
Durham, UK

LESLIE J. FRANCIS
Professor of Practical Theology
University of Wales, Bangor, UK

ASHGATE

© The editors and contributors, 2005

All rights reserved. No part of this publication may be reproduced, stored in a retrieval system, or transmitted in any form or by any means, electronic, mechanical, photocopied, recorded, or otherwise without the prior permission of the publisher.

Published by
Ashgate Publishing Limited
Wey Court East
Union Street
Farnham
Surrey GU9 7PT
England

Ashgate Publishing Company
Suite 420
101 Cherry Street
Burlington, VT 05401-4405
USA

Ashgate website: http://www.ashgate.com

British Library Cataloguing in Publication Data
A reader on preaching : making connections. – (Explorations in practical, pastoral
    and empirical theology)
    1. Preaching
    I. Day, David, 1936–   II. Astley, Jeff   III. Francis, Leslie J.
    251

Library of Congress Control Number: 2004007477

Reprinted 2006, 2009, 2012

ISBN 978 0 7546 5009 6 paperback

MIX
Paper from
responsible sources
FSC
www.fsc.org   FSC® C018575

Printed and bound in Great Britain by the
MPG Books Group, UK

Contents

Preface

This publishing project began in Durham some years ago when David Day, then Principal of St John's College with Cranmer Hall, and Jeff Astley, Director of the North of England Institute for Christian Education (NEICE), collaborated in developing a bibliographical database of journal articles on preaching. They were assisted in this work by Paul Cubitt, a postgraduate student at St John's.

The database became available in an interactive form as part of the BIBCEREP database housed at NEICE, and in hard copy as a joint publication by NEICE and the St John's College Centre for the Study of Christian Communication (*Resourcing the Word: A Select Bibliography on Preaching*, 1997). The great majority of the articles identified at this time were in journals that were not readily available to students, teachers or preaching practitioners. As a response, Astley and Day joined forces with Leslie Francis (of the University of Wales, Bangor) to produce this anthology. The unholy editorial trinity embarked on the long task of selecting, sourcing, editing and compiling a collection of good quality writing on the principles, theology and process of preaching, in order to make this material more accessible to a wider readership. The editors were greatly assisted in the task of identifying suitable material by an international network of correspondents, which included Peter Adam, Walter J. Burghardt, David G. Buttrick, Charles Campbell, Richard Lischer, John S. McClure, John Stott, Roger Van Harn and Stephen Wright. We are grateful to these scholars for widening our own perspectives on preaching and making us aware of the wide range of articles in this field. Our thanks also go to those who have helped to shape this text for publication, including Sarah Lloyd and Ellen Keeling from Ashgate Publishing; Brad Embry, Evelyn Jackson and Declan O'Sullivan from NEICE; Paul Cubitt from St John's College, Durham; and Jane Lankshear and Mandy Robbins from the University of Wales, Bangor.

Jeff Astley
David V. Day
Leslie J. Francis

Foreword

The Bishop of Durham, the Rt Revd Dr N. T. Wright

'Oh, the *sermon*.' The tone of voice is patronizing, almost sneering. Some people, the speaker implies, still like that kind of thing, and we can't decently abolish it altogether. But it is, at best, a necessary evil, something to be got over as quickly as possible. The shorter the better, and don't make a fuss about it.

I have heard that tone of voice often enough. Sometimes people scoff at sermons simply because none of their regular pulpit-occupiers can preach their way out of a paper bag. Sometimes, more worryingly, they are making a direct attack on the underlying theology of preaching, the idea that a fresh word from God should strike a path through the congregation and make us think new and dangerous thoughts.

Equally, there are plenty of churches that know they should have a sermon, and preferably a good solid one, but have forgotten exactly what it is. It isn't a lecture, though it may contain some elements of teaching laid out systematically. It isn't a string of friendly anecdotes (a sort of Sunday Morning at the London Palladium) with a spiritual point added for good measure. It isn't simply an exposition of Scripture, though Scripture should be part of its very fabric, woven in by one of the many appropriate means. A sermon, as Barth used to insist, is an *event*. Something *happens* when a sermon is preached.

Does it work automatically? No, of course not. We can hardly hold an *ex opere operato* theory of the sermon, though God in his mercy can and does speak to people even through badly prepared, poorly pondered and stumblingly delivered sermons. (My teacher, the Congregationalist George Caird, used to say that Anglican sermons could usually do with another half an hour in the oven.) It is tempting to go for an *ex opere operantis* theory instead, since a sermon demands the full personal engagement of the preacher at every level. The well-known phenomenon of the 'parsonic voice' comes, I fear, when preachers are not fully engaged, when they allow a gap to open up between what they feel bound to say and what they truly believe. But the success of the sermon is never simply a function of the preacher's skill. That could, and sometimes does, lead to personality cults.

No: the sermon does what it does because the true God is a speaking, communicating God whose warm, creative breath became human in Jesus of Nazareth. The sermon, through the Spirit's power, is part of the continuing work of God in becoming incarnate. More: as the incarnate God died and was raised, so the sermon by its very existence, as well as in anything specific it might say, announces God's judgment on the careless and idolatrous world, and plants the seeds of new creation. The very fact of the sermon is part of a truly biblical theology of the church, the people who live under God's word. The content, infinitely variable at one level, must, however implicitly, reflect this structural role.

No wonder those whose theology avoids the sharp edges of Calvary and Easter don't want to give the sermon more than grudging admission. No wonder, too, that those who have made Christianity comfortable allow the sermon to decline into a spiritual pep talk or a vaguely Christianized comment on current affairs. No wonder, though, that those who take seriously their calling to listen with every fabric of their being to the living God, and to speak with all their skill of his love and grace in the Gospel, find it exhausting but exhilarating. My hope and prayer is that this book will be of real help in challenging the first two approaches, and in encouraging and directing the third.

+Thomas Dunelm
Epiphany 2004

Six Feet Above Contradiction? An Overview

David Day

Surveying the field

The articles which are reprinted in this volume mirror the revolution which has taken place in homiletics over the last 30 years. There is widespread agreement that the beginning of this revolution may be dated from the publication of Fred B. Craddock's *As One Without Authority*.[1] In that book Craddock set many hares running and homileticians have been in hot pursuit ever since.

Clearly a collection of this length cannot aspire to an exhaustive treatment of recent developments but the articles touch upon most of the main movements and new emphases of the homiletical revolution. Even so, it must be conceded that there is virtually nothing on black preaching, preaching within the Roman Catholic tradition or preaching in Africa, the Far East or South America. Indeed, most contributors reflect the American scene, largely because it is in the United States that most of the serious thinking and writing about preaching has taken place. Professors of homiletics are relatively numerous in America, universities foster higher degree research in homiletics and an active conference scene ensures that current theories (and fads) are subject to critical scrutiny and debate. Despite the efforts of the College of Preachers, Spurgeon's College[2] and the Proclamation Trust, no one could pretend that preaching receives the same attention in the United Kingdom. Chairs in homiletics are virtually unknown, few theological colleges devote much time or serious research to the subject in their curricula and little academic work has been published since the great classics of the past.[3]

A volume such as this is of considerable value, therefore, not least because there is welcome evidence in the United Kingdom of a revival of interest in the preacher's craft and a renewed willingness to work at the business of sermon design and delivery. Certainly, no writer in this collection assumes that the sermon will be prepared hastily on a Saturday evening or concluded in eight minutes flat. The authors thus constitute conversation partners for British preachers, resourcing their work and inviting them to pursue the study of homiletics with greater energy and rigour. Moreover, since most of the articles appeared first in journals which are difficult for the British reader to access, the collection offers a convenient overview of the volume of work, theoretical and practical, that has been produced in recent years on the subject of preaching. In many cases the authors published the article as a first draft of material which appeared later as part of, or as the main thesis of, a book. Taken as a whole then, the *Reader* will serve as a map of the present state of homiletics.

One way of characterizing the contents is to see them as an extended conversation on the twin themes of communication and power.

The issue of communication

In terms of communication, the 1960s saw the widespread marginalization of the sermon, precisely because the monologue seemed a grossly inadequate tool of communication. Experimental forms of communication took centre stage. Many of these experiments flourished briefly and then withered, but the issue they were intended to address has persisted. Communication theory lays heavy emphasis on what the listener brings to the party and presses traditional preaching to take more seriously the role of the congregation as processors of what is heard. The concept of feedback has become correspondingly important. At the same time, in a media-saturated society visual immediacy and shortened concentration spans also demand a new mode of address.

Parallel with these developments the last 30 years have seen growing dissatisfaction with conventional wisdom about the sermon. The driving force behind this feeling is a desire to be more faithful to the gospel. It has produced a fresh examination of the role of the scriptures, and a wish to articulate more precisely the homiletical move from text to sermon, exploring the question, 'In what way can this ancient text speak to us today?' This concern has also focused on the craft of the sermon and has led to a search for rhetorical strategies which will be responsive to the nature of the scriptures and the gospel, together with a concentration on image, form, structure, narrative and movement.

The Issue of power

Questions of power have arisen in a variety of ways. For example, a recent book by David Norrington[4] has brought to the surface what many had suspected for some time. Arguing that preaching disempowers the people of God, he calls for a new emphasis on the congregation as partners in the enterprise. The demand for dialogue and conversation reappear, but now not so much as communicative strategies as ways of dismantling the privileged position of the preacher.

The allegation that the preacher is 'six feet above contradiction' has had the effect of putting the nature of the sermon under scrutiny. It has provoked inquiry into the ethics of preaching, raised issues of manipulation and led to the questioning of rhetoric as a contaminated tool. Of course, all this is in conflict with those who hold a high view of pulpit authority. From within an authoritative tradition the message can be transmitted from on high, almost thrown like a stone at the congregation. It is fair to say, however, that reflection on the preacher as a human being has led to some interesting suggestions about vulnerability and woundedness as valuable elements in the message.

Even at the end of the 30-year period male preachers are still very much in the majority and this has given a new dimension to the debate about the sermon as an instrument of oppression. Is it but another example of male dominance? What effect have feminist theology and feminist homiletics had on preaching? Do women bring something distinctive and different to the preaching event?

These issues of communication and power are being worked through in different ways within four main foci of inquiry – Scripture, the sermon, the preacher and the hearers.

Focusing on scripture

There has been a return to the scriptures as the proper subject matter for preaching. This is not to say that topical and thematic sermons are never to be found, but writing on preaching increasingly finds home ground in the biblical text. A specific passage is likely to define the scope of the sermon. This development marks a move away from *texts* in the sense of single verses, often used as pegs on which to hang blessed thoughts, and *topics*, as the free-ranging exploration of themes suggested by the passage. It is only fair to observe that Edward Farley has argued against the current fashion of preaching from a passage.[5] In his view preachers are unhelpfully restricted by their need to build a bridge from the what-is-preached of the passage to a specific congregation. He observes that biblical preaching as evidenced by the New Testament consists of preaching the gospel not bits of Scripture. However, at present Farley seems not to have carried most homileticians with him.

The commitment to the scriptures as the proper source of the sermon usually carries with it a commitment to a canonical view of the Bible. This too marks a move away from historico-critical interests in the pre-history of the text or a concern with 'what really happened'. For example, fishing, in the style of the Jesus Seminar, for authentic words and deeds of Jesus supposedly to be found floating around in the text of the Gospels leaves the preacher with very little worth preaching about. By contrast, the acceptance of the canon as the corpus of material by which the church is shaped and nourished has encouraged a renewed interest in redaction criticism as a tool for discovering the distinctive purposes of each Gospel.

An emphasis on Scripture as canon has encouraged an interest in the Bible as a literary work, to be read as a cunningly crafted piece of persuasion. For example, Craddock's commentary on Luke's Gospel in the *Interpretation* series points out that Luke is primarily a preacher.[6] Once this is accepted, literary rather than historical questions come to the fore. A Gospel is a portrait of Jesus and the preacher wants to see the lineaments of this portrait as clearly as possible. The question of how far this portrait corresponds to the historical Jesus is not without interest, but in the first instance the preacher wants to see Jesus *through Luke's eyes.* If Luke's witness to Jesus is of fundamental importance, then the kind of commentaries which will be prized are those which take the readers into narrative criticism, which use social and cultural information to help them feel the force of actions and words within the story, and which show how this specific unit of material contributes to Luke's larger purpose.

Related to this interest is the recognition that Scripture is not primarily a receptacle of information about God and the world. Scripture was written with the intention of effecting change. It does things as well as says things; it has a function as well as a focus. 'What is this text trying to do?' has become a critical question.

Homiletics has accepted the hermeneutical principle that texts are polyvalent, that is, they are open to many meanings, and that the standpoint of the preacher materially affects the reading of the text. At the same time, it has not abandoned the hermeneutic of retrieval: 'What did this text mean?' is still a proper question to ask.

A focus on hermeneutics in the service of homiletics has led to widespread suspicion of the notion that every biblical text contains a main idea which may be distilled and ought to be the proper subject of the sermon. Most preachers have come to terms with the idea that many texts exhibit *movement* and that the 'meaning and the message' are carried not only by ideas and propositions but also, and sometimes more powerfully, by genre, form, sequence and linearity.

Focusing on the sermon

There has been a renewed interest in the sermon as proclaiming a word of grace, rather than giving information or offering the listeners second-hand opinions on current political issues or ethical debate. This development has reinstated the ministry of the word and has located the sermon firmly within worship. It ought not, therefore, to be supplanted by discussion groups or viewed solely as a preliminary to the real business of the sacrament. James Thompson has vigorously pleaded for the reinstatement of the sermon as a vehicle of pastoral direction and care, deploring the tendency to separate preaching from the work of the pastoral counsellor.[7] Others have argued for attention to be given to the proper place of the sermon within the Eucharist. In this regard the writings of Walter Burghardt and Mary Catherine Hilkert are significant.[8]

A vigorous debate has taken place about how to make the move from text to sermon in a responsible way. This has involved criticism not just of classical approaches, often heavily dependent on allegorization and spiritualization, but also of more recent methods such as using the passage to identify one preachable theme or distilling 'the main idea'.[9] It is widely acknowledged that there is no failsafe method of effecting the transition, a sermon cannot be 'read off' from a biblical text. There is a greater willingness to recognize that even the first reading of the biblical text takes place in the presence of the (unseen) congregation and that the preacher brings to the passage a set of pre-suppositions which affect his or her reading of it. It is likely that more attention will be given to the importance of a leap of imagination on the part of the preacher which will effect a fresh hearing of the text for a specific congregation.[10]

While preachers have always come to the Bible for the content of their sermons they are now encouraged to study the scriptures for help with method and style. Ever since Thomas Long's slim volume on preaching the biblical forms, there has been a willingness to listen to the biblical text not just for what it says but also for the way it says it.[11] As a result sermon construction has become more responsive to the genre, form, mood and shape of the scriptural passage and is more likely to take account of those elements when plotting the form, movement and mood of the sermon.[12]

There has been a new interest in the craft of the sermon which has been underpinned by serious theoretical reflection. Conventional lore and 'tips for preachers' have received critical scrutiny. David Buttrick's magisterial work on *Homiletic* marks a watershed in the application of theory to the practice of sermon construction.[13] But even before him, Craddock's *Preaching* had opened up the subject in new ways.[14] The systematic study of design and technique has disposed of much traditional pulpit wisdom. A brisker, more rigorous, empirical and theoretical inquiry has made problematic much that used to be confidently asserted about sermon structure, openings, humour, personal anecdotes, illustrations and endings. A notable concern has been that of sermon shape and form. Eugene Lowry's two volumes have probably done as much as anything to bring this issue to prominence.[15] Can the shape of the sermon reflect the movement of the gospel itself? Lowry believes it can and should. At the same time the power of story and its presence in the Bible has given narrative preaching a new importance. Calvin Miller, William Bausch, Richard Eslinger and Lowry himself have all made significant contributions to this debate.[16] Particularly noteworthy has been the move to reinstate rhetoric. Denying the existence or disparaging the importance of rhetoric are moves made only by those who are naïve or disingenuous. Sermons aim to do something, they are in the business of persuasion. Homiletics needs to take account of rhetoric in order to ensure that it is used skilfully, self-consciously, purposefully, responsibly and with integrity.[17]

Focusing on the preacher

The pulpit is a place of power and it is not surprising that much writing has concentrated on the role of the preacher, particularly when he is male, white and western, himself a representative of the mighty who are due to be put down from their seats. There is little in this volume about black preaching or about preaching which takes place in a non-western context, but the articles on women as preachers raise some of the issues which need to be addressed. A good deal of interest centres on whether preaching by women is distinctively different from that by men. A collection of sermons by Heather Walton and Susan Durber suggests that it may be.[18] The sermons encourage us to conclude that women bring different attitudes and assumptions into the pulpit, that they have developed new ways of doing theology and handling biblical texts and, in many cases, demonstrate distinctively different styles of preaching. The authors argue that ways of speaking which men have found 'new' (use of imagination, self-conscious taking account of context, telling of stories) have always been characteristic of women, and that as women begin to find their own voice in the pulpit so their hearers will hear old texts in fresh and enlivening ways and be drawn to consider some topics which have never been adequately treated before.

Perceiving the preacher as a figure of power and authority raises ethical issues. The pulpit can easily become a place of manipulation or self-display. Alvin Rueter's article in this volume identifies areas where the preacher can easily and undetectably be less than honest. Some discussion has centred on the question of authority. Is there a proper authority which flows from the nature of the preaching task and is to be contrasted with mere authoritarianism? In what accents should the preacher speak? Is the sermon to be proclaimed and declaimed, or should preachers attempt a more dialogic stance in keeping with the image of companions on a journey? Are sermons to be so tightly structured and clearly organized that no one could penetrate beneath the surface, or should they reveal something of the wrestling with the text which went into their preparation? How far should the preacher expose his or her humanity? This issue has surfaced even in the discussion of something as apparently trivial as the personal anecdote. This is much beloved of preachers yet Buttrick and Eslinger both counsel against its use. In their view, personal revelations are fraught with danger. Displaying the preacher as hero or victim distracts the listeners from the central purpose of the sermon. In the case of intimate revelations the congregation is either desperate to leave the church or wants to offer the preacher therapy. The impact of such anecdotes will overpower the point they are intended to illustrate. Against this view, Troeger and Hans van der Geest suggest that the preacher's acknowledgement of his or her humanity and the willingness to reveal woundedness and vulnerability are crucial to making contact with the congregation. For them personal authenticity is the pre-condition of theological credibility.[19]

Focusing on the hearers

A good deal of work in this area has concentrated on the power of the mass media and has evidenced anxiety about the context in which preaching takes place. If we live in a media-saturated society, can traditional modes of communication continue to operate effectively? The work of Jolyon Mitchell, a sample of which is included in this collection, takes seriously the need to adapt our preaching to a new kind of situation. He argues that we must move from 'single camera to multi-camera discourse', from proclamatory to conversational discourse, from visual to multi-sensorial discourse. Many of the ideas which appear in this article have been developed in much greater detail in Mitchell's book, *Visually Speaking*.[20]

At the beginning of this introduction it was suggested that communication theory has highlighted the critical role played by those who receive the message. No communication has taken place, it may be claimed, until the message has been processed. The listeners are not passive; they are not receptacles into which the communication may be poured. As every preacher knows, sometimes to his or her chagrin, each listener processes the message in a personal and idiosyncratic way. This is often a cause for concern if not despair. It has led to a renewed interest in strategies for ensuring that the preacher gain insight into the thought worlds of the congregation and take account of differing personality types within a single group of listeners.[21] The issues of feedback after the sermon and collaboration before the sermon have also been the subject of a number of studies. For example, Roger van Harn has explored the idea of 'pew rights' and the shift in perspective which occurs when the sermon is seen from the standpoint of the listeners.[22] His 'daily diary' technique constitutes a strategy for both collaboration and feedback. Leonora Tubbs Tisdale has recommended that the preacher 'exegete the congregation'. In her view, those who design sermons are to become 'amateur cultural anthropologists, studying and interpreting the symbols of congregational life in order to gain greater understanding of congregational subcultural identity'.[23] Can this interest in the congregation be taken further? Communication is only part of what is at stake; is it possible to address the issue of empowerment? Here John McClure's work has been seminal. 'The roundtable pulpit' offers a way in which the hearers can directly affect the substance of what is to be preached and can be, as it were, at the preacher's elbow throughout the preaching of the sermon.[24]

How do sermons do their work? Does it matter that they are so quickly forgotten? There has been a modest amount of empirical work devoted to this question, of which some is included in this volume. But much still proceeds on the basis of experience and reflection. As a result, a good deal of attention has been given to the power of imagination, the construction of images and the turn towards narrative to which reference has already been made.[25] Walter Brueggemann is an Old Testament specialist who has concerned himself with issues of preaching. He asks what it is about sermons which changes people, and concludes his reflections by giving pride of place to images:

> In a conversation wherein doctrinal argument and moral suasion are operative, people in fact change by the offer of new models, images and pictures of how the pieces of life fit together – models, images and pictures that characteristically have the particularity of narrative to carry them. Transformation is the slow, steady process of inviting each other into a counterstory about God, world, neighbor, and self.[26]

Preaching normally takes place in the context of worship and the life of the church. In some traditions the sermon has been magnified at the expense of the sacrament, in others it has been reduced to a few thoughts as a preliminary to the main business. It is unfortunately not unknown for sermon and sacrament to be pulled apart so that there is no particular connection between them. Buttrick's article in Part 6 of this collection represents the concern of many scholars, from a variety of traditions, to articulate the function of the sermon in joining Word, Eucharist and Community in one celebration. Against preaching which assumes that the congregation needs to be battered, cajoled, persuaded and reconverted, recent writing on liturgical preaching has rightly stressed the sermon's role in the formation of community identity.[27]

Conclusion

If this survey approximates to anything like the actual state of affairs, then the study of preaching and writing about homiletics is in good health. Obviously, in itself that is not enough. Every preacher hopes not just that the homiletics industry will flourish but that the sermon will be similarly healthy, able to perform its function under God of giving life and nourishment to the hearers. Some recent publications suggest a new confidence in preaching.[28] Authors write optimistically about scrutinizing the post-modern context and discovering how messages are communicated by those who live in a radically different world. Others indicate that we have hardly begun to allow the insights of women and black preachers to affect the way we preach. A number of writers have started to explore more deeply the question of congregational interaction with the preacher, particularly in contexts of cultural diversity. All such contributions witness to a continuing conversation that is not aridly theoretical but which informs the practice of preaching and is, in turn, informed and shaped by it.

Notes

1 Fred B. Craddock, *As One Without Authority*, Enid, OK, Phillips University Press, 1971; reprinted Nashville, TN, Abingdon, 1979.

2 A welcome initiative is the MTh in Preaching offered jointly by the College of Preachers and Spurgeon's College.

3 See, for example, the writings of Martyn Lloyd Jones, W. E. Sangster, John Stott, Colin Morris and

Donald Coggan. For more recent works on preaching within a British context, see Christopher Green and David Jackman (eds), *When God's Voice is Heard*, Leicester, Inter-Varsity Press, 1995; David Brindley, *Story, Song and Law,* Swindon, British and Foreign Bible Society, 1996, David Day, *A Preaching Workbook,* London, SPCK, 1998.

4   David C. Norrington, *To Preach or Not to Preach?*, Carlisle, Paternoster, 1996.

5   Edward Farley, 'Preaching the Bible and Preaching the Gospel', *Theology Today*, 51, 1, 1994, pp. 90–104, and 'Towards a New Paradigm for Preaching', in Thomas G. Long and Edward Farley (eds), *Preaching as a Theological Task: World, Gospel, Scripture*, Louisville, KY, Westminster, John Knox, 1996, pp. 165–75. But see a reply from Ronald J. Allen, 'Why Preach from Passages in the Bible?', in the same volume, pp. 176–88.

6   Fred B. Craddock, *Luke: Interpretation, a Bible Commentary for Teaching and Preaching*, Louisville, KY, John Knox, 1990.

7   James W. Thompson, *Preaching like Paul: Homiletical Wisdom for Today*, Louisville, KY, Westminster, John Knox, 2001.

8   Walter J. Burghardt, *Preaching, The Art and The Craft*, New York, Paulist, 1987, especially pp. 108–18; Mary Catherine Hilkert, *Naming Grace: Preaching and the Sacramental Imagination*, New York, Continuum, 1998.

9   See David Buttrick, *A Captive Voice: The Liberation of Preaching*, Louisville, KY, Westminster, John Knox, 1994.

10   Jerry Camery-Hoggatt, *Speaking of God: Reading and Preaching the Word of God*, Peabody, Hendrickson, 1995.

11   Thomas G. Long, *Preaching and the Literary Forms of the Bible*, Philadelphia, Fortress, 1989.

12   See David Day, 'Preaching the Epistles', *Anvil*, 14, 4, 1997, pp. 273–82 and Stephen Wright, *Preaching with the Grain of Scripture*, Cambridge, Grove Books, 2001.

13   David Buttrick, *Homiletic: Moves and Structures*, London, SCM, 1987.

14   Fred Craddock, *Preaching*, Nashville, TN, Abingdon, 1985.

15   Eugene L. Lowry, *The Homiletical Plot: The Sermon as Narrative Art Form*, Atlanta, GA, John Knox, 1980, and *The Sermon: Dancing the Edge of Mystery*, Nashville, TN, Abingdon, 1997.

16   Calvin Miller, *Spirit, Word and Story: A Philosophy of Marketplace Preaching*, Grand Rapids, MI, Baker, 1996; William J. Bausch, *Storytelling the Word: Homilies and How to Write Them*, Mystic, CT, Twenty-Third Publications, 1996; Richard L. Eslinger, *Narrative and Imagination: Preaching the Worlds that Shape Us*, Minneapolis, MN, Fortress, 1995; Eugene L. Lowry, *How to Preach a Parable: Designs for Narrative Sermons*, Nashville, TN, Abingdon, 1989.

17   See, for example, Lucy Lind Hogan and Robert Reid, *Connecting with the Congregation: Rhetoric and the Art of Preaching*, Nashville, TN, Abingdon, 1999.

18   Heather Walton and Susan Durber (eds), *Silence in Heaven: A Book of Women's Preaching*, London, SCM, 1994.

19   For a stimulating discussion of the importance of the preacher's character, see Andre Resner, Jr, *Preacher and Cross: Person and Message in Theology and Rhetoric*, Grand Rapids, MI, Eerdmans, 1999.

20   Jolyon P. Mitchell, *Visually Speaking: Radio and the Renaissance of Preaching*, Edinburgh, T. & T. Clark, 1999.

21   See the article by Leslie Francis in this volume (Chapter 7) and his *Personality Type and Scripture: Exploring Mark's Gospel*, London, Mowbray, 1997.

22   Roger E. Van Harn, *Pew Rights: For People who Listen to Sermons*, Grand Rapids, MI, Eerdmans, 1992.

23   Leonora Tubbs Tisdale, *Preaching as Local Theology and Folk Art*, Minneapolis, MN, Fortress, 1997, p. 57.

24   John S. McClure, *The Roundtable Pulpit*, Nashville, TN, Abingdon, 1995.

25 See in particular Thomas H. Troeger, *Imagining a Sermon*, Nashville, TN, Abingdon, 1990.

26 Walter Brueggemann, *The Bible and Postmodern Imagination*, London, SCM, 1993, pp. 24–5.

27 See again Mary Catherine Hilkert, *Naming Grace*, and David J. Schlafer, *What Makes this Day Different?: Preaching Grace on Special Occasions*, Boston, MA, Cowley, 1998.

28 See for example, Graham Johnston, *Preaching to a Postmodern World: A Guide to Reaching Twenty-First Century Listeners*, Leicester, InterVarsity Press, 2001; Roger Standing, *Preaching for the Unchurched in an Entertainment Culture*, Cambridge, Grove Books, 2002; Cyril S. Rodd, *Preaching with Imagination*, Peterborough, Foundery, 2001; Jane V. Craske, *A Woman's Perspective on Preaching*, Peterborough, Foundery, 2001; Cleophus J. LaRue, *The Heart of Black Preaching*, Louisville, KY, Westminster, John Knox, 2000; James R. Nieman and Thomas G. Rogers, *Preaching to Every Pew: Cross-Cultural Strategies*, Minneapolis, MN, Fortress, 2001; Richard L. Eslinger, *The Web of Preaching: New Options in Homiletic Method*, Nashville, TN, Abingdon, 2002; Tim Stratford, *Interactive Preaching*, Cambridge, Grove Books, 1998; John Leach, *Responding to Preaching*, Cambridge, Grove Books, 2001; Richard Bewes, *Speaking in Public Effectively*, second edition, Fearn, Christian Focus, 2002.

Part 1

TRENDS IN PREACHING

Introduction to Part 1

In the first article in this reader, Thomas Long traces the developments in preaching over the 21 years between 1962 and 1983. He examines four key elements: the Bible, the congregation, the preacher and the sermon. Long notes the revolutionary impact which new emphases in biblical studies have had on the perception of the preacher's task, discerning a new respect for the canonical form of the text, its social context and literary character. As far as the congregation is concerned, homiletics is increasingly inclined to see listeners as active participants in the sermon rather than passive recipients. This has led to a new interest in the dynamics of communication and the congregation as 'co-artists'. At the close of the article Long explores the image of the preacher as explorer, contrasting this with the traditional image of 'herald'. The analogy of the explorer, excitedly calling his hearers to follow him on a journey which he has already undertaken, suggests that the sermon has an unfinished aspect and functions, like the preacher, as witness to an encounter.

Many of these insights were later developed by Long, notably in his *Preaching and the Literary Forms of the Bible* (Philadelphia, Fortress, 1989) and *The Witness of Preaching* (Louisville, KY, Westminster/John Knox, 1989).

Thomas G. Long, 'The Distance We Have Traveled: Changing Trends in Preaching' was first published in *Reformed Liturgy and Music*, 17, 1983, pp. 11–15.

In the second article, Walter Brueggemann, Old Testament specialist and theologian, surveys the present situation under 16 theses. He argues that many features of the contemporary scene – knowledge as the servant of those who wield power, the tendency of the historical-critical understanding of the Bible to distance text and interpreter, the pluralism of the local congregation, the diversity of possible meanings to be found in any biblical text, the power exercised by the dominant account of reality, the way in which human transformation occurs – require a different kind of preaching. Individual and specific biblical texts are construed as alternative visions of how the world is, subverting the dominant script and grasped through the imagination. Preaching is therefore the offer of images by which experience can be reorganized, the congregation is an audience which may at any point become participants, and narrative is the primary mode by which such world-making takes place. Preaching invites listeners to hear 'a counter-script which, over time, may authorize and empower counter-life'. Preaching would do well to take on this role since the 'old givens of white, male, Western, colonial advantage no longer hold.'

See also Brueggemann's *The Bible and Postmodern Imagination: Texts Under Negotiation* (London, SCM, 1993).

Walter Brueggemann, 'Preaching as Reimagination' was first published in *Theology Today*, 52, 3, 1995, pp. 313–29.

1   The Distance We Have Traveled: Changing Trends in Preaching

Thomas G. Long

Sometimes when we are cleaning out a cluttered desk drawer or leafing through a scrapbook rediscovered in a box in the attic, we run across a long-forgotten snapshot, a photograph which not only brings back memories but also marks the distance we have traveled between then and now. There is our son, now in college perhaps or maybe the Navy, bravely but wobbly peddling down the driveway on a new Christmas bicycle. There is a picture of the house before we added the porch. Or there we are, pounds lighter, wearing yesterday's dress or a five-inch-wide tie, standing in front of a convertible with the 'top down'. One comes face-to-face both with life's continuities and with its immense changes.

Not long ago I reread Professor J. J. Von Allmen's seminal essay on Reformed preaching, *Preaching and Congregation*[1] and felt as if I had found a photo under the yellowed papers in the desk drawer. Published over twenty years ago – before the winds of the sixties had achieved full strength, before Vatican II, before SALT talks, before Apollo moon shots, before acid and punk rock, before Watergate, before preaching itself went from bullish to bearish and back to a chastened bullishness – Von Allmen's work stands as a reassuring reminder of that which endures about preaching in the Reformed tradition and a somewhat startling indicator of how very much has changed in two decades about our understanding of preaching.

What I want to comment on are some of the differences I think can be observed between preaching as it is now practiced and the 1962 snapshot found in Von Allmen. I do this not because I believe Von Allmen's work to be obsolete but, rather, because of my profound respect for it as a high water mark in Reformed homiletics.

In order to spot the changes which have occurred we will need some categories, and Von Allmen is helpful here. He provides us with something of a line drawing of the preaching event itself. Imagine two dots spaced some distance from each other on a sheet of paper. One of these dots we will label 'The Word of God', by which Von Allmen would mean the story of God's mighty acts as given in the Bible. The other dot will be labeled 'The Congregation', the hearers, those to whom the Word is addressed. Now imagine a bold arrow drawn from the dot labeled 'The Word' to the dot labeled 'The Congregation'. This arrow marks the path traveled by the preacher in the preparation and delivery of the sermon. The arrow is, in a sense, the sermon itself, and it is important to note that it moves in only one direction: *from* Word *to Congregation. There you have it: a simple picture of the essential ingredients of preaching – Bible, Congregation, Preacher, and Sermon – bound together in a system of interrelationships.*[2] Let's take each of these ingredients and explore some of the transformations which have occurred in the last two decades.

The Bible in preaching

For Von Allmen the Bible is the source of all authentic preaching, and the role of the Bible in the preaching of the Church is as a dynamic, event-provoking presence. Preaching cannot claim to be biblical simply because it gums together a lot of biblical quotes, like peanuts in a Snickers bar. Nor can it claim to be biblical by virtue of its presentation of great biblical doctrines, like 'salvation' or 'providence'. *Preaching is biblical when it somehow makes the biblical events present for contemporary hearers, when it enrolls the congregation in the biblical story.*

In my view, the past two decades have, if anything, underscored and solidified Von Allmen's claim for the primacy of the Bible in preaching. While it is still possible, of course, to find preachers who use the Bible as a whip or a sourcebook for scholastic doctrines or who bounce around like a ball in a roulette wheel from one 'culturally relevant' issue to the next, only occasionally stumbling across a biblical text in an embarrassed moment of half-recognition, more and more preachers are finding renewed excitement in honest struggling with the biblical materials. Part of this is due, no doubt, to the emergence of an (almost) common lectionary and to the accompanying wealth of relatively inexpensive exegetical aids which the new lectionary has fostered.

But most of the renewed enthusiasm about biblical preaching has resulted from recent developments in the methods of biblical interpretation, and here we begin to mark some of the distance between us and Von Allmen:

(1) First of all, *redaction criticism* is finally making its way into the preacher's tool box. Twenty years ago most well-trained preachers would begin their work on, say, a passage in the Gospel of Luke like a medical pathologist. First they would remove the passage in question from the corpus of Luke, and then they would proceed to dissect the text using the instruments of historical criticism. They would unpack the structure of the sentences, do definitive examinations of each of the major words in the passage, measure the scars inflicted on the passage during its journey through the oral tradition, and reconstruct the impact the text may have had upon the original Lukan audience. The goal of all of this inquiry was to discover the theological center of gravity of the text, the main theological claim which governed the shape of the entire text. Von Allmen put it this way: ' . . . [We] should identify the main point, the principal *scopus* of the text and make it the governing aim of our sermon'.[3]

This process was not bad, of course, but it was severely limiting. What was lost was a sense of how this one passage fit into the whole fabric of Luke's gospel. If Luke is simply stringing texts together like beads on a string, then we can remove one of those beads and study it alone without regard for the rest. But if Luke is an artist, carefully choosing, polishing, and arranging the beads, then we must appreciate the function a single bead plays in the whole necklace.

Redaction criticism attempts to approach biblical texts with an eye to the way in which a writer has utilized those texts in the totality of his literary document.

One impact of the use of redaction criticism is the tendency among preachers to respect the canonical form of a biblical text, that is to say, the way the passage comes to us in the Bible. Preachers are far less tempted to use the methods of historical criticism to strip a text down to 'what Jesus *really* said' before Luke got hold of it. Moreover, preachers are more sensitive to the variety of witness in the scripture. Preaching on the parable of the Lost Sheep, for example, becomes a different experience when one uses the Lukan text (where the parable is given as a counter to the grumbling of the Pharisees and the scribes) rather than the Matthean text (where the parable appears as part of an address to the disciples about pastoral care).

(2) A second change which has occurred in biblical interpretation in the last twenty years involves an *increased recognition of the social and political contexts of the biblical documents.* The emphasis in the Reformed tradition upon the theological content and value of the Bible often pushed Reformed preaching toward a sort of disembodied biblical theology, abstracted from the social

forces which gave it birth. Congregations would hear sermons on the freedom from bondage offered in Christ or the ethics of 'rendering unto Caesar' with little awareness of the political issues of slavery and imperial power which originally gave those texts their bite.

Preachers are being increasingly exposed to biblical commentaries and other resources which make it abundantly clear that the Bible was not written in a theological think tank but by people whose faces were weathered by the economic, political, and social climate of their day. To be sure, older critics were not blind to the social forces at work in the Bible, but the surprise has been the discovery of just how fully the biblical documents are embedded in the sociological context. To try to understand and preach from the Bible without using sociological categories would be like trying to understand Martin Luther King's 'I Have A Dream' speech without taking into account the civil rights movement.

An example of the sort of sociologically-grounded resource available to preachers is John Elliott's study of I Peter, *A Home for the Homeless*.[4] First Peter is filled with the language of exile. Various translations of the letter call the recipients 'strangers', 'aliens', 'refugees', and the like. Elliott points out that traditional biblical scholarship, conducted with only minor attention to sociological concerns, tends often to spiritualize this language. *All* Christians are strangers and exiles, goes the argument, since their true home is a heavenly one. Maybe so, but that is not, according to Elliott, what the text of I Peter has in mind. The language of exile in the letter, he maintains, is not cosmological but sociological. That is to say, the author of I Peter writes to a group of actual exiles in Asia Minor. Perhaps they were rural villagers displaced to the cities, or perhaps they were immigrant craftsmen and traders working in a strange land, but, in any case, they were dislocated persons estranged from any sense of belonging and deprived of social and legal status. Elliott writes:

> Conversion to Christianity at first appeared to offer [them] a 'place of belonging', fraternal assistance, and participation in a community of equals – benefits which were denied these strangers in the larger society indifferent to their needs and suspicious of their presence. The vehemence, however, with which the local communities had reacted to the Christian sect had made increased suffering rather than security the lot of these believers.[5]

Viewed from this perspective, then, I Peter has an ethical as well as a theological cutting edge. Rather than casting our gaze toward the heavenly home, the letter directs our vision to the Church, a place where the displaced of society need no longer feel isolation but can be received as brothers and sisters. The Church is, in the deepest sense of the word, a home for the homeless. While it may be more comfortable to preach to a suburban congregation on 'Heaven is Our Home', a grasp of the full context of I Peter pushes the preacher toward a more risky proclamation.

(3) A third development in biblical studies which has influenced preaching has been *the recent and growing interest in literary-critical approaches to the Bible*. In one sense this marks the most radical shift of all, since it implies a move from a concern with the history of a biblical text to a concern for poetics, the literary, and communicative impact of a text.

One, perhaps overly simple, way to describe this change is to imagine that one is present for a performance of *King Lear*. One way to understand this play, of course, is to inquire about its history. We can discover much about Shakespeare, the social and cultural context of his day, the peculiarities of his use of language, the historical allusions in the play itself, and so on. This would be an attempt to comprehend the play's meaning by looking *behind* the play itself, an historical inquiry. Another place to look for the play's meaning, however, is *in front* of the play, that is to say in what the play 'does' to the audience. Does it make them weep? Does it evoke pessimism? Do they somehow find themselves 'in' the play, caught up in the plot and characters? From this vantage point it hardly matters whether the play is by Shakespeare or Ibsen, 350-years-old or the latest piece on Broadway. Its meaning is to be found in what it creates through the dramatic interaction with the audience.

In similar fashion, literary critics of the Bible tend to focus upon the power of biblical texts to act in a literary fashion upon hearers and readers. As a matter of practice, the literary and historical approaches are usually used in complementary fashion in a search for some common ground between what the text *meant*, as an historical document, and what the text *does*, as a literary document.

One sample of how literary criticism operates can be found in recent studies of the Book of Jonah. Biblical scholar John Dominic Crossan, among others, has moved beyond traditional historical concerns to argue that the book has the literary structure of a parable and is ingeniously designed to pull a 'double reversal' on the reader:

> The hearer expects the prophets to obey God and pagans such as the Ninevites, especially, to disobey God. But the speaker tells a story in which a prophet disobeys and the Ninevites obey beyond all belief.[6]

If this is true, then, the Book of Jonah does far more for the hearer than to convey an idea; it overthrows a world which the hearer previously imagined to be secure and impregnable.

In terms of preaching, the literary-critical approach to the Bible not only expands the meaning potential of texts, it also offers an intriguing possibility for a biblical sermon: the sermon may seek not only to say what the text says, it may also seek to do what the text does. Recent attempts to compose sermons which are themselves parables or to formulate sermons which are in some way 'storyshaped' are outgrowths of the appreciation of the literary character of the Bible itself.

The congregation in preaching

Contemporary understandings of the task of preaching share Von Allmen's high view of the congregation's place in the preaching event. For Von Allmen, no sermon could be adequately prepared without keeping in view the real persons who would hear the sermon. He even suggested that the preacher, in the early stages of preparation, write down the names of four or five members of the congregation and keep them in mind as insurance against allowing the sermon to drift into vague generalities, applicable to people *en masse* but pertinent to no one in particular.[7] Von Allmen also urged his readers to recognize that most of our preaching is not *missionary* preaching (that is, preaching to the world) but preaching in and to the Church. 'Conversion must be recalled', he insisted, 'not proposed; the Church is to be awakened, not founded. . . . '[8]

More recent views of the congregation's role are not so much departures from Von Allmen's view as much as they are extensions of it. Von Allmen called on us to trust our hearers to be Christians; contemporary homiletics further asks us to trust them as co-creators of the sermon. When Von Allmen drew his picture of preaching, he lined a heavy arrow from Bible to Congregation. He did not draw any arrow, however faint, in the other direction because he wanted to insure that the agenda for preaching was set by the Bible and not by people's perceived needs, real or illusory. In failing to do so, however, he ran the risk of obscuring an important truth about preaching: *those who hear the gospel are not passive receivers of information, they are active participants in the gospel story.* As one notable homiletician, Fred B . Craddock, put it:

> It is not a matter of saying truth is subjective but it is a matter of asking whether there is truth inseparable from its appropriation. Whatever may be [one's] theology of the Word as Truth complete and valid and final apart from all human grasp of it, the fact is [one] cannot employ such theology as a working principle for preaching.[9]

One thing this means for preaching is a renewed interest in human communication as a proper area of theological investigation. Older students of preaching, Von Allmen included, were properly concerned that preachers might become fascinated by the techniques of secular rhetoric, thus replacing theological *substance* with homiletical *style*. It has now become clear, though, that a concern for the substance of the gospel carries with it a concern for how people hear the message, become involved in it, and make use of it in their lives. Listen as one teacher of preaching, J. Randall Nichols, describes the communication dynamics in preaching:

> When a message begins, a kind of mental search mission starts in the minds of hearers. From their vast internal computers of stored experience comes a set of meanings, images, and previous understandings to which the unfamiliar incoming message is referred for translation, so to speak. . . . As soon as that happens, which as a rule takes something like a billionth of a second, communication has become essentially a receiver phenomenon. The meaning of the message is not 'transmitted', as we sometimes mistakenly say; it is, so to speak, 'transgenerated' in the awareness of the hearer, reassembled in the context of his or her own story.[10]

A preacher, then, who preaches to a congregation of 150 people does not preach one sermon but rather provides the basis for the creation of 150 more or less similar sermons. The preacher, to be sure, leads and guides the process, but the hearer shapes the finished work. Some preachers, of course, are uneasy with this phenomenon, distressed that every hearer cannot 'remember the points of the sermon' or otherwise replicate the exact intentions of the preacher. To the contrary, though, the co-artistry of the hearer ought to be celebrated as intrinsic to the gospel. Indeed, as communication becomes more and more univocal, it also becomes less and less human.

The preacher and the sermon

In a sense, by describing some of the changes which have occurred in our understanding of the use of the Bible and the role of the congregation in preaching, we have already implied something of the distance we have traveled in our understanding of the person of the preacher and the character of the sermon. I would like to try to flesh this out a bit with a homespun analogy.

Imagine that the biblical text for next Sunday's sermon is not a piece of literature but a deep and mysterious cave. The preacher is a trained explorer of caves who descends into this one, flashlight and ropes in hand, filled with the spirit of adventure and the anticipation of discovery. Others have explored this cave before, indeed the preacher has read their accounts, studied their maps, been excited by the sights they have seen, marveled at the treasures they have discovered, and is impelled by their assurances that there are new treasures yet to be found. The preacher moves ever deeper into the cave, sometimes ambling easily through wide passageways, other times wedging his way through an opening barely large enough to squeeze through. He wanders down alluring grottos, only to find they end in cold, blank walls. He shines his light across chasms too wide for him to cross with the equipment he has. He inches his way down a high and narrow ledge, once almost losing his footing and tumbling into the black infinity below. Suddenly, he turns a corner and there it is, what he has been looking for all along. Perhaps it is a waterfall, tumbling from a great height to the floor below. Or perhaps it is an enormous stalactite, an icicle eons old which overwhelms him by its sheer size. Or maybe his flashlight has illumined a wall of gems, filling the dark space with dancing fire and color. He stands before the sight in a moment of awe and silence. Then, knowing what he must do, he carefully retraces his path, scrambles to the mouth of the cave, and with the dirt of the journey still on his face and his flashlight waving excitedly, he calls to those who have been waiting on him, 'Come on. Have I got something to show you!'

The point of that little story is, I suppose, obvious. We are less and less impressed by preachers who present the Christian faith as a finished business, fully explored and only needing to be taught.

While it may be tempting to see the preacher as a 'herald', delivering the King's message to the people accurately and carefully, being sure not to alter it in the slightest, the 'herald' image finally will not do. The preacher is really more a 'witness', one who sees and experiences and tells the truth about what has been seen and experienced. There is, to be sure, a truth outside of and larger than the preacher's experience, and it is, in part, the experience of being in the presence of that ineffable truth which forms the content of the witness. In other words, there are dimensions of the gospel which have not been experienced by the preacher, but the preacher points to these and tells the truth about them: They are there, but I have not yet fully experienced them.

This understanding of the preacher has led contemporary homiletics quite naturally to the image of storytelling as a way of understanding the sermon itself. This image, while undeniably powerful and suggestive, may be a bit misleading, since it could imply that every sermon ought to *be* a story or be *full of* stories. Sermons are not, however, always stories in the technical sense, but they are, in a way, story-like. They have movement and plot; they create identification and evoke experience. They are stories in the sense that the preacher, who has encountered the biblical text in some new way, witnesses to – tells the story of – that encounter. Fred Craddock describes it this way:

> Why not re-create with the congregation his [sic] inductive experience of coming to an understanding of the message of the text? For obvious reasons it would not, of course, be an exact re-creation . . . but the minister may be surprised at the mental ability of his [sic] people to chase an idea through paradoxes, dilemmas, myths, history, and dramatic narrative if the movement of the chase corresponds to the way they think through the issues of daily life.[11]

The sermon, then, becomes not an essay, a lawyer's brief, a debater's rebuttal, or a piece of religious rhetoric; it becomes a journey . . . a journey which the preacher has taken once in the study and now guides for the congregation.

So, we have looked at the faded snapshot of preaching so skillfully developed by Von Allmen, and we have compared the lines and creases then and now. Preaching is not just getting older; in at least a few ways, it's getting better!

Notes

1   Jean-Jacques Von Allmen, *Preaching and Congregation*, Richmond, VA, John Knox, 1962.

2   It should be said that this schematic represents only part of the preaching event as understood by Von Allmen. Preaching is conducted in the faith that, as human preachers speak from the Bible to congregations, God also speaks in and through that event.

3   Von Allmen, 1962, p. 53.

4   John H. Elliott, *A Home for the Homeless*, Philadelphia, Fortress, 1981.

5   Elliott, 1981, p. 101.

6   John Dominic Crossan, *The Dark Interval: Towards A Theology of Story*, Niles, IL, Argus Communications, 1975, p. 76.

7   Von Allmen, 1975, p. 52.

8   Von Allmen, 1975, p. 11.

9   Fred B. Craddock, *As One Without Authority*, Nashville, TN, Abingdon, 1979, p. 70.

10 J. Randall Nichols, *Building the Word: The Dynamics of Communication and Preaching*, New York, Harper & Row, 1980, pp. 69–70.

11 Craddock, 1979, p. 125.

2 Preaching as Reimagination

Walter Brueggemann

In what follows, sixteen theses are set forth and developed, suggesting that evangelical preaching finds itself now in a quite new cultural, epistemological context.

(1) *Ours is a changed preaching situation, because the old modes of church absolutes are no longer trusted.*

It is not that the church's theological absolutes are no longer trusted, but that the *old modes* in which those absolutes have been articulated are increasingly suspect and dysfunctional. That is because our old modes are increasingly regarded as patriarchal, hierarchic, authoritarian, and mono-logic. The mistrust that flies under all these adjectives, however, is due to a growing suspicion about the linkage between knowledge and power. The mistrust of conventional authority, now broad and deep in our society, is rooted in the failure of positivism, positivism that is scientific, political, or theological. Many are increasingly aware that 'absolute knowledge' most characteristically means agreement of all those permitted in the room.[1] Such 'absolutism' in 'truth', moreover, characteristically has pretensions to 'absolute power' as well, surely an adequate reason for suspicion. Those at the margins of dominating knowledge will no longer permit the practitioners of dominating power to be supervisors of absolute knowledge.

(2) *Along with the failure of old modes of articulation, we now face the inadequacy of historical-critical understanding of the biblical text as it has been conventionally practiced.*

I do not say the failure or bankruptcy of historical criticism but its inadequacy, for historical criticism has become, in Scripture study, a version of modes of absolutism among the elitely educated. It is increasingly clear that historical criticism has become a handmaiden of certain kinds of power.[2] This not only refers to the control of the agenda through academic politics, but it also recognizes that the rise of criticism is deeply related to the banishment of the supernatural and to the dismissal of tradition as a form of truthfulness.[3]

One can note that in academic circles, where methodological discussions are conducted, there is a growing tension between old-line historical criticism, which serves to distance the text from the interpreter, and the emerging criticisms (sociological, literary, and canonical).[4] A probable general-ization can be made that critical scholars who most resist change and who regard the transfer of social power and influence as only modes of political correctness cling most passionately to older modes of historical criticism, whereas scholars who advocate and benefit from redistributions of interpretive power engage in sociological and literary criticism. Indeed, old-line historical criticism is our particular form of positivism in the biblical, interpretive guild and so receives its share of the suspicion I have more generally noted in thesis 1. I am aware that moves from historical criticism are easily judged to be obscurantism, advocacy, or ideology, but those labels only have lethal con-notations in the context of self-satisfied positivism.

(3) A great new reality for preaching is pluralism in the interpreting community of the local con-gregation.

All but the most closed and sheltered liturgical congregations are indomitably heterogeneous.[5] That emerging pluralism, moreover, can no longer be overcome by absolute assertion. For such absolute assertion, whether by strong pastoral authority or by denominational dictum, can only serve to excommunicate those who see and take and experience reality otherwise. The more frantic our zeal to maintain the oneness and wholeness of 'our truth', the more divisive does such practice become.

An honest facing of pluralism can only be pastorally and usefully engaged by an open-ended adjudication that takes the form of trustful, respectful conversation.[6] Such a conversation is joined with no participant seeking to convert the other and no participant knowing the outcome ahead of time but only entering with full respect for the good faith of others and the willingness to entertain the troublesome thought that new 'truth' received together may well be out in front of any of us. While such an approach sounds like relativism, an answering objectivism is destructive not only of the community but of any chance to receive new truth together. Preaching thus must be conducted in a context where one makes proposals and advocacies but not conclusions.[7]

(4) Pluralism as the perspective and orientation of the community that hears and interprets is matched by an emerging awareness of the polyvalence of the biblical text.

Texts are open to many meanings, more than one of which may be legitimate and faithful at the same time. This is evident, in its most simple form, in the awareness that many preachers on any given occasion preach many sermons on the same lectionary texts. While not all such sermons may be legitimate and faithful, many of them would qualify as such, without mutual exclusiveness. Notice that such a polyvalence flies in the face of old-line historical criticism, which tried to arrive at 'the meaning' of the text.[8]

The claim of polyvalence is an invitation for Christians to relearn from Jewish interpretive tradi-tion.[9] Indeed, Jewish interpretation does not seek to give closure to texts but can permit many read-ings to stand side by side, reflecting both the rich density of the text and the freedom of interpretation. Such a way of reading reflects the mode of midrashic interpretation, a Jewish affir-mation that the voice of the text is variously heard and is not limited by authorial intent.[10]

It is now suggested, moreover, that midrashic interpretation is strongly, even if unwittingly, reflected in Freud's theory of psychoanalysis and in his practice of dream interpretation.[11] Freud understood that dreams are endlessly open to interpretation. In this regard, the reading of dreams is not unlike the reading of texts. At the same time, it is important to note that dreams are no more unreal fantasies than are texts but contain a profound truth that is available only upon a rich reading. It is unhelpful for the text interpreter, and therefore the preacher, to give heavy closure to texts because such a habit does a disservice to text and to listener, both of which are evokers and practi-tioners of multiple readings.

(5) Reality is scripted, that is, shaped and authorized by a text.

Paul Ricoeur has done the most to show us that reality lives by text.[12] By 'text', Ricoeur means written discourse that is no longer in the control of the 'author' but makes its own testimony and insists upon interpretation. Interpretation, moreover, is 'to appropriate *here and now* the intention of the text.'[13] But such intention is derived not from the 'author' of the text but from the work within the act of interpretation.

That text may be recognized or invisible. It may be a great religious classic or a powerful philo-sophical tradition or a long-standing tribal conviction.[14] It is an account of reality that the commu-nity comes to trust and to take for granted as a given that tends to be beyond reexamination. This text describes reality in a certain way and shape. In a world where there is more than one text, that is, a world of plurality, a given text may describe, but if another text intrudes, it is possible for that text to redescribe reality.[15]

It is important, on the basis of this thesis, for the preacher to recognize that there are no 'textless' worlds. Such an assertion may be much disputed; at a practical level, however, it is no doubt true. People come to the preaching moment with texts already in hand that describe the world. The preacher who interprets the text, who 'appropriates here and now the intention of the text', does not act in a vacuum. There are always rival and competing texts, in the face of which the biblical text may be a counter-text that does not primarily describe but subversively redescribes reality.

(6) *The dominant scripting of reality in our culture is rooted in the Enlightenment enterprise associated with Descartes, Locke, Hobbes, and Rousseau, which has issued in a notion of autonomous individualism, resulting in what Philip Rieff calls 'The Triumph of the Therapeutic.'*[16]

It is difficult to take in the radical shift of assumptions in 'world making' that occurred at the beginning of the seventeenth century.[17] The collapse of the hegemony of medieval Christianity, hastened by the Reformation, the Thirty Years War, and the rise of science, produced, as Susan Bordo has made clear, a profound anxiety about certitude.[18] It was clear that certitude would no longer be found in 'the truth of Christ', for confessional divisions had broken that truth. Believers henceforth could appeal only to reason guided by the spirit, or the spirit measured by reason, clearly a circular mode of truth. Indeed, Descartes introduced his massive program of doubt as an attempt to link the new truth to the claims of Christianity. What emerged was the individual knower as the decontextualized adjudicator of truth.[19]

That autonomy in knowledge, moreover, produced autonomy in action and ethics as well, so that the individual becomes the norm for what is acceptable. The end result is a self-preoccupation that ends in self-indulgence, driving religion to narcissistic catering and consumerism, to limitless seeking after well-being and pleasure on one's own terms without regard to any other in the community.[20]

While this scripting of reality has profound critical thought behind it, the practice of this script is embraced and undertaken by those in modern culture who have no awareness of the text, of its rootage, or its intention.[21] Thus it is clear that very many folk in our culture who come to preaching events are reliant upon this 'text of reality' that is permitted to describe the world. The preacher perforce preaches in a world shaped by this text.

(7) *This scripting tradition of the Enlightenment exercises an incredible and pervasive hegemony among us.*

(a) In economics, this text-generated ideology issues in consumerism, which operates on the claims that more is better, that most will make happy, and that each is entitled to and must have all that one can take, even if at the expense of others. Such a value system, of course, must discredit the claims of any other who is a competitor for the goods that will make me happy. Television advertising is a primary voice in advocating this view of reality, and television is closely allied with spectator sports, which move in the same direction.[22] Witness the 'shoe contracts' of college coaches.

(b) In political affairs, this same ideology is rooted in the privilege of European superiority and colonialism, although in recent time that political dimension of the text has found its primary expression in the notion of Pax Americana. That ideology assumes that the world works best if the United States adjudicates from a position of dominant power, which, in turn, guarantees and endlessly enhances the privileged position of the United States in terms of prosperity and standard of living. Thus the public administration of power guarantees the private capacity to consume without limit. The deepness of this claim is evident in the political requirement of a commitment to a strong America.

In political affairs, this vision of political hegemony perhaps was given authoritative voice by Elihu Root, Secretary of State under Theodore Roosevelt, and his expansionist notions. Root, in turn, was the mentor to Henry Stimson who moved the United States, almost single-handedly through his advocacy and political mechanizations, to take responsibility for the world.[23] Stimson, in turn, was the patron and mentor of the 'Wise Men' who guided foreign policy, produced the Cold War, and finally overreached in Viet Nam.[24]

But of course the end is not yet. The United States, as the remaining superpower, can have it all its own way, so it thinks, finding itself most often on the side of the old colonial powers and allied with the forces of reactionism in order to preserve the old hegemony that goes unexamined.

(c) The Enlightenment text, as practiced in the Euro-American world, thus provides an unchallenged rationale for privilege and advantage in the world in every zone of life. This not only means political ascendancy and economic domination but also makes its adherents the norm for virtue. In turn, this shows up even in the church, where it is assumed that the Western church is the privileged norm by which to test the rest of the church. In the end, even truth is tied in some way to Western virtue.

(d) This defining text of the West is exceedingly hard on and dismissive of those whose lives do not measure up to the norms of competence, productivity, and privilege. This text has resulted in a kind of social Darwinism in which the fast, smart, well-connected, and ruthless are the 'best' people.[25] And the counterpart is impatience with those who are not so competent-productive-righteous. Very many of the enormous social problems and social inequities in our society are legitimated by this text.

(e) This definitive text exercises great authority over the imagination, even of those who set out to resist its claim and power. As Karl Marx saw, it exercises a powerful attraction for those who do not share in its promised benefits but are in fact its victims. Marx's dictum is 'The ideas of the dominant class become the dominant ideas.'[26] Marx, moreover, understood well that in the end, the dominant class does not need to exercise force but holds sway by 'hegemonic theatre.'[27] I suspect that just now the lottery is a tool of such imagination, which proposes that any may succeed in this system. Is this a great system or what?!

(8) *We now know (or think we know) that human transformation (the way people change) does not happen through didacticism or through excessive certitude but through the playful entertainment of another scripting of reality that may subvert the old given text and its interpretation and lead to the embrace of an alternative text and its redescription of reality.*

Very few people make important changes in their description of the world abruptly. Most of us linger in wistfulness, notice dissonance between our experience and the old text, and wonder if there is a dimension to it all that has been missed.[28] Most of us will not quickly embrace an alternative that is given us in a coercive way. Such coercion more likely makes us defend the old and, in general, become defensive.

Victor Turner noted that there is an in-between time and place in social transformation and relocation, which he termed 'liminality.'[29] Liminality is a time when the old configurations of social reality are increasingly seen to be in jeopardy, but new alternatives are not yet in hand.

What we need for such liminality is a safe place in which to host such ambiguity, to notice the tension and unresolve without pressure but with freedom to see and test alternative textings of reality. It is my impression that very much preaching, which is excessively urgent and earnest, does not pay much attention to what we know about how we change or how anyone else may receive change when it is given. The text entrusted to the preachers of the church is all about human transformation, but the characteristic modes of presentation, in many quarters, contradict the claim of the text and are the enemies of transformation.

An inviting, effective alternative does not need to be toned down in its claim or made palatable. It does, however, need to be presented in a way that stops well short of coercion that is threatening and evokes resistance to hearing or appropriating the new text. Preaching is not only the announcement of the alternative but the practice of that very liminality that does not yet know too much.

(9) *The biblical text, in all its odd disjunctions, is an offer of an alternative script, and preaching this text is the exploration of how the world is if it is imagined through this alternative script.*

This thesis reminds us of two important recognitions, First, the biblical text is indeed a profound alternative to the text of the Enlightenment and therefore alternative to the dominant text with which most of us came to church. For a very long time we have assumed that the 'American Dream', which is our version of Enlightenment freedom and well-being, coheres with the claims of the gospel.[30] It is the U.S. that is God's agent in the world, God's example, and God's most blessed people. I imagine that even those of us who reject blatant forms of this claim have been schooled effectively in the notion in some lesser ways. Now we are coming to see, belatedly we are required to see, that the American Dream as it is now understood has long since parted company with the claims of the gospel. Whereas the dominant text finds human initiative at the core of reality, the gospel witnesses to holiness as the core, and whereas it is the self that arises out of the hegemonic text, in the gospel it is the neighbor. The preacher and the congregation will be much liberated for serious preaching if it is understood that all of us, liberal and conservative, are in fact conducting an adjudication between these two competing texts, between which there is diminished overlap and between which we do not want to choose. The preacher must show how this counter-text of the gospel is a genuine alternative.

The second notion here is that the preacher, from this text, does not describe a gospel-governed world but helps the congregation imagine it.[31] Every text that describes and redescribes presents something that is not in hand, until the text is appropriated and all reality is passed through the text. Something like this must be the intent of Wallace Stevens in his enigmatic statement:

> Poetry is the supreme fiction, madame . . .
> But fictive things Wink as they will.[32]

The preacher traffics in a fiction that makes true. But that is why preaching is so urgent and must be done with such art. This world of the gospel is not real, not available, until this credible utterance authorizes a departure from a failed text and appropriation of this text.

Such an imaginative act of making fiction real is expounded well by Garrett Green in his assertion that 'as' is the 'copula of imagination.'[33] I take Green to mean that an event or object must be interpreted 'as' something before it becomes available. First, such a notion means that there are no available uninterpreted events or objects. They are beyond reach until interpreted, and when interpreted, they are seen or taken according to that 'as.'[34] Second, there is no right answer in the back of the book. Thus, formally, any interpretive 'as' has as much claim as any other. What the preacher is doing is proposing that the world and our lives be seen or taken *as* under the aegis of the gospel. Such an imaginative 'as' means a break with the world and our lives taken 'as' under the aegis of Enlightenment construal. It is, of course, our usual assumption that the Enlightenment descriptions of reality are given.[35] They are not, according to Green, given but only a powerful, long-sustained 'as', which is now to be countered by this evangelical 'as.'

(10) *The proposal of this alternative script is not through large, comprehensive, universal claims, but through concrete, specific, local texts that, in small ways, provide alternative imagination.*

I have no doubt that every preacher and every interpreter of biblical texts operates with something like a 'systematic theology.'[36] Of course. But such systematic thinking, which is essential to some provisional coherence about reality, is not the primary mode of the biblical text. In fact, our macro-vision in systematic theology is stitched together selectively from little texts that refuse long-term stabilization. Of course, there is deep disagreement about this proposition. 'Canonical criticism', as proposed by Brevard Childs, assumes long-term stabilization of a larger reading.[37] While there is some truth in that claim, it is equally (or more pertinently) true that continual study, reading, and reflection upon the text causes that stabilization to be constantly under review and change. Thus, the insistence upon concrete, specific, local presentation is parallel to the nature of the text itself, which is put together of small parts, the precise relation of which to each other is not self-evident. The interpretive act is itself a major set of decisions about how the parts relate to each other this time.

Thus, the preacher, if taking the text seriously, does not sound the whole of 'biblical truth' in preaching but focuses on one detailed text to see what it yields of 'as.' It can be a great relief to the preacher not to have to utter a universal truth with each utterance, and it may be an assurance to the church that it is not given to pronounce universally on every issue that comes along.[38] It is enough to work with the local detail in the interest of transformation.

As examples of such 'local work', we may cite almost any part of the Bible. In the powerful memories of Genesis 12–50, the action is quite local around one family, the members of which are known by name and in considerable detail.[39] Perhaps more poignantly, the parables of Jesus focus remarkably on detail of one time and place.[40] Helpful dimensions of this accent on the concrete are offered by Sandra Schneiders in her programmatic use of the phrase 'paschal imagination', in which she shows how the text moves beyond the subject/object split to world construal and construction.[41] And Jacob Neusner shows how very small acts of piety and ritual are ways in which practitioners can 'imagine themselves to be Jews.'[42] Such detail was perhaps not necessary when Christianity recently occupied a hegemonic position in our society, and one could deal in unnuanced summaries. Now, however, with the dehegemonization of Christianity, we are back to the little pieces that in various ways make a claim against the dominant text. The preacher can understand the act of a single sermon as providing yet another detail to the very odd and very different description of reality being enacted over time in the congregation.

(11) *The work of preaching is an act of imagination, an offer of an image through which perception, experience, and finally faith can be reorganized in alternative ways.*

The alternative voiced in textual preaching intends to show that this scripting of reality is in deep conflict with the dominant description of reality, so that the scripts are shown to be in deep tension with each other, if not in contradiction. If an alternative is not set forth with some clarity and vigor, then no choice is given, and no alternative choice is available. There is, of course, a long history of suspicion about imagination going back to Aristotle and suggesting that imagination is an inferior and unreliable source of knowledge.[43] With the failure of Enlightenment notions of 'objectivity', imagination has made an important comeback as a mode of knowledge. Gaston Bachelard has elaborated in powerful ways the creative function of imagination in the generation of knowledge.[44] Of his work, Richard Kearney writes that, in contrast to Sartre,

> Bachelard . . . conceives of the imagination not as privation, but as audition – an acoustics of the *other* than self. His poetical model of imagination is two-dimensional: at once a giving and a taking, a projection and a discovery, a centrifugal exodus towards things and a centripetal return to the self. This notion of an 'interlacing rhythm' which spans the breach between subjectivity and being epitomizes the Bachelardian theory of poetics.[45]

According to Bachelard, it is imagination that 'valorizes' an alternative, and that, of course, is what preaching intends to do. Such a mode of preaching requires a break with our more usual modes of didactic, doctrinal, or moralistic preaching.

More recently, John Thiel has argued that imagination is a reliable mode of theological knowledge.[46] He, of course, knows that imagination is available for distortion but asserts that it is no more available for distortion or less reliable for knowing than is reason, a long-trusted practice in theological reflection.

It is thus my notion that the preacher and congregation can reconstrue the time and place of preaching as a time and place for the practice of imagination, that is, the reimagination of reality according to the evangelical script of the Bible. Such preaching does not aim at immediate outcomes but, over time, intends, detail by detail, to make available a different world in which different acts, attitudes, and policies are seen to be appropriate. To aim at this 'underneath' dimension of faith is consistent with Ricoeur's conclusion that the 'symbol gives rise to thought.'[47] I would paraphrase Ricoeur to say that 'the image gives rise to a new world of possibility', and the preaching for which I contend is aimed at the image-making out of the text that may give rise to a church of new obedience.[48]

(12) *Because old modes of certitude are no longer trusted, the preaching of these texts is not an offer of metaphysics but the enactment of a drama in which the congregation is audience but may at any point become participant.*

In *Texts Under Negotiation*, I have already articulated what I think is at issue in the move from metaphysical to dramatic thinking.[49] It is clear that dramatic modes of thought are more congenial to the way in which the Old Testament proceeds and in which the primal testimony of the New Testament is expressed. Characteristically, biblical faith may assume a metaphysic, but it is of little interest and of little value for the generation of faith. What counts, characteristically, is the dramatic turn of affairs to which the community bears witness and responds in praise, joy, and obedience. The result is that, in the text itself, God is a character at play and at risk; in the preaching moment, the congregation may see itself as among the characters in the drama.

This means that the preacher, in the drama of the sermon, must 'undo' much of the metaphysical preoccupation of the church tradition, to see whether the world can be imagined in terms of God's action in the ongoing account of the world, the nations, Israel, and the church. Such freedom and vitality as drama, which von Balthasar has shown to be definitive, is matched in yet another image offered by Frances Young.[50] Young proposes that the Bible is a musical score and that, in each interpretive act, the score must be 'performed' with the freedom and discipline always required of good performance. Moreover, Young proposes that much interpretation is a 'cadenza' in the score, which gives the interpreter (here preacher) a good bit of room for maneuverability and idiosyncracy.

(13) *This dramatic rendering of imagination has narrative as its quintessential mode, the telling of a story, and the subsequent living of that story.*

The claim that narrative is a privileged mode in Christian preaching is, of course, not a new idea. After paying attention to the 'testimony' of Israel and the early church, as in the earlier work of G. Ernest Wright, Reginald Fuller, and C. H. Dodd,[51] more recent study has considered the epistemological assumptions in the use of the genre of narrative and has concluded that, in this mode, reality itself has something of a narrative quality, that reality is an ongoing theater that has a plot with a beginning, middle, and end and has characters who remain constant but also develop, change, and exercise great freedom.[52] As Dale Patrick has shown, God in the Bible (like Jesus in the New Testament) is an ongoing character in a narrative who is endlessly re-rendered in the Bible and whom the preacher subsequently re-renders.[53] The constancy of God is the constancy of a character in a narrative who must change in order to remain constant and who necessarily violates our conventional notions of immutable transcendence.

Moreover, it is clear that the living of human life is embedded in a narrative rendering. Thus Hayden White has argued, persuasively in my judgment, that history is essentially a rhetorical activity in which past memory is told and retold in alternative ways, ways that may be intentional but that also take into account the vested interests of the narrating community.[54] And Alasdair MacIntyre has shown decisively that alternative ethical systems cannot be understood or assessed apart from the narrative world in which they are told, received, and valued.[55] Thus, narrative is not a secondary or auxiliary enterprise; it is an act whereby social reality is constituted. Amos Wilder has championed the view long held by serious rhetoricians that speech, and specifically narrative speech, is constitutive of reality, so that narrative is indeed 'world-making.'[56]

To be sure, there are many texts in the 'script' of the Bible available to the preacher that are not narrative. Given my presuppositions, these are the most difficult to preach. It is my impression, nonetheless, that every text in any genre has behind it something of a narrative that generates it and through which the texts in other genres are to be understood. Thus, for example, the Psalms are notoriously difficult preaching material. I suspect that the preacher characteristically either presents a narrative situation that is critically recoverable (as in Psalm 137) or imagines such a context that led this speaker to speak thusly. In the case of the Psalms, some of the superscriptions, even if not historically 'reliable', provide a clue for such narrative construal.[57] And in the letters of Paul, a critically recoverable or homiletically imagined narrative context serves the preaching of the letters.

Such a mode of preaching has the spin-off effect of a drama being enacted, a story being narrated, and a plot being worked out. Such a mode holds the potential of showing the congregants that their lives (and life together) also constitute a drama being enacted and a story being told, in which we are characters with work to do, options to exercise, and loyalties to sustain or alter. This mode of preaching not only reconstrues the shape of the Bible but also reconstrues human life. It moves away from an essentialist focus to see that much of life is a rhetorical operation, and that we are indeed 'speeched into newness.'[58]

(14) *The invitation of preaching (not unlike therapy) is to abandon the script in which one has had confidence and to enter a different script that imaginatively tells one's life differently.*

The folk in the Bible are shown to be those who have often settled into a narrative that is deathly and destructive. Thus, the early Hebrews settled for a slave narrative as their proper self-presentation. That narrative is disrupted by another narrative that has Yahweh the liberator as the key and decisive agent. The decision about staying in Egypt or leaving for the promise is a decision about which narrative in which to participate, whether to understand the 'plot of life' according to the character Pharaoh or according to a different plot featuring Yahweh.[59] Likewise, the New Testament narratives portray many folk either in a narrative of hopelessness and despair or in one of self-righteousness and arrogance. In each case, they are invited into an alternative narrative, which is the narrative of the life-giving kingdom of God.

In *Texts Under Negotiation*, I have already suggested the analogue of psychotherapy.[60] I have no wish to 'psychologize' preaching but only to suggest an analogue. In such a parallel, I do not understand the conversation of psychotherapy as simply one of self-discovery, but I envision an active 'therapist' who, together with the one in need, conducts a conversation in which an alternative account of his or her life may emerge. And if such an alternative narrative emerges, then the needful person in therapy has the opportunity and the task of adjudicating between the old narrative long since believed and the new narrative only now available. Such a person may eventually decide that the old narrative (from childhood) is not only destructive and paralyzing but false, and a new one may be chosen that renarrates life in health. Many alternatives of one's life or the life of the world are made available in the process.

Mutatis mutandis, the task of the preacher is to exhibit this particular narrative script of the Bible and to show how and in what ways life will be reimagined, redescribed, and relived if this narrative is embraced. The old-fashioned word for this process is 'conversion.' In my book *Biblical Perspectives on Evangelism*, I have shown in some detail what this might mean for the study and proclamation of the Bible.[61] It is in this context that Peter Berger and Thomas Luckmann understand the social construction of reality as a process of 'switching worlds.'[62] Nobody can switch worlds unless an alternative world is made richly available with great artistry, care, and boldness.

(15) *The offer of an alternative script (to which we testify and bear witness as true) invites the listener out of his or her assumed context into many alternative contexts where different scripts may have a ring of authenticity and credibility.*

That is, the place wherein I know myself to be living is not the only place where I could live. That is why it is important to pay attention to the several *contexts* of Scripture texts that may be either critically recoverable or textually evoked. Thus, I know myself to be living in a crime-threatened suburb in which I hear of the poor but, on most days, do not see them. In the text of Deuteronomy (to take one easy example), however, I do not listen in a threatened suburb. My 'place' is different. The claimed location of this text is the River Jordan whereby 'we' are about to enter the land of promise, a land filled with threatening Canaanite social structures and seductive Canaanite religion. As I listen, I have important decisions to make, according to Deuteronomy, mostly concerning neighbors. Or alternatively, to take the critical judgment about Deuteronomy, I live in seventh-century Jerusalem under the danger and threat of Assyria where the temptation is strong to accommodate and compromise until one's identity is gone.[63] In listening to this text, I can be at the Jordan or in Jerusalem only for a brief period, and then I return to the 'reality' of suburbia. But being transported briefly by rhetoric invites me to re-see and redescribe my own setting, perchance to act differently. Thus, the hearing of a counter-script invites to a countercontext which, over time, may authorize and empower counter-life.

(16) *Finally, I believe that the great pastoral fact among us that troubles everyone, liberal or conservative, is that the old givens of white, male, Western, colonial advantage no longer hold.*

The trust in those old givens takes many forms. It takes the form of power whereby we have known who was in charge, whom to trust and obey. It takes the form of knowledge, for we could identify the knowing authorities who had a right to govern. It takes the form of certitude, because the world was reliably and stably ordered. And those in control or authority had great finesse in conducting the kind of 'hegemonic theatre' that kept the world closely ordered and coherent.[64]

No special argument needs to be made about the demise of that world, even though a lot of political and ecclesiastical mileage is available out of the claim that the old world can be sustained even longer. The demise of that hegemony touches us in many different ways, personal and public, but there is in any case a widely shared sense that things are out of control. That sense is widely shared not only by beneficiaries of the old patterns of certitude but also by many of its perceived victims. Nothing seems to be reliable as it used to be. And that sense of things being out of control invites all kinds of extreme notions of fear and anxiety that eventuate in acts and policies of brutality.

In that context, preachers are entrusted with a text, alternative to the failed text of white, male, Western hegemony, which mediates and valorizes a viable world outside that given, privileged advantage of certitude and domination. It turns out that the script we have trusted in the Enlightenment (and in the older Euro-American) tradition is an unreliable script, even though we have been massively committed to it. And now, we are wondering, is there a more adequate script out of which we may reimagine our lives? Although few would articulate their coming to worship on such grounds, I believe people are haunted by the question of whether there is a text (and an interpreter) that can say something that will make sense out of our pervasive nonsense.[65] It is my conviction that neither old liberal ideologies nor old conservative certitudes nor critical claims made for the Bible will now do. Our circumstance permits and requires the preacher to do something we have not been permitted or required to do before. Ours is an awesome opportunity: to see whether this text, with all of our interpretive inclinations, can voice and offer reality in a redescribed way that is credible and evocative of a new humanness, rooted in holiness and practiced in neighborliness.

Notes

1 See Richard Rorty, *Philosophy and the Mirror of Nature*, Princeton, Princeton University Press, 1979, p. 335 and *passim*.

2 I am aware that the term 'handmaiden' is beset by a history of sexism. I use it here intentionally and in recognition of what it implies for historical criticism.

3 On the presuppositional, intellectual, and ideological revolution wrought in the rise of criticism, see Paul Hazard, *The European Mind: 1680–1715*, New York, World Publishing, 1963; and Susan Bordo, *The Flight to Objectivity: Essays on Cartesianism and Culture*, Albany, NY, SUNY Press, 1987.

4 On what I call 'the emerging criticism', see Steven L. McKenzie and Stephen R. Haynes (eds), *To Each Its Own Meaning: An Introduction to Biblical Criticisms and Their Applications*, Louisville, KY, Westminster/John Knox, 1993.

5 It is conventional to view most worshiping congregations as profoundly homogeneous and that is no doubt true. But within such homogeneous communities, it is increasingly the case that there are wide-ranging convictions and opinions, so wide-ranging that it is often difficult to identify any basis of consensus. Such heterogeneity is very different from a kind of diversity rooted in a shared core of perspective.

6 See David Lochhead, *The Dialogical Imperative: A Christian Reflection on Interfaith Encounter*, Maryknoll, Orbis, 1988, and especially David Tracy, *Plurality and Ambiguity: Hermeneutics, Religion, Hope*, San Francisco, Harper & Row, 1987.

7 Alasdair MacIntyre, *Three Rival Versions of Moral Enquiry: Encyclopaedia, Genealogy, and Tradition*, Notre Dame, IN, University of Notre Dame Press, 1990, has observed that even in such a formidable situation as the Gifford Lectures, a changed epistemological climate now permits the lecturer only to make a proposal but not to announce a conclusion to be received by the audience.

8 See the famous distinction made by Krister Stendahl, 'Biblical Theology, Contemporary', in *The Interpreter's Dictionary of the Bible*, vol. 1, Nashville, TN, Abingdon, 1962, pp. 418–32; and the critical response of Ben Ollenburger, 'What Krister Stendahl "Meant": A Normative Critique of "Descriptive Biblical Theology"', in *Horizons in Biblical Theology*, 8, 1986, pp. 61–98.

9 See especially Susan A. Handelman, *The Slayers of Moses: The Emergence of Rabbinic Interpretation in Modern Literary Theory*, Albany, NY, SUNY Press, 1982.

10 Ibid., pp. 21, 34, and *passim*. See also Moshe Idel, 'Infinities of Torah in Kabbalah', in Geoffrey H. Hartman and Sanford Budick (eds), *Midrash and Literature*, New Haven, CT, Yale University Press, 1986, pp. 141–57; and, more generally, the entire volume.

11 See Handelman, 1982, pp. 141–52 and *passim*.

12 Paul Ricoeur, 'From the Hermeneutics of Texts to the Hermeneutics of Action', in *From Text to Action*, Evanston, IL, Northeastern University Press, 1991, pp. 105–222. See also Richard Harvey Brown, *Society as Text: Essays on Rhetoric, Reason, and Reality*, Chicago, University of Chicago Press, 1987.

13 Ricoeur, 1991, p. 121.

14 On the classic, see David Tracy, *The Analogical Imagination: Christian Theology and the Culture of Pluralism*, New York, Crossroad, 1981.

15 See Paul Ricoeur, 'Biblical Hermeneutics', *Semeia*, 4, 1975, p. 127 and *passim*. In a very different frame of reference, see also the notion of construal and reconstrual in David H. Kelsey, *The Uses of Scripture in Recent Theology*, Philadelphia, Fortress, 1975.

16 Philip Rieff, *The Triumph of the Therapeutic: Uses of Faith After Freud*, New York, Harper & Row, 1966. More generally on the Enlightenment, see Bordo, 1987, and Stephen Toulmin, *Cosmopolis: The Hidden Agenda of Modernity*, New York, Free Press, 1990. In Walter Brueggemann, *Texts Under Negotiation: The Bible and Postmodern Imagination*, Minneapolis, MN, Fortress, 1993, chapter 1, I have tried to assess the significance of the changes in Enlightenment consciousness for biblical interpretation.

17 In addition to Paul Hazard, *The European Mind*, see Klaus Scholder, *The Birth of Modern Critical Theology: Origins and Problems of Biblical Criticism in the Seventeenth Century*, Philadelphia, Trinity Press International, 1990.

18   Bordo, 1987, suggests that the loss of 'mother church' required finding another certitude that could nurture like a mother.

19   On the emergence of the individual self in the Cartesian program, see Charles Taylor, *Sources of the Self: The Making of the Modern Identity*, Cambridge, MA, Harvard University Press, 1989.

20   For a positive alternative to such individualism, see Paul R. Sponheim, *Faith and the Other: A Relational Theology*, Minneapolis, MN, Fortress, 1993.

21   See Milton L. Myers, *The Soul of Modern Economic Man*, Chicago, University of Chicago Press, 1983, on the 'text' of Hobbes behind the work of Adam Smith.

22   See Neil Postman, *Entertaining Ourselves to Death: Public Discourse in the Age of Show Business*, New York, Penguin, 1986; and Postman, *Technology: The Surrender of Culture to Technology*, New York, Random House, 1993.

23   See Godfrey Hodgson, *The Colonel: The Life and Wars of Henry Stimson, 1867–1950*, New York, Alfred A. Knopf, 1990.

24   See Walter Isaacson and Evan Thomas, *Wise Men: Six Friends and the World They Made*, New York, Touchstone, 1988. Of the 'Wise Men' Kai Bird, *The Chairman, John J. McCloy: The Making of the American Establishment*, New York, Simon and Schuster, 1992, p. 663, writes: 'As men possessing a measure of *gravitas*, McCloy and other Establishment figures always claimed they could rise above the private interests they represented and discern the larger public good. Ultimately, the claim is not sustainable.'

25   In *Darwin*, New York, Warner, 1991, Adrian Desmond and James Moore make a compelling case that social Darwinism was not remote from the awareness of Darwin himself. He knew where he was located socially as he did his research.

26   See the discussion of David McLellan, *The Thought of Karl Marx: An Introduction*, London, Macmillan, 1971, pp. 41–51.

27   Concerning the role of 'social theatre' in the establishment and maintenance of social relations, see E. P. Thompson, *Customs in Common*, New York, New Press, 1991, pp. 86–7 and *passim*.

28   See Leon Festinger, *A Theory of Cognitive Dissonance*, Stanford, CA, Stanford University Press, 1962.

29   Victor Turner, *The Ritual Process: Structure and Anti-Structure*, Ithaca, NY, Cornell University Press, 1969. For an exposition and critique of Turner's work, see Bobby C. Alexander, *Victor Turner Revisited: Ritual as Social Change*, Atlanta, Scholars Press, 1991.

30   The basic study of this coherence is Robert Bellah, 'Civil Religion in America', *Daedalus*, 96, 1967, pp. 1–21. See his larger discussion in *The Broken Covenant: American Civil Religion in Time of Trial*, New York, Crossroad, 1975. Part of the power of Martin Luther King, Jr. was that he was still able to appeal to this coherence.

31   In Brueggemann, 1993, pp. 2–25, I have suggested that the work of Scripture interpretation is to fund counter-imagination.

32   Wallace Stevens, 'A High-Toned Old Christian Woman', in *The Collected Poems of Wallace Stevens*, New York, Vintage, 1954, p. 59.

33   Garrett Green, *Imagining God: Theology and the Religious Imagination*, San Francisco, Harper & Row, 1989, pp. 73, 140, and *passim*.

34   David J. Bryant, *Faith and the Play of Imagination: On the Role of Imagination in Religion*, Macon, GA, Mercer University Press, 1989, p. 115, helpfully explores what it means to 'take as.'

35   On the 'myth of the given', in addition to Thomas Kuhn, *The Structure of Scientific Revolutions*, Chicago, University of Chicago Press, 1962, see also the important work of Mary Hesse and Michael Arbib, *The Construction of Reality*, Cambridge, Cambridge University Press, 1986.

36   The claim of David R. Blumenthal, *Facing the Abusing God: A Theology of Protest*, Louisville, Westminster/John Knox, 1993, pp. 47–54 and *passim*, that we live '*seriatim*', has much to commend it. But it is likely an overstatement for anyone.

37   See Brevard S. Childs's most recent statement in *Biblical Theology of the Old and New Testaments: Theological Reflection on the Christian Bible*, Minneapolis, Fortress, 1992, pp. 70–94 and *passim*.

38   Toulmin, 1990, pp. 186–201, has nicely argued positively for a retreat from universal assertion.

39   See for example, Gabriel Josipovici, *The Book of God: A Response to the Bible,* New Haven, CT, Yale University Press, 1988, pp. 75–89, and his treatment of the Joseph narrative.

40   John R. Donahue, *The Gospel in Parable*, Philadelphia, Fortress, 1988, has provided a rich study of the parables and fully understands the parabolic character of gospel truth. He observes the cruciality of such speech when living in a 'desert of the imagination' (p. 212).

41   Sandra M. Schneiders, *The Revelatory Text: Interpreting the New Testament as Sacred Scripture*, San Francisco, Harper, 1991, pp. 102–108.

42   Jacob Neusner, *The Enchantments of Judaism: Rites of Transformation from Birth through Death*, New York, Basic, 1987, p. 214: 'We are Jews through the power of our imagination.'

43   On the history of imagination, see Green, 1989, chapter 1; Richard Kearney, *The Wake of Imagination*, Minneapolis, University of Minnesota Press, 1988; and *Poetic of Imagining: From Husserl to Lyotard*, San Francisco, Harper, 1991.

44   Kearney, 1991, pp. 88–111, provides a useful entry to Bachelard. It is from Kearney that I have taken my lead here. Of the work of Bachelard, see *The Poetics of Space*, Boston, Beacon, 1969; and *On Poetic Imagination*, ed. Colette Gandin, New York, Bobbs Merrill, 1971.

45   Kearney, 1991, p. 95.

46   John E. Thiel, *Imagination and Authority: Theological Authorship in the Modern Tradition*, Minneapolis, Fortress, 1991.

47   The statement is programmatic for Ricoeur. See, for example, Paul Ricoeur, *The Conflict of Interpretations*, Evanston, IL, Northwestern University Press, 1974, p. 288.

48   On imagination as the originary point of possibility, see Paul Ricoeur, *The Philosophy of Paul Ricoeur*, ed. Charles E. Reagan and David Stewart, Boston, Beacon, 1978, pp. 231–38.

49   Brueggemann, 1993, pp. 64–70.

50   Hans Urs von Balthasar, *Theo-Drama: Theological Dramatic Theory,* Vol. 1, *Prolegomena*, San Francisco, Ignatius, 1988; Vol. 2, *Dramatis Personae: Man in God*, San Francisco, Ignatius, 1990; Francis Young, *Virtuoso Theology: The Bible and Interpretation*, Cleveland, Pilgrim, 1993.

51   G. Ernest Wright, *God Who Acts: Biblical Theology as Recital*, London, SCM, 1952; G. Ernest Wright and Reginald H. Fuller, *The Book of the Acts of God: Christian Scholarship Interprets the Bible*, Garden City, NY, Doubleday, 1957; and C. H. Dodd, *The Apostolic Preaching and Its Developments*, New London, Hodder & Stoughton, 1944.

52   See, for example, Owen C. Thomas (ed.), *God's Activity in the World: The Contemporary Problem,* Chico, CA, Scholars Press, 1983; James B. Wiggins (ed.), *Religion as Story,* New York, University Press of America, 1975; and Stanley Hauerwas and L. Gregory Jones (eds), *Why Narrative? Readings in Narrative Theology,* Grand Rapids, MI, Eerdmans, 1989.

53   On dramatic rendering as it pertains to theological discourse, see Dale Patrick, *The Rendering of God in the Old Testament*, Philadelphia, Fortress, 1981.

54   Hayden White, 'The Politics of Historical Interpretation: Discipline and De-Sublimation', in W. J. T. Mitchell (ed.) *The Politics of Interpretation*, Chicago, University of Chicago Press, 1983, pp. 119–43; and White, *The Content of the Form: Narrative Discourse and Historical Representation*, Baltimore, Johns Hopkins University Press, 1987; and White, *Metahistory: The Historical Imagination in Nineteenth Century Europe*, Baltimore, Johns Hopkins University Press, 1973.

55   Alasdair MacIntyre, *Whose Justice? Which Rationality?,* Notre Dame, University of Notre Dame Press, 1988.

56   Amos Wilder, 'Story and Story-World', *Interpretation*, 37, 1983, pp. 353–64. See my summary on 'world-making' in Brueggemann, *Israel's Praise: Doxology Against Idolatry and Ideology*, Philadelphia, Fortress, 1988, pp. 1–28, 157–60.

57 Brevard S. Childs, 'Psalm Titles and Midrashic Exegesis', *Journal of Semitic Studies*, 16, 1971, pp. 137–50.

58 On the cruciality of rhetoric, see the suggestive distinction between 'rhetorical man' and 'serious man' made by Richard A. Lanham, *The Motives of Eloquence: Literary Rhetoric in the Renaissance,* New Haven, CT, Yale University Press, 1976, pp. 1–35. And see the comments on Lanham's distinction by Stanley Fish, 'Rhetoric', in Frank Lentricchia and Thomas McLaughlin (eds), *Critical Terms for Literary Study,* Chicago, University of Chicago Press, 1990, pp. 206–9. Such arguments suggest that the privilege long assigned to Plato and Aristotle against the Sophists may be usefully re-examined.

59 See, for example, Numbers 11:4–6; 14:1–4; Exodus 16:3.

60 Brueggemann, 1993, pp. 21–5.

61 Walter Brueggemann, *Biblical Perspectives on Evangelism: Living in a Three-Storied Universe,* Nashville, TN, Abingdon, 1993.

62 Peter L. Berger and Thomas Luckmann, *The Social Construction of Reality: A Treatise in the Sociology of Knowledge,* Garden City, NY, Doubleday, 1967, pp. 156–7.

63 For a standard summary of critical judgments about Deuteronomy, see Patrick D. Miller, *Deuteronomy,* Louisville, KY, John Knox, 1990, pp. 2–17.

64 See Thompson, 1991.

65 See Walter Brueggemann, 'As the Text "Makes Sense": Keep the Methods as Lean and Uncomplicated as Possible', *Christian Ministry*, 14, 1983, pp. 7–10.

Part 2

PREACHING SCRIPTURE

Introduction to Part 2

How to make the move from biblical text to sermon is a question that has been vigorously discussed for many years. Thomas Long queries the conventional wisdom on the subject – break open the text, extract its key idea, turn towards the congregation and apply the idea to contemporary life. The labour of exegesis will seldom get the preacher beyond the point of 'what the text used to mean'. The leap into contemporary application, which is often presented as no more than a step across a puddle, requires, in fact, a leap across a historical chasm. Any analogy between then and now is far from obvious and the text may function as little more than a Rorschach blot. Against this, Long argues that the connection between the text and the contemporary world is not scientific or procedural but poetic. Meaning is given only as 'the interpreter brings together the two poles, the ancient text and the present situation, and allows the spark of imagination to jump between them'. Two worked examples – from James chapter 5 and Mark chapter 1 – demonstrate how everything the preacher knows about the text, and everything he or she knows about the world, come together 'in a volatile, exciting, and free-ranging moment of imaginative encounter'.

Thomas G. Long, 'The Use of Scripture in Contemporary Preaching' was first published in *Interpretation*, 44, 4, 1990, pp. 341–52.

In his article on preaching the epistles, David Day examines the assumption that their real message resides in the content of the biblical text and can be detached without loss from the form in which it is expressed. He argues that such a view can result in vital elements being ignored or passed over. An exclusive concentration on content may underrate rhetorical strategies, complexity, movement and specific context. The preacher who is concerned to hear not just what a passage says but also how it says it will take account of characteristic features of the epistles such as their personal reference, occasional nature, mood, structure, linearity, function and the highly situation-specific nature of their theology. If Scripture is given as content-embodied-in-a-form then the sermon should echo that form. He gives examples from the epistles of how form, technique, mood and function, 'conversational theology' and narrative might affect the construction of the sermon and argues that Scripture might be usefully approached not just as a theological resource but also as a model for communicative method.

David V. Day, 'Preaching the Epistles' first appeared in *Anvil*, 14, 4, 1997, pp. 273–82.

What is the relevance of the Old Testament for the Christian preacher and how should it be handled? This question has usually been seen as a Christological one. In our next article, Walter Brueggemann looks at the issue from an ecclesial point of view. The Old Testament consists of a challenge to live as an alternative community with an alternative identity. Most texts urge Israel to choose against the prevailing power structures and for the way of radical trust in Yahweh. She is endlessly engaged in either conforming to the existing culture or deciding to embrace the life and identity of the Yahwistic covenant. Either/Or is the theme of the Old Testament. Brueggemann illustrates this theme from two classic formulations: Joshua 24 and Second Isaiah. The importance of preaching resides in the fact that the *either/or* is never obvious but depends on the utterance of witnesses to make the choice clear. 'Where there is no speaking and hearing of an alternative world, there is no faith, no courage, no freedom to choose differently'. Preaching is an urgent task because the *Or* of faith is still needed in our culture.

Walter Brueggemann's 'An imaginative "Or"' was first published in the *Journal for Preachers*, 23, 3, 2000, pp. 3–17.

In the next article, Edward Farley addresses what he calls the impossible task of preaching week by week. He believes that the problem is caused by the preacher's subjection to 'the prevailing paradigm of preaching'. This paradigm assumes that the proper way to view the Bible is as a collection of 'passages' containing the 'word of God' that have to be related to the situation of the congregation by means of rhetorically-crafted sermons. This paradigm is markedly different from New Testament preaching, which preached not passages but the gospel. In fact, the content of most biblical passages is not the gospel. Nor is the word of God necessarily found in a lectionary passage. Some passages even contain material which the preacher might want to preach against and division into passages fragments the larger unity of the biblical book. What really happens in a sermon is that the preacher moves from the lesson in life to a constructed preachable message in the passage, while speaking as if the movement were the reverse. After considering flawed attempts to correct the failed paradigm, Farley grants that the church should continue to teach the Bible but argues that she should preach the gospel, that is, 'to bring to bear a certain past event on the present so as to open up the future'. The preacher will still need to enter the world of the Bible, but it is the gospel which is to be preached not the passage.

For a critique of Farley's position see Ronald J. Allen, 'Why Preach from Passages in the Bible?', in Thomas G. Long and Edward Farley (eds), *Preaching as a Theological Task*, Louisville, KY, Westminster/John Knox, 1996, pp. 176–88.

Edward Farley, 'Preaching the Bible and Preaching the Gospel' was first published in *Theology Today*, 51, 1, 1994, pp. 90–103.

The final article in Part 2 draws on Jungian psychology to propose a method of biblical hermeneutics and preaching that takes seriously the psychological functions of sensing (S), intuition (I), feeling (F), and thinking (T). Leslie Francis names this the SIFT method. It addresses four distinct questions to each passage of Scripture, which are shaped by these four psychological functions.

Leslie Francis has written extensively on psychological type, including a series of books (co-authored with Peter Atkins) applying his SIFT method to passages from the Gospels.

Leslie J. Francis, 'Psychological Type and Biblical Hermeneutics: SIFT Method of Preaching' first appeared in the journal *Rural Theology*, 1, 1, 2003, pp. 13–23.

3   The Use of Scripture in Contemporary Preaching

Thomas G. Long

Once upon a time any preacher who wished to take up the challenge of responsible biblical preaching could at least be clear about the task. Not every preacher, to be sure, aspired to be a 'biblical' preacher, and certainly not all who aimed at preaching biblical sermons actually did so; but there was little uncertainty about the mission. A great host of biblical scholars, theologians, and homileticians had gathered in the vast convention hall of 'biblical theology', and because of their efforts, preachers were the beneficiaries of a virtual consensus regarding the proper method for interpreting Scripture for preaching. Biblical texts were viewed as sealed containers with urgent theological ideas inside. So, the preacher's job, simply put, was to crack the seal, reach inside the textual vessel, draw out the ideas (thus, *exegesis*), and then produce a sermon somehow applying those ideas to the contemporary situation.

Producing biblical sermons, therefore, involved two clear and distinct movements. First, the preacher turned toward the ancient text, withdrawing its internal meanings. Then, the preacher swiveled one hundred and eighty degrees toward the congregation, attempting to state the implications of those meanings for the current situation. The order was crucial and the direction of the flow immutable: first the text, then the contemporary situation. Though sometimes difficult to perform and demanding specialized skills, this two-step procedure was nonetheless elegantly simple in design.

When preachers were taught this text-to-sermon method, they were sternly warned against inadvertent contamination of the process. The danger, they were told, was that when reaching into the textual vessel, the preacher could accidentally introduce some foreign element into the text from the modern scene (the dreaded *eis-egesis*),[1] thus polluting the purity of the biblical witness. The only way to avoid this was for the preacher to don a set of sterile surgical gloves, namely through a rigorous application of the methods of historical-critical exegesis, procedures designed to sublimate contemporary presumptions in favor of a nonintrusive viewing of the text in its own historical milieu.

Nowadays, however, things are not so plain and simple for the biblical preacher. The devotees of the 'biblical theology' movement have long since left the convention hall and broken into smaller, sometimes rival, caucuses, or given up the cause altogether. Moreover, the alleged neutrality of historical-criticism has been unmasked as itself biased, the product of a set of ideological assumptions about the nature of meaning.[2] In other words, the surgical gloves, as it turns out, were not sterile. Not only that, rival methods of interpretation – feminist, liberationist, and postmodernist, just to name a few – have risen on the hermeneutical skyline. We have moved in textual interpretation from village simplicity to urban complexity, and the consensus regarding interpretational method has broken down. Indeed, any who attempt to keep an alert, watchful eye on recent developments in biblical studies have, of late, felt like observers of political trends in eastern Europe. They gaze in astonishment as almost everyday some seemingly fixed boundary is shifted, some unexpected factor appears in the equation, some reigning world view is overturned, some previously silent, or silenced, voice begins to command attention. The landscape of biblical hermeneutics has been altered rapidly, radically, and with profound effect upon biblical preaching.

Commenting on the rise in recent biblical studies of the newer, politically-fueled hermeneutical methods and the interest among biblical scholars in the social sciences, literary criticism, and other cross-disciplinary endeavors, Stephen D. Moore states: 'It is an exciting and confusing time for biblical studies. . . . The spectacle of so many biblical scholars, many of them old enough to know better, climbing over the neighbor's fences has elicited bemused headshaking in some of their colleagues and outright disapproval in others'.[3]

What is, in Moore's words, 'exciting and confusing' for biblical scholars is also exciting and confusing for biblical preachers, too. The question is, Does the confusion finally overpower the excitement and the promise of new insight? To be sure, all of the recent ferment in biblical hermeneutics can, of course, be quite disorienting for the preacher. No longer is there a well-traveled, brightly-lit, four-lane highway from text to sermon. Many paths lead from the text toward the pulpit, some of them unpaved, poorly marked, and all of them fraught with uncertain stretches. On the other hand, the energetic eruption of multiple and alternative approaches to biblical interpretation may also serve to energize the task of biblical preaching. Indeed, it seems more evident every day that when the dust settles in biblical studies it will be seen that biblical hermeneutics has, for the most part and in its own way, edged ever closer to the concerns of homiletics, with the result that we may well be on the verge of an exciting and hopeful renewal of biblical preaching. That, at least, is the idea I would like to explore in this article.

Coming clean about imagination

Working preachers, for the most part, do not keep up with the hottest news from the hermeneutical front, nor are they likely to have a well-thumbed copy of the latest inscrutable tome from Derrida on the nightstand. Nevertheless, they are in touch, at least intuitively, with the changes rippling across the surface of biblical hemeneutics because they are active and intentional practitioners of the art of interpretation. In fact, if any university-style literary critic wished to venture beyond the walls of Poetry 101, the pages of the *New York Review of Books*, and other hothouse hermeneutical environments into some rough and tumble social arena where textual interpretation actually shapes the practical life of a group of people, then one could hardly find a better test case than the parish minister preaching in the context of corporate worship. Week in and week out preachers stand up before congregations of people and actually interpret ancient texts, and one simply cannot do this without feeling in one's bones the stresses and strains of the task and without discerning through constant use the design flaws in any model of interpretation. The 'hermeneutical textbook' of working ministers is the demanding, ceaseless, urgent, and electric moment of preaching, with all its ambiguities, and this textbook yields considerable wisdom to those who study its pages carefully.

For example, conscientious biblical preachers have long shared the little secret that the classical text-to-sermon exegetical methods produce far more chaff than wheat. If one has the time and patience to stay at the chores of exegesis, theoretically one can find out a great deal of background information about virtually every passage in the Bible, much of it unfortunately quite remote from any conceivable use in a sermon. The preacher's desk can quickly be covered with Ugaritic parallels and details about syncretistic religion in the Phrygian region of Asia Minor. It is hard to find fault here; every scrap of data is potentially valuable, and it is impossible to know in advance which piece of information is to be prized. So, we brace ourselves for the next round of exegesis by saying that it is necessary to pan a lot of earth to find a little gold, and that is true, of course. However, preachers have the nagging suspicion that there is a good deal of wasted energy in the traditional model of exegesis or, worse, that the real business of exegesis is excavation and earth-moving and that any homiletical gold stumbled over along the way is largely coincidental. Stephen Moore's image of the work of traditional biblical studies also fits the preacher toiling away at the task of classical histor-ical-critical exegesis, namely, that it is at first like army boot camp, turning flabby faith and ill-informed biblical piety into firm muscle, but that it soon slips 'little by little into the anesthesia of a desk job, adrift in the sea of paperwork that is the mainstay of biblical studies in peace time: the thou-sands of small-scale jobs collectively undertaken, which issue in thousands of small-scale findings'.[4]

More important, alert biblical preachers have been aware for some time that there is a bit of deception, a touch of legerdemain, built into that classical text-to-sermon process. The preacher takes the text and puts it through the paces of a good exegetical process. The grammar of the text is analysed, word studies are conducted, the probable *Sitz im Leben* is established, and so on. The handle is turned, the wheels spin, the gears mesh, and in the end out pops a reasonably secure version of what the text *meant* in its historical context or, to put it more bluntly, what the text *used to mean*.

Now, so what? The exegesis yielded the information that Paul responded in such and such a way to a question in Corinth about meat offered to idols, a question that would never in a million years occur to anyone in Kingsport, Tennessee, or Fresno, California. So what? We find that Jesus told the parable of the prodigal son to defend his ministry against the criticism of the Pharisees. So what? The preacher must answer that question, of course, but is given scant help for doing so. The preacher is simply told that now the gap must be bridged from the history of the text to the urgency of the contemporary situation. It is presented as an obvious next step, a child's leap across a puddle, but the honest preacher knows that the distance between what the text *used to mean* and what the text may *now mean* yawns wide, and the leap seems difficult indeed.

The standard and most often traveled homiletical bridge between then and now, between the ancient text and the modern context, is analogy: the claim that something in the historical circum-stances of the text is like something in our world. Thus the preacher skips sprightly across the ana-logical span, asserting in the sermon, 'Aren't we just like those Pharisees?' or 'Even today the church faces a crisis much like the Corinthians faced in their controversy over the eating of meat, do we not?' But herein, the astute preacher knows, lies the little deception, the wave of the magician's wand. The analogies do not really hold. No, to be precise, we are *not* 'just like' the Pharisees, and no, as a matter of fact, we *do not* face a crisis that is 'much like' the one the Corinthians faced. First-century Pharisees are as extinct as mastodons, and the meat-offered-to-idols controversy would be unrecognizable to the officers of any present-day church. The historical discontinuities between us and the characters who populate the pages of the Bible, between their world and ours, are at least as striking as the continuities.

A student of mine, who had just returned from a seminary-sponsored trip to Palestine, confided to me that the trip had thrown his preaching into profound disarray. Far from the experience of some other visitors to the Holy Land, who come back whistling 'I walked today where Jesus walked', this student returned deeply impressed with the differences between the historical circumstances of the Bible and his own situation. 'I used to preach about Abraham and Sarah', he said, 'as if they were people who could have lived on my street, who grew up in our neighborhood, who could have been comfortable at worship in our church. I now know that Abraham and I inhabit different worlds, and the gulf between us is unimaginably vast. I don't know what to say in the pulpit any more about somebody like Abraham.' What had happened was that this preacher had become suddenly aware of what seems to be a subtle truth-in-advertising problem in much biblical preaching, a shell game that quickly substitutes our world for the biblical world, as if the gap of history could be bridged through the alleged analogical symmetry of the constant human situation.

Some years ago, in an often cited essay entitled 'The Use of the Bible in Modern Theology',

Oxford theologian [Dennis] Nineham spotted the same apparent 'now you see it, now you don't' move from text to contemporary context.[5] While serving on a World Council of Churches task force on biblical hermeneutics, Nineham participated in several group exercises in which teams of scholars engaged in the interpretation of sample biblical texts. The members of these groups agreed, Nineham noted, on the philological, lexicographical, and other procedures necessary to establish the historical meaning of texts. Beyond that, however, the group participants parted company, since some of the scholars, Nineham observed, assumed that these historical textual meanings were, theologically speaking, the Word of God and, as such, would also inevitably prove to have contemporary meaning. In short, Nineham was satisfied to ascertain what the text *meant*, but some of his colleagues were persuaded on theological grounds that more was demanded, that the exegetical task was incomplete until the exegete had moved at least halfway down the homiletical pathway and determined what the text *means* for today. Nineham strenuously objected to this:

> A lot of this did not seem to me self-evident. Many statements in ancient texts have *no* meaning today in any normal sense of the word 'meaning'. No doubt if you reflect long enough over any ancient statement – even, let us say, an historical inaccuracy in some ancient Egyptian annals – interesting reflections of some sort will occur to you; but my colleagues seemed to mean something more positive and direct than that. When pressed, they were not prepared to assert it as a universal principle that every biblical statement has a contemporary meaning, but it clearly surprised some of them that the question should be raised as an open one; and I suppose their attitude is reflected in much contemporary preaching, in which we seek to explicate '*the* meaning' (for today) of a short biblical passage.[6]

The point of dispute here is absolutely crucial for biblical preaching, and at the risk both of oversimplification and of getting involved in a scrap that is none of my business, I would like to attempt to step between Nineham and his colleagues. On the one hand, as a preacher, I am in sympathy with Nineham's colleagues who assume that Scripture, theologically described, provides access to the eventful Word of God and that the exegetical task is unfinished until it has moved the text into the contemporary arena. Indeed, biblical preaching is based upon the confident hope and the profound promise that the church's engagement with Scripture yields, in the words of Elizabeth Achtemeier, 'an active, effective . . . community-formed word' for today.[7] On the other hand, Nineham has a point, too. What sense can there be in claiming that some ancient text (say the instructions in Lev. 13 for the priestly treatment of itching diseases) has a ready and apparent meaning for today? Nineham was perplexed, and rightly so, by his colleagues' confident and methodical march from the historical meanings of texts to assertions about their pertinence for the contemporary world.

In my view, though, Nineham's satirical picture of the interpreter, musing long and hard over some flawed scrap of ancient Egyptian scribbling and finally having 'interesting reflections of some sort' says more than he knows, and something more positive than he intends. Nineham aims, of course, to make a nasty crack, to portray this so-called act of interpretation as essentially arbitrary and negative, to depict the interpreter as arriving at meanings that are actually utterly extraneous to the text. He implies that biblical interpreters falsely believe themselves to be moving smoothly from ancient to contemporary meanings, while they are really treating texts as Rorschach blots or as inert crowbars that simply pry loose meanings already present in the interpreter's mind. Taken another way, though, Nineham has simply stumbled over the truth that between an ancient text and any contemporary application of that text stands an act of imagination on the part of the interpreter. Acts of the imagination, because they are exercises in freedom, can, of course, be arbitrary, but they are not necessarily so. Imaginative acts of interpretation call admittedly use texts as pretexts, but they can be truly guided by texts as well.

It is here, precisely at the juncture between human imagination and textual interpretation, that contemporary biblical hermeneutics becomes the true friend of the preacher. One of the hallmarks of recent biblical interpretation has been the discovery of the role of human imagination, both the imagination employed by those authors who composed or compiled the biblical text and the imagination required of those who read and interpret it.

If one is caught up in the assumptions that proper exegesis is somehow 'scientific' and that biblical texts have stable meanings that can be discovered, carefully transported into the present, and applied, then the very thought that the interpreter's imagination might be running loose in the process is, as Nineham intended, an embarrassment. Yet it is precisely the breakup of the idea that any hermeneutical method is neutral or 'scientific' that has freed good biblical preachers (and biblical scholars as well) to admit what they have intuitively known all along: The connection between the ancient text and the contemporary world is not procedural but poetic, not mechanical but metaphorical. The 'meaning for today' of a biblical text is not lying there in the text itself, waiting to be uncovered; it is given only as the interpreter brings together the two poles, the ancient text and the present situation, and allows the spark of imagination to jump between them.[8]

To be specific and also to return to earlier examples, when preachers say, 'Aren't we just like the Pharisees today?' or when they treat Abraham and Sarah as if they were neighbors down the street, they are not really forging an exact analogy, or moving with precision between discrete historical eras. Rather they are depending upon the creative capacity of the hearer to enter imaginatively into the world of a character in a story. When the preacher joins the text about the meat controversy at Corinth to, let us say, a local dispute about religion in the public schools, this connection is not obvious or mechanical; it results from the preacher's exercise of imagination, and its aptness must be judged on grounds other than strict, mathematical logic.

To see preaching as an imaginative regeneration of a biblical text also opens our eyes to the role played by imagination both in the creation and canonization of the text itself and in the minds of those who will hear the sermon. As Walter Brueggemann states, 'The process of forming, transmitting, and interpreting the biblical text is a creative process at its beginning, midpoint and ending.'[9] In other words, imagination is present all along the line: The text was formed by a set of imaginative acts (the beginning), the preacher employs imagination to relate the text to the present situation (the midpoint), and those who listen to the sermon (the end of the textual process) are not blank tablets upon which the sermon is written but are 'engaged in a constructive act of construal, of choosing, discerning and shaping the text through the way the community chooses to listen.'[10]

What difference does it make to the preacher to see the entire text-to-sermon process infused with acts of imagination on the part of the textual authors, canonizers, preachers, and hearers of sermons? Plenty, as it turns out. First, think about how imagination operates in the minds of the people in the pews. If we recognize that the hearers are engaged in an imaginative act of listening, taking our sermons and refiguring them in their minds, creating yet a new text out of the ancient text presented through the creative medium of the sermon, then we, as preachers, are freed from the need to exercise undue control over or to expect precise results from what is heard in the sermon. If two hundred people hear the sermon, then we can be assured, and reassured, that two hundred at least slightly different versions of the sermon will be heard. Moreover, while preachers are called to careful and faithful attention to biblical texts, attending to them with all of the tools and skills at their disposal, they are freed from the paralyzing fears associated with *eisegesis*. The text must be listened to, lived with, encountered on its own ground; but a sterile, presuppositionless, methodical move from text to sermon is neither possible nor desirable. The ever new and unpredictable event of the Word occurs in the imaginative *pas de deux* involving our world and the text. This interactive character of biblical interpretation has found support in the recent emphasis in biblical hermeneutics upon the role of the *reader*. Readers of texts, it is claimed, do not simply receive the words of texts in linear fashion, as if texts were sending out bits of processed information like linked sausages. Reading is a much more active and creative event; the reader enters into the passageways and gaps of the text, climbs up and down the syntactical ladders, moves backward and forward in the text. As this occurs the reader is guided toward an event of understanding that is both old (the product of the text's fixed pattern) and new (a function of the reader's artistry).[11] As Brueggemann maintains, 'The sermon is not an act of reporting on an old text, but it is an act of making a new text visible and available. This new text in part is the old text, and in part is the imaginative construction of the preacher which did not exist until the moment of utterance by the preacher.'[12]

Indeed, the old two-step notion – first the text, then the application – was wrong-headed to begin with. Preachers do not draw pure biblical ideas from texts and then figure out what they might mean for today. In the act of interpretation, everything we know and experience about our present world and everything we know and experience about the ancient text come together in a volatile, exciting, and free-ranging moment of imaginative encounter. Interpreting a text for preaching is much like going to a powerful and provocative play. When we experience the play, everything about ourselves and our world is simultaneously present and involved. We do not suspend our present concerns as we watch the play in the theater, as if it were some isolated dramatic event that we could observe with clinical detachment, and then walk back out into the sunshine and only at that moment try somehow to apply what we have seen to the way we live in the everyday world. Our ongoing concerns are already present, bristling and alert, as we watch, indeed, they are our points of access into the play. The boldest way to put this is that a certain kind of *eisegesis*, the kind that renders us completely present before the text and passionately concerned to hear a Word that addresses our world, is not a sin to be avoided, but rather is an earnestly sought prerequisite to productive *exegesis*. Argentinean biblical scholar J. Severino Croatto, writing from a liberation theology perspective, claims as much:

> One does not 'emerge' from a text (ex-egesis, from *ex* and *hegeisthai*, 'to lead, to guide') with a pure meaning, gathered from within, as a diver might swim to the surface with a piece of coral in hand, or as one might take something out of a bag or trunk. One must first 'get into' the text – a matter of *eis*-egesis – with questions that are not always those of its author, from a different horizon of experience.... [A]ny reading can only be a *re*reading of the meaning of a text.[13]

The imagination of the text

So, listeners exercise imagination in the hearing of sermons, and preachers exercise imagination in the interpretation of texts and in the construction of those sermons, but the most exciting gift of recent biblical hermeneutics to the text-to-sermon process has been the emphasis upon the imaginative dimensions of the text itself. Texts are no longer viewed as inert containers, jars with theological ideas inside, but as poetic expressions displaying rhetorical and literary artistry. Biblical texts are something like sermons in the sense that they not only intend to *say* things, but they intend to *do* things, to engender effects in the readers or hearers. Preachers are required to do more than to reach inside the textual vessel to retrieve the concept it contains, like a prize in a box of Cracker Jacks. They are invited to do 'close readings' of biblical texts, tracking the grooves of textual syntax and genre, keeping their eyes open for the rhetorical strategies expressed in the linguistic designs of the text.

This means that those who wish to be faithful biblical preachers must be eclectic in the methods of exegesis and interpretation. Rather than always attempting to pick the lock of the text with the blunt instrument of historical-criticism (or any other single method, for that matter), the preacher will rattle every door and try every window in an effort to enter the textual environment and to experience the total impact of the text.

Take, as an example, the fifth chapter of the Book of James. Suppose we were developing a sermon based upon that text. The text begins with what appears to be a direct and forceful denunciation of the wealthy: 'Come now, you rich, weep and howl for the miseries that are coming upon you. . . .' Clear enough, then, the sermon, if it is to be faithful to the text, should also be a diatribe against the rich, and the only decision left for the preacher to make is the identity of the target. Shall we take on the Trumps, the Exxons, or the local country club set?

But wait. A closer look at the text reveals a curious, and apparently nonsensical, shift in tone. After six verses of screaming threats, the text suddenly, at verse 7, soothes, 'Be patient, therefore . . . until the coming of the Lord. . . .' This abrupt turn in the rhetorical road may cause the modern reader to skid out of control, unless we bring into the picture a bit of historical and sociological data. What was the economic condition of the first recipients of the letter of James? Were they rich, or poor? Internal evidence would lead us to the conclusion that they were poor, or, at the very least, not rich (see 2:6).

If that is the case, we can begin to piece together the rhetorical strategy of the text, and we can begin to make sense of the seeming non sequitur in the text. Brother James is, in effect, preaching an epistolary sermon to a congregation of Christians who are, among other things, on the low side economically. At one dramatic point in the sermon (5:1), James strides away from the pulpit, flings open a window of the little sanctuary, and begins to shout toward the Manor House, 'Come now, you rich, weep and howl. . . . Your gold and silver have rusted. . . .' The congregation watches and listens in stunned silence as their pastor shouts dire warnings toward the rich, toward the powerful, toward the folks who control the society. 'Behold', thunders James, 'the wages of the laborers who mowed your fields, which you kept back by fraud, cry out. . . .' Now the congregation begins to get into the sermon. An 'amen' from a laborer in the back pew is heard, then another 'amen' and another, until the tiny church is filled with a chorus of amens.

Suddenly James stops, and when the echo of his last ringing shout dies out, the church is filled with an electric silence. James pulls a handkerchief out of his coat, wipes his dripping brow, walks slowly back to the pulpit, looks at every waiting eye, and in a reassuring voice, calm and low, says, 'Be patient, children, until the coming of the Lord'.

What we have discovered is that the *primary* rhetorical effect of our text is eschatological reassurance of the oppressed Christian community. This particular 'reading' of the text involved an interplay of various critical methods, historical, sociological, and rhetorical. Now, the effect of this reading upon the contemporary respondent will depend, of course, upon where that reader is positioned. For those Christian groups who today suffer at the hands of the rich and powerful, the text speaks again its word of encouragement. If, poetically speaking, we are in the Manor House, we hear the strong warnings coming from the little church, but we also 'overhear' the word of promise to the disadvantaged congregation. All of these levels of meaning in the text allow for a variety of sermonic approaches, none of them alike, but all of them faithful to this text.

Or again, to observe the variety of methods that can helpfully come into play in textual interpretation for preaching, look at the use of symbolic theological language in Mark 1:35–39, the passage that reports the event of Jesus' early morning praying in a 'lonely place'. The often preached sermon on this text, blind to the rhetorical aspects of the passage, talks sweetly of Jesus' busy ministry in Capernaum the day before (1:21–34) and his need for prayerful replenishment through quiet time. In other words, this conventional and predictable sermon tells us that the text shows a Jesus who, in the midst of his business, finds a tranquil time and a solitary place to pray – and so should we.

Yet the careful reader of Mark's Gospel will not make such a mistake in reading. When the text tells us that Jesus 'went out to a *lonely place*', the attentive reader will recognize this place. The word translated 'lonely place' is the word for 'desert' or 'wilderness', and even though we are only a few verses into Mark's Gospel, we have already encountered that word, and that place, four times: In Isaiah's voice of one crying in the 'wilderness' (v. 3), in John the Baptist's appearing in the 'wilderness' (v. 4), and twice in the brief account of Jesus' temptation (vs. 12–13). The 'wilderness', in short, has already become a technical literary and theological term, a place where momentous and decisive events occur, a place where the holy and the demonic vie for power.

So, when our text tells us that Jesus went into the 'wilderness' to pray, if we are paying attention, we do not think of this wilderness, this lonely place, as a tranquil, carefree spiritual oasis. To the contrary, the author has posted all of the signs along the way to alert us to the critical character and to the dangers of this place. This is the arena of temptation, the place where decisions of vocation and repentance must be made, the arena of decision between the call of God and the sirens of destruction. Sure enough, while Jesus is at prayer, the tempter comes: Simon and his companions find him and say, 'Every one is searching for you.' Every one wants you back in Capernaum, wants you to continue to be the local wonder-worker. Come back.

The question for the reader now becomes: Will Jesus go back, or will he not? Will he allow the 'way' Isaiah proclaimed to become changed from a straight path to a cul-de-sac, or not? Now comes the answer: 'Let us go on to the next towns, that I may preach there also', states Jesus, 'for that is why I came out.' Or, to put it theologically, let us go to Golgotha instead of remaining in Capernaum. The crisis has been faced, the temptation has been met, and Jesus has remained faithful to his messianic call.

The responsible and attentive sermon on this passage, then, will not coo piously of the virtues of prayer moments in the quiet garden before breakfast but will speak of prayer in the 'wilderness', prayer when the chips are down, when the temptations are fierce, when the possibilities of doing other than our calling are brightly attractive and deeply compelling. The key to this 'reading' is the interaction of theological and rhetorical aspects of the passage, the way in which the text evokes the crisis of Jesus' vocation and, by implication, ours, through its use of symbolic theological language.

The preacher who yearns for a clear and simple text-to-sermon method, who wants to 'paint by the numbers' homiletically, will surely be frustrated in the volatile environment of contemporary biblical hermeneutics. On the other hand, the preacher who is willing to risk the white-water ride through the spray-filled canyons of the text will surely see wonders there and on Sunday morning will testify about what was seen with breathless excitement.

Notes

1   For an intriguing homiletical case on behalf of a certain style of eisegesis, see the chapter entitled 'An Eisegesis Revival', in J. Randall Nichols, *Building the Word: The Dynamics of Communication and Preaching*, San Francisco, Harper & Row, 1980, pp. 26–30.

2   See, as one among many examples of recent challenges to the alleged neutrality of historical-criticism, Edgar V. McKnight, *Post-Modern Use of the Bible: The Emergence of Reader-Oriented Criticism*, Nashville, TN, Abingdon, 1988, esp. pp. 44–53. Following the argument of Van A. Harvey, McKnight claims, 'By the nineteenth century, the assumptions of the historical-critical method had penetrated so deeply into Western consciousness that it was impossible even to think about the assumptions. These had become "a part of the furniture" of Western mentality' (p. 47).

3   Stephen D. Moore, *Literary Criticism and the Gospels: The Theoretical Challenge*, New Haven, CT, and London, Yale University Press, 1989, p. xiii.

4   Moore, 1989, p. 176.

5   Dennis E. Nineham, 'The Use of the Bible in Modern Theology', *The Bulletin of the John Rylands Library*, 52, 1, 1969, pp. 178–99.

6   Nineham, 1969, p. 181.

7   Elizabeth Achtemeier, *Preaching from the Old Testament*, Louisville, Westminster/John Knox, 1989, pp. 28–9.

8   On the role of imagination in the theological interpretation of Scripture done within the context of the
    church, see David Kelsey, *The Uses of Scripture in Recent Theology,* Philadelphia, Fortress, 1975.
    Particularly helpful is Kelsey's discussion of the controls exercised upon imagination, both by biblical
    texts seen as Scripture and by the communal and social placement of the interpreter (pp. 170–75, 192–7).

9   Walter Brueggemann, 'The Social Nature of the Biblical Text for Preaching', in Arthur Van Seters (ed.),
    Preaching as a Social Act: Theology and Practice, Nashville, TN, Abingdon, 1988, p. 127.

10 Brueggemann, 1988, p. 128.

11 See the discussion of the role of the reader (reception theory) in Terry Eagleton's masterful survey,
    Literary Theory: An Interpretation, Minneapolis, University of Minnesota Press, 1983, chapter 2. For a
    readable analysis of the current debate on the capacity of the text to guide the process of reading and, thus,
    interpretation, see Robert Scholes, *Textual Power: Literary Theory and the Teaching of English,* New
    Haven, CT, and London, Yale University Press, 1985. For a direct application of the reader criticism and
    literary criticism to biblical studies, see John Barton, *Reading the Old Testament: Method in Biblical
    Study*, Philadelphia, Westminster, 1984, especially chapter 12.

12 Brueggemann, 1988, p. 128. In *Texts of Terror: Literary-Feminist Readings of Biblical Narratives,*
    Philadelphia, Fortress, 1984, Phyllis Trible makes much the same point regarding biblical storytelling
    when she claims that '[s]torytelling is a trinitarian act that unites writer, text, and reader in a collage of
    understanding' and '[A]lone a text is mute and ineffectual. In the speaking and the hearing new things
    appear in the land' (p. 1).

13 J. Severino Croatto, *Biblical Hermeneutics: Toward a Theory of Reading as the Production of Meaning*,
    Maryknoll, NY, Orbis, 1987, p. 66.

4　Preaching the Epistles

David Day

Further, in this method of preaching only three statements, or the equivalent of three, are used in the theme – either from respect to the Trinity, or because a threefold cord is not easily broken, or because this method is mostly followed by Bernard, or, as I think more likely, because it is more convenient for the set time of the sermon. A preacher can follow up just so many members without tiring his hearers; and if he should mention fewer, he would occupy too little time.[1]

So wrote Robert of Basevorn in 1322. I am not sure he got it right, and, in consequence, I want to look afresh at the way we preach the Epistles, with special reference to the Paulines.

The threefold cord and all that

The Epistles are the heartland of the evangelical preacher. Here we are at home. We know Paul. For many, it is from Paul's Epistles that 'the canon within the canon' is derived. His doctrine of justification by faith is central to the gospel. Evangelicals, standing in a long tradition of expository preaching, are most comfortable when they preach from an Epistle.

It is that 'long tradition' which interests me. To its credit it takes the subject matter with immense seriousness; this is the content which is to be faithfully expounded. However, it has also sponsored a characteristic style of preaching, with the result that evangelical preachers are initiated not only into what to say but also into how to say it. Evangelicals often tease one another about the 'three points and a poem' sermon form. It has been neatly satirized by Cathy Fox as the 'Barbour, Brogues and Bible school of preaching'. At its pyrotechnical limit it can take your breath away. Marvel at Oswald Chambers' exposition of Ecclesiastes 3:1–15 under the headings: Dispensational Durations, Dispositional Distresses (subdivided into personality and ploughing; precious and pernicious healing; priestesses of death and delight; pleasures and pains – domestic and devotional; profitless and prosperous commerce; programmes of speech and silence; requited and unrequited love), Decrees of Despair, Discretions of Deity (reasonableness; rehabilitation)![2]

I don't want to suggest that this is anything other than a caricature but it is related, albeit distantly, to sermons preached up and down the country most Sundays in the year. It is undeniable, of course, that the formula can actually help people hear and remember. From forty years ago I recall a sermon outline, *Adam behind a tree, Christ on a tree, Zacchaeus up a tree*. Most of us could preach that sermon from the headings alone. Nevertheless, the conception of the three (or fourteen) point sermon with its formulaic mnemonic raises for me an intriguing question: *What happens to a text when it is reshaped in a form which is substantially different from the original?*

For it seems to me that the traditional way of preaching the Epistles assumes that *the real message of the Epistle resides in its content and can be detached from the form in which it is expressed without much being lost*. The corollary of this is that, provided the content is preserved, whatever form the sermon takes will not seriously affect the message. In other words, we can hear the original message just as clearly through the new form (ie the sermon form) as we heard it in the

43

original. But this assumption is surely open to question. Write the message of Paul in the form of a limerick and you will effect a *new* hearing of the original.

It is at least possible that when the original text is reformulated in the sermon, vital features may be obscured or disappear completely. Let me suggest some ways in which sermons which do not take this possibility into account become problematical:

First, they tend to focus on *content*, treating language mainly as propositional statements and distilling doctrine from the words. Unfortunately, this concentration on content as units of information can blind the exegete to the significance of *rhetorical strategies*. It is not just what you say but also the way that you say it.

Furthermore, many books in this tradition of preaching advocate the isolation of one central thought as the key to understanding a passage. The passage is thus seen as a mini essay on a theme. This thematic idea will persist through the various stages of shaping a sermon and will summarize the preacher's message to the congregation. Doubtless there are many advantages in identifying *one thought* which will control the sermon. The disadvantage is that it will underrate *complexity* and subordinate many important ideas. It is just possible that there is more than one crucial thought in the text.

A third problem area concerns the tendency to *extract points* and devise headings. Despite the gains in terms of clarity, however, the freeze-framing entailed by headings and points ignores the *movement* of a passage. In a plea against undue analysis Jerry Camery-Hoggatt asks for balance: 'This is like unravelling the strands of a rope and looking at them individually, and it is a helpful procedure because it can give us a fix on the variety of things we must know if we are to read well. But something more must happen. The rope must be rewoven and viewed whole.'[3]

A final problematical feature of preaching in this tradition lies in its tendency to *systematize* the message. Here key concepts are loosed from their moorings and incorporated into a bigger system, thought of as 'Pauline theology' or 'biblical truth'. This process is flawed when it fails to give proper weight to *the situation* which evoked the letter. Epistles are essentially the products of specific occasions. When the distinctive message of the passage is flattened out, the result justifies Anthony Thiselton's warning: 'To try to cut loose "propositions" in the New Testament from the specific situation in which they were uttered and to try thereby to treat them "timelessly" is not only bad theology; it is also bad linguistics.'[4]

A personal journey

My own journey into dissatisfaction began when, as a member of a study group, I undertook to read Mark's Gospel as if I had never read the other three. I began to realise how much I had missed. It was not just a matter of noticing the flattening and systematizing that goes on unconsciously as a result of knowing the other gospels. I had failed to see the distinctive portrait of the passion given in Mark or even to be provoked into asking, 'What is Mark hoping to achieve here?' I think I had seen Mark as a repository of doctrinal truths in the form of narrative and not as [a] skilfully constructed sermon. The portrait of Christ that emerged – as utterly rejected and forsaken (no penitent thief, no cry of triumph or prayer of forgiveness etc.) – was fresh and deeply moving.

The next stage of the journey came when I had to prepare a series of sermons on the Letter to the Colossians. I had worked on an address on the thanksgiving and the prayer in chapter one. Suddenly I was confronted with what many take to be a hymn, followed soon afterwards by personal disclosure and testimony. Later came a vigorously polemical affirmation of the supremacy of Christ, a lyrical description of the body of Christ and some brisk, no-nonsense practical injunctions in the form of 'housetables'. At this point I found myself thinking, 'How can I preach all this *as if it were the same kind of material*?'

The conversion was complete when, encouraged by Walter Moberly's study of Micaiah ben Imlah, I started to look at the story from a preacher's standpoint. How does one puncture the complacency of a king who has hardened his heart? By means of a three point sermon, of course. What we might expect is something like, *Your prophets deluded; your people defeated; your plans demolished* (or possibly, *your glory departed*). Or, if you prefer, *You say, They say, God says*. However, as we know, Micaiah eschews evangelical tradition and comes up with an audacious homiletical *tour de force*. In his own creative way he addresses Craddock's question, 'What has to be done in order to get this message heard?'[5] In other words, Micaiah is prepared to take the communicative task seriously.

Thus three lessons emerged which I can express in shorthand as: this specific biblical passage carries a distinctive message; don't read or preach passages with diverse forms, moods and functions as if they were all the same kind of material; Learn from the homiletical freedom which the Bible exemplifies.

The characteristics of the Epistles

With these three maxims in mind I now turn to the Epistles and try to identify significant features. Some of the characteristics which I list below are not unique to the epistolary genre but are to be found in any literature. Nevertheless, I suggest that all ought to be taken into account by the preacher who is concerned to hear everything the text is saying and not limit himself or herself to the subject matter.

i   *Personal reference*. An Epistle is more direct and conversational than a Gospel. The evangelists hide themselves behind their story. In the Epistles we are in direct contact with the author. (This is true even of pseudepigraphy precisely because the fiction of the author is sustained.) Epistles are one step nearer to preaching (conventionally understood) than the Gospels. Thus Amos Wilder tries to capture the authentic Paul as heard in his letters:

> Paul writes always as one thwarted by absence and eagerly anticipating meeting or reunion. He is distressed by circumstances which prevent face-to-face address: 'I could wish to be present with you now', he writes to the Galatians, 'and change my tone, for I am perplexed about you' (4:20). Even in writing he falls into the style of direct oral plea and challenge. The very nature of the gospel imposes upon him ways of expression that suggest dramatic immediacy: devices and rhythms of the speaker rather than the writer; imagined dialogue; the situation of a court hearing or church trial with its accusations and defenses; the use of direct discourse; challenges not so much to understand the written words but to listen and behold; queries, exclamations and oaths.[6]

How many sermons on the Epistles attempt to recapture or reproduce 'queries, exclamations and oaths'?

ii   *Occasion*. Epistles are time-conditioned and situation specific. This feature of the Epistle justifies the considerable effort which has gone into establishing the date and provenance. If you don't grasp what caused the question you will probably have a problem with the answer. Work on the particular occasion is never wasted, nor is the attempt to learn more about the historical background. And, of course, very often the occasion which provoked the letter will lie within the text itself.

iii   *Mood*. Even in the eighteenth century Charles Simeon recommended that budding preachers mark *the spirit* of the passage ('it may be tender and compassionate, or indignant, or menacing').[7] Paul fighting for his life in 2 Corinthians needs to be heard differently from Paul arguing like a rabbi in Galatians 3. A hymn to Christ (Phil. 2:6–11) creates a different atmosphere from an argumentative diatribe (Rom. 3:1–9). Should not preachers take the mood into account when trying to read the passage faithfully and imaginatively?

iv *Structure*. Yet the historical context does not tell us much about the literary structure. There are forces at work in the text which we believe can be exposed after careful study. How has this passage been organised? What are the determinants of the argument? The current interest in Pauline rhetoric is a timely acknowledgement that Epistles, again like sermons, are crafted works. Faithful reading invites us to ask, 'How does this passage work?'

v *Linearity*. Epistles were written first to be read aloud. Rhetoric originates in speech and its primary product is a speech act, not a text. Kennedy writes, 'the rhetorical qualities inherent in the text were originally intended to have an impact on first hearing and to be heard by a group. This would have cut down the hearers' capacity to scan back and forth as with a written text and invites us to take sequence seriously. For this reason we 'need to read the Bible as speech'.[8] As we read an Epistle we need to read word by word, trying hard not to hear later sections until they arrive. This keeps us open to being surprised. Jerry Camery-Hoggatt remarks: 'The tendency of the text to keep the reader off balance is a problem for the critic who would reduce the meaning of the Bible to the objective information it yields, but it is an asset to the reader who seeks a transforming encounter with the word of God.'[9]

vi *Function*. Epistles are like sermons in that they are intended to effect change, even transformation. They are not intended just to give information, especially not general information about the world. We need to highlight their persuasive function and ask, 'What is this passage trying to do?' just as much as 'What is it trying to say?'

vii *Conversational theology*. To call Paul unsystematic may almost seem like heresy but it is intended to highlight the fact that the apostle usually does his theology 'on the hoof'. There is a delightful passage in Austin Farrer's *The Glass of Vision* where he describes Paul as 'a very unsystematic systematic theologian, no doubt, too impulsive and enthusiastic to put his material in proper order or to standardize his terminology. Still, what of that? Anyone who has a decent modern education can do it for him: we, for example, will be rewarded a research degree for doing it.'[10] If Paul's theology is highly situation specific, partly called forth by the exigencies of the occasion, always in the process of being formed, then what might be the implications for the preacher?

If these seven features of the Epistles are significant, then form, mood, function, linearity etc. are new partners round the table at the point of exegesis. To understand a passage is more than to extract its content (though that is involved, of course). We need also to be responsive to the effect on the meaning of the passage of all these other elements and ensure that when we read the text faithfully and imaginatively we incorporate the rhetorical intention of the text into our understanding of its message.

Preaching Paul after him

I want to suggest, in addition, that the features I have isolated ought also to affect any sermon which claims to expound the text. I argue this partly because it seems to me to be demanded of us as an aspect of faithfulness to Scripture. Scripture is given to us as *content-embodied-in-a-form*. In this respect it matches God's revelation of himself in Jesus. Incarnation appears to be God's preferred method of communication. It is precisely because we respect the method that we take these apparently irrelevant and disposable features into account. When a message is embodied you cannot jettison the body without loss.

Many readers will recognise a debt to Thomas Long at this point. He suggests, for example, that sometimes the sermon should replicate the passage's shape or form; sometimes it should try to produce an equivalent effect on the modern listener as the passage did on the original hearers; sometimes, the forces which organize the sermon should be the same as those which control the passage and so on.[11]

It may help to set out some examples of how this might work. First, how might we take account of the *form* of a passage? How, for instance, should we preach the 'hymn' (if such it is) to the cosmic Christ in Colossians 1:15–20 (with 21–23)? Randolph Tate notes the 'pervasive lyric quality' of the section. The language is 'structured, cadenced, compressed, intense, economical, and with unusual grammatical qualities'.[12] In the light of these comments it is not enough just to tell the congregation that Jesus is the first in creation and the first in redemption, especially since at the end Paul suddenly puts the Colossians into this cosmic picture with a sharply personal, 'And *you* . . . he has reconciled'. Hymns don't work like systematic theology. Here the tone is exalted, the scope cosmic, the language in overdrive; surely the sermon itself should sound like a hymn, certainly it should evoke exultation and worship from the congregation.

My second example emphasizes *technique* and is drawn from the Epistle to the Romans. It is a commonplace that Paul's letters contain traces of the literary form known as diatribe, that is, an imaginary conversation between the writer and an opponent, a device which allows the author to set up objections and then answer them in dialogue form. Neil Elliott reconstructs Romans 3:1–9 along these lines:[13]

Paul:	What then is the advantage of being a Jew? Or what is the benefit of circumcision?
The Jew:	Much in every way! First, they were entrusted with the oracles of God.
Paul:	What now? If some were disobedient, their unfaithfulness does not nullify God's integrity, does it?
The Jew:	May it never be! Let God be proven true, though every human being be false, as it is written . . .
Paul:	But if our wickedness, my Jewish friend, serves to show the justice of God (that is, if our transgressions provide God an opportunity to be 'merciful' to us), what shall you and I conclude? Surely not that God is unjust who bears wrath?

And so on through to the end of verse 9.

What interests me here is not so much the question of whether Elliott's reconstruction of the diatribe is correct in every detail, as the diatribe as a rhetorical technique. Here we have a sermon design which could easily be translated to the contemporary pulpit and with care it may work as well for us as for Paul's readers.

My third example focuses on *mood and function*. Simeon argued in relation to the spirit of the passage, 'Whatever it be, let that be the spirit of your discourse.' His advice is worth heeding, even though its essential soundness is more clearly seen when it is ignored. For we readily concede the inappropriateness of a sermon mood which jars with that of the original, where, perhaps, the sermon is flippant and the Bible grave, or informative where the Bible is passionate. If part of the preacher's task is to help the congregation hear the passage as it was intended to be heard then there will be many occasions when the mood and tone of the sermon should be matched to the mood and tone of the original.

Colossians 1:24–2:8 is a case in point. This passage comes at the end of an argument which will culminate in the impassioned appeal, 'See to it that no one makes a prey of you!' In it Paul the pastor and Paul the man shine through. Instances of the personal pronoun increase and the tone is in marked contrast to the later part of the letter. The rhetoric works because Paul is bold enough to show the Colossians something of himself, his pain and toil, and his understanding of how that pain and toil is for them. The logic of the early part of the letter seems to be something like: Don't rubbish what has already happened. God has been at work. (To thank God for someone is to recognize that he has been at work in their lives.) I am praying for you. (*Telling* people that you are praying for them is a pastoral strategy.) Don't let me down. Woven in with this is Paul's exultation at the inexhaustible riches of Christ, framed in a cosmic vision and heavy with eschatological overtones. His craft sets personal disclosures within a cosmic perspective, in such a way that they become a powerful appeal. 'Shall all this be for nothing? Do not let anyone lead you astray!'

The task set before the preacher is not just to tell the congregation that this is what Paul felt but to reproduce within twentieth-century listeners the feeling of being present at a conversation where someone is personally involved, pastorally in anguish, trying to effect a change in a specific situation by every rhetorical means at his disposal. Can the sermon take the congregation through the 'narrative' of the argument, allowing them to ride the same roller coaster of emotions, and giving them the same experience as the original (or implied) readers of being entreated, encouraged, amazed, moved and ultimately convinced? To take mood, technique and purpose seriously would suggest that the attempt should be made.

Fourthly, what can we say about preaching *conversational theology*? I have already argued that Paul was an unsystematic theologian: some of the classic passages of doctrine were designed as answers to specific problems. John Goldingay observes, 'It is characteristic of the Epistles to look at contemporary issues and problems and to reflect on them in the light of the gospel, of scripture, and of the revelation that has come to the writers in the course of this reflection'.[14] It is time that sermons recaptured something of that sense of occasional theology, done in relation to an issue. Can the preacher bring the congregation into the workshop, as it were? Can they experience a Christian discerning and articulating the truth 'as he runs'?

Too many sermons serve the dish up ready cooked and then, as a listener, I have no idea what the ingredients are nor how the recipe works. I lose sight of the man wrestling, turning, twisting and pulling in everything he can lay his hands on in order to commend Christ. Here is Paul exploring a vivid image of Christ and his work, bouncing it off a telling quotation from Scripture imaginatively used, throwing in a piece of inspired logic to tease out its implications, confirming it by personal testimony, linking it up with a practical precept which flows from this insight. Sermons which open this process up to the congregation communicate the excitement of theology on fire, the practical power of Christian truth glimpsed, hammered out, half systematized, vigorously applied to real issues, reflecting a vision of the world rather than the propositions of the textbook.

Finally, is there a place for taking *narrative* seriously and incorporating it into the sermon? Story preaching has been enthusiastically embraced by the guild of homileticians yet it is still seen as applicable primarily to Gospel and OT material. One can understand why since, at first sight, the Epistles appear short on story. However, Paul does give us personal accounts of his life and ministry (Gal 1; Phil. 3:4–14; 2 Cor. 11:22–12:10). This material is essentially narrative and can be preached in that style. Here is Craddock preaching on the sentence, 'you have heard of my former life in Judaism, how I persecuted the church of God' (Gal. 1:13).

Then imagine how the young Paul feels. Generations and generations of being the people of God and now someone in the name of Jesus of Nazareth gets this strange opinion that it doesn't matter anymore, that Jews and Gentiles are alike. You must sense how Saul feels. All your family and national traditions, all that you have ever known and believed, now erased completely from the board? Every moment in school, every belief held dear, every job toward which your life is pointed, now meaningless? Everything that grandfather and father and now you believed, gone? Of course, he resolves to stop it. The dark cloud of his brooding bitterness forms a tornado funnel over that small church, and he strikes it, seeking to end it. In the name of his fathers, in the name of his country, in the name of God, yes.[15]

Lowry observes, 'When a given sermon text consists essentially of a report, the preacher is often at a loss to know how to handle it homiletically. The expository style of preaching with which I was raised "solved" the problem simply by going through the text verse by verse, phrase by phrase, and word by word. We often gained valuable information – *if* we could stay hooked to the sermon'.[16] Craddock turns to the story mode, feels free to explore Paul's motivation, though in a controlled way, and thus sets up a problem looking for a solution. The Pauline material is embedded within a number of vignettes of bitter people which intensify the problem. We stay hooked because we need a resolution – which comes in a concluding story of the grace of God.

Autobiographical passages invite story treatment but other kinds of material may also be treated in this way. For example, Paul's technical terms often contain a story within them – redemption, justification, reconciliation are stock examples of ideas which begin in situations familiar to the readers and which point towards stories – of the slave trade, the law court or the family. One of Whitefield's favourite techniques was to preach the great doctrines in the form of stories but the stories were there already in embryo, they did not have to be imported into the text. We could do worse than follow his example.

I have suggested that sermons should reflect the nature of the epistolary material which they aim to expound. The Epistles are themselves an invitation to experiment with Craddock's question: 'What has to be done in order to get this message heard?' We have much to learn from those who in their own time preached sermons designed to change people's lives.

My final point is an extension of this idea. We are used to searching the Bible for content but oddly reluctant to turn to it as a model for method. Truly biblical preaching should display the same freedom in communication as that which is found in the Bible. I am inclined to think, on the basis of listening to many sermons, that in practice the range of strategies commonly employed is much more limited than the Bible warrants. A rich treasure house is open to us: we can use all the forms found in the Psalter, cries of lament, complaint and accusation, hymns of praise and thanksgiving, meditations on wisdom; we can also employ proverbs and pithy aphorisms, and parables, provocative stories with no tidy explanation at the end; apocalyptic literature gives us a world of images and pictures and encourages us to use the vision as a tool of communication; the prophets remind us of the power of metaphor and symbolic action. These forms are known to most preachers as ways in which the biblical revelation has come to us; they are less familiar as possible homiletical techniques. But a friend of mine still remembers the electric atmosphere when the late David Watson took a paper on which was written 'God's offer of free forgiveness' and tore it to pieces to the accompaniment of 'Too busy', 'Not interested', 'Too good to be true' – one tear per comment. The strategy was worthy of Jeremiah breaking the pot.

I come across students, loyal disciples of Robert de Basevorn, who fall naturally upon the conventional sermon form. Nevertheless there are others, not few in number, who would like to express in their preaching something of the freedom which the Bible licenses but who are inhibited by anxieties about whether this is 'real preaching' or not, either because they have too fixed a model of what constitutes exposition or because they are too apprehensive about what the congregation will say. Perhaps it is a time to be bold.

Notes

1   Robert of Basevorn, *The Form of Preaching*, quoted in Richard Lischer (ed.), *Theories of Preaching*, Durham, NC, Labyrinth, 1987, p. 220.

2   O. Chambers, *Shade of his Hand*, London, Marshall, Morgan and Scott, 1962, p. 21.

3   Jerry Camery-Hoggatt, *Speaking of God*, Peabody, MA, Hendrickson, 1995, p. 163.

4   Anthony C. Thiselton, 'Semantics and New Testament Interpretation', in I. Howard Marshall (ed.), *New Testament Interpretation*, Exeter, Paternoster, 1979, p. 79.

5   Fred B. Craddock, *Preaching,* Nashville, TN, Abingdon, 1985, p. 182.

6   Amos N. Wilder, *Early Christian Rhetoric,* quoted in Lischer, 1987, p. 241.

7   Charles Simeon, *Horae Homileticae,* Vol. 21, p. 307.

8   George A. Kennedy, *New Testament Interpretation through Rhetorical Criticism,* Chapel Hill, NC, University of North Carolina Press, 1984, p. 6.

9   Camery-Hoggatt, 1995, p. 164.

10   Austin Farrer, *The Glass of Vision,* Westminster, Dacre, 1948, p. 45.

11   Thomas G. Long, *Preaching and the Literary Forms of the Bible,* Philadelphia, Fortress, 1989, pp. 127-35.

12   W. Randolph Tate, *Biblical Interpretation,* Peabody, MA, Hendrickson, 1991, p. 118. See also p. 133.

13   Neil Elliott, *The Rhetoric of Romans*, Sheffield, JSOT, 1990, pp. 139 ff.

14   John Goldingay, *Models for Scripture*, Grand Rapids, MI, Eerdmans; Carlisle, Paternoster, 1994, p. 330.

15   Fred Craddock, *Praying through Clenched Teeth,* in Eugene Lowry, *How to Preach a Parable,* Nashville, TN, Abingdon, 1989, pp. 142-8.

16   Lowry, 1989, p. 162.

5   An Imaginative 'Or'

Walter Brueggemann

Perhaps the assigned theme, 'preaching from the Old Testament', is intended to raise the sticky christological issue about finishing up OT texts with Jesus. The question is difficult and I should say where I am. I believe the Old Testament leads to the New and to the gospel of Jesus Christ. It does not, however, lead there directly, but only with immense interpretive agility. It does not, moreover, lead there singularly and necessarily in my judgment, because it also leads to Judaism and to the synagogue with its parallel faith. I shall bracket out of my consideration the christological question with the recognition, put in trinitarian terms, that in the Old Testament we speak of the Father of the Son.[1] As we confess the fullness of the Father manifest in the Son, so we may confess the fullness of God manifest to Israel in the Father. This is a question of endless dispute, but I owe it to you to be clear on my own conviction.

I

Rather than the christological question, I shall focus on the ecclesial question. I understand preaching to be the chance to *summon and nurture an alternative community with an alternative identity, vision, and vocation, preoccupied with praise and obedience toward the God we Christians know fully in Jesus of Nazareth.* (This accent on alternative community resonates with the point being made in current 'Gospel and Culture' conversation, much propelled by Lesslie Newbigin's focus on election, that God in God's inscrutable wisdom has chosen a people whereby the creation will be brought to wholeness.)[2] Two other beginning points make the community-forming work of the Old Testament peculiarly contemporary for us.

First, it is crucial to remember that the Old Testament is zealously and pervasively a Jewish book. Jews, and Israelites before them, are characteristically presented and understand themselves to be a distinct community with an alternative identity *rooted theologically and exhibited ethically* – alternative to the Egyptians, the Canaanites, the Philistines, the Assyrians, the Babylonians, the Persians, and the Hellenists – not only alternative but always subordinate to and under threat from dominant culture.[3] Thus I understand the intention of the Torah and prophets – and differently I believe also wisdom – to be insisting upon *difference* with theological rootage and ethical exhibit. The God question is decisive, even if back-grounded, but the urgency concerns maintenance of communal identity, consciousness, and intentionality.

Second, with the disestablishment of Western Christianity and the collapse of the social hegemony of the church, the formation of a distinctive community of praise and obedience now becomes urgent as it had not been when the Western church could count on the support and collusion of dominant culture. If the church in our society is not to evaporate into an ocean of consumerism and anti-neighborly individualism, then the summons and nurture of an alternative community constitutes an emergency. Thus with a huge *mutatis mutandis*, I propose that as the Jews lived in a perennial emergency of identity, so the church in our time and place lives in such an emergency.[4] In both cases,

51

moreover, a primal response to the emergency and a primal antidote to assimilation and evaporation is the chance of preaching. In reflection upon the Old Testament and the ecclesial emergency, I will consider three theses.

II

The summons and nurture, formation and enhancement of an alternative community of praise and obedience *depends upon the clear articulation of an either/or, the offer of a choice and the require-ment of a decision that is theologically rooted and ethically exhibited, that touches and pervades every facet of the life of the community and its members.*[5] The choice is presented as clear. I believe that this *either/or* belongs inevitably to an alternative community, because an alternative identity requires an endless intentionality. For without vigilance the alternative cannot be sustained. I have reflected upon Old Testament texts around this theme; my impression is that there are only rare texts that are 'holding actions'. Everything in Israel's text urges an alternative.

The alternative that must be embraced in order to be Israel includes the summons to Abraham and Sarah to 'go', for without going there will be no land and no future, no heir and no Israel. The summons to slaves in Egypt through Moses is to 'depart', for if there is no 'departure' there is no promised land. Moses worries, moreover, that if Israel does not believe, it will not depart and will not be Israel (Ex. 4:1).[6] Less instantaneous but certainly pervasively, the prophets endlessly summon Israel to an alternative covenant ethic, lest the community be destroyed. And even in the wisdom tradi-tions, the restrained advocacy of wisdom and righteousness is in the awareness that foolishness will indeed bring termination. Perhaps the most dominant statement of *either/or* that belongs characteristi-cally to the faith perspective of the Old Testament is the context at Mt Carmel where Elijah challenges Israel: 'How long will you go limping with two different opinions? If the Lord is God, follow him; but if Baal, then follow him' (I Kings 18:21). We are told first, 'The people did not answer him a word' (v. 21b). But at the end they said, 'The Lord indeed is God; the Lord indeed is God' (v. 39). This text knows that Israel, in order to be the people of Yahweh, must be endlessly engaged in an intentional decision for Yahwism, a decision that fends off the powerful forces of the dominant culture.[7]

I wish now to consider in some detail two classic formulations of *either/or* that occur at pivotal points in Israel's life. The first of these is Joshua 24, a much discussed text that von Rad regarded as an ancient credo that is situated as the culmination of the Hexateuch.[8] The meeting at Shechem over which Joshua presides is set canonically just as Israel is situated in the land. Joshua 1–12 concerns control of the land, albeit by violence, and Joshua 13–21 concerns division of the land among the tribes. I read this moment as Israel's arrival at security, well-being, affluence, and rare self-congrat-ulations. The text is presented as a *bid to non-Israelites* to join up.[9] I shall consider that a fictional staging, so that the text is in fact a *bid to Israelites* in their new affluence to reembrace the faith of the Yahwistic covenant. The text (and Joshua) know that there are indeed attractive alternatives, alternatives that Israel must resist.

As von Rad saw most clearly, vv. 2–13 is a recital of Israel's core memory.[10] It includes the ancestors of Genesis (vv. 2–4), the Exodus (vv. 5–7a), the wilderness sojourn (v. 7b), and the entry into the land (vv. 8–13). This latter theme ends:

> I gave you a land on which you had not labored, and towns that you had
> not built, and you live in them; you eat the fruit of vineyards and oliveyards
> that you did not plant. (v. 13)

It is all gift!

After this recital, the speaker (here Joshua the preacher) makes his bid for allegiance to this particular narrative construal of reality: 'fear and serve Yahweh in completeness and in faithfulness'. Negatively: 'put away the other gods'. Positively: 'serve Yahweh'. *Choose*: If Yahweh ... if not then, option (a) is the gods of the Euphrates valley, option (b) is the Amorite gods in the land. Choose! Then says the preacher, 'those in my household will serve Yahweh', and will put our lives down in the Yahweh narrative just recited. But if you refuse this narrative, then put your life down somewhere else and live with the consequences. No doubt the entire Hexateuch has pointed to this moment. The Pentateuch consists of the live narrative of Yahweh that generates a world of gift and liberation and demand about which decisions must be made.[11]

Then follows in vv. 16–24 a dialogue about church growth. The exchange of Joshua and the community is a negotiation about the *either/or*.

> People (vv. 16–18): Far be us from us to serve other gods ... we will serve Yahweh;[12]

> Joshua (vv. 19–20): You cannot do it. It is too hard and Yahweh is more ferocious than you imagine (No growth seduction here).

> People (v. 21): No, we are committed. We will serve Yahweh.

> Joshua (v. 22a): You are witnesses ... you are on notice.

> People (v. 22b): Yes we are.

> Joshua (23): with an imperative:

> Negative: put away foreign gods.[13]

> Positive: extend your hearts to Yahweh.

> Conclusion (v. 25):

> Joshua made a covenant with Torah demands.

This particular crisis of *either/or* is negotiated and Israel comes to be, yet again, an intentional alternative community, alternative to the gods of the land.

The second case of *either/or* that I cite is in II Isaiah. This wondrous text is situated in the exile. That is, the context is exactly the opposite of Joshua 24. There it was excessive security in the land. Here it is complete displacement from the religious, cultural supports of Jerusalem, set down in an ocean of Babylonian seductions and intimidations, with effective Babylonian economics and seemingly effective Babylonian gods. No doubt many deported Jews found it easier to be a Babylonian Jew, and for some that status was only a transition to becoming Babylonian. The lean choice of remaining Jews embedded in Yahweh depended upon having the *either/or* made plain, for without the *either/or*, cultural accommodation and assimilation go unchecked.

It is precisely the work of II Isaiah to state the alternative, so that Jews tempted by Babylon have a real choice available to them. The text of II Isaiah is well known to us (unfortunately Handel reworked it so that the *either/or* is not at all visible). The recurring accent of II Isaiah is that it is now the emergency moment when Jews may and must depart Babylon. In our historical criticism, we have focused much on Cyrus and the overturn of Babylon by the Persians, so that the emancipation of the Jews is a geo-political event. No doubt there is something in that. But I suggest not so much, because the primal departure from Babylon is not geographical, but imaginative, liturgical, and emotional: imagine Jewishness, imagine distinctiveness that has not succumbed to the pressures and seductions of the empire. From this familiar poetry of departure and distinctiveness, I will mention four characteristic elements.

1. The initial announcement, 'comfort, comfort', is an assertion to Jews displaced by Yahweh's anger that caring embrace by Yahweh is now the order of the day: 'For a brief moment I abandoned you, but with great compassion I will gather you' (54:7). The Jews in exile are addressed as the forgiven, as the welcomed, as the cherished. They had pondered, for two generations, rejection by Yahweh. But to be forgiven, welcomed, and cherished invites the reembrace of Jewishness. The poet, moreover, draws out the scenario of wondrous, jubilant, victorious procession back to Jerusalem, back to Jewishness, back to alternative identity (40:3–8). It is in this reassertion and reenactment of Jewishness that the glory of Yahweh is revealed before all flesh. These Jews in this uncommon identity, moreover, are surrounded by the God who leads like a triumphant general and the God who does the rearguard pickup in order to salvage the dropouts:

> See, the Lord comes with might,
> and his arm rules for him . . .
> He will feed his flock like a shepherd;
> he will gather the lambs in his arms,
> and carry them in his bosom,
> and gently lead the mother sheep. (40:10–11)

The purpose of the poetic opener is to permit the community to reexperience the embracive quality of Jewishness welcomed in its peculiarity.

2. In order to create imaginative space for Jewishness, the poet employs two kinds of rhetorical strategies.[14] First, it is important to debunk the vaunted powers of Babylon. This is done by teasing and mocking the gods of the empire. In 46:1–2, the gods are mocked as dumb statues that must be carried around on the backs of animals, like so many meaningless floats in a May day parade. The ridicule is like the old humor at the chiefs of the Soviet Union or the mocking of 'whitey' that Black people have had [to] do for their own health and sanity. Or the poet holds a mock trial in order to show how weak and ineffectual are the imperial gods who are passive, silent, dormant, all failures who can do neither good nor evil (41:21–29). The intention of such speech is to dress down the powers of domination, to exhibit courage in the face of power, to show that the choice of Babylon that looks so impressive is in the end sheer foolishness.

3. This debunking is matched by the vigorous reassertion of Yahweh as the most reliable player in the struggle for the future. In the salvation oracles, this poet has Yahweh repeatedly say to terrified Jews, 'fear not'. 'Fear not, I am with you'. 'Fear not, I will help you'. 'Fear not', be a Jew. The poet knows that the empire traffics in fear and intimidation with its uniforms, its parades, its limousines, its press conferences, its agents with dark glasses, and its intrusions in the night. All is for nought, because Yahweh is the great Equalizer who creates safe space and overrides the threat of dominant claims.

4. Finally, looking back on the highway of chapter 40 and the fearless safe return that the dumb Babylonian gods cannot stop – nothing can stop resolved Jewishness – the poem announces the departure: 'Depart, depart, go out from there' (52:11)!

They could remember the ancient 'departure' from Egypt. They remembered every passover by means of unleavened bread. The lack of leavening recalled that they left in a hurry, with no time for the yeast to rise. This is a like emergency and a like departure. Except,

For you shall not go out in haste,
and you shall not go in flight;
for the Lord will go before you,
and the God of Israel will be your rear guard. (52:12)

No rush. Leave at your convenience. First class passengers may board at their leisure for the journey back to full, alternative Jewishness: 'For you shall go out in joy, and be led back in peace' (55:12).

They might not depart the emotional grip of Babylon on the day they first hear the poem; but the poetry lingers. Alternative identity, even in places of threat and seduction, is embraced as the invitation does its proper work.

III

The *either/or* of distinctive identity for praise and obedience is not self-evident in the nature of things, but *depends completely and exclusively upon the courageous utterance of witnesses who voice choices and invite decisions where none were self-evident*. My accent on the urgency of preaching the *either/or* is grounded in my conviction that Israel lives by a certain kind of utterance without which Israel has no chance to live. It is for this reason that I have insisted in my recent book on Old Testament theology that Old Testament claims for God finally do not appeal to historical facticity or to ontology, but rely upon the utterance of witnesses to offer what is not self-evident or otherwise available.[15] This is indeed 'theology of the word', by which I mean simply and leanly and crucially *utterance*.

I take as my primary case II Isaiah, admittedly an easy case; but I would extrapolate from II Isaiah to claim the entire Old Testament is utterance that expresses *either/or* that is not self-evident.[16] The massive hegemony of Babylon – political, economic, theological – had, so far as we know, well nigh driven Jewishness from the horizon; and with the elimination of Jewishness it had vetoed Yahweh from the theological conversation. It is the intention of every hegemony to eliminate separatist construals of reality that are endlessly inconvenient and problematic, and certainly a separatism as dangerous as Jewishness that endlessly subverts. The tale of Daniel, perhaps later but clearly reflective of the Babylonian crisis, tells the tale of how Nebuchadnezzar is enraged that Jews should refuse imperial allegiance and hold to their odd alternative claim (Dan. 3:13–15).

This power of hegemony, moreover, matched the exiles' own sense of things, for they also had concluded that Yahweh was not engaged or worth trusting:

Why do you say, O Jacob,
and speak, O Israel,
'My way is hidden from the Lord,
and my right is disregarded by my God'? (40:27)

But Zion said, 'The Lord has forsaken me,
my Lord has forgotten me'. (49:14)

Is my hand shortened, that I cannot redeem?
Or have I no power to deliver? (50:2)

It is in such an environment of hegemony-cum-despair that the utterance of *either/or* takes place. It is the utterance of *either/or* that shapes the perceptual field of Israel anew, to become aware of resources not recognized, of dangers not acknowledged, and of choices that had not seemed available. I shall consider this new, subversive voice of *either/or* in two waves. First, II Isaiah himself, perhaps someone who had arisen out of a continuing seminar on the text of I Isaiah, is now moved to generate and extrapolate new text. 'Moved', I say, because some think it was by an out-of-the-ordinary confrontation in 'the divine council': when the voices say 'Cry . . . what shall I cry . . . get you up on a high mountain, herald of good tidings', the one moved by divine imperative is none other than II Isaiah, who moves out from this theological experience to reshape the lived emergency of Israel.

It is this poet who gives to the rhetoric of the synagogue and church the term 'gospel'.[17] Indeed, I suggest provisionally that gospel is the offer of an *either/or* where none seemed available. So in 40:9:

> Get you up to a high mountain,
> O Zion, herald of *gospel tidings*,
> lift up your voice with strength,
> O Jerusalem, herald of *gospel tidings*,
> lift it up, do not fear.

The gospeler is twice named. The gospeler, moreover, is given the utterance to be sounded: 'Behold, your God', or in NRSV, 'Here is your God'. It is the exhibit of Yahweh as God of the exiles in a context where Babylon had banished the God of the exiles so that there were only Babylonian gods available. The news is that Yahweh is back in play, creating choices. Yahweh is back in play on the lips of the one moved to new utterance.

That text in 40:9 is matched in 52:7 in a better known utterance:

> How beautiful upon the mountains
> are the feet of the *gospel messenger*
> who announces peace,
> who brings *gospel news*,
> who announces salvation,
> who says to Zion, 'Your God reigns'.

Again the term gospel is twice used, and again the lines are given: 'Your God reigns', or better, 'Your God has just become king'. The line is a quote from the Psalms (see 96:10), but the utterance here is an assertion that in the contest for domination, the gods of the empire have been defeated and the God of Israel is now the dominant force in creation. The poet creates an environment for choice, for decision, for homecoming, for new, faithful action, none of which is available or choosable without this utterance.

It is, however, the second layer of utterance in this poetry that interests me, namely that the Israelites are summoned by the poet to be witnesses, to give testimony about the Yahwistic alternative about which they did not know and which the Babylonians certainly could never tolerate. In 43:8–13, the poet offers a contest among the gods. Negatively he invites the Babylonians to give evidence for their gods: 'Let them bring forth their witnesses' (v. 9). Then in v. 10: 'You are my witnesses', you exiles. You are the ones who are to speak my name, confess my authority, obey my will, accept my emancipation, tell my miracles. The exiles who themselves had thought there was no *or* to the Babylonian *either* are now called to testify to this Yahwistic *or*. There are two quite remarkable features to this poem authorizing Israel's testimonial utterance about an alternative that the empire cannot tolerate.

First, the summons and authorization to testify is interwoven with *the substance of testimony* that is to be given:

Before me no god was formed,
nor shall there be any after me.
I, I am the Lord,
and besides me there is no savior . . .
I am God, and also henceforth I am He;
there is no one who can
deliver from my hand;
I work and who can hinder it? (vv. 10b–11, 13)

What is to be said is that Yahweh is the alpha and the omega, the first and the last, the creator, the one who is utterly irresistible. Note well that this extravagant claim allows no room for any Babylonian gods. In the statement of the *either/or*, the Babylonian *either* is dismissed as an irrelevant fantasy. There is only the Yahwistic *or* as an option.

Now we might suspect that this is a frontal assault to convince the Babylonians. Perhaps so. But the second feature I observe in v. 10 is this:

You are my witnesses, says the Lord,
and my servant whom I have chosen,
so that you may know and believe me
and understand that I am he.

Notice: You are my witnesses . . . in order that . . . *you may know, believe, understand!* The giving of testimony is to claim the ones who testify. Israel is to enunciate the Yahwistic option so that they themselves should trust and embrace that option. This is surely the most direct claim I know concerning Paul's assertion that faith comes from what is heard (Romans 10:17); where there is not speaking and hearing of an alternative world, there is no faith, no courage, no freedom to choose differently, no community of faith apart from and even against the empire.

The other remarkable text is 44:8, followed by the negative of 44:9. It is clear that vv. 8 and 9 belong to quite different literary units; they are joined together perhaps to make the point about utterance. Verse 8 asserts yet again, 'You are my witnesses'. The last two lines of the verse, just as we have seen in chapter 43, outline the utterance that is to be uttered: 'Is there any god besides me? There is no other rock; I know not one'.

The testimony is that there is not only a choice outside Babylon. It is the only real choice. The new feature here, after chapter 43, is the first line of the verse to the witnesses now being recruited: 'Do not fear, or be afraid'. One can imagine a lawyer briefing a witness, perhaps a witness who is a whistle blower against a great corporation, who must say in court what the company cannot tolerate: 'do not be afraid'. Or one can imagine a women in a rape trial who must give evidence, but is terrified both of the shame and of the continuing threat of the rapist: 'do not fear'. The lawyer must encourage and reassure. Every witness, every serious preacher, every exile who speaks against hegemony knows the fear. And Yahweh says, state the *or*, because it is true. Many witnesses discover, of course, that Yahweh in the end has no 'witness protection program', but the witness is often compelled to give evidence nonetheless.

The negative of v. 9 is surprising. Verses 9–20 constitute an odd unit that mocks the makers of idols, the Babylonians who manufacture powerless gods. Verse 9 speaks of idols and then of witnesses, that is, the Babylonian gods and the Babylonians who champion them or Jews who trust those imperial gods too much. The idols are, with the NRSV, 'nothing'. The term looks like a simple rejection. But the Hebrew *tôhû* = chaos. The Babylonian gods are embodiments of chaos, forces of disorder. This is a remarkable claim, for the empire had claimed to be a great sponsor of order and well-being. But here it is clear: the spiritual force of the empire is against *shalom*, against peace and order and well-being. The *tôhû* of Babylon of course is to be contrasted with the power of the true creator God, Yahweh. Finally it is asserted that the witnesses who champion the gods of *tôhû* neither see nor know. They are so narcoticized and mesmerized by the empire that they cannot see what is going on. The contrast is total, no overlap between these two god offers. The exiles can choose either *the gods of the empire* who will never deliver the well-being they claim to sponsor, or *the God of the news* who stands against all things fearful. The battle for Jewishness in exile is acute, a battle now replicated in the battle for baptism in an ocean of military consumerism that generates endless layers of chaos in the name of prosperity.

To be sure, II Isaiah is an easy case for *either/or* through utterance. But I would argue that the theme is pervasive in the text of this people always struggling for its identity. Perhaps you noticed in my longish comment on Joshua 24 that Joshua and his counterparts finally get serious precisely about testimony. He says to them: 'You are witnesses against yourselves that you have chosen the Lord, to serve him' (v. 22). The answer, 'Witnesses'. The Hebrew is terse, without a nominative pronoun. My point is a simple one. Everything depends upon utterance. The dramatic occasions of teaching and preaching where the *either/or* is spelled out and sometimes embraced, are serious occasions, serious not simply because of formal oath or because we claim to be speaking true, but serious elementally because *what we say* and *how we say* is the world we receive. Israel's serious oath is to choose the *or* of Yahweh and to hold to it (see also v. 27).

It would be nice if the *either/or* were simply out there in the landscape. Israel, however, knows better. It is here, in speech. If it is not uttered, it is not available. If it is not uttered, it is not. This point, that human possibility resides in utterance, it seems to me, is crucial not only for preaching, but more generally in a technological society.[18] Our technological mindset wants to thin, reduce, and eventually silence serious speech. The urgency of preaching and all the utterance of the church and the synagogue, I suggest, is that we know intuitively that where there is not face-to-face truth-telling, we are by that much diminished in the human enterprise. And Joshua insists, Israel must stand by its utterance.[19]

IV

While the *either/or* may be uttered frontally, *the or of Yahweh is characteristically spoken in figure*, because it is a possibility 'at hand' but not yet in hand.[20] The *either/or* of Yahwism is directly utterable, and I have cited cases of such direct utterance. Characteristically, however, it is not done tersely and confrontationally, because such utterance is too lean, gives the listeners few resources for the tricky negotiation between options, and because the *either/or*, having no one shape or form, is always different with different folk in different circumstance. Moreover, while the *either* of hegemony is visible and can be described in some detail, the *or* of Yahweh does not admit of flat description because it is not yet visible, not yet in hand, always about to be, always under construal, always just beyond us. Indeed, if the *or* of Yahweh could be fully and exhaustively described, the prospect is that it would become, almost immediately, some new hegemonic *either*, as is often the case if creeds are heard too flatly, if liturgies are held too closely, if ethics is turned to legalism, if piety becomes self-confidence and pride. It is this open act of imagination in the service of a demanding, healing *or* that is the primary hard work of the preacher and the wonder of good preaching that is communicated in modes outside hegemonic certitude.

I will return to my two major cases and then in conclusion note three other places where one can see some playfulness at work in utterance.

1. I have characterized Joshua 24 as a primary model of *either/or* in which testimonial utterance is evident. That utterance of either/or in solemn assembly by Joshua culminates in v. 25: 'So Joshua made a covenant with the people that day, and made statutes and ordinances for them at Shechem.'

The verse tells us almost nothing of what constitutes the new obedience to which Israel is pledged after this hard-won decision to embrace Yahweh's *or*. I suggest that because Joshua 24 is about the immediate settlement in the land, the Torah of Deuteronomy is the figurative articulation that fleshes out the *either/or* announced in Joshua 24. For the sake of that connection, I make two critical observations. First, it is generally agreed that Deuteronomy constitutes the norm for the 'history' offered in Joshua, Judges, Samuel, and Kings, the 'Deuteronomic' account of Israel's life in the land.[21] Thus the linkage between Deuteronomy and Joshua 24 is entirely plausible; Joshua 24:25 alludes to that Torah. Second, because Deuteronomy is 'Deuteronomic', we are free to say that its framing is fictive, that the staging of the speech of Moses at the Jordan is an invitation for Israel that has embraced the Yahwistic *or* against the Canaanite *either* to conjure what the land of promise would be like were it alternatively organized and practiced in covenant. This delivers us from needing to insist that Israel enacted all these laws, but it also permits us to see the 'laws' as acts of imagination in which each successive generation of *or* is to explore how to take this text into its own concrete life and practice.

I shall comment on three texts from Deuteronomy. The ones I have selected are perhaps easy cases, but the point will be more generally clear. Joshua counts on the clear *either/or* worked in detail by Moses:

1. *Either* let the economy work unfettered so that the rich become richer, *or* read Deut. 15:1–18 on the 'Year of Release'.[22] Moses, in this text, anticipates and imagines that the economy of the land of Canaan does not need to be organized in exploitative 'Canaanite' ways, but could be reorganized in neighborly Israelite ways. He offers a scenario for a society in which poor people must work off their debts (no doubt at high interest rates), but a neighborly ethic proposes that at the end of six years, the debt is cancelled and the poor person is invited back into the economy.

– Moses said, 'There will always be poor people', so you must take this seriously and keep doing it all the time (v. 11);

– Moses said, If you do it effectively, you can eliminate such demeaning poverty and 'the poor will cease out of the land' (v. 4);

– Moses said, 'Do not entertain mean thoughts and begin to count toward the seventh year and act in hostility' (v. 9);

– Moses said, do not only cancel the debt but give the poor a generous stake so that they can reenter the economy viably, not from the bottom up (vv. 7–10);

– Moses said, if this seems outrageous to you, remember that you were bond-servants in Egypt and you were released by the generous power of Yahweh your redeemer who brought you out (v. 18).

This is the most radical *or* in the Bible, insisting that the economy must be embedded in a neighborly human fabric. Almost all of us choose the *either*, imagining that Joshua's *or* is not relevant to an urban, post-industrial economy. But there it sits, always a summons, always a reminder, always an invitation. And Joshua had already said, 'I tried to talk you out of this *or*; I told you it was too difficult for you.'

2. *Either* let legitimate authority run loose in self-serving acquisitiveness, *or* read Deut. 17:14–20 on monarchy. It is the only law of Moses on kingship. Moses agrees only reluctantly to let Israel have a king; he thought kingship a bad idea and all available models of centralized power were bad. Then he says, but if you must, your king, your Israelite, covenantal, neighborly king shall be different. This king, embedded in covenant, must not accumulate silver or gold or horses or chariots or wives. Moses knows the three great seductions are money, power, and sex, all of which make com-

munity impossible if they are accumulated. And so he offers an *or*. The king, when in office, shall sit all day, every day, reading Torah, meditating day and night on what Yahweh intends, on how covenantal community can curb raw power.

Israel, like every government since, has found it difficult to choose this *or*. The kings of Israel characteristically took the *either* of raw power, as has every kind of power ... priests, parents, teachers, deans, bishops, corporate executives. In Israel, the primal example of the power of greed is Solomon, gold, gold, gold, 300 wives, 700 concubines, and later it was said, 'Do not be anxious, even Solomon in all his vast royal apparatus was not as well off as a bird'.[23] The *or* is about power and governance and greed; in the end, however, it is about anxiety, getting more, keeping more while the land is lost in dread, terror, and devouring.[24]

3. *Either* it is every man [sic] for himself at the expense of all the others, *or* read Deut. 24:19–22. It is about the triangle of *land-owner*, *land*, and *landless*, and how they will live together. The *either* of Canaanite agriculture is just a 'labor pool' of those nameless ones without any leverage or fringe benefits, who work but fall farther and farther behind, until they drop into welfare and then out of welfare into drugs, alcohol, sometimes a threat to us, often an inconvenience, always a nuisance and embarrassment. *Or*, says Moses, in your economic operations, leave enough for *the alien, the widow, the orphan*. Leave the sheaves of wheat when you are 'bringing in the sheaves', for *the alien, the widow, the orphan*. When you beat your olive trees, leave enough for *the alien, the widow, the orphan*. When you gather grapes, leave some for *the alien, the widow, the orphan*. The triad is like a mantra for this *or* of covenant because Moses knows that the powerful are in common destiny with the powerless. The haves are linked to the future of the have-nots. Moses had already said, 'Same law for citizens and undocumented workers' (Lev. 19:34). Moses knew that in a patriarchal society women without husbands and children without fathers are lost to the community, as bad off as outsiders.

The *or* requires a break with the orthodoxy of individualism. It requires a rejection of the notion of the undeserving poor. It requires a negation of all the pet ideologies whereby unburdened freedom is the capacity to disregard neighbor. And it is all there in the deep command of Yahweh ... not socialism, not liberalism, not ideology, just an alternative life.[25]

Our Christian strategy for disposing of the Mosaic is to dismiss it as legalism, certain we are justified by grace alone, except that this obedience belongs to the center of an alternative community. The *or* is demanding but not obvious. The mantra of this community is endlessly 'love God, then love neighbor, neighbor, neighbor.'

2. I have characterized Isaiah 40–55 as a primary model of *either/or* testimonial utterance for this special community almost succumbing to Babylon. It was to this little community without confidence and almost without conviction that the poet declared on Yahweh's behalf:

> because you are precious in my sight,
> and honored, and I love you,
> I give people in return for you,
> nations in exchange for your life. (Is. 43:4)

II Isaiah, however, only provides the trigger for liturgical, emotional, imaginative, perhaps geographical homecoming. When the Jews did come back to Jerusalem in 537 or 520 or 444, II Isaiah gave little guidance. But then, II Isaiah never comes without III Isaiah. I propose that III Isaiah, Is. 56–66, is the figurative articulation that fleshes out the *either/or* of II Isaiah.[26] There is now a great deal of ferment about the book of Isaiah. It is increasingly likely, in scholarly judgment, that the old, deep separation of II and III Isaiah cannot be sustained. And therefore in its canonical shaping, one may see Isaiah 56–66 as an attempt to enact the glorious vision of II Isaiah, but enactments must always come to detail.

1. *Either* be a community of like-minded people who are convinced of their own purity, virtue, orthodoxy, and legitimacy, excluding all others, *or* read Is. 56:3–8. There were all around the edges of restored Judaism inconvenient people who had no claim to purity, virtue, orthodoxy, or legitimacy. There were late-comers, not good Jews with pedigrees, who had joined in, drawn to the faith, perhaps Samaritans or whatever, but surely not 'qualified'. Worse than that, there were people with marked, scarred, compromised genitals, people who had sold out to Babylon in order to become willing eunuchs with access to power. Of these Moses long ago in Deut. 23:1 had declared that people with irregular sexual disposition were excluded. It is there in the Torah. All around were hovering people not like us, claiming and pushing and yearning and even believing . . . What to do?

Says the *or* of III Isaiah, have a generous spirit and a minimum but clear bar of admission. Tilt toward inclusiveness with only two requirements: that they keep covenant, that is submit to the neighborly intention of Yahweh; that they keep sabbath, rest from the madness of production and consumption as a sign of confidence in Yahweh's governance. That's all! It is the *or* of inclusiveness, no other pedigree, no sexual transposition, no other purification, an *or* that says the community is not made in the image of our strong points. The community teems with people who score irregularly on every Myers-Briggs notion of how we are and how we ought to be.[27]

2. *Either* become a punctilious community of religious discipline, engaging in religious scruple with amazing callousness about the real world of human transaction, *or* read Isaiah 58:1–9 and consider an alternative religious discipline of fasting that is not for show or piety or self-congratulations. Practice fast that commits to the neighbor, specifically the neighbor in need, the neighbor boxed in injustice and oppression. Break the vicious cycles of haves and have-nots that produce hungry people and homeless people and naked people, the most elemental signs and gestures of exposure, vulnerability, and degradation, produced by a system that does not notice.

Conventional religious disciplines that feel like virtue are disconnected. The practitioners of such self-congratulation, all the while, exploit and oppress and quarrel; they are uncaring, unthinking, unnoticing. And now the *or* of engagement moves to solidarity with the exposed and the vulnerable. The NRSV says 'they are your kin', but the Hebrew says 'flesh', your own flesh of flesh and bone of bone, self of self. That is who they are.

When the lines of separation between haves and have-nots are broken by true fast, then, says III Isaiah, then, only then, not until then:

> *Then* your light shall break forth like the dawn,
> and your healing shall spring up quickly;
> your vindicator shall go before you,
> the glory of the Lord shall be your rear guard.
> *Then* you shall call, and the Lord will answer;
> you shall cry for help,
> and he will say, 'Here I am'. (vv. 8–9)

Then, then, then, then . . . it is the *or* of communion. There is, however, no communion with Yahweh until there is community with neighbor.[28]

3. *Either* cling to the old status quo of social arrangements and miss God's newness, *or* read Isaiah 65:17–25. The *or* of poetic imagination asserts that the old heaven and the old earth and the old Jerusalem, the old holy city and every old holy city and every old city and every old power arrangement is on the way out and is being displaced. The *or* of world renewal and urban renewal is a fantasy. The community of *or* engages in a strong act of vision: 'We have a dream.' It is a dream of joy and well-being, a dream in which there are no more cries of distress, no more infant mortality, no more social dislocation when people build houses and lose them by taxation, war, ethnic cleansing, or Olympic committees, where people do not plant gardens and have to move before

harvest time. In the world coming there is no more anguish in childbirth. And to top it all, there is reconciliation of creation, lions and lambs, immediate communion with and attentiveness from Yahweh who answers before we call.

The poet offers a breath-taking *or*. He has been radical in chapters 56 on eunuchs and 58 on poor people. But now in chapter 65 he no longer has time for the conventions of reality as he is off on a poetic, evangelical fantasy of what might be and what will be and what is at hand, but not in hand. He imagines, against the lovers of the old city who had felt but not yet noticed the brutal dysfunction of the old city. All will be changed. The poet can scarcely see its shape, but he has no doubt that its coming shape is a healing of all old abrasions and despairs. This *or* will never happen among us while we are bound to what was. Thus the poem is more like a parable than a blueprint, but a parable to be ingested by reforming Judaism, a parable,

> about a banquet,
> about a rich man and a barn,
> about a man with two sons,
> about a neighborly foreigner who paid the bills,
> about a nagging widow,
> about day laborers who get full pay.[29]

None of that is visible yet. Indeed none of that is possible . . . yet – except for those who depart the way things are for the One who will make things new.

V

I am taking an ecclesial agenda because for too long, so it seems to me, christological certitude in the church has much of the time been permitted to silence, trump, and give closure to the Old Testament. I have wanted to suggest that faithful Christian exposition could do otherwise. I regard the preacher's engagement with the Old Testament as urgent:

– because the *or* of faith, so deeply pondered by ancient Israel, is needed in the face of our dominant *either*;

– because in a technological society, it is mostly left to the preacher, who labors at it locally, to voice the human options in a crisis of flatness;

– because preachers, more than any others, have endless opportunity for the tease of detail whereby the *or* of the gospel may be received and embraced.

The *or* is an impossible possibility. Both Israel and the church have always known that. That is what makes preaching both foolish and urgent.[30]

Notes

1   Jon D. Levenson, *The Death and Resurrection of the Beloved Son: The Transformation of Child Sacrifice in Judaism and Christianity,* New Haven, CT, Yale University Press, 1993, has explored Jewish antecedents to the Christian foundation of 'Father-Son'.

2   For a critical summary of Newbigin's accent on ecclesiology, see George R. Hunsberger, *Bearing the Witness of the Spirit: Lesslie Newbigin's Theology of Cultural Pluralism,* Grand Rapids, MI, Eerdmans, 1998.

3　See Walter Brueggemann, 'Ecumenism as the Shared Practice of a Peculiar Identity', *Word and World*, XVIII, 1998, pp. 122–35.

4　See my discussion, Walter Brueggemann, *Cadences of Home: Preaching Among Exiles*, Louisville, KY, Westminster/John Knox, 1997.

5　The either/or I will exposit is essentially that of the Deuteronomic theology that speaks with conviction that one choice is good and one is bad (see Deuteronomy 30:15–20). That is to say that the *either/or* of the Deuteronomist is completely without the irony of which Søren Keirkegaard can write: 'Marry, and you will regret it. Do not marry, and you will also regret it. Marry or do not marry, you will regret it either way. Whether you marry or you do not marry, you will regret it either way. Laugh at the stupidities of the world, and you will regret it; weep over them, and you will also regret it. Laugh at the stupidities of the world or weep over them, you will regret it either way. Whether you laugh at the stupidities of the world or you weep over them, you will regret it either way. Trust a girl, and you will regret it. Do not trust her, and you will also regret it. Trust a girl or do not trust her, you will regret it either way. Whether you trust a girl or do not trust her, you will regret it either way. Hang yourself, and you will regret it. Do not hang yourself and you will also regret it. Hang yourself or do not hang yourself, you will regret it either way. Whether you hang yourself or do not hang yourself, you will regret it either way. This, gentlemen, is the quintessence of all the wisdom of life.' (*Either/Or I*, trans. Howard V. Hong and Edna H. Hong, Princeton, NJ, Princeton University Press, 1987, pp. 38–9.)

6　It is instructive that in both narratives of Abraham (Genesis 15:6) and Moses (Exodus 4:1), the key term is '*men* = 'trust'. It is 'trust' that makes the 'or' of Yahweh choosable against the 'either' that characteristically seems given and easy to embrace.

7　Of that intentional decision, Jacob Neusner, *The Enchantments of Judaism: Rites of Transformation from Birth Through Death*, New York, Basic Books, 1987, p. 212, writes, 'All of us are Jews through the power of our imagination.'

8　Gerhard von Rad, *The Problem of the Hexateuch and Other Essays*, New York, McGraw-Hill, 1966, pp. 73–74, 96, to be sure, takes chapter 24 to be an early credo and Joshua 21:43–45 to be the culmination of the Hexateuch. The placement of chapter 24, however, is important to the argument concerning its significance, even if he regards it as early.

9　See Walter Brueggemann, *Biblical Perspectives on Evangelism: Living in a Three-Storied Universe*, Nashville, TN, Abingdon, 1993, pp. 48–70.

10　Von Rad, 1966, pp. 6–7.

11　On narratives producing worlds, see Amos Wilder, 'Story and Story-World', *Interpretation*, XXXVII, 1983, pp. 353–64.

12　The term 'far be it from' is an exceedingly strong expression, suggesting the complete inappropriateness of the action, for such an action would profane and render its subject unworthy. See a usage with reference to Yahweh's own action in Genesis 18:25.

13　On this negative command, see the parallel in Genesis 35:1–4. Some scholars, following Albrecht Alt, suggest that a ritual performance is here envisioned whereby the foreign gods are dramatically banished from the community.

14　The fundamental rhetorical analysis is that of Claus Westermann, 'Sprache und Struktur der Prophetie Deuterojesajas', *Neudrucke und Berichte aus dem 20. Jahrhundert*, ThB 24 Altes Testament, München, Kaiser Verlag, 1964, pp. 92–170.

15　See Walter Brueggemann, *Theology of the Old Testament: Testimony, Dispute, Advocacy*, Minneapolis, Fortress, 1997, pp. 117–44.

16　It is evident that 'testimony' is a way to make a claim from 'below', when one lacks the tools and authority to make a more established sort of claim for truth. See my comments on Ricoeur and Wiesel in *Theology of the Old Testament*.

17　See Brueggemann, 1993, especially pp. 26–30.

18　The most fundamental analysis is that of Jacques Ellul, *Technological Society*, New York, Random

House, 1967. See more specifically to our point, Jacques Ellul, *The Humiliation of the Word*, Grand Rapids, Eerdmans, 1985.

19 On the integrity of speech and matching speech to life, see Wendell Berry, *Standing by Words: Essays*, San Francisco, North Point Press, 1983, pp. 24–63.

20 In recent time, Paul Ricoeur has understood most clearly and most consistently that serious religious language must be spoken in 'figure', thus his accent on imagination. Speech that is not in 'figure' runs the prompt risk of idolatry, of producing what can be controlled. See the several essays in his book nicely entitled, *Figuring the Sacred: Religion, Narrative, and Imagination*, ed. Mark I. Wallace, Minneapolis, Fortress, 1995.

21 See a summary of this scholarship by Terence E. Fretheim, *Deuteronomic History, Interpreting Biblical Texts*, Nashville, TN, Abingdon, 1983.

22 On this pivotal command, see Jeffries M. Hamilton, *Social Justice and Deuteronomy: The Case of Deuteronomy 15*, SBL Dissertation Series 136, Atlanta, Scholars Press, 1992.

23 See Walter Brueggemann, 'Faith with a Price', *The Other Side*, 34, 4, 1998 pp. 32–35.

24 The 'or' of covenantal power is nicely put in the words of Jesus in Mark 10:42–44.

25 On neighborliness extended to outsiders and the weak insiders, see Luke 4:26–27.

26 See Grace I. Emmerson, *Isaiah 56–66*, Old Testament Guides, Sheffield, Sheffield Academic Press, 1992, and Elizabeth Achtemeier, *The Community and Message of Isaiah 56–66*, Minneapolis, Augsburg, 1982.

27 The New Testament counterpart to such 'foreigners and eunuchs' is perhaps 'publicans and sinners', on which see Mark 2:15–17.

28 On neighborly attentiveness as a condition of well-being, see Matt. 25:31–46.

29 Among the most helpful treatments of the parables is John R. Donahue, *The Gospel in Parable: Metaphor, Narrative and Theology in the Synoptic Gospels*, Philadelphia, Fortress, 1998.

30 This is a slightly abbreviated version of my address to the annual meeting of The Academy of Homiletics on December 3, 1998, in Toronto.

6   Preaching the Bible and Preaching the Gospel

Edward Farley

The impossible task

Most would agree that preaching is at the center of Protestant churchly life. Likewise, most would agree that something is not quite right about the preaching that goes on in the churches. A few ministers have the reputation of being 'good preachers'. Most of us do not. The sermon is for many preachers the stone of Sisyphus to be rolled back up the hill each Sunday and for their parishioners something to be endured. Ministers who attend church while on vacation typically think they did not hear 'good preaching'. The books about preaching are filled with phrases like the 'crisis of preaching'. There are the usual explanations for all of this: the multiple pressures on the minister's time, the decline of both the orientation to and the time for study, and the failure of theological education.

Assessing the quality of contemporary preaching is not my topic. These things do suggest that something is not quite right in the land of preaching. We need not think this is due to a lack of gifts of the minister, the decline of genuine religious life in the United States, or the quality of teaching and writing in current homiletic theory. Present-day homiletics probably offers the most sophisticated analyses of preaching Christendom has ever seen. The reason there is something not quite right with preaching is that a notion of preaching prevails in Christendom that poses to the preacher a task impossible to carry out, a problem impossible to solve. That impossible-to-solve problem is the subject of this essay.

When something has been around long enough and is a matter of almost universal consensus, the fact that it is an *interpretation*, one among many possible ways of seeing and thinking, becomes invisible. It simply seems 'true' 'right', the 'only possibility'. But everything we human beings do, think, and believe is interpretation. What we think reflects our community's past, our gender experience, our very personal angle on things. Interpretation attends how we use the Bible, how we conceive church education, and how we think of preaching. Interpretations that have cumulated over centuries in particular images and concepts tend to have the character of paradigms. To think of salvation simply as an individual going to heaven is one paradigm of salvation; social liberation from oppression is another. Preaching, too, exists in the expectations of (Protestant) congregations, in the attitude of their preachers. and in the literature (homiletics) about preaching by way of a prevailing paradigm. It is the aim of this essay to analyse that paradigm and show why it is a failed paradigm, fostering an impossible task upon the preacher.

The prevailing paradigm of preaching

The Christian movement has always existed in relation to a collection of sacred writings, the Hebrew Scriptures in the time of its formation, and the two testament canon from the second century to the present. The sense of being subject to the collection was reaffirmed in the

Reformation. In Protestant Christendom, therefore, the only authentic preaching is biblical preaching. This general conviction is not, however, the prevailing paradigm of preaching. This paradigm arises as one way to conceive what it means to preach biblically. The paradigm is clearly rooted in Jewish midrash, the several ways of interpreting Scripture in ancient Judaism.[1] The major elements of the paradigm are as follows:

(1) What is preached is the Bible or the biblical message.[2]

(2) The Bible is a collection that becomes available to preaching only as it is divided into passages (text, pericopes). Hence, to preach the Bible means to preach it as so divided. Specific passages then are *what* is preached. Preaching is not preaching unless it is 'on' a passage.[3]

(3) Since the Bible itself is not divided into such passages, the work of dividing must be done to the Bible, either by the individual preacher or by an institution, as in the lectionary. The boundaries of the passage will be whatever the dividers determine it to be.

(4) What is preached is not simply our own human, private convictions, speculations, or beliefs but the Word of God, some truth of God that has a claim on us, that consoles us, evokes our action, prompts our belief, or salvifically transforms us.

(5) Since the Bible (the Word of God) is present to preaching only in the form of a passage on which one preaches, each passage must necessarily and in an a priori way contain a truth of God that summons, consoles, and the like, distributed into discrete units (passages), the Word of God (revelation, authority), bestows on each passage something preachable. Whatever and wherever the passage is, however small (a verse) or large, and however arbitrarily its boundaries are drawn, something about the passage must be preachable. This something is the *that-which-is-preached*, the what of preaching.

(6) Preaching itself is an orally delivered message to a congregation in a liturgical setting. The congregation in its situation is the *that-to-which* of preaching.

(7) Preaching to a congregation takes into account the situation of the congregation, its cultural setting, and the problems of its members. This is the *that-in-the-light-of which* of preaching.

(8) In old-line churches and in the homiletics of their theological schools, this orally delivered message exists in the form of a piece of writing, the crafted sermon with its introduction, movement through major points, narratives, and metaphors. In this crafted sermon, the above three concerns come together in the form of a writing meant to be delivered orally.

This paradigm poses to the preacher a two-sided task, First, the preacher must connect that-which-is-preached (the content of the passage) to the situation of the congregation. This means connecting the *whatever* is preachable in the passage with something in the present. Second, the preacher must create the rhetorical vehicle, the (written) sermon that renders this connection into language. One kind of homiletic theory focuses on the problem of discerning the preachable content in the passage, thus on exegesis. A second kind of homiletic theory focuses on the moment of application, the situation and problem to which the sermon is addressed. A third kind of homiletic theory focuses primarily on the rhetorical problem, the skill of finding the rhetorical moves that best fit the passage and its preachable content. It is my impression that the most recent wave of homiletic theory is primarily of the third type. The paradigm here can be expressed in the form of a metaphor of building a bridge.[4] The preacher's task is to build a bridge from that which is preached (the truth of the specific passage) to the situation of the congregation. The construction of the crafted written sermon sets the problem of traversing the bridge.

A failed paradigm

The bridge paradigm reflects both a way of thinking about preaching and a way of thinking about the Bible. As a way of thinking about preaching, the bridge paradigm is clearly a departure from primitive Christian preaching as we find it described on the pages of the New Testament.[5] It is somewhat anachronistic to compare what we now call preaching with the *kērussō* of Paul and other itinerant evangelists. With certain exceptions, present-day preaching is part of a weekly Christian liturgical event. Jesus' preaching was that of an itinerant prophet proclaiming the impending reign of God. Early Christian preaching continued this itinerant tradition, proclaiming the good news of salvation through Jesus. One thing is clear in the New Testament accounts. That which is preached is not the content of passages of Scripture. It is the gospel, the event of Christ through which we are saved. To think that what is preached is the Bible and the content of its passages is a quite different way of thinking about preaching.

How did the church get from the preaching of the gospel to the preaching of passages of the Bible? I can only leave that complex problem to the historians. Some developments that contributed to the change do seem evident. Dividing the Scriptures into passages one interprets is already part of early Judaism, both in the Qumran community and in what later was called rabbinic Judaism. The early Christian community always presupposed the 'Scriptures', the Hebrew Bible, and, with the help of Marcion and Irenaeus, developed a second authoritative collection.The ecclesia, or congregation, was modeled on the Jewish synagogue and it retained the practice of a weekly gathering for worship at which they read and expounded a passage of Scripture. As new generations of believers arose, separated by decades from the event of Jesus, the church circulated written accounts of that event as well as written pastoral advice by Paul and others. We have, then, several things coming together to dispose the church to interpret preaching as taking its start from biblical passages: the tradition of the kerygma of the apostles, the Jewish paradigm of authoritative passages, the reading of passages in a liturgical setting, and the addition of a new literature about the event of Jesus and the beginning of the church. When these things merge, we have a shift from the preaching of the gospel, or of the kingdom of God, or of Jesus as Lord to a preaching of the contents of the new two testament Scripture.

Why is this a radical departure from the preaching of the gospel? The Hebrew Scriptures are a vast collection of historical memory spread over a thousand years. The collection records a myriad of themes, events, personages, poetry, and laws. These things are not, as such, the gospel. The New Testament collection is a literature that records and attests to the event of Jesus and the early decades of the life of the ecclesia. Neither are these things as such the gospel. It is not apparent on the face of it why passages about what Peter did in his controversy with Paul, or a piece of advice from Timothy to a congregation, or a genealogical list would be *that-which-is-preached*. One can see why such things might find their way into the church's memory by way of teaching. The New Testament is the church's founding document, recording as it does the birth event of the church. But it does not, in its discrete passages, describe what the church is called to proclaim, namely the good tidings. To regard it so is, therefore, to regard not the gospel but the Bible (in its passages) as that which is proclaimed. And surely it is a subterfuge to say, as some have, that one preaches the gospel through preaching a passage or that preaching a passage *is* preaching the gospel. If one preaches the passage on the basis of a rigorous exegesis of its contents, what one cannot do is to ignore the distinctive content therein. That would be to abandon the paradigm and acknowledge that it is not the passage being preached. For it is surely clear that the content of most biblical passages is not as such the gospel.

The other aspect of the bridge paradigm is a way of thinking about the Bible. The bridge paradigm requires us to think of the Bible as a collection of passages, each of which necessarily contains a preaching word or truth of God. This is of course the paradigm of ancient Judaism. Peshar and rabbinic midrash assume it. The dividing of the printed Bible into chapters and verses gave a huge boost to this way of thinking of the Bible. Many modern Protestant churches and their ministers distinguish themselves from fundamentalism. Accordingly, they reject notions of biblical inerrancy and methods of establishing belief by verse proof-texting. They criticize such proof-texting as unhistorical, as interpreting the matters of Scripture out of context. They have thus become accustomed to historical-critical and literary methods of interpreting the Bible. In the face of such commitments, we must pose a question. Given a rejection of biblical inerrancy and the acceptance of historical-critical methods, what is the basis of the claim that something preachable is necessarily in the text or lectionary chosen by the preacher? Why is a word or truth of God *necessarily* present in a passage of the Bible chosen by a lectionarist or by the preacher? Such an assumption seems more arbitrary and more incoherent than the fundamentalist view. For fundamentalists, a passage, any passage no matter how you determine its boundaries, is authoritative because the words of the Bible are themselves inspired. It makes no difference whether they have the form of a verse or larger passage. Whatever the Bible says is true. But why would someone who thinks that the Bible originated historically, contextually, and editorially, thus reflecting the human and even corrupted perspectives of its writers, think that any passage one happens to select must contain something in or about it that is proclaimable? If I correct an illegitimate proof-texting citation of Romans 8:1 by making it a part of Romans 8:1–10, do I now have an intrinsically inerrant and authoritative unit, something God placed in the passage? If criticism of an out-of-context verse arises from historical sensibility, then isolating a *passage* and regarding it as the unit of authority has the same problem. The whole paradigm of necessarily true passages breaks on the rocks of historical consciousness and requires a fundamentalist element to make it work.

It is clear that to divide the Bible into necessarily true passages is only one way among many ways of thinking about the Bible, of being 'biblical', of placing oneself under the power and influence of Scripture. Surely we can be moved and influenced by the Iliad, King Lear, or *The Color Purple* without dividing these great works into pericopes and assigning a necessary truth to each one. Why must this be done to Jeremiah or Paul? Ironically, the effect of this atomism and leveling of Scripture into passages is to suppress the power and beauty of that literature. If the Bible is not in fact an aggregate of 'passages' or texts (even as King Lear and *The Color Purple* are not), then so to construe it is to distort it. To see a letter of Paul, a Gospel, or a prophetic tract as an aggregate of discrete units is surely to miss the writing as an argument, a polemic, a set of imageries, a theological perspective, a narrative. The very thing that gives the writing its power is its unity, its total concrete vision, its total movement. This is the ironical side of the bridge paradigm and its pretension to preach 'biblically'. The weekly application of something in the passage to life casts a dark veil over the Scriptures. One becomes used to thinking of Scripture as an aggregate of thousands of small units, each with its lesson for life. Lost here is the grandeur, beauty, and moral vision of the pentateuchal narratives, the prophetic theology, the radicality of Jesus' message, and the dramatic birth of the early Christian movement.

Is the problem simply that passages are the arbitrary creation of lectionarists and preachers? If this were the case, the solution lies in the direction of letting the Bible itself determine its passages. There are of course natural passages in any literature that lend themselves to selection, memorization, and interpretation: Hamlet's soliloquy, the Grand Inquisitor passage from *The Brothers Karamazov*. In the Bible we find many natural rhetorical units: specific stories, parables, psalms, confessional formulas, aphorisms, laws, sermons, collections of laws (the decalogue), miracle stories, and speeches. Have we evaded the fundamentalist element when we limit our selection to these natural rhetorical units? Is there something about these units that guarantees each one contains a preachable truth of God? Again, in the absence of a fundamentalist argument, there is nothing about the content of these units that requires or guarantees such a truth. Some of them may offer a kind of perennial wisdom we recognize and can expound. Others might foster anti-Semitism or patriarchal bias or an oppressive sexual ethic. In other words, some might contain contents that Christian preaching would want to oppose, not proclaim.[6]

Insofar as that which is preached must be a preachable truth of God in a delimited passage of the Bible, the preacher who would 'preach on' this preachable something faces an impossible task. The preacher sets out to locate that something in or about the passage. Let us call it X, the preachable element about the passage. Because the passage is a delimited piece in a larger writing and because there is no guaranteed verbal inerrancy about the writing at any level, there may be no X (preachable truth) in the passage. Or the content of the passage may be something one should preach against. Or the passage may have a moralizable content, something that lends itself to a 'lesson for life'. To the degree that there is nothing preachable in the text, the preacher who still must find a way from the text to the sermon must invent X. Something about the text is latched onto as that which is preached: a word, a phrase, an action, the text as narrative. Whatever this is, it must be made into a lesson for life. Since what most biblical passages are up to, judged on strict exegetical grounds, is not to provide such lessons, the preacher must wring an X out of the exegeted passage. The passage then is not so much 'preached on' as something that provides a jumping off place for the sermon.

More typically, because the lectionarist or preacher has selected the passage on the grounds of its preachability, the passage will contain an X that promises to be a lesson for life. This something rarely has anything to do with what exegesis would discover. Almost all biblical passages are part of a larger flow of writing as in a letter, a narrative, or a list of laws. To discover the lesson for life, the preacher must abandon exegesis and move to 'interpretation'. The interest of interpretation is to cross the bridge by applying X to the life situations of the congregation. Exegesis may disclose that the story of the temptation of Jesus reflects the problem the early church had in its claim that Jesus was Messiah in the face of the fact that his life story was not that of a messianic king. But the preacher, looking for a preachable X in the story, finds it by showing how Jesus' temptation to self-glorification is a lesson for our lives. But the preacher has to abandon exegesis to make this move. To alter a phrase from the controversy over the Vietnam war, the preacher must kill the passage in order to preach on it. The application then has the character of a stipulation, an invention, a making up something about the passage.

Thus, the preacher is not really starting with the text but with the lesson for life she knows is pertinent to the congregation. Rhetorically, the sermon may sound like it marches from the passage to the situation. Actually, the route is the reverse, from the situation, the in-the-light-of problem, to a constructed X of the text. The passage or its preachable X is not really that-which-is-preached, but the rhetorical occasion that jump-starts the sermon. Interpreting the passage then is a modification of the exegeted content so that the passage's lesson for life can be applied.

This imaginative stipulation of the preachable X is so deeply rooted in Protestant preaching that it takes place almost unconsciously, with little awareness that it is a stipulation. But the very fact that the stipulation or construction of the preachable X is necessary in order to preach 'on' the passage shows that the bridge paradigm is a failed paradigm. It has failure built into it from the beginning. The reason for the failure can be stated simply. There is nothing about arbitrarily selected passages of the Bible that in some necessary or a priori way contains that-which-is-proclaimed. If that is the case, the bridge paradigm fosters onto the preacher a task impossible to fulfill. This does not mean there is no 'good preaching' or even marvelously gifted preachers. These are the preachers who if not solving the impossible problem have surmounted it with personal power, eloquent style, and profound insight into the situation. They have found a way to preach the gospel even within the confines of the bridge paradigm. Many of the rest of us are simply nonplussed by the sermon and flounder about assembling stories and quotations into the weekly message.

Attempts at correction

The bridge paradigm pervades the Protestant pulpit and dominates its homiletic literature.[7] It seems to be fixed permanently in the practice and consciousness of Protestant Christendom. At the same time, it is a paradigm with an unhappy conscience. Preachers and homileticians sense something not quite right about preaching and work hard to reconceive and correct. The corrections do not, however, identify the bridge paradigm itself as the source of the problem but, rather, certain deployments of the paradigm. Recent homiletic theory is critical of traditional preaching, but its revisionings fall within the bridge paradigm.[8] Corrections are offered along at least the following four lines:

The first type would correct the violation of the text by means of rigorous exegesis. It makes a heroic effort to avoid making the text into something it is not. It thus sets the passage in its context and attends to historically and linguistically retrieved contents. But the more rigorous and successful the exegesis is carried out, the greater the distance between what is discovered in the passage and the preachable X. Surely the *what* of preaching is not what historical exegesis is able to retrieve from a selected passage.

The second correction, perhaps the most recent phase of contemporary homiletic theory, draws on literary, structuralist, semiological, and rhetorical analyses. These homileticians are severely critical of conventional preaching and of the old homiletics. Criticized is the rationalistic notion that a pericope is a static field from which one distills a single idea.[9] Opposed also is the notion of the Bible as a source of propositional truths that prompts 'deductive preaching', or the notion that the sermon is an engineering project that assembles textual and other elements.[10]

These critics do sense something problematic in the effort to go from passage to sermon. That problematic something is not, however, the bridge paradigm itself but false ways of making the journey. They especially oppose the effort to find a single preachable point *in* a passage. That smacks of fundamentalism. Instead, one should view the passage in a different way. Attend not to the distilled point but to the passage as a narrative, as a dynamic movement, as a moving and distinctive rhetoric. It is evident that such proposals do in fact correct our ways of reading the Bible. We do falsify a passage by reducing it to its 'point'. Any passage of writing will contain movement and, also, as deconstructionists argue, self-differentiation. What is not evident is why a passage's movement, dynamic rhetoric, or narrative is in some necessary way the *what* of preaching. What is gained by regarding the passage as a whole the preachable X instead of some point in the passage? What gives a selected passage that a priori feature? Why cannot a passage even as a movement be anti-Semitic, irrelevant, vacuous, or sexist? Even in this more total and dynamic correction, we find ourselves trying to wring some lesson for life out of the passage.

The third attempt to save the passage arises when homiletics joins with contemporary hermeneutics. Few would dispute the general insight of such hermeneutics. The interpretation and use of texts is never simply a passive reception of objective content. It is a human act that reflects the interests and agendas of the interpreter. In interpretation, the interpreter's world and the world of the text merge in what Gadamer calls a fusion of horizons. Hermeneutics helps make interpreters aware of their pre-understandings and agendas so as to place them in the service of interpretation. These interests can serve as a hermeneutic key that breaks the hold of the authoritarian text and uncovers new possibilities in it.

Such keys are existential relevance, liberation and social praxis, and a genealogy of the past. The entanglements of the interpreter's world and the world of the text appear to be an unavoidable part of all interpretation. What is not so clear is how this insight solves the problem of the stipulated preachable X. Hermeneutics can so orient the preacher to the selected passage that it is made to speak, for instance, of liberation. But this clearly is a usage of the passage, not a genuine preaching of the passage.

The fourth attempt to save the passages is a more general version of hermeneutics. It recalls for us that what we preach is the gospel, the Word of God, or Jesus Christ. One version of this argues that the passage becomes the Word of God as the Spirit works in the event of preaching. The problems of the isolated passage are solved if we connect what we preach to the gospel. But what does this mean specifically? The Word of God, gospel, or Jesus do not displace the preachable X of the passage. If they did, the passage would be superfluous. And it would be simply odd to pretend that the preachable X (for example, a piece of advice of Paul to the Corinthians) *is* itself the good tidings.

These responses to the problem of preaching indicate an uneasiness about making that-which-is-preached to be passages of the Bible. But they do not break with the bridge paradigm. Their proposals to reform preaching take place within the paradigm and as such tend to keep the paradigm and its problems hidden from view.

A counter view

What else might preaching be than the bridging of passage and situation? The bridge paradigm is so deeply rooted in the Protestant consciousness that for many an alternative is unthinkable. Paradigms of this sort are so basic, so tied up with other paradigms (such as how one thinks about the Bible) that they do not arise overnight or even with the work of individuals. Alternative paradigms will probably be the work of historical periods or ecclesial and theological movements. We can, however, make a beginning at an interpretation of preaching minus the bridge paradigm.

According to the bridge paradigm, what we preach is not the gospel but the Bible, the preachable *whatever* of a selected passage. There is a rationale for this view. The apostles proclaimed the gospel because they were in direct proximity to Jesus. With the rise of the New Testament canon, our only access to Jesus is by way of these writings. Accordingly, we must preach this literature, our one and only path to Jesus. I would offer a counter view. The Christian church is summoned to the apostolic task of preaching the good news, and to preach biblical passages is to reject that summons. I do think that the church's teaching faces a broader task, and it makes complete sense to say that the church is summoned to teach the Bible; its history, books, theologies, narratives, and the like. But we preach, that is, proclaim, the gospel. What then is 'gospel', the good tidings?

Let us begin with a cautionary remark. Gospel is not a thing to be defined. It is not a doctrine, a delimited objective content. The summaries in Acts and in Paul of what is proclaimed, the formulas of the kerygma, attest to this. Phrases like the kingdom of God, Jesus as Lord, Christ crucified do have content, but that content is not simply a quantity of information. To proclaim means to bring to bear a certain past event on the present in such a way as to open the future. Since the present is always specific and situational, the way that the past, the event of Christ, is brought to bear so as to elicit hope will never be captured in some timeless phrase, some ideality of language. Preaching the good tidings is a new task whenever and wherever it takes place. From the hearer's perspective, preaching the gospel is a summons to faithful existence in the face of whatever happens, whatever is to come.

Preaching, the bringing to bear of a past event on a present situation so as to open up the future, has a specific temporal structure. We find that structure in the Hebrew prophets who brought the event of exodus liberation, promise, and covenant to bear on Israel's situation, opening up a future of both impending judgment and mercy. For the apostolic preaching, Jesus' life, death, and resurrection as set in the story of Israel was the past that opened up a new aeon. And this is ever the content and structure of the proclamation of the Christian church: the bringing to bear of the event of Jesus onto the present in such a way that the present is both judged and drawn in hope toward redemption.

This structure of preaching does not describe all that happened when the Christian movement became both a church and a teaching. Both things were necessary if the attestation to Jesus were to survive. The church was pressed to distinguish its teaching from the multitude of religious, philosophical, and cultural traditions of the Mediterranean basin. To do so it developed the kerygma into a conceptual framework that interpreted the kerygma in the Mediterranean cultures and beyond. The kerygma became embodied in a doctrinal framework that includes apocalyptic, cosmological, ethical, juristic, and even mythical elements. In the course of Christian history, other frameworks have arisen for interpreting the kerygma (salvation through Jesus) in the historical setting. It is important to recognize this constant theological, cultural, and conceptual enfleshment of the kerygma so as not to identify the kerygma itself, the good tidings, with one of these frameworks. Preaching is not bringing to bear the conceptual solutions of Tertullian, Aquinas, or Calvin onto the present so as to open up the future. Preaching will of course always reflect these past attempts to understand and conceptualize the kerygma. But *that which* is preached is not these historical interpretations. Even as we do not preach the Bible, neither do we preach Augustine or Barth. We preach the good tidings.

Do these comments then release those who preach from biblical and theological study and reflection? To be so released implies that the gospel is a rather thin recitation of verbal formulas. We must return to our question. What is gospel? It is of course good tidings. The Christian gospel is good tidings about 'salvation through Jesus'. And to attest to that is always to bring it in relation to the concrete cultural, political, and individual situations in which the preaching takes place. Does 'salvation through Jesus' have any content on its own? We recall the prophetic appeal to the exodus deliverance, the covenant, and the torah. Entangled in these apparently simple terms is a whole cluster of deep symbols concerning justice, community, evil, law, grace, and many other things. 'Salvation through Jesus' retains virtually all of these deep symbols plus others. Minimally, we have as a content of the gospel a radical version of human social, historical, and individual sin and a paradigm of redemption. If this is the case, the gospel is not simply a clear and given content. It is the mystery of God's salvific working. Thus, we never master it, exhaust it, presume we comprehend it. Rather, we continue to struggle to fathom its reality. Gospel is not simply given all at once like a gift-wrapped package. It is something to be proclaimed, but the summons to proclaim it is a summons to struggle with the mystery of God's salvific action and how that transforms the world. To proclaim the gospel then is to enter the world of the gospel, struggling with questions of suffering, evil, idolatry, hope, and freedom.

The world of the gospel does have certain recurring themes. even a certain structure. This structure is partly temporal, a bringing of a past event to bear on the present so as to open the future to redemption. It is centrally about the future, what can be, what historical evils and fates do not have to be. Looked at another way, the gospel is – and this is its prophetic element – a disruption, an exposure of corporate oppression and individual collusion, and, at the same time, an uncovering of redemptive possibilities. To say it is the good news of the kingdom of God is to say both of these things. And those who find themselves proclaiming these good tidings will surely be drawn to understanding the reality and power of the deep symbols in the world of the gospel. This is why preaching the gospel summons the preacher to biblical and theological study and reflection. For we enter the world of the gospel by way of the world of the Bible and the world of the interpretation of the Christian faith. To understand the gospel and the world of the gospel is to struggle critically with the truth and reality of these things. It is in other words a theological task.[11] Even so, that which is preached remains the good tidings, not 'theology' or the Bible.

I have argued that we preach not the Bible but the gospel. And I have argued that to make the *what* of preaching the materials (points, movement, etc.) of a passage is to substitute something else for the gospel. Does this mean that preaching cannot and should not be done in connection with the

Bible? I would hope not. First, it seems evident that to struggle with the world of the gospel in its mystery and reality is to be launched into the world of the Bible. Second, the Bible can surely be used to set forth something in the world of the gospel. But note the order here. The sermon is first of all a preaching of the gospel, not a preaching of a passage. The Bible and its usage is ordered to that. The fourth Gospel's metaphor of life may powerfully help one understand what redemption means in the world of the gospel. The eloquent praise of creation in Isaiah may also figure in the world of the gospel as it counsels against any hopeless rejection of finitude and the world. But it is the gospel not the passage that sets the themes and aim of the sermon. Third, if the gospel replaces passages as the *what* of preaching, then the Bible can be present in preaching not simply in the form of passages or texts but in its many dimensions. The preacher can draw from the world of the Bible stories (Nathan's rebuke of David), symbols (covenant, kingdom, messiah), metaphors (shepherding, light, the law court), social realities (ecclesia), comparisons (faith as it is expressed in Jesus' teaching and in Romans), moral insight (Paul on idolatry), and editorial slants (Luke on the poor). Here the Bible is remembered, interpreted, and used not simply as an aggregate of passages but in its many and rich dimensions. Accordingly, such preaching may be more truly 'biblical' than the preaching that proceeds from an artificial division of the Bible into passages.

Notes

1 Jacob Neusner outlines three different meanings of midrash: midrash as a collection or document, midrash as a process of interpretation or method, and midrash as 'the explanation, by Judaic interpreters, of the meaning of individual verses of Scripture. The result of the interpretation of a verse of Scripture is called midrash exegesis.' *Invitation to Midrash: The Workings of Rabbinic Bible Interpretation,* San Francisco, Harper & Row, 1989, p. 5.

2 Thus, according to Karl Barth, 'The purpose of preaching is to explain the Scriptures', and 'keep to the text and confine his discourse to expounding it', *Preaching the Gospel,* Philadelphia, Westminster Press, 1963, p. 43.

3 'It is this man's duty to proclaim to his fellow men what God himself has to say to them, by explaining to them in his own words a passage from Scripture which concerns them personally'. Barth, 1963, p. 9. In the same vein, 'It might be a lectionary choice or a text with an arresting idea rising with a challenging voice during your morning devotions and saying, "preach on me".' Donald Macleod, *The Problem of Preaching,* Philadelphia, Fortress, 1987, p. 46.

4 The bridge metaphor is sometimes given explicit articulation. According to Reginald Fuller, the preacher should allow the text to establish the pattern and structure of the sermon. Thus, preachers 'are concerned with two poles – the text and the contemporary situation. It is their task to build a bridge between these poles', *The Use of the Bible in Preaching*, Philadelphia, Fortress, 1981, p. 41.

5 The account of the primitive preaching that has obtained almost the status of a classic is C. H. Dodd, *The Apostolic Preaching and its Development,* New York, Harper & Row, 1964.

6 See Clark Williamson and Ronald Allen, *Interpreting Difficult Texts: Anti-Judaism and Christian Preaching,* Philadelphia, Trinity, 1989, for a strong statement on this point. Because of anti-Semitic elements in the New Testament, preaching, they say, can and sometimes should be against the text. They do not, however, draw the conclusion that the presence of anti-Semitic texts shows that texts or passages have no a priori, necessary truth of God and, therefore, breaks the whole paradigm of preaching 'on' passages.

7 For a survey of the major representatives, see Richard L. Eslinger, *A New Hearing: Living Options in Homiletic Method*, Nashville, TN, Abingdon, 1987. A few examples from current homiletic literature indicate that the bridge metaphor is more or less taken for granted. Eugene Lowry works to reconceive the sermon as a plot bringing theme and problem together. Yet his account of the stages of preparing the sermon seems to presuppose that a discrete text is what one is working with. Thus he speaks of problem texts and solution texts, texts that are themselves narratives and those that are not (*The Homiletic Plot:*

The Sermon as Narrative Art Form, Atlanta, John Knox, 1980). In some passages, Robert Jensen seems to be departing from the bridge paradigm. He says that preaching, by definition, is a preaching of Christ, 'the announcement of the marvelously good news (gospel) that God calls outcasts, sinners and aliens to his Kingdom.' Yet on the same page he will also say that preaching is 'the proclamation of specific biblical texts' (*Telling the Story: Variety and Imagination in Preaching,* Minneapolis, Augsburg, 1980, p. 8). For David J. Randolph, 'The structure of the sermon should be faithful to the biblical confession of which it is the execution, following the particular form which best conveys the intention of the text' (*The Renewal of Preaching,* Philadelphia, Fortress, 1969, p. 24). According to Fred Craddock, 'We remind ourselves at this point, then, that the route from text to proclamation is an old and difficult one, but not such as to discourage the preacher but rather should help him to see that interpretation is not an alien and abusive intrusion on Scripture' (*As One Without Authority: Essays in Inductive Preaching,* Enid, OK, Phillips University Press, 1974, p. 120).

8   There are exceptions. One of the most notable is Thor Hall's Sprunt Lectures, *The Future Shape of Preaching,* Philadelphia, Fortress, 1971. In his view, a sermon is not a literary assemblage of materials representing the route from text to sermon. It is a medium of communication that sets forth the preacher's 'depth of concern', and the way the gospel confronts the people in a situation so that the congregation is moved to new images of the situation and themselves. He calls preaching the event of the church's ongoing encounter with the gospel (p. 129). See also David Buttrick's forthcoming *Preaching to Captives: Essays in the Liberation of Preaching,* chapter 12.

9   See Eslinger's chapter on David Buttrick.

10   See Eslinger's chapter on Fred Craddock and on E. L. Lowry.

11   The bridge paradigm connects preaching to some fields of theological study and not others. To prepare a sermon one must exegete the passage, think about the situation of its application, and attend to rhetorical crafting. Three 'disciplines' are pertinent to this process: biblical studies, cultural (sociological, psychological) studies, and rhetorical studies. Hence, the encyclopedia of disciplines for preaching differs from the standard four-fold pattern of studies in theological seminaries, which is Bible, history, theology, and practical theology. The three-fold requirement of the bridge paradigm shows why theology itself, the critical and constructive struggle with truth questions as they pertain to the world of faith, has no place in preaching. We have here the anomaly of Reformed and Lutheran traditions with their emphasis on theology marginalizing theology in their paradigm of preaching. But if it is the gospel and not biblical passages that are preached, surely preaching call for theological work and reflections.

7 Psychological Type and Biblical Hermeneutics: SIFT Method of Preaching

Leslie J. Francis

Introduction

There is now a well established understanding of biblical preaching as hermeneutical dialogue between the text of scripture and the worldviews of both the preacher and the listener (Astley, 2002, 2003). Such an understanding of biblical preaching places weight on critical interrogation both of the text itself and of the worldviews of preacher and listener. The study of these two intellectual activities clearly belong to very different academic domains. Critical interrogation of the text is properly the professional business of biblical studies. Critical interrogation of the worldviews of preacher and listener is properly the professional business of psychology. If biblical preaching is indeed to be understood as hermeneutical dialogue of this nature, then there is a good case for the study of preaching to be equally balanced between the professional expertise of biblical studies and the professional expertise of psychology. The balance between these two disciplines in the current debate appears, however, to be heavily weighted in favour of biblical studies.

The aim of the present essay is to approach the understanding of biblical preaching as hermeneutical dialogue from the perspective of psychology, and to do so by drawing on the broad psychological tradition known as *individual differences* (see, for example, Eysenck and Eysenck, 1985). Within this broad tradition, particular attention will be given to the theory of *psychological types* (see, for example, Jung, 1971). Building on Jung's theory of psychological types Leslie J. Francis and Peter Atkins have developed the SIFT method of preaching, with reference to the four psychological functions of sensing (S), intuition (I), feeling (F), and thinking (T). The SIFT method of preaching has been displayed in three volumes exploring the gospel readings from the Revised Common Lectionary for the years of Matthew (Francis and Atkins, 2001), Mark (Francis and Atkins, 2002), and Luke (Francis and Atkins, 2000).

Individual differences

Preachers are trained to take individual differences seriously. The sermon prepared for the children attending the family service differs both in content and in presentation from the sermon prepared for the adults attending evensong. Individual differences like the age and the sex of the congregation are easy to recognise.

Personality psychology has a long history of charting less obvious individual differences. Personality differences may also have important implications for teachers and for preachers. It has, for example, long been recognised that introverts and extraverts prefer to learn in different ways, and as a consequence of their own learning preferences may prefer to teach others in the way that they themselves would prefer to be taught (see for example, Lawrence, 1993).

Extraverts prefer to learn in groups and are stimulated by group activities and group projects. They need space to *talk* about their ideas. Some schools, especially primary schools, concentrate on a lot of group learning. As a consequence, extraverts pull ahead and do better at their schools.

Introverts prefer to learn by individual study and are stimulated by finding things out for themselves. They need space to *think* about their ideas. Some university courses concentrate on equipping students to learn by themselves. As a consequence, introverts pull ahead and do better at their universities.

The very way in which the activity of preaching is set up may discriminate in favour of a preference for introversion. Introvert preachers prefer to plan what they want to say well in advance of saying it. In public situations introvert preachers prefer to deliver a statement rather than to engage in spontaneous dialogue. Introvert congregations prefer to listen to a point of view and then to go away to think about it. Introvert congregations do not relish the idea of being asked to participate publically in making their responses known.

Psychological type

The distinction between introversion and extraversion concentrates on different preferences for *methods* of learning. Jung's classic analysis of psychological type goes beyond looking at methods of learning to examine preferences for what most powerfully captures the attention in the *content* of learning.

Jung's analysis of individual differences draws attention to two primary psychological processes which he describes as the perceiving functions and as the judging functions. The perceiving functions are concerned with the way in which information is acquired. Jung distinguishes between two very different ways of perceiving which he characterises as sensing and as intuition. Each individual, Jung maintains, will prefer either sensing or intuition and, as a consequence of this preference, will develop that function and neglect the other. Individuals who prefer sensing will approach scripture in a very different way from individuals who prefer intuition.

The judging functions are concerned with the way in which information is evaluated and assessed to make decisions and to inform actions. Jung distinguishes between two very different ways of judging which he characterises as feeling and as thinking. Each individual, Jung maintains, will prefer either feeling or thinking and, as a consequence of this preference, will develop that function and neglect the other. Individuals who prefer feeling will approach scripture in a very different way from individuals who prefer thinking.

According to this account each individual will have a preferred perceiving function (either sensing *or* intuition) and a preferred judging function (either feeling *or* thinking). Jung's analysis of psychological types then proceeds one step further and argues that for each individual one of these two preferred functions (either the preferred perceiving function *or* the preferred judging function) will emerge as the strongest psychological characteristic. Each individual will develop most strongly one of their preferences, for sensing, for intuition, for feeling, or for thinking. This becomes the individual's dominant function.

This understanding of psychological type and dominant preference has key implications both for the preacher and for the listener. If Jung is right and the church congregation contains a mix of sensers, intuitives, thinkers, and feelers, these four groups would be attracted first to different parts of the scriptures they hear read and to different messages focused by the preacher.

If preachers are as alert to individual differences in psychological type as they are to the more obvious individual differences, like age and sex, they stand a better chance of addressing the *whole* congregation.

If preachers remain oblivious to the theory of psychological type they will preach out of their own preferred mode and possibly ignore the needs of three quarters of their congregation. Preachers who are strongly committed to just one perspective may begin to attract people of similar preferences to their church and watch others slip away.

Jung's theory of psychological type has been operationalised through a number of self-assessment psychological inventories, the two best known of which are the Myers-Briggs Type Indicator (MBTI: Myers and McCaulley, 1985)[1] and the Keirsey Temperament Sorter (KTS: Keirsey and Bates, 1978). Jung's theory and the derived instruments have in recent years proved to be useful tools both for a theoretically-based approach to practical theology and for a data-driven approach to empirical theology. Theoretical discussions in practical theology have applied this psychological model to illuminate areas like prayer preferences (Michael and Norrisey, 1984; Keating, 1987; Duncan, 1993), communicating the gospel (Butler, 1999), styles of ministry (Oswald and Kroeger, 1985), and understanding congregations (Baab, 1998). Empirical research projects in practical theology have applied these psychological instruments within two different types of studies: those concerned with establishing the type profile of specific religious groups, and those concerned with modelling the religious correlations or preferences associated with different psychological types.

Within the first category of studies, attention has been given to type patterns among different churches or denominational groups (Ross, 1993, 1995; Calahan, 1996), seminarians and others in training for ministry (Harbaugh, 1984; Holsworth, 1984; Francis, Penson and Jones, 2001), Jewish rabbis and Christian clergy (Greenfield, 1969; Nauss, 1989; Francis, Payne and Jones, 2001), and members of religious orders (Cabral, 1984; Bigelow, Fitzgerald, Busk, Girault and Avis, 1988). For example, Francis, Payne and Jones (2001) found among a sample of 427 male Anglican clergy in Wales clear preferences for introversion over extraversion, for sensing over intuition, for feeling over thinking, and for judging over perceiving. The two predominant types among male Anglican clergy in Wales emerged as ISFJ and ESFJ, which together accounted for 33% of the clergy. What these two types hold in common are preferences for sensing (S), feeling (F), and judging (J).

Within the second category of studies, attention has been given to the relationship between psychological type and such factors as preferences for different forms of prayer (Ware, Knapp and Schwarzin, 1989), biblical interpretation (Bassett, Mathewson and Gailitis, 1993), religious attitudes (Ross, Weiss and Jackson, 1996), styles of spirituality (Francis and Ross, 1997), charismatic experience (Francis and Jones, 1997), patterns of Christian belief (Francis and Jones, 1998), tolerance for religious uncertainty (Francis and Jones, 1999), and mystical orientation (Francis and Louden, 2000; Francis, 2002). For example, Francis and Jones (1997) found among a sample of 368 committed Christian adults that Christians who preferred thinking scored higher on the index of charismatic experience than Christians who preferred feeling.

Sensing types

Individuals who prefer sensing perceive information primarily through their five senses. They attend to practical and factual details, and are in touch with physical realities. They observe the small details of everyday life and attend to actual experience. They prefer to let the eyes tell the mind.

Sensing types often have acute powers of observation, good memory for facts and details, the capacity for realism, and the ability to see the world as it is. They tend to rely on experience rather than theory and prefer to put their trust in what is known and in the conventional.

Sensing types usually reach their conclusion step by step, observing each piece of information carefully. They are not easily inspired to interpret the information in front of them and they may not trust inspiration when it comes. They learn best about new ideas and theories through practical applications.

When sensing types hear a passage of scripture, they want to savour all the detail of the text and may become fascinated by descriptions that appeal to their senses. They tend to start from a fairly literal interest in what is being said.

Sensing types may want to find out all they can about the passage and about the facts that stand behind the passage. They welcome preachers who lead them into the passage by repeating the story and by giving them time to observe and appreciate the details.

Sensing types quickly lose the thread if they are bombarded with too many possibilities too quickly.

Intuitive types

Individuals who prefer intuition perceive information primarily by seeing patterns, meanings, and relationships. They tend to be good at reading between the lines and projecting possibilities for the future. They prefer to focus on the 'big picture'. They prefer to let the mind tell the eyes.

Intuitive types have the ability to see abstract, symbolic, and theoretical relationships, and the capacity to see future possibilities. They tend to put their reliance on inspiration rather than on past experience. They trust their intuitive grasp of meanings and relationships.

Individuals with a preference for intuition are aware of new challenges and possibilities. Their interest is in the new and untried. They are often discontent with the way things are and wish to improve them. They dislike doing the same thing repeatedly.

When intuitive types hear a passage of scripture they want to know how that passage will fire their imagination and stimulate their ideas. They tend to focus not on the literal meaning of what is being said, but on the possibilities and challenges implied.

Intuitive types may want to explore all of the possible directions in which the passage could lead. They welcome preachers who throw out suggestions and brainstorm possibilities, whether or not these are obviously linked to the passage, whether or not these ideas are followed through.

Intuitive types quickly become bored with too much detail, too many facts and too much repetition.

Feeling types

Individuals who prefer feeling make decisions and judgements primarily based on subjective, personal values. They tend to place people, relationships, and interpersonal matters high on their agenda. They develop good skills at applying personal priorities. They are good at weighing human values and motives, both their own and other peoples'. They are characterised by qualities of empathy, sympathy, and trustfulness.

Feeling types like harmony and will work hard to bring harmony about between other people. They dislike telling other people unpleasant things or reprimanding other people. They take into account other people's feelings.

Feeling types are often sympathetic individuals. They take a great interest in the people behind the job and respond to other people's values as much as to their ideas. They enjoy pleasing people.

When feeling types hear a passage of scripture they want to know what the passage has to say about personal values and about human relationships. They empathise deeply with people in the story and with the human drama in the narrative.

Feeling types are keen to get inside the lives of people about whom they hear in scripture. They want to explore what it felt like to be there at the time and how those feelings help to illuminate their Christian journey today. They welcome preachers who take time to develop the human dimension of the passage and who apply the passage to issues of compassion, harmony, and trust.

Feeling types quickly lose interest in theological debates which explore abstract issues without clear application to personal relationships.

Thinking types

Individuals who prefer thinking make decisions and judgements primarily based on objective, impersonal logic. They tend to place truth and reason high on their agenda. They often develop good powers of logical analysis. They tend to use objective and impersonal criteria in reaching decisions and to follow rationally the relationships between cause and effect. They may develop characteristics of being firm-minded and reasonable. They may sometimes appear sceptical.

Individuals with a preference for thinking tend to prize integrity, truthfulness, and fairness. They are usually able to put people in their place when they consider it necessary. They are able to take tough decisions and to reprimand others. They are also able to be firm and tough-minded about themselves.

Thinking types need to be treated fairly and to see that other people are treated fairly as well. They are inclined to respond more to other people's ideas than to other people's feelings. They may inadvertently hurt other people's feelings without recognising that they are doing so.

When thinking types hear a passage of scripture they want to know what the passage has to say about principles of truth and justice. They get caught up with the principles involved in the story and with the various kinds of truth claims being made.

Thinking types are often keen to do theology and to follow through the implications and the logic of the positions they adopt. Some thinkers apply this perspective to a literal interpretation of scripture, while other thinkers are more at home with the liberal interpretation of scripture. They welcome preachers who are fully alert to the logical and to the theological implications of their themes. They value sermons which debate fundamental issues of integrity and righteousness.

Thinking types quickly lose interest in sermons which concentrate on applications to personal relationships, but fail to debate critically issues of theology and morality.

The SIFT method

The SIFT method of preaching addresses to scripture in a systematic way the four sets of questions posed by an understanding of Jung's account of the four primary psychological processes: sensing, intuition, feeling, and thinking. Each preaching event takes all four perspectives and does so in a recognised fixed order of progression.

There are two main, interrelated but distinct theological reasons behind this approach. The first theological reason is grounded in an application of individual differences. It is recognised that different individuals in the congregation will be able to relate more easily to one of these four functions than to the other three. Faith in a God who creates diversity and who rejoices in individual differences demands that each psychological type should be properly included and embraced in the act of preaching.

The second theological reason is grounded in an appreciation of the quest for wholeness and completeness. Although each individual may prefer (and therefore develop) one of the four functions, human development presses towards properly embracing and developing all four. It is precisely in humanity's encounter with the creator God revealed through the text of scripture that the individual is challenged to love God with *all* his or her mind: with sensing, with intuition, with feeling, and with thinking.

The first step in the SIFT method is to address the sensing perspective. It is the sensing perspective which gets to grip with the text itself and which gives proper attention to the insights of biblical scholarship. The first question asks, 'How does this passage speak to the sensing function? What are the facts and details? What is there to see, to hear, to touch, to smell, and to taste?'

The second step in the SIFT method is to address the intuitive perspective. It is the intuitive perspective which relates the biblical text to wider issues and concerns. The second question asks, 'How does this passage speak to the intuitive function? What is there to speak to the imagination, to forge links with current situations, to illuminate issues in our lives?'

The third step in the SIFT method is to address the feeling perspective. It is the feeling perspective which examines the human interest in the biblical text and learns the lesson of God for harmonious and compassionate living. The third question asks, 'How does this passage speak to the feeling function? What is there to speak about fundamental human values, about the relationship between people, and about what it is to be truly human?'

The fourth step in the SIFT method is to address the thinking perspective. It is the thinking perspective which examines the theological interest in the biblical text and reflects rationally and crucially on issues of principle. The fourth question asks, 'How does this passage speak to the thinking function? What is there to speak to the mind, to challenge issues of truth and justice, and to provoke profound theological thinking?'

Conclusion

The SIFT method of preaching has been developed on the basis of three principles. The first principle is that an understanding of biblical preaching as a hermeneutical dialogue between the text of scripture and the worldviews of preacher and listener properly involves the discipline of psychology as a key tool in the analysis and development of the place of preaching in the Christian community. The second principle is that the Jungian notion of psychological type provides an insightful and accessible model of the human psyche which is of practical relevance to the preaching process. The third principle is that there is good theological justification for the preaching event to address all four of the psychological functions identified by Jung in response to the first of the great commandments to love the Lord God with all our heart, with all our soul, and with *all our mind*.

A programme of empirical research is now needed to assess the impact of the SIFT method of preaching on local congregations.

Note

1   The Myers-Briggs Type Indicator and MBTI are registered trademarks of Consulting Psychologists Press, Inc.

References

Astley, J. (2002), *Ordinary Theology: Looking, Listening and Learning Theology*, Aldershot, Ashgate.

Astley, J. (2003), 'Preaching and Listening', *Journal of the College of Preachers*, July, pp. 39–45.

Baab, L. M. (1998), *Personality Type in Congregations: How to Work with Others more Effectively*, Washington, DC, Alban Institute.

Bassett, R. L., Mathewson, K. and Gailitis, A. (1993), 'Recognising the Person in Biblical Interpretation: An Empirical Study', *Journal of Psychology and Christianity*, 12, pp. 38–46.

Bigelow, E. D., Fitzgerald, R., Busk, P., Girault, E. and Avis, J. (1988), 'Psychological Characteristics of Catholic Sisters: Relationships between the MBTI and other Measures', *Journal of Psychological Type*, 14, pp. 32–6.

Butler, A. (1999), *Personality and Communicating the Gospel*, Cambridge, Grove Books.

Cabral, G. (1984), 'Psychological Types in a Catholic Convent: Applications to Community Living and Congregational Data', *Journal of Psychological Type*, 8, pp. 16–22.

Calahan, C. A. (1996), 'Keirsey's Temperament Types and Religious Preference for a Conservative Church Setting', *Perceptual and Motor Skills*, 82, p. 674.

Duncan, B. (1993), *Pray Your Way*, London, Darton, Longman & Todd.

Eysenck, H. J. and Eysenck, M. W. (1985), *Personality and Individual Differences: A Natural Science Approach*, New York, Plenum.

Francis, L. J. (2002), 'Psychological Type and Mystical Orientation: Anticipating Individual Differences within Congregational Life', *Pastoral Sciences*, 21, pp. 77–99.

Francis, L. J. and Atkins, P. (2000), *Exploring Luke's Gospel: A Guide to the Gospel Readings in the Revised Common Lectionary*, London, Mowbray.

Francis, L .J. and Atkins, P. (2001), *Exploring Matthew's Gospel: A Guide to the Gospel Readings in the Revised Common Lectionary*, London, Mowbray.

Francis, L. J. and Atkins, P. (2002), *Exploring Mark's Gospel: An Aid for Readers and Preachers using Year B of the Revised Common Lectionary*, London, Continuum.

Francis, L. J. and Jones, S. H. (1997), 'Personality and Charismatic Experience among Adult Christians', *Pastoral Psychology*, 45, pp. 421–8.

Francis, L .J. and Jones, S. H. (1998), 'Personality and Christian Belief among Adult Churchgoers', *Journal of Psychological Type*, 47, pp. 5–11.

Francis, L. J. and Jones, S. H. (1999), 'Psychological Type and Tolerance for Religious Uncertainty', *Pastoral Psychology*, 47, pp. 253–9.

Francis, L. J. and Louden, S. H. (2000), 'Mystical Orientation and Psychological Type: A Study among Student and Adult Churchgoers', *Transpersonal Psychology Review*, 4, 1, pp. 36–42.

Francis, L. J., Payne, V. J. and Jones, S. H. (2001), 'Psychological Types of Male Anglican Clergy in Wales', *Journal of Psychological Type*, 56, pp. 19–23.

Francis, L. J., Penson, A. W. and Jones, S. H. (2001), 'Psychological Types of Male and Female Bible College Students in England', *Mental Health, Religion and Culture*, 4, pp. 23–32.

Francis, L .J. and Ross, C. F. J. (1997), 'The Perceiving Function and Christian Spirituality: Distinguishing between Sensing and Intuition', *Pastoral Sciences*, 16, pp. 93–103.

Greenfield, M. (1969), 'Typologies of Persisting and Non-Persisting Jewish Clergymen', *Journal of Counselling Psychology*, 16, pp. 368–72.

Harbaugh, G. L. (1984), 'The Person in Ministry: Psychological Type and the Seminary', *Journal of Psychological Type*, 8, pp. 23–32.

Holsworth, T. E. (1984), 'Type Preferences among Roman Catholic Seminarians', *Journal of Psychological Type*, 8, pp. 33–5.

Jung, C. G. (1971), *Psychological Types: The Collected Works*, Volume 6, London, Routledge and Kegan Paul.

Keating, C. J. (1987), *Who We Are is How We Pray: Matching Personality and Spirituality*, Mystic, CT, Twenty-Third Publications.

Keirsey, D. and Bates, M. (1978), *Please Understand Me*, Del Mar, CA, Prometheus Nemesis.

Lawrence, G. (1993), *People Types and Tiger Stripes*, Gainesville, FL, Center for Applications of Psychological Type.

Michael, C. P. and Norrisey, M. C. (1984), *Prayer and Temperament: Different Prayer Forms for Different Personality Types*, Charlottesville, VA, The Open Door.

Myers, I. B. and McCaulley, M. H. (1985), *Manual: A Guide to the Development and Use of the Myers-Briggs Type Indicator*, Palo Alto, CA, Consulting Psychologists Press.

Nauss, A. H. (1989), 'Leadership Styles of Effective Ministry', *Journal of Psychology and Theology*, 17, pp. 59–67.

Oswald, R. M. and Kroeger, O. (1988), *Personality Type and Religious Leadership*, Washington, DC, Alban Institute.

Ross, C. F. J. (1993), 'Type Patterns among Active Members of the Anglican Church: Comparisons with Catholics, Evangelicals and Clergy', *Journal of Psychological Type*, 26, pp. 28–35.

Ross, C. F. J. (1995), 'Type Patterns among Catholics: Four Anglophone Congregations compared with Protestants, Francophone Catholics and Priests', *Journal of Psychological Type*, 33, pp. 33–41.

Ross, C. F. J., Weiss, D. and Jackson, L. M. (1996), 'The Relation of Jungian Psychological Type to Religious Attitudes and Practices', *International Journal for the Psychology of Religion*, 6, pp. 263–79.

Ware, R., Knapp, C. R. and Schwarzin, H. (1989), 'Prayer Form Preferences of Keirsey Temperaments and Psychological Types', *Journal of Psychological Type*, 17, pp. 39–42.

Part 3

STRUCTURE AND COMMUNICATION

Introduction to Part 3

The preceding part has explored some of the issues which arise over the connection between Bible and sermon. In the first article in Part 3, Fred Craddock, one of the most influential preachers and homileticians of the last 25 years, provides a worked example. How precisely is the passage from text to sermon to be negotiated? What is the role of the commentary? Craddock takes the reader through the process of preparing a sermon, from first invitation to finished version. In so doing he illustrates many of the theoretical principles later to be found in his book, *Preaching* (Nashville, TN, Abingdon, 1985).

Fred B. Craddock, 'From Exegesis to Sermon: 1 Corinthians 12:4–6' is reprinted from the *Review and Expositor*, 80, 1983, pp. 417–25.

In the next article, Thomas Long argues that recent advances in homiletics have led us to see a sermon 'as a dynamic organism in which each part affects – and is affected by – all the others'. Nowhere is this clearer than in its introduction. Following J. Randall Nichols, Long suggests that the introduction serves as the basis of an agreement between preacher and congregation about how the message is to be handled. The important question to ask, therefore, is not if the introduction is brief, interesting or raises the issue, but 'When has the contract been set?' In six observations Long sketches out the beginnings of a theory of introductions.

Thomas G. Long, 'Pawn to King Four: Sermon Introductions and Communicational Design' comes from *Reformed Review*, 40, 1, 1986, pp. 27–35.

Peter Stevenson's article surveys some of the issues which arise when considering the current interest in narrative preaching. Narrative preaching is a proper response to the prominence of narrative in the Bible, which with many texts will ensure that there is an appropriate connection between sermon form and biblical genre. Lowry's work on narrative preaching has highlighted the importance of plot, and sermons which move the hearers from conflict through complication and sudden shift to unfolding. Such plotting seeks to engage the imagination as well as the intellect. Drawing on the insights of narrative theology, Stevenson suggests that preaching should aim to make plain the God who is an agent in the biblical narratives. Such narratives are theocentric and should not be allowed to collapse into sermons which merely lay out 'good examples for believers to follow'. In the final sections Stevenson commends preaching which works with liturgy as the re-enactment of the grand story and, citing Schlafer, suggests that preachers identify their preferred preaching voice, while being prepared to broaden their repertoire.

For the writers who form the basis of this survey article, see Sidney Greidanus, *The Modern Preacher and the Ancient Text* (Leicester, IVP, 1988); Eugene L. Lowry, *The Homiletical Plot* (Atlanta, GA, John Knox, 1980) and *The Sermon: Dancing the Edge of Mystery* (Nashville, TN, Abingdon, 1997); David J. Schlafer, *Your Way with God's Word: Discovering your Distinctive Preaching Voice* (Boston, Cowley, 1995).

Peter K. Stevenson, 'Preaching and Narrative' is from *Evangel*, 17, 2, 1999, pp. 43–8.

Dwight Stevenson's article offers an amusing but telling examination of 11 sermon surrogates, ranging from moralistic harangue and aesthetic artefact to ecclesiastical commercial and monologue and soliloquy. The author argues that clearing these substitutes for genuine preaching out of the way may be the first step to preaching not just in word but in power.

Dwight E. Stevenson, 'Eleven ways of Preaching a Non-Sermon' was first published in the *Lexington Theological Quarterly*, 10, 1975, pp. 19–28.

8　From Exegesis to Sermon: 1 Corinthians 12:4–6

Fred B. Craddock

The editor [of *Review and Expositor*, the original journal] graciously invited me to contribute to [the] issue devoted to 1 Corinthians by selecting a passage from the epistle, providing a brief exegetical analysis, and offering in full a sermon growing out of that exegesis. For this exercise to be most helpful, it seemed to me that it should correspond as nearly as possible to an occasion of preparation and preaching in the work of the local minister. In other words, to provide an exegesis and sermon for an editor or even for unknown readers of [a] journal would be an exercise lacking in concrete context and reason. Sermons are not delivered into the air but to particular persons for particular purposes. What follows, then, is a brief description of a time and place and gathering to which I was invited to preach, an account of the exegetical work involved in preparation, and the sermon itself.

It is my hope that this procedure, which addresses the readers indirectly rather than directly, will be more, not less, meaningful. After all, is this not the nature of the impact upon us of the New Testament itself? Paul wrote to the Corinthians, not to us, but those who listen carefully to what he said to the Corinthians find themselves addressed by his words.

The listeners

The invitation to preach came by both phone call and letter from the pastor of a suburban church. I had never been to that church, and I knew the pastor only slightly. He enjoyed the reputation of being a very nourishing pastor, having both the discipline of continuing study and the skills for communicating. His request was that I preach for his congregation on a Wednesday evening. The sermon would mark the end of an eight-week series of Wednesday evenings devoted to a study of 1 Corinthians. The pastor himself had led the series, focusing on major issues in the epistle, with each session consisting of a lecture followed by discussion. Attendance, he said, had been about 150 consistently, and I could expect the same. The sermon would be preceded by a fellowship dinner. Emphasis at the dinners is upon family participation, but children and youth go to their own programs following the meal. The adults remain in fellowship hall for the message, which is set between a hymn and a prayer. The pastor said they tried to honor the fact that it was a school night and conclude by 8:15. This would give me approximately twenty-five minutes. In response to my questions, he provided other details: dishes would be cleared; acoustics were not good, but there was a good public address system; a lectern would be set on the head table; most of the people brought Bibles and were engaged in reading and listening; the people enjoyed each other on these Wednesday evenings together. He told me I was correct in assuming they wanted me to preach from 1 Corinthians, in fact, from 1 Corinthians 12. Why that chapter? Was there a charismatic group in the church, or a problem with speaking in tongues? No, that was not an issue, but chapter 12 elicited most interest and most questions. Was I expected to deal with the whole chapter in twenty-five minutes? Certainly not, I was to choose from it a portion or a theme and develop.that. 'Use your own judgment; we have spent one evening on the chapter', he said. 'You can assume some familiarity and much interest.' Jokingly I commented on his confidence in allowing

a visitor to speak on a text and a subject which many found problematic and eve:
laughed, said he was not worried, and we concluded the conversation.

I felt comfortably clear about the listeners and the context. Those of us who are not ;
therefore, always guest preachers always need this and any other information that wil
appropriate. Let me pause, however, to say that pastors also should think through these same questions
as a regular procedure of preparation. Familiarity can blind a pastor and create as much distance from
the listeners as exists between a visiting speaker and the congregation. No minister remains in a
church long enough to outgrow the need to do an exegesis of the listeners in preparation for preaching.

It was important to me to ponder the fact that I would be preaching on a text and in a subject area
to which the hearers had been recently and thoughtfully exposed and with which they were generally familiar. To be honest, earlier in my ministry I would have regarded their familiarity as an
obstacle to my preaching. Regardless of how much I and others encouraged and exhorted the church
to study the Scriptures, the plain fact is that much time in sermon preparation was in pursuit of what
might be new and unfamiliar, some text or subject or approach that would 'get them' because none
of my predecessors had ever dealt with it, at least not in that way. In other words, the assumption
was that the power of preaching lay in its novelty, in leaping off the pinnacle of the temple each
Sunday. That assumption is false, nourished by the ego of the preacher who competes with rather
than building upon what previous ministers have done. The message is the church's message;
blessed is the church familiar with the message, and blessed is the preacher who accepts that familiarity as a boon to the pulpit. The most positive responses come often from those who know something about the subject. We go hear lecturers whose books we have read; we attend concerts hoping
to hear the songs we have heard; we offer supportive 'Amens' only to those whose messages we
recognize as our own.

With these matters in mind, I moved to 1 Corinthians 12.

Exegesis

The first task of exegesis is selection of the text. Although good preaching that can qualify as biblical preaching may back off from the text and develop major themes running through a body of
scripture, it is generally.the best procedure to have the sermon grow out of what is said in a particular text. In this way the preacher is giving the Bible to the people in a concrete way so that they can
own both sermon and text. Such preaching also models for the listeners how they can honestly and
fruitfully for themselves interpret scripture. And, of course, preaching of this type has its authorization in the text and not in the person of the speaker. Having said that, it remains the case that
sermons which seemingly linger near the text can be offering another agenda entirely, one only
apparently with the blessing of the text itself.

The choice of text in this case seems to be made relatively easy by the request that I preach from
1 Corinthians 12. In part this is true, but no preacher should week by week be foraging around in the
sixty-six books looking for Sunday's text. A planned program of preaching is essential if the people
and the program are to be adequately nourished with a balanced diet.

Given the limits of one chapter, decision still must be made as to what unit within that chapter
will be the point of attention. In order to qualify, the unit should be of manageable size, should
contain subject matter central and not marginal to the overall discussion of the passage, and should
have its own integrity. By having its own integrity I simply mean that the text for the sermon should
have a clear beginning and ending, expressing its own message. Otherwise, vague limits tend to lack
the discipline to control the range of the sermon and increase the possibilities of that kind of
preaching familiar to us all which wanders far afield from the intent or content of the text.

.he chapter before us provides several units: verses 1–3, verses 4–6, verses 7–11, verses 12–13, .erses 14–26, and verses 27–31. I rejected 27–31 because this unit really has its completion in chapter 13. I decided against 7–11 and 14–26 because these discuss the particular gifts being exercised in a congregation. The value of that presentation would depend very much on the transfer of the discussion from Corinth to the congregation to which I am to speak. As a stranger I do not know about this transference; I trust the pastor has handled it. It is now clear to me that Paul offers in this chapter two kinds of assessment and control in the church's exercise of spiritual gifts: practical and theological. The theological could be discussed by a visitor more fruitfully than the practical. The three remaining units are theological 1–3, 4–6, 12–13. It is my judgment that verses 4–6 are not only a clear and distinct unit but that they state what is more central to the whole discussion than either verses 1–3 or 12–13. In fact, a treatment of 12:4–6 could well embrace the contents of the other two units, while neither of the other two have the breadth of thought to include verses 4–6 implicitly or explicitly. It is settled: the sermon text is 1 Corinthians 12:4–6.

Having checked the Greek text to see if there are any significant variants in the passage that require attention (footnotes in good English translations are helpful in this regard), I proceed to a careful, open-minded, inquisitive, somewhat naive reading of the text. No commentaries or lexicons yet. Let all one's faculties of mind and heart be exposed to the text, while jotting down impressions, questions, and issues triggered by the text. The commentaries and other aids come later, after the preacher is knowledgeable enough about the text to regard scholars as colleagues, not masters, and after the text has raised its own questions to be taken to those who write on this passage.

Verses 4–6 are carefully structured in triads: varieties of gifts, varieties of service, varieties of working (RSV), as well as the same Spirit, the same Lord, the same God. The trinity is present but not in the traditional form (God, Son, Spirit). The reverse order indicates an approach more functional than formal, one beginning with the immediate experience of the Corinthians. Variety in the church's experience of the Spirit is not a fact to be tolerated; it is a given in the very nature of God's equipping the church. That variety, however, is not 'anything goes' but is governed by the same Spirit, the same Lord, the same God. Why are Jesus and God brought into the discussion when the topic is gifts of the Spirit? Is Paul here quoting a trinitarian formula or creed that actually arose in another context? Are gifts, services, and workings synonymous here, or are the meanings quite different? What does it mean that God inspires (works in) them all in everyone? This expression is not used of the Spirit or of the Lord (Jesus). It is interesting that the Corinthians asked Paul about 'spiritual things' (or spiritual persons, the noun ending here being the same for neuter, masculine, and feminine) in verse 1 and that Paul answers in verse 4 by first changing the word to *gifts* (*charismata*). *Gifts* relates one's activity to a source, a given, while *spiritual* is a general and often unclear description of a kind of person or activity.

It was apparently important for Paul that the Corinthians see their activity in relation to the source of their life and work and not simply as a quality (spiritual) they possessed. Nowhere in the text is Paul inclined to deny the reality or the source of the various ministries being performed in the church. He seems primarily concerned that the gifts be set in proper theological and practical contexts. The first theological guideline is the confession 'Jesus is Lord' (v. 3). No gift is of the Holy Spirit which denies that. Another theological guideline is the understanding that, regardless of background, we are all members of the one body of Christ (vv. 12–13). No gift is of the Holy Spirit which violates that. In verses 4–6, however, somehow the whole experience of charismatic gifts in the church is set within the trinitarian formula: Spirit, Christ, God. What really does this mean? Were the Corinthians so caught up in the Holy Spirit that Jesus and God were neglected or treated as peripheral to their immediate experience? If so, exactly what correction is being made, what reminder is being given, by Paul's tying the Spirit to Christ and to God?

It is clear by now that the last question is the one to govern the sermon. Verses 4–6 do not alter in any way the preceding or succeeding discussions of the nature and function of gifts of the Spirit. This unit simply affirms the variety of such ministries while repeatedly insisting on one single source. This unit calls these ministries gifts, services, and workings (energizings), all of which are terms of function, not titles or offices or positions. And clearly in all this the unit is controlled by the triadic formula: same Spirit, same Lord, same God. Apparently it is very important that the expression close with reference to God as energizer (inspirer) 'all in all'. That last phrase seems to set gifts, Christians, ministries, church, everything in the ultimate and final context. One suspects that charismatic ministries in Corinth had gotten 'out of hand' because they were being performed 'out of context'.

At this point I go to the commentaries. I usually begin with that of Hans Conzelmann because of its great detail and its references to other helpful sources. From there I turn to the works of C. K. Barrett, F. F. Bruce, Carl Holladay, and Walter Schmithals. These studies help with the overall argument of 1 Corinthians and provide a clear structure within which chapter 12 is set. This chapter is a part of the larger unit in which Paul answers questions about which the Corinthians had written (7:1). The opening phrase of 12:1, 'Now concerning spiritual gifts', is the literary clue that Paul is still responding to their list of questions. Since the religions of their pagan background involved 'spiritual gifts' and ecstatic experiences, including tongues, it is no wonder that the activities in their new religion were confusing many. How is all this different from our old religion? Chapter 12 is a part of a smaller unit (chapters 10–14) dealing with the confused and distressing state of worship and the assembled life of the church. The discussions center primarily on the Lord's Supper, the role of women in the assembly, and the exercise of gifts, most especially glossolalia. So problematic and significant is this last subject that Paul devotes to it chapters 12–14.

Although there is [a] difference in scholarly opinion about whether much is to be made of differences between gifts, services, and workings, most commentators remark upon the fact that the *charismata* in relation to the Spirit are called *gifts*, in relation to Jesus Christ are called services or ministries, and in relation to God are called workings. And although there is disagreement as to whether Paul is here quoting a trinitarian formula or creating the expression for the situation, there is general consensus that Paul is concerned that Holy Spirit talk and activity not be isolated from faith and obedience to Jesus Christ and from the foundational conviction that all life and all activity is energized by God, who is source and sustainer of everything. The expression 'all in all' or 'all in everyone' (RSV) is found rather often in Paul (1 Cor. 8:6; 15:28; Rom. 11:36; Col. 1:15–20) and was in his day a technical term for the totality, all that is, visible and invisible, in heaven and on earth. In other words, Paul begins his discussion of charismatic gifts with a crisp, clear statement of the frame of reference. We are, he says, talking about a variety of gifts from the one Holy Spirit, a variety of services and ministries in obedience to Jesus Christ, and a variety of workings or activities nourished by the one God whose creating and sustaining energy operates not only in the Corinthian church but in all the universe, in all creation.

For a congregation which has already studied 1 Corinthians 12 I am now ready to prepare a sermon developing the theme of verses 4–6: one function of the doctrine of the Trinity is to inform and to provide norms for the life and activity of the church.

The sermon

Long before 1 Corinthians was a book in our New Testament it was a letter from a missionary to a congregation on the frontier, far from the church's hearth and home. The church was born in Judaism, nurtured on tradition, scripture, and common faith in God, scaffolded by temple and synagogue until the foundation and walls were well fixed. But out on distant frontiers the background was pagan, and there were no mothers and fathers in the faith to give clarity and stability. There were preachers passing through, to be sure, but that's just it; they were passing through. The church had experiences for which they had no texts and problems for which they had no precedents. Some concerned members wrote to the missionary who started the church, and their questions were many, touching on marriage, divorce, litigation, support of local shrines, proper foods, leadership of women, order of worship, and the nature of a resurrected body. What a list! And among the questions was this one: What are activities of the Spirit?

Unlike some of us, Paul was not intimidated or thrown on the defensive by the question. He welcomed it as deserving a careful answer. After all, Paul spoke often of the Holy Spirit and regarded the Spirit as the prompter of the confession of faith, the source of Christian character, and the enabler of Christian ministry. Certainly he did not wish to shut down their enthusiasm. Himself a man of abundant energy, he would have considered lifelessness a complete contradiction of Christian faith. Paul, however, knew the difference between enthusiasm and indulgence. Just as there is indulgence of the flesh there is indulgence of the spirit, and to bless that wallowing in one's feelings with claims about the Holy Spirit could be dangerous for both the believer and the church. Everything truly genuine has its counterfeits and everything truly Christian has its pornographers.

In answering the letter from Corinth, Paul is not at all interested in dealing with events in the church services there as a question of whether these Spirit activities really happened. Whether an unusual, an extraordinary, or even a miraculous event really happened is a question we would ask, not they. We operate as though believing something really happened is faith and believing it did not happen is doubt. More to the point in the early church, however, was the question, did God do it? Did the Holy Spirit do it? In other words, they assumed extraordinary events occurred; the issue was whether they were acts of God. Jesus spoke of those who prophesied, cast out demons, and worked wonders who were not of God. In Samaria, one Simon the sorcerer wowed the people, but he did not have the Holy Spirit. And, of course, we recall from the Old Testament how the magicians in Egypt matched Moses frog for frog, louse for louse.

Before he can answer the question as to whether certain activities and behavior patterns are of the Holy Spirit, Paul feels the need to change the word used in the letter to him. They inquired about 'spiritual things'; Paul wants to talk about 'gifts'. Some years ago someone broke into the church, pried open the door to the room where the vocabulary is kept, and stole one of the richest words the Christian community possessed. The word was *charisma*. It was peddled on the street and soon came to be used by everybody for everything: an exciting personality, a particular hairstyle, photogenic face, stimulating speech, provocative style of leadership. The word is a form of *charis*, grace, from which we get eucharist, and is the background word for charity. Charisma is gift, and it is Paul's insistence that when we talk of these matters, we call them what they are – gifts of God. Apart from that association with God and grace, we might as well be discussing magic and horoscopes.

And the word for Paul is plural, *charismata*; there are varieties of gifts. By its repetition it can be assumed that diversity of gifts is Paul's insistence. Perhaps the divided and confused state of the congregation was prompting some of them to wish to quiet dissenting voices, to bring order and unity to the church by demanding that all have the same gift, the same grasp of the Holy Spirit. And surely that thought comes to sincere minds: whatever it takes to still the storm, whatever it takes to clear up the chaos, let's do it. Politicians call it granting emergency powers to the leader; it means a benevolent dictatorship, temporarily! Let us not deny it; that it is a swifter, cleaner, easier path to unity makes this a tempting solution. But Paul says no. Even a quarreling church must not relinquish its diversity, opting for unity on the grounds of one common experience. And the reason? Because diversity is not a condition we tolerate, up to a point; diversity, is a given in the very plenitude of God, whose grace is boundless.

But what if things are out of hand? The answer, says Paul, does not lie in tighter control but in setting the experience of the church back into proper context. That context – are you ready for this? – is the Trinity. 'Now there are varieties of gifts, but the same Spirit; and there are varieties of service, but the same Lord; and there are varieties of working, but it is the same God who inspires them all in everyone' (vv. 4–6).

My first response is: How clever of Paul! Why can't I be that quick witted? When called upon to deal with an incendiary issue, surrounded by persons with high emotional investment who have already decided the conclusion of the discussion, introduce the Trinity. One can escape before the fog lifts!

We expect more from Paul, however, and we get it. Nothing could be more appropriate to the understanding and enriching of one's experience of the Spirit than the clear association of that experience with Jesus Christ and with God. Look closely at the text for a moment. Notice the order is not Father, Son, and Holy Spirit. That would be proper for a class lecture perhaps, but Paul begins with his listeners and with their experience of the Spirit. Here we have doctrine with a reason. Notice also that the accent is not upon the nature of the Trinity but upon function: *gifts* of the Spirit, *service* of Jesus Christ, and *energizing* of God. Here we have doctrine with a will to do. But still the question remains: What has the Trinity to do with charismatic activity?

First, let us remind ourselves that it is Paul more than any other New Testament writer who personalizes and internalizes the experience of the Holy Spirit in the church. But Paul is aware of the dangers here. A subjective experience without an outside point of reference can easily become a trap, a tender trap to be sure, but a trap of feeling, mood, intuition, sensation. Certainly no one wants to go on record as opposing heartfelt religion, but what happens to the gospel's engagement with law, science, business, politics, and all human affairs if the game is moved to a new park where only feeling can play – the heart? Who will keep the store open and try to transact a little business for the Kingdom? Some may sincerely think the heart became the stronghold of the faith, but in reality it became a hiding place.

Paul provides a guard against such a reduction of our faith by adding to the first article of his affirmation, 'There are varieties of gifts but the same Spirit', a second: 'There are varieties of service but the same Lord'. He has already said that the Holy Spirit inspires the confession, 'Jesus is Lord' (v. 3), but here it must be repeated: all experiences of the Holy Spirit must come under the guidance and instruction of the incarnation, God's act in history, in Jesus, for human beings, for the salvation of the world. This is to say that the life of the Spirit which I now experience is a continuation of that life which was in the world, sharing, giving, serving, suffering, dying. Spirituality that stands under the cross does not waste its enthusiasm into the air but harnesses it in service for the common good. From time to time in the history of the church Christian spirituality has tried to hide from the historical Jesus by evaporating Jesus through mystical interpretations of the gospel records. Jesus is born in our hearts; the Sermon on the Mount is observed in our hearts; Jesus enters triumphantly into our hearts; the temples of our hearts are cleansed; Jesus is crucified in our hearts; and if you ask me how I know he lives, he lives within my heart. What hearts! But in the meantime, back in the world. . . .

And finally, Paul provides an even larger context, encompassing both Spirit and Jesus: 'And there are varieties of working [empowering, enabling], but it is the same God who inspires [works in] them all in everyone.' The phrase 'all in everyone' is really not large enough to convey what Paul says. The phrase means the complete totality, all that there is. Earlier Paul has used the expression to speak of God as the One from whom are 'all things' (8:6); and later he will say that after death is defeated, Christ will turn the Kingdom over to God and God will be 'the Totality' (15:28).

Now Paul is making us think big thoughts here. He is asking us to be aware that all worship and activity of the Christian community is responsible finally to God. No claims, real or imagined, about the influence of the Holy Spirit can justify behavior or preaching or teaching that is not appropriate to the one God, Creator, Redeemer, and Sustainer of all life. He is asking us to grasp the dimensions of the realm of the Spirit's work. If God is energizing the totality, then the arena of the Spirit's activity is too narrowly defined if it excludes any of God's creation. Those members of the Corinthian church, or any church, who removed from the list of 'spiritual' concerns all issues domestic, sexual, legal, or social were, and are, in error. If the Holy Spirit means anything, it means something where people live. Paul is also allowing us to catch the hope of the final vision. That final vision was of a God who had reclaimed all things, of a time when the realm of creation and the realm of redemption would be coextensive. This is no faint wish; even now God is at work enabling the totality. The church which catches that vision is inspired by the Spirit to sing with Paul: 'From God and through God and to God are all things. To God be glory forever'.

Before saying amen, however, let us warn ourselves one last time. I spoke earlier of persons hiding from the world by centering upon experiences of the Spirit within the heart. Let's be fair. There is no less a danger of hiding in the totality, the world in general, life in general. Many Christian programs have been discouraged and finally aborted by those who immobilized the church with broad descriptions of how great the need, how deplorable the conditions, how urgent the pleas from all over the universe. Overwhelmed by the totality, the church can easily disregard as puny and ineffective the cup of water, the loaf of bread, the small chapel, the family altar, the covey of children listening to a Bible story on Sunday evening. Hear a parable:

It came to pass that there was a certain minister who preached to his little flock of 'the world today', 'the twentieth century', and 'the human race'. A layman complained of not being addressed by the sermons, but his complaints were turned aside with admonitions against small-mindedness and provincialism. In the course of time, the minister and the layman attended together a church conference in a distant city. When the minister expressed anxiety about losing their way in the large and busy metropolis, the layman assured him there was no reason to fear. With that word, he produced from the rear seat of the car a globe of the world.

Of course, God is at work in all things. Of course, the whole of creation is the object of God's love. Of course, Christ was lifted up on the cross to draw all people to himself. But I thought I heard him say, as he was hanging there, 'Take my mother home'.

9   Pawn To King Four: Sermon Introductions and Communicational Design

Thomas G. Long

One of the many recent advances in contemporary homiletical theory has involved the acknowledgement of the inter-relatedness of the various aspects of sermon development. It is no longer thought sufficient to divide the process of sermon construction into separate 'stages', such as 'exegesis', 'theological analysis', 'outlining', 'illustrating the sermon', 'delivery', and so on. We discuss these aspects, of course, but only in the full awareness that, when all is said and done, they are not, in fact, discrete, but rather interpenetrating, realities and that each has much to do with all of the others.

How the preacher encounters and understands the biblical text, at one end of the process, for example, already bears (or should bear) upon delivery, at the other end. For instance, a biblical text which achieves its impact through irony or poetic imagery calls for something more than a flat-footed, schoolmaster's delivery. A text which embraces a confident and ringing affirmation of the gospel calls the preacher, not to deliver a 'book report' on the text, but rather to an embodiment of the text's assurance (or at least an involved response to the text's boldness). In one sense there is nothing new about all of this. Good preachers have known for a long time that tugging at any single thread in the sermonic fabric causes the whole cloth to gather. What is new is that the concept of the inter-relatedness of the sermon development process has moved from intuitive practice to the level of theory. The fact that biblical scholars themselves are now doing such things as looking for 'literary patterns' and 'rhetorical cues' in texts only brings confirmation, theoretical precision, and methodological refinement to what preachers have long been doing by the seat of their pants and the hems of their skirts.

Sermon unity: a new perspective

This grasp of the inter-relatedness of the various portions of the sermon development process has also transferred to the sermon itself. Sermons are now viewed as dynamic organisms, in which each part affects – and is affected by – all the others. This makes it inadequate to think, for example, of 'finding an illustration to plug into a sermon', as if sermons were like chandeliers into which pieces, like bulbs, could be inserted and replaced at will, as if a change in one part of a sermon did not affect the whole.

This view of sermonic unity is not really new, either. Sermons have never really been seen, except in some exceedingly scholastic homiletics texts, as consisting of a set of ideas or units strung together, sharing a common theme, but otherwise disconnected. There has always been at least some awareness that the various facets of the sermon work together in some common act of communication. There is fairly good evidence that even the synogogue sermons of the first century, which almost surely were the models for early Christian preaching, were constructed according to a

93

rather sophisticated theme which involved the interlacing of the Torah and Prophetic readings toward the goal of demonstrating what the one had to say about the other. This afforded no little opportunity for the best of the rabbinical orators to show off, flaunting their creative skills and dazzling the hearers with the many layers at which the law and the prophets could be seen to speak to each other.

What is new in recent homiletics is the degree of theoretical precision which is beginning to be brought to bear upon the task of understanding how one portion of the sermon serves, and is served by, the others. Sermons are now seen to be 'systems of communication', a ghastly phrase to be sure, but a helpful analytical abstraction nonetheless. Nowadays, when a teacher of preaching tells a student that a certain kind of 'illustration' is needed at such and such a point in the sermon, this advice does not have to be made on the basis of some mechanical pattern of sermon design (e.g., 'each "point" should have an illustration') or on some pseudo-psychological understanding of communication (e.g., 'the congregation needs a "break" between points'). It can be made out of a larger vision of the communicational work of the whole sermon and how it is that each aspect of the sermon picks up a piece of that total task.

Introductions: a test case

One place we can see the impact of this revisioning of the sermon is in the way contemporary homileticians discuss the traditional topic of sermon structure, or 'outlines'. Some of them find the word 'outline' to be hopelessly mired in pedantic and deductive conceptions and refuse to use it at all, preferring a more fluid notion, like 'plot' or 'shape'. Even when the term 'outline' is retained, though, it is clear that the focus of the discussion has changed. The older preaching texts tended to discuss outlining as the way in which the *content* of the sermon was arranged. The newer texts make the shift from content to *communication*. A sermon outline, plot, shape, or whatever term is used, is not merely a description of the way in which the sermon's content is arrayed. It is a description of the process of communication between preacher and hearers. Sermons are designed in specific patterns not merely because the content assumes a certain form (e.g., 'There are four claims this text makes about faith . . . '), but because of the ways in which people listen. The main question is not, 'How can this material be divided?', but rather, 'How can people best hear this material?'

An examination of the role of sermon beginnings, or 'introductions', can serve as a revealing test case of this newer integrative approach to preaching theory. An 'introduction' is not simply the way the content of the sermon begins. It is also the way in which a certain phase of the communication between preacher and hearer begins. We need, then, to ask about the role beginnings play in the whole process of sermon communication.

Sermon introductions in recent homiletics

When George Buttrick said that preachers should prepare a sermon introduction which is 'brief, interesting, and raises the issue',[1] he said everything – and nothing. Properly exegeted, Buttrick's rule perhaps says all that can or should be said on the subject. The problem, however, is that considerable exegesis is needed to appreciate the value of the rule, and Buttrick's dictum has often been employed in a clumsy manner. If Buttrick is merely giving a three-fold check list, then the first item ('brevity') is mis-identified, the second ('interesting') is obvious, and the third ('raises the issue') is biased toward an overly cognitive approach to preaching. Good sermon introductions usually *are* brief, but this is not because brevity is a self-contained virtue. Introductions are *doing* something in and for the whole sermon which can, in most cases, be done best when they are brief, but it is this communicational action which must be named, not the by-product of brevity. If being 'uninteresting' is the alternative, then introductions surely ought to be 'interesting', but so should 'middles' and 'conclusions'. What needs to be specified is the particular kind of interest which introductions have as their task to arouse. To say that introductions should 'raise the issue' of the sermon comes closer to the kind of specificity needed, as long as 'the issue' is not misconstrued to read 'state the thesis' or some similar language of ideational abstraction.

In his recent book *Fundamentals of Preaching*, John Killinger borrows Buttrick's formula (translated as 'brief, arresting, and conductive') and adds a virtue to the list: memorable.[2] This is an interesting addition, mainly because Killinger may be on to more than he is aware. What Killinger really wants to say, I think, is not that sermon *introductions* ought to be memorable, but that *sermons* themselves ought to be memorable and that introductions can contribute to that characteristic. In other words, introductions are evaluated on the basis of their contributions to the sermon as a whole, rather than in isolation from the other aspects of the sermon.

Grady Davis, whose *Design for Preaching* served as a standard homiletics textbook for many years, also followed Buttrick in regard to introductions, but advanced the discussion by doing so in a far more sophisticated and complex manner than most. Davis conceived of a sermon on the model of a sentence. Each sermon consists of a subject (what the sermon is about) and a predicate (the one main thing which the sermon says about the subject). The predicate is further divided into a series of assertions, two to six claims which develop the subject and which form the logical flow, or continuity, of the sermon. Davis elaborates this basic 'design' in four ways. First, he identifies three possible functions, or purposes, of a sermon: proclamation, teaching, and therapy. Second, he names five different organic forms, or organizing principles, for sermons: a subject discussed, a thesis supported, a message illumined, a question propounded, and a story told. Third, he specifies four types of sermon continuity, or flow: deductive, inductive, logical, and chronological. Finally, he suggests three tenses, or modes, of preaching: imperative, conditional, and indicative.

Taken seriously, of course, Davis' scheme is an immensely complex model of preaching, and the usefulness of some of his categories justly deserves challenge. It would take more space than we have here to elaborate upon and criticize Davis' schema, and that is not our main concern. The crucial point we wish to make is that Davis was among the first to discern the organic communicational unity of sermons and to attempt to mold homiletical practice around that theoretical vision. When he gets around to introductions, he remains faithful to his theory, maintaining that 'the introduction should be thought of as the first two minutes of a twenty- to twenty-five minute experience by the people of the sermon's thought.'[3] In other words, the introduction is the first in a series of communicational moves, each linked to the others, one phase in a comprehensive experience of listening. Davis knows that the introduction is a piece of the sermon fabric not to be considered apart from the whole garment. It sets the stage for the complete sermon and, as such, establishes limits on the style, tone, form, and purpose of the rest of the sermonic communication.[4]

The next real advance in understanding the role and communicative value of sermon introductions comes from human communication science, as brokered into the homiletical field by J. Randall Nichols in his *Building the Word*. Nichols maintains that the purpose of an introduction is . . .

> . . . to establish between preacher and hearers a 'contract for communication', a shared agreement that in the message to follow we will be talking about certain things in certain ways, trying to get certain points of understanding or action, and each contributing this or that to the unfolding process.[5]

Now, at first glance, this appears to be a nice restatement of Davis. In the introduction we talk about certain things (the subject) in certain ways (the organic form), to get certain points of under-standing (the assertions), and so on. But what sets Nichols' view apart is the crucial distinction he makes between 'communication', *per se*, and 'meta-communication', or communication *about* com-munication. Nichols is aware, of course, that introductions have communicational value in that they have 'some informational relationship to the "body" of the message', but that is not what concerns him. His interest, and his contribution, is the realization that introductions serve a meta-communica-tional purpose, that is, they serve as the basis of an agreement between the preacher and the hearers 'about how we will handle and what we will make of the message content which is to come'. As such, the introduction to the sermon is analogous to the 'contract' made between a pastoral coun-selor and the counselee 'to work toward certain goals and in certain ways between care giver and receiver'.

What we have in Nichols, then, is a genuine innovation in homiletical theory: a thoroughgoing analysis of sermon introductions done from a communicational vantage point. Nichols has his eye on the listening process, on what happens between the preacher and the hearer. This view of the introduction allows Nichols to dismiss two of Buttrick's time-worn criteria as misplaced categories. 'The communication question to ask', claims Nichols, 'is "When has the contract been set?" rather than "How long should the introduction be?"' So much for brevity. Nichols has gone beneath the superficial quality to discern the communicational dynamic. As for the demand that the introduction be 'interesting', Nichols states the following:

> Time after time we have heard that the purpose of an introduction is to 'get people's attention'. Now really, when was the last time anyone saw a preacher step into the pulpit at sermon time and *not* have everyone's attention . . . We do not need to 'get it', but we surely do need to *use* it by establishing a contract for com-munication.[6]

Nichols acknowledges – and addresses – two potential objections to his view of introductions. First, there is the objection that clearly setting out the contract of the sermon will spoil those sermons which are built around a discovery process of communication. Revealing everything in the beginning would, in effect, ruin the surprise. This would not only be a disappointment for the preacher, but, more important, for the hearers as well, who relish such experiences. Nichols answers that this objection misses the communication/meta-communication distinction. The introduction can contract with the hearers to join with the preacher in a thinking-through process toward an as-yet-undisclosed point. Thus, the contract is clear while, at the same time, the surprise remains intact.

The second objection addressed by Nichols is an aesthetic one, namely that the business of setting a contract inevitably involves the kind of technical, cards-on-the-table language which could mar a poetic and lyrical sermon. Nichols concedes that this is on occasion true (though not as often as would-be homiletical poets think). He suggests that these rare occasions can be handled by announcements about the nature of the sermon in the bulletin, elsewhere in the service of worship, or as a preface to the sermon itself.

Nichols' main point seems to be that listening to sermons is demanding work and that hearers have the need and right to know what they are in for. The introduction recognizes and respects the work of the listener by stating the nature of the task and inviting the hearer to accept his or her end of the cooperative task of co-creating the communication event of preaching.

A critique

Nichols' work is clearly the most advanced statement to date on the nature of sermon introductions. A sermon is not primarily a literary product; it is essentially an act of proclamation. Whatever literary and aesthetic merits a sermon may possess, they must be subordinated to the larger concern that the sermon communicate something to those who hear. By introducing communicational concepts into the discussion, Nichols has refashioned the agenda in a helpful way and cleared the homiletical landscape of much clutter. Any further advance in understanding what a sermon introduction should be must begin by considering Nichols' position.

Without taking away from Nichols' contributions, which are significant, I want to raise two objections to his view on the way toward making what I hope will be a constructive proposal regarding the role sermon introductions play in sermons:

1. I will begin by conceding the main point: introductions *do* involve what Nichols calls 'meta-communication' in that they signal to the hearer certain cues about the communication event which is to follow. Meta-communication, however, is not a characteristic of introductions alone, but rather occurs throughout the sermon. What conventional homiletics has called 'transitions' are often particularly high in meta-communicational content. It is not strictly accurate, then, to suggest that the introduction is *the* place in the sermon where meta-communication occurs. What does happen there might best be termed 'introductory meta-communication', which, in a way, sends us back around to our original question: What can be said about the special role of introductions?

2. Nichols recognizes that meta-communication can be 'sometimes overt and sometimes implicit', but he clearly pushes toward the more explicit variety, complaining that 'we probably err in introductions more on the side of subtlety than overdirection'. One is left with the impression that there are two almost discrete *classes* of statements: communicational ones, which involve certain kinds of information, and meta-communicational ones, which are directions or proposals for how the first class of statements shall be handled. Nichols knows that introductions contain examples of the first class of statements, but these do not attract his interest much. It is the second class of statements which is really important in an introduction, since a cluster of such statements can serve as the contractual agreement for the communicational tasks of preacher and listener throughout the sermon. This not only deprives us of Nichols' wisdom about what introductions ought to be in terms of communication content, but it also obscures the fact that meta-communication is most often a simultaneous, and not a separate, activity in human communication. I do not need (or want) formal instruction in meta-communication to know that 'Dearly Beloved, we are gathered here in the presence of God . . . ' is a piece of information which has to be handled differently from 'Did ya' hear the one about the sailor and the parrot?' These statements, like most human utterances, contain their own meta-communicational cues.

The point here is not that meta-communication ought to go on; it *does* go on whether we want it to or not. Part of Nichols' argument and contribution is that preachers need to become aware of this process and, to some degree, control it. Agreed, but I would insist that, most of the time, effective meta-communication occurs not by stepping aside and uttering several examples from a special class of meta-communicative statements, but rather by recognizing and regulating the meta-communicational overtones inherent in ordinary communication.

Sermon introductions: a proposal

So, what can we say about sermon introductions which would employ the insight of communication theory while at the same time avoiding some of the problems of Nichols' approach? I want to make six observations about sermon introductions. More observations need to be made before this can come close to a complete *theory* of introductions, but perhaps the bare outlines of a theory can already be seen here:

1. If there is anything which should have been made clear by the above discussion it is that it is

not appropriate to speak about sermon introductions in isolation from their placement in the overall network of sermonic communication. An introduction gets the conversation going between the preacher and the hearers, and it already anticipates where that conversation will move. The way in which a sermon begins governs, to some degree, how that sermon can develop and how it can end.

2. This means that all homiletical descriptions of 'good' introductions which are based upon the identification of self-contained virtues (such as 'brevity' or 'memorability') can be dismissed. Introductions cannot be 'good' in and of themselves, but only in reference to the effectiveness of their role in the whole sermon.

3. This also means that introductions function as the first 'step' in the sermon journey toward a 'destination'. The term 'destination' can be defined in communicational terms as a certain form of psychological awareness which is present in the hearer at the end of the sermon and which the sermon played an important role in creating. It can be further described with reference to the familiar triad, knowing-being-doing. The preacher hopes that at the end of a sermon the hearers will know some things they did not previously know, feel some things they did not previously feel, be ready to act in certain new ways, or some combination of these. There is, in other words, a certain psychic distance to be traveled, and the sermon is a kind of guided journey from 'here' to 'there'. The introduction must, of course, begin 'here', but it must also anticipate 'there'.

4. An introduction begins 'here' when it raises, implicitly or explicitly, some issue, problem, question, need, or situation which is recognized and construed to be important by the hearer. This is not to say, à la Fosdick, that introductions are condemned to the presentation of 'life situations'. Indeed, the introduction may be a description of Assyrian cultic practices, but it must include signals to the hearer about why listening to this material is pertinent and worthwhile and at least some hint about how this material will be valuable to the sermon event as a whole. Listening to a sermon is active not passive, and part of the activity of listeners involves their continual attempt to answer two questions: Where does this material fit in the overall 'logic' of the message, and what does this material have to do with me? Introductions don't have to spell out the answers to those questions, but if they ignore them completely, they do so at great peril.

Introductions are also 'here' when they guide the hearer through the first step of the sermon journey in the way in which *these* listeners can take that step. This involves strategy . . . and pastoral sensitivity. To begin a sermon with a detailed background exegesis of a biblical text may make perfectly good sense with one congregation, and yet be communicational suicide with another.

5. Introductions anticipate the 'there' of the sermon when they help to shape in the hearer's mind a more or less accurate impression of where the sermon will go. Nichols is also helpful in describing how this works:

> When a message begins, a kind of mental search mission starts in the mind of the hearers. From their vast internal computer of stored experience comes a set of meanings, images, and previous understandings to which the unfamiliar incoming message is referred for translation, so to speak. That is the 'story', like the accompaniment roll of a player piano, or a film clip backing up the commentary of the evening television news. As soon as that happens, which as a rule takes something like a billionth of a second, communication has become essentially a receiver phenomenon. The meaning of the message is not 'transmitted', as we sometimes mistakenly say; it is, so to speak, 'transgenerated' in the awareness of the hearer, reassembled in the context of his or her own story.[7]

Since hearers listen faster than speakers speak, they are 'running ahead', anticipating where the message is going, deciding if, in fact, they wish to go there. The introduction provides clues – both of the communicational and meta-communicational variety – about this journey. Indeed, implicit in each introduction is more of a 'covenant' than a contract: a promise made in the context of trust that, when this sermon is done, we will have arrived together in a more or less agreed upon place. I keep saying 'more or less' because I want to protect the value of unpredictability and surprise in communication. If the hearer is always able to guess exactly where the preacher is going, then boredom sets in. If the preacher is always arriving at some spot different from that predicted by the hearer, then the preacher is viewed as idiosyncratic and, thus, communicationally untrustworthy. Nobody wants the weekly experience of checking their luggage in the sermon introduction to Miami, only to arrive in Denver. Occasionally, it's an adventure; weekly, it's a hassle.

In order to see how this process of listener anticipation works, consider the following sermon introduction:

> The story of Noah and his ark is not something we grown-ups take very seriously. We tend to regard it as a story for children, and we have our children making replicas of the ark in Sunday school. But it is a very strange thing, really, that we should regard this as a children's story (which is to say a fairy tale), because it is a dark and frightening story. Furthermore, it is a story about ourselves and our world – a story that is quite modern.[8]

Now a hearer listening to this sermon introduction is moving ahead of the preacher, guessing where this sermon will be going, deciding whether to accompany the preacher on this particular journey. In this case, the listeners would have every reason to guess that, when this sermon is concluded, the preacher will have helped them to take the Noah story more seriously by a) exposing its 'dark and frightening' side and b) connecting it meaningfully to the real issues of their personal and social lives. In fact, in this introduction the preacher has made a 'covenant' with the hearers to do just that. If the preacher fails to do those things, then the communicational covenant is broken. If, sermon after sermon, the preacher breaks covenant with the hearers, the implicit and necessary trust between them is damaged.

Is the above introduction a *good* one? The answer must be a tentative 'yes'. It does begin 'here' by naming an issue in the hearers' lives (i.e., their current understanding of the Noah story), and it does anticipate 'there' (i.e., by promising to expose a new and important understanding of that story). So far, so good. We cannot yet say, though, that this is an effective introduction, because this assessment must be made in light of the *whole* sermon. Was the covenant fulfilled? Was the inquisitive, exploratory tone set by the introduction maintained throughout the sermon? In short, an introduction is effective only when it plays a consistent and satisfactory role in the total network of the sermon's communication.

6. One thing implied in the above analysis of the example introduction is that introductions have certain 'tonal' qualities (what Nichols would call implicit meta-communication) which are important clues for the hearers about the nature of the overall sermon and, which, in fact, should be consistent with the rest of the sermon. An introduction which raises the theodicy problem in intellectual terms promises a sermon in which preacher and hearer grapple with the issues. To spend the rest of the sermon sloshing around in emotional stories and tearful examples would be, among other infractions, a betrayal of the covenant established in and through the introduction.

It is clear that the understanding of the sermon as an integrated communicational event cannot be confined to a discussion of introductions. It has clear implications for every aspect of the sermon – illustrations, transitions, conclusions, and all the rest. All of the parts of the sermon work together as a system, creating a unified event in the experience of the listeners. Viewed this way, the task of creating the sermon becomes admittedly more complex, more demanding pastorally, and more subject to local and congregational criteria than to 'universal' literary canons. But this perspective also rescues the sermon from the arena of written discourse, where it has learned much, but to which it finally does not belong, and brings it home again to the world of oral communication.

Notes

1   Buttrick as quoted in O. C. Edwards, Jr, *Elements of Homiletic,* New York, Pueblo 1982, p. 74. Buttrick
    varied his rule from time to time, occasionally adding a fourth element: appropriateness to the particular
    sermon. (See H. Grady Davis, *Design for Preaching*, Philadelphia, Fortress, 1958, p. 189.)

2   John Killinger, *Fundamentals of Preaching*, Philadelphia, Fortress, 1985, p. 83.

3   Davis, 1958, p. 188.

4   We do not have to look very far to see the impact of Davis' theory on such modern homileticians as
    Craddock and Lowry, both of whom have built entire theories (whether they knew it or acknowledged it or
    not) on a single aspect of Davis' design (for Craddock, inductive logic, and for Lowry, narrative conti-
    nuity). See Fred B. Craddock, *As One Without Authority*, Nashville, TN, Abingdon, 1978, and Eugene L.
    Lowry, *The Homiletical Plot. The Sermon as Narrative Art,*, Atlanta, John Knox, 1980.

5   J. Randall Nichols, *Building the Word: The Dynamics of Communication and Preaching*, San Francisco,
    Harper & Row, 1980, p. 101.

6   Nichols, 1980, pp. 102–3.

7   Ibid., pp. 69–70.

8   Vance Barron, 'To Keep Hope Alive', in *Sermons for the Celebration of the Christian Year,* Nashville, TN,
    Abingdon, 1977, p. 14.

10   Preaching and Narrative

Peter K. Stevenson

During the last 30 years there has been a growing interest in 'narrative preaching'. This interest, most noticeable in north America, has arisen out of the interplay of a number of factors. In part it arises from the fact that people enjoy stories. The preacher, struggling to attract people's attention, knows the story's power to enliven the sermon. Long-suffering hearers welcome the stories which help them make sense of what the preacher is saying.

More significantly, a greater appreciation of the literary characteristics of the Bible has drawn attention to the different genres of biblical material which call for a variety of hermeneutical strategies.[1] As Frances Young puts it, an 'awareness of the Bible as a canon of literature, representing different styles from different periods, must be the starting-point for appropriate interpretation. Each genre within the Bible will have its proper mode of performance. Narrative, poetry, prophecy, law, wisdom, hymns, prayers, visions – all these require different approaches'.[2]

Generic preaching

What is true for biblical interpretation in general has some clear implications for preachers as well. If God has chosen to communicate his word in and through such a variety of literary forms, then at the very least that provides a basis for believing that God's word can be communicated in and through different forms of sermons. More positively it suggests that the God who chooses to communicate his living word in such a multiplicity of ways, intends that preachers should exercise similar amounts of creativity in designing and using a wide range of sermon styles as they communicate the living word for today. If Christian preaching is to allow the Bible to function in an authoritative way, then the specific characteristics of the text should be allowed to mould not only the content of the sermon but the form as well. Recognizing the link between the genre of a biblical passage and the form of the sermon does not imply, for example, that all sermons on Paul's epistles must take the form of a letter read out to the congregation. It does suggest, however, that it would be a mistake to try to force all scriptural materials into three-point, propositional sermons. If all biblical passages are forced to fit into one set sermon form, the danger will be that the listeners will find such sermons predictable and dull.

Differing genres of material would appear to call for different styles of preaching.[3] Goldingay, for example, argues that an understanding of the ways in which stories engage their readers, can help preachers use similar strategies to preach biblical stories effectively.[4] If such a link exists between the genre of the passage and the form of the sermon then this suggests that narrative approaches to preaching are vital because 'of all the biblical genres of literature, narrative may be described as the central, foundational, and all-encompassing genre of the Bible.'[5]

This recognition of the literary characteristics of the biblical materials has coincided with a growing sense of unease about approaches to preaching which major on the deductive, didactic and propositional. This discomfort leads some to conclude that the time has come to get rid of the sermon. Advocates of 'narrative preaching' recognize the force of these sorts of criticisms but respond not by abandoning the sermon, but by advocating an alternative form of preaching. In place of the deductive sermon which directs people about what to believe, they argue the need for a more indirect, inductive approach to preaching. This begins with people's experience and draws them into the experiential event of the sermon within which the hearers begin to experience transformation.

It is the coming together of these sorts of factors which has helped to create interest in forms of narrative preaching. To talk about '*narrative preaching*', however, is to run the risk of arousing all sorts of mixed emotions. For some the phrase 'narrative preaching' conjures up images of content-less sermons which are little more than a series of amusing stories. From another perspective the word 'narrative' is sometimes taken as short-hand for dramatic monologues, where the preacher re-tells a biblical story from the perspective of one of its characters. As part of the preacher's reper-toire, the ability to re-tell biblical stories in a lively way is clearly a useful skill, but on its own this style of communication does not appear to have the resources necessary to sustain the faith and witness of the church. This article neither aims to provide a D-I-Y guide to performing dramatic monologues, nor seeks to provide a comprehensive treatment of all the issues connected to preaching and narrative. Such an overview would be difficult in the absence of any agreed defini-tion of 'narrative preaching'. The more limited aim here is to look at the related themes of 'preaching' and 'narrative' and to highlight some topics which seem to have practical relevance to the contemporary preacher.

The homiletical plot

Having argued that there should be a connection between sermon form and biblical genre, it may seem strange now to have to explain that much of the writing about narrative preaching does not actually concentrate on the best ways of handling biblical narrative! In part this is because homileti-cians who emphasize narrative are also concerned with the structures which they perceive to underlie sacred and secular forms of narrative. One of the structural features within all kinds of nar-rative writing is the *plot*. So it comes as no surprise to be told that 'each story has a beginning, a middle, and an end; that is, stories are structured. Each story has a plot of some kind. We are pre-sented with a problem that is to be solved; quite likely there are difficulties to be overcome on the way or consequences when the main events are over.'[6]

It is a short step from here to go on to suggest that sermons should also have a clear dramatic plot. Eugene Lowry[7] is an influential advocate of narrative preaching and at the heart of his approach there is a marked emphasis upon what he calls 'the homiletical plot'. For him it is clear that a 'sermon is not a doctrinal lecture. It is an *event-in-time*, a narrative art form more akin to a play or novel in shape than to a book. . . . I propose that we begin by regarding the sermon as a homiletical plot, a narrative art form, a sacred story.'[8]

At the heart of his homiletical plot is the sense that there is a problem, or a conflict which builds up in intensity through the sermon until the gospel provides the key to resolving the conflict. In *The Homiletical Plot* Lowry outlines five stages through which the preacher moves in the course of a sermon:

1 Upsetting the equilibrium
2 Analysing the discrepancy
3 Disclosing the clue to resolution
4 Experiencing the gospel
5 Anticipating the consequences.[9]

The sermon upsets the equilibrium of the hearers by identifying a problem from the human condition. This is explored progressively in the second stage of the sermon. This leads on to the turning point when the good news of the gospel is brought to bear on this problem. This leads on to illustrations which enable the hearer to experience this good news for themselves. The sermon finishes by considering the implications of this experience for our living. This schema is simplified in his latest book where the dynamics of the plot are unfolded in four movements, *Conflict, Complication, Sudden Shift* and *Unfolding*. Rather than the preacher removing all elements of suspense at the start by telling the congregation what is coming next, this form of preaching engages its hearers in a more dramatic way and entices them to keep listening to discover where it will all lead. This kind of sermon cannot be dismissed as a bundle of stories strung together for there is a clear structure which provides a sense of progression as the sermon moves through these stages.

Such an approach to preaching can claim a biblical basis in the example of Jesus who taught in parables. In common with many gospel parables this form of narrative preaching is an indirect method of communication in that the sermon concludes by inviting and encouraging the hearers to work out the ending for themselves. This emphasis has been welcomed by many because it provides a plausible alternative to a more traditional 'three-point' approach to preaching. Whereas some forms of propositional preaching may be in danger of appealing only to the intellect of the hearers this approach operates in a more holistic way in that it seeks to engage the imagination and the emotions of the hearers as well.

Such an approach is not without its own set of difficulties. Indeed there would appear to be the real possibility that the preacher who always adopts a narrative approach is just as much in danger of downplaying the variety within Scripture, as the one who constantly resorts to a more didactic style of preaching. Whilst it is true that Jesus taught in parables which often provoked his hearers to work out the application of the story for themselves, it would be misleading to say that this is the only way in which Jesus taught and preached. The Sermon on the Mount shows that there were occasions where Jesus was happy to operate in a more didactic manner.

A detailed critique of this style of narrative preaching has been advanced recently by Charles Campbell[10] who feels that the emphasis upon formal matters of *plot* tends towards a neglect of more significant issues about the *character* of the one who is at the heart of Christian preaching. The important thing is not that we can be like Jesus in the way we preach in parables but that the character of Jesus should be at the heart of all preaching. As several forms of narrative preaching adopt an inductive method, beginning from human experience and leading individuals on towards an experience of transformation, Campbell feels that the end result is that human experience dictates the terms of the discussion carried out in the sermon. This need not be the case as within Lowry's schema it would also be possible to begin with a problem within the biblical text, or between two apparently contradictory passages, and to move on to seek a biblical resolution to that particular problem.

The homiletical plot may not solve all the problems facing the contemporary preacher, but it suggests another viable way of structuring sermons which merits further exploration and experimentation.

Preaching and narrative theology

In a study of the way that theologians use Scripture to support their theological position David H. Kelsey suggests that theologians tend to use Scripture in one of three main ways[11]. Some adopt what he calls a *doctrinal approach* to Scripture, viewing it mainly as a source of doctrines and concepts. Another group of writers, he suggests, pursue a more *symbolic approach* because they see Scripture as an important collection of images and symbols. These both 'express' past revelatory events and also have the power to change people's lives by 'occasioning' a revelatory encounter with God. Other writers, such as Karl Barth, employ what Kelsey describes as the *rendering an agent approach*. Such a narrative approach to biblical interpretation, seen also in the work of writers such as Frei, Lindbeck and Thiemann,[12] is constantly seeking to draw the reader's attention to the nature and character of God who is the prime agent at work within the biblical narrative. The task of theology therefore is to reflect upon this agent and say what must be said about him today.

If biblical materials perform the function of revealing the character of God in this kind of way then this also has implications for the preacher. Preaching must surely be a practical form of Christian doctrine and there is a case for saying that any preaching which performrns this crucial function of drawing attention to the character of God is a practical form of narrative theology. Whatever form the sermon may take it can claim to have a narrative dimension if it narrates the truth about the character of God.

In a helpful section about *Preaching Hebrew Narrative*,[13] Greidanus notes 'the pervasive presence of God' within the narrative scene. Indeed 'even in scenes where God, in a particular frame, is not one of the "characters" or is not represented by one of the characters, the scene as a whole will undoubtedly reveal the presence of God, for the human characters act out the scene against the backdrop of God's promises, God's enabling power, God's demands, God's providence.'[14]

The pervasive presence of God is expressed in a memorable phrase by Ronald Thiemann who says, as he comments upon the Old Testament accounts of David's accession to kingship, that '*God is not so much absent from as hidden within the biblical narrative*'.[15] Other places within the biblical narrative where the pervasive, but hidden, presence of God can be identified, are the Joseph cycle and the Book of Esther. In the Joseph cycle God is not a prominent actor, but at the end of the day Joseph affirms his belief that God has been at work (Gen. 50:20). In Esther the name of God is not even mentioned, but the book was preserved because the people believed that the hidden God had been at work to protect and deliver his people.

Although the biblical narratives are clearly *theocentric*, Greidanus notes that many preachers tend to drift into an *anthropocentric* use of narrative passages. If God is the prime character in Hebrew narrative, *even when he is not mentioned*, then this implies that biblical preaching must avoid the temptation to use these narratives simply as sources of good examples for believers to follow. Theocentric materials call for theocentric sermons which are far more concerned with what a passage reveals about who God is than exhortations about what I must do.[16] This suggests that sermons on the Joseph narratives should not be primarily concerned to portray him as a glowing example for Christians to imitate but should point much more in the direction of the sovereign God who is constantly at work in the midst of the tangled family affairs involving Joseph and his brothers. To argue that appropriate use of narrative calls for more theocentric preaching is another way of pleading for putting the gospel back into preaching.

Incredulity towards metanarratives

Undergirding the work of preaching lies the gospel story which is the grand narrative of the church.[17] The postmodern suspicion of metanarratives raises questions about the validity of this, or of any other, world view. Such incredulity towards metanarratives need not be seen as a prohibition upon telling the story of salvation, because it can also be viewed as an invitation, in a world of competing stories, to tell the Christian story in attractive and compelling ways.

In an earlier generation the preacher could probably assume that most people in society had a basic understanding of the grand narrative, but those days are long since gone. Perhaps even more unsettling for the preacher are the comments from confessing Christians which reveal that many believers have a very limited understanding of the grand narrative which is at the heart of the life and mission of the church.

Within such a context one aspect of the preacher's task is to find ways of telling this story of salvation. Andrew Walker argues that a renewal of liturgy has a vital part to play in telling the gospel story to a generation which has forgotten it or never heard it. For 'liturgy is the regular, unceasing dramaturgical re-enactment of the story. We become more like Christ as together we worship him, feed on him, learn of him. This is essential for maintaining a faithful witness to the gospel. Old churches can sometimes be run by luke-warm or apostate priests, but however much damage they may cause from pulpit or pastoral guidance, they will always be counteracted by the discipline of liturgical tradition.'[18]

Walker's comments are relevant to preachers whatever their churchmanship for they alert us to the importance of the liturgical background to preaching. They are a reminder that congregations learn not only through sermons but also through the whole experience of worship. In an age where so many know so little about the church's grand narrative, a creative and biblical use of liturgy provides another way of telling the gospel story. Perhaps this is an encouragement for those in less liturgical traditions to review the whole shape of the worship service, and the overall scheme of preaching throughout the year, to check that the gospel story in all its richness is proclaimed in the prayers, songs and readings as well as in the preached word. The danger otherwise is that well prepared, God-centred preaching will be undermined by anthropocentric patterns of worship.

Images, narratives and arguments

David Schlafer asserts that 'throughout all the varieties of Scripture forms three basic related, but distinctive motifs can be consistently found. Whether a text is a hymn of praise, a terse teaching, a historical account, a parable, or a theological essay, it communicates by using images, narratives and arguments.'[19] This recognition leads him to observe that when it comes to constructing the sermon one of these three – image, story, or argument – serves as the integrating principle which gives shape to the whole sermon. In his opinion, effective sermons normally employ only one central strategy. 'One of the three is chosen as the means best suited for *this* preacher at *this* time with *this* text for *these* people. Images, stories and arguments serve as sermon-shaping strategies, as vehicles for an experience of the Word that is genuinely sacramental.'[20] This would tend to suggest that a closely argued piece of writing such as 1 Corinthians 1:18–25 will be best treated in a sermon which develops a careful argument, whereas an episode from the Gospels may best be presented in a more narrative style.

Schlafer moves on from this to suggest that preachers may have a preferred way of working and may see themselves as either a *poet*, a *storyteller* or an *essay writer*. 'No preacher is exclusively a poet, storyteller or essayist, of course; effective preachers regularly use elements of each in all of their sermons. But most preachers have a voice which is centred more in one mode of discourse than another. If a preacher operates incessantly from one mode, listeners will begin to typecast the sermons and lose interest.'[21]

At the outset it was argued that it is essential to recognize the different genres of material which cry out to be handled and performed in different ways. Whilst the thrust of this article has been about handling narrative texts in appropriate ways, this implies the need to treat other kinds of texts sensitively as well. Similarly the invitation to see the preacher as a poet, a storyteller or an essayist, does not prove that one approach is better than the other. Rather it suggests that there is a need, both to recognize the style which we are most familiar with, and to broaden our repertoire by developing other styles of preaching as well.

Notes

1   See for example, Gordon D. Fee and Douglas Stuart, *How to Read the Bible for All Its Worth*, London, Scripture Union, 1983.

2   Frances Young, *The Art of Performance*, London, Darton, Longman & Todd, 1990, p. 27.

3   A helpful treatment of these issues can be found in Thomas G. Long, *Preaching and the Literary Forms of the Bible*, Philadelphia, Fortress, 1989.

4   John Goldingay, *Models for Interpretation of Scripture*, Carlisle, Paternoster, 1995, chapter 5: 'How stories preach'.

5   Sidney Greidanus, *The Modern Preacher and the Ancient Text*, Leicester, IVP, 1988.

6   Goldingay, 1995, p. 76.

7   See Eugene L. Lowry, *The Homiletical Plot*, Atlanta, John Knox, 1980; *Doing Time in the Pulpit: The Relationship Between Narrative and Preaching,* Nashville, TN, Abingdon, 1985; *How to Preach a Parable: Designs for Narrative Sermons*, Nashville, TN, Abingdon, 1989; and *The Sermon: Dancing the Edge of Mystery*, Nashville, TN, Abingdon, 1997.

8   Lowry, 1980, pp. 24–5.

9   Lowry, 1980.

10 Charles L. Campbell, *Preaching Jesus: New Directions for Homiletics in Hans Frei's Postliberal Theology,* Grand Rapids/Cambridge, Eerdmans, 1997.

11 David H. Kelsey, *The Uses of Scripture in Recent Theology*, London, SCM, 1975.

12 Hans W. Frei, *The Eclipse of Biblical Narrative*, New Haven and London, Yale University Press, 1974; *The Identity of Jesus Christ,* Philadelphia, Fortress, 1975; 'The "Literal Reading" of Biblical Narrative in the Christian Tradition: Does It Stretch or Will It Break?', in Frank McConnell (ed.) *The Bible and the Narrative Tradition*, New York and London, Oxford University Press, 1986, pp. 36–77; *Types of Christian Theology,* New Haven and London, Yale University Press, 1992. George A. Lindbeck, *The Nature of Doctrine: Religion and Theology in a Postliberal Age,* London, SPCK, 1984; 'Theology and Ecumenism since Vatican II', in David F. Ford (ed.), *The Modern Theologians: An Introduction to Christian Theologies in the Twentieth Century*, Oxford, Blackwell, 1989. Ronald F. Thiemann, *Revelation and Theology*, Notre Dame, University of Notre Dame Press, 1985; 'Radiance and Obscurity in Biblical Narrative', in Garret Green (ed.), *Scriptural Authority and Narrative Interpretation*, Philadelphia, Fortress, 1987, pp. 21–41.

13 Greidanus, 1988, pp. 188–227.

14 Ibid., p. 199.

15 Thiemann, 1987, pp. 21–41.

16 Greidanus, 1988, pp. 216–21. See also Goldingay, 1995, chapters 2–5.

17 For a helpful outline of the church's grand narrative, see Andrew Walker, *Telling the Story*, London, SPCK, 1996, pp. 12–19.

18 Ibid., pp. 194–9.

19 David J. Schlafer, *Surviving the Sermon: A Guide to Preaching for Those Who Have to Listen,* Boston, Cowley, 1992, p. 63.

20 Ibid., p. 65.

21 David J. Schlafer, *Your Way with God's Word: Discovering Your Distinctive Preaching Voice*, Boston, Cowley, 1995, p. 57. In chapter 6 he suggests some ways in which the preacher might identify his or her preferred mode of preaching.

11   Eleven Ways of Preaching a Non-Sermon

Dwight E. Stevenson

We learn from our mistakes – if we can detect and correct them. As a teacher of preaching I early discovered the power of negative examples, when exposed to peer-evaluation and followed by positive examples. From this we can safely say that a person will be a better preacher from knowing the ways in which a sermon can misfire – more especially, by knowing the ways in which his own sermon may go wrong.

This can happen in fundamental ways, so basic as to constitute a negation of the sermon as such. We might call these violations 'counterfeit sermons', or 'sermon surrogates'. Counterfeiting in the pulpit happens more frequently than we like to think, most of the time without conscious intention. (All the more reason, then, to study the art of detecting it.) Here, the mistake is not an error *within* the sermon; rather it is the gross error of substituting a non-sermon for the genuine article. There are no less than eleven ways in which to do this.

1. *Moralistic harangue*. This non-sermon leads all the rest. We who stand at the pulpit have our reasons for developing a moralistic harangue. Because our people are not living up to their obligations, institutional and moral, we exhort them 'in season and out of season'. To put the matter less delicately, we punish them. We whip them. The New Testament, it is true, counsels us to 'reprove, rebuke, exhort' but we do not always do this 'with all long suffering and patience'. (2 Tim. 4:2 ASV). What is more, we do not always do it against a background of good news and sound teaching plus the family-like solidarity of the Christian community in which alone it can be accepted. Pulpit convention permits us – it may even require us – to be the voice of wrath. People come to church expecting to take their medicine; and we come prepared to administer it.

The amazing thing is that people put up with it, and may even welcome it. Why? There are reasons. For one thing, a great many people do not like themselves very much; in a vague way they feel guilty (without ever coming right out to admit it); and they want to be punished. Thus they can be at peace again with a soothed conscience. But they do not want to be punished too severely, nor driven to genuine repentance. A tongue-lashing from an authorized preacher seems to fill the bill exactly. It is a fine way of paying for sin without repenting of it. The tongue is a lash that does not draw blood.

John Steinbeck has given this theme classic treatment in his autobiographical *Travels With Charlie in Search of America*. He describes his reaction to an old-fashioned fire and brimstone sermon which he heard in Vermont.

> He [the preacher] spoke of hell as an expert, not the mush-mush hell of these soft days, but a wellstoked, white-hot hell served by technicians of the first order. This reverend brought it to a point where we could understand it, a good hard coal fire, plenty of draft, and a squad of open-hearth devils who put their hearts into their work and their work was me. I began to feel good all over. For some years now God has been a pal to us, practicing togetherness, and that causes the same emptiness a father does playing softball with his son. But this Vermont God cared enough about me to go to a lot of trouble to kick the hell out of me. He put my sins in a new perspective. Whereas they had been small and mean and nasty and best forgotten, this minister gave them some size and bloom and dignity. I hadn't been thinking very well of myself for some years, but

if my sins had this dimension there was some pride left. I wasn't a naughty child but a first rate sinner, and I was going to catch it.

I felt so revived in spirit that I put five dollars in the plate, and afterward, in front of the church, shook hands warmly with the minister and as many of the congregation as I could. It gave me a lovely sense of evil-doing that lasted clear through Tuesday.[1]

It is clear that there is a kind of satisfaction for those who take their medicine under such punitive preaching, Steinbeck's irony notwithstanding. It provides a substitute sermon difficult to distinguish from the real thing. The trouble is that it transforms the light of the gospel almost wholly into heat – and the work of the sermon as life-giving light has been usurped. There is simply no time for illumination.

2. *Aesthetic artifact.* There is an art of preaching, of course, but it is more like the art of gardening than the art of painting or sculpture. And in any case, in this artistry the aim is not a beautiful sermon, any more than the aim of gardening is a beautiful hoe. The aim is human life captured by the beauty of holiness that was seen in Christ. The literary quality of our sermon manuscripts, in most cases, will be less like the plays of Shakespeare and the Dialogues of Plato than like the morning newspaper, which today is eagerly sought and read and tomorrow is cast into the wastebasket. And perhaps we would be better preachers if we had something of the discipline of the journalist who writes with all possible care, knowing that twenty-four hours hence his words will be as dead as a corsage the morning after the dance. The minister who regards his sermons as works of art and who is busy turning the sanctuary of his church into an art gallery for the exhibition of his masterpieces is in the wrong calling. The sermon is not an intellectual object to be admired for its aesthetic worth. Neither is it an intellectual object to be remembered, like a grocery list.

Several years ago a reader of *The British Weekly* wrote a letter to the editor which, as I remember, went something like this:

Dear Sir: I notice that ministers seem to set a great deal of store by their sermons and to spend a great deal of time in preparing them. I have been attending services quite regularly for the past thirty years and during that time if I estimate correctly, I have listened to no less than three thousand sermons. But, to my consternation, I discover that I cannot remember a single one of them. I wonder if most church goers are not in a like case? And if so, I wonder if ministers' time might not be more profitably spent on something else? Sincerely yours. . . .

This letter, as you can imagine, kicked up quite a dust storm. The battle of angry pens raged for several weeks. Then somebody wrote a letter that quietly put an end to the controversy. It went something like this:

Dear Sir: I have been married for thirty years. During that time I have eaten 32,850 meals mostly of my wife's cooking. Suddenly I have discovered to my amazement that I cannot remember the menu of a single one of those meals! And yet, I received the nourishment from every one of them; and I have the distinct impression that without them I would have starved to death long ago. Sincerely yours. . . .

Enough on this subject. A minister is not hanging masterpieces in an art gallery; neither is he nailing up menus on a bulletin board. Rather, he is a waiter, serving the bread of life to hungry people.

3. *Pontifical pronouncement.* Someone years ago referred to ministers in the high pulpits of Scotland as 'standing six feet above criticism'. Undeniably the minister is an authority figure. He may take himself seriously as such, endeavoring to do his peoples' thinking for them. And, from the congregational side, he may be accepted gratefully as such by the immature and the timid who do not want to take the risks of maturity. Still from the congregational side, however, those who want

to think and grow will be repelled. Sometimes they will rebel violently, rejecting not only the religion of the pulpit pundit who offended them but all ministers and all churches, supposing them to be the same. We could dwell at length upon the covert self-righteousness of such preachers, their pompousness, their cynical estimate of people, their unrecognized hostilities. And in the same way we could linger over the subversion of religion by the immature into pseudo-security. The temptation from both sides is great, and subtle.

4. *Museum lecture*. A sermon, in the nature of the case, begins in scripture. The tragedy is that it so often ends where it begins. It is like a tour through ancient ruins. At best it is mildly interesting and informative. At worst it is dusty, dull and boring. The preacher in such a case seems to know all about the Red Sea and the ancient Jordan, but nothing about the Great Lakes and the Mississippi basin. A true sermon, as John Knox has so helpfully observed, deals not simply with 'an ancient event', but also with 'the always new life of the spirit'.[2] Thus, it has not a single focus, but two foci. There is the contemporaneity of the scripture to be recognized, its timelessness, timeliness and relevance to be acknowledged. Otherwise even the most precise knowledge *about* the Bible is spiritual illiteracy.

5. *Palliative prescription*. Jeremiah satarized this kind of preaching (among the false prophets):

They have healed the wound of my people lightly,
saying 'Peace, peace,'
when there is no peace. (Jer. 8:11)

Jeremiah, of course, was talking about a religion of easy assurance. On this same subject, under the label of 'Cheap Grace', Dietrich Bonhoeffer wrote, 'Cheap grace is the preaching of forgiveness without requiring repentance, baptism without church discipline, communion without confession, absolution without personal confession. Cheap grace is grace without discipleship, grace without the cross, grace without Jesus Christ, living and incarnate.'[3]

The preacher who is rightly warned away from moralism with its verbal punishments is always in danger of falling into the trap of cheap grace. The assurance of pardon, when spoken from the pulpit, so seldom conveys the reality of pardon to the listening heart. The man in the pew may feel remorse, and even derive some satisfaction from the bitter sweet of self-pity, but he will resist genuine repentance with all his might. As long as that continues he will also be resisting grace; the minister should be on guard against trying to bring it about by incantation. What is required is a costly one-to-one communication which can never be achieved by spraying a congregation with words. This is one point at which preaching without pastoral involvement simply becomes an impertinence.

6. *Palace propaganda*. The mould for this kind of preaching was set by the four hundred court prophets of Ahab who told him what he wanted to hear as he and Jehoshaphat contemplated war against Syria (1 Kings 22:5–6). If a cross section of the world were present in our congregations, rich and poor, black and white, workers and management, we would perhaps be safeguarded against pleasing the ears of the power elite. However, congregations these days tend to draw their membership from a single economic class, race and social stratum. And the temptation to comfort the comfortable and lie to the self-deceived is almost irresistible. As corrective, Helmut Thielicke has suggested that we ought to preach all sermons as if all classes and conditions of men were actually present – to save us from special pleading and rescue the people from blessing their prejudices with a text.

7. *Theological lecture*. A Christian man should be able to give a reason for the faith that is in him, as Paul advised Timothy. For the minister, this means theological preaching. But woe to the man who mistakes dogma for faith and a reasoned system of doctrines for the power of an ultimate

concern. Young preachers, in particular, are in danger of identifying faith with dogma, and of developing their theology before they have had their doxology. The observations of Harry Emerson Fosdick on the last years of his teaching at Union Theological Seminary (New York) pinpoints this danger as he experienced it in 'the men who had never known theology until they learned it first in neo-orthodoxy! In a few cases especially I never had heard at Union such homiletical arrogance, such take-it-or-leave-it assumption of theological finality, such cancellation of the life and words of the historic Jesus by the substitution of a dogmatic Christ'.[4] When talk about God rises out of first hand encounter with God something very different happens. The preaching is doctrinal without sounding doctrinaire; in fact, it may not even sound like theology at all because it arises out of life and leads back into life as good tidings for modern man.

8. *Argumentation and debate*. Jesus told his disciples that they were to be his witnesses, not his lawyers. And they were. But not a few of their successors have behaved as though Christ were desperately in need of an attorney for the defense or even a prosecutor. This pulpit posture grows out of a prior identification of faith with formulated dogma – that is with the sermon surrogate just identified as *theological lecture*. It is but a short step from lecture to debate. Born on the American frontier at a time when forensic debate was in high fashion, the religious movement with which I am identified often fell into this trap. Even before reading particular sermons of its early advocates one might safely predict that those preachers would level their guns in the course of a single sermon, first to the right against the legions of Calvinism, and then to the left against the equally dangerous *batallions* of Arminianism. Barton Warren Stone, one of the 'big four' of the Disciples of Christ, early called attention to the blight of this debating spirit:

> Seldom do we see in the same person a warrior and an humble, devoted Christian. *Rara avis in terra.* Such acquire a controversial habit and temper. They may proselyte many to their opinions, and greatly increase their numbers; but the children are like the parents, lean and pygmie things. [Such preaching, like 'an ecclesiastical duel' between two speakers, tends to smother the spirit of devotion and true religion.] . . .
>
> In these public debates but few persons attend who have not their minds prepossessed in favor of one side or the other. A few sophisticated persons may be proselyted to your opinions, but one renewed soul is of more value than a score of such proselytes; and such renewed souls are made by the truth uttered in the spirit, and heartily received and obeyed.[5]

Attack begets counterattack. Argumentation arouses controversy; and controversy fathers division. Barton Warren Stone, early in the nineteenth century, and Isaac Errett in its third quarter labored to supplant such ecclesiastical warfare with something constructive. Thereby, according to one historian, the denomination was saved 'from becoming a fissiparous sect of jangling legalists'.

9. *Eulogy*. There is perhaps little preaching today that is compounded purely of praise – to the church, to Jesus Christ, to the Christian way of life. But there have been instances of it, and it may return. Such preaching sounds as though it has only one text: 'Wonderful Counselor, Mighty God, Everlasting Father, Prince of Peace' (Isaiah 9:6). It is closely allied to what Harry Elmer Barnes characterized forty years ago as 'the Jesus Stereotype' – the problems of mankind concretely stated and painfully experienced, but nothing from the Christian side but booming generalities: 'Jesus is the answer!' A steady diet of syrup can be as deadly as acid. Unless the question 'How?' can interrupt such preaching and bring it up short we will surely be where Barnes thought we were – in 'The Twilight of Christianity'.

10. *Ecclesiastical commercial*. I am here likening some preaching to television commercials – a sales pitch for the program of the institution. Ministers get into this position quite naturally, by yielding to the pressure of their administrative role in running a complex organization. In wide reaches of the church, it seems to be assumed that the sermon is the chief instrument for the promo-

tion of the program. After this promotional work is completed, if there is any time left for the proclamation of the gospel and for Christian teaching, well and good; but if not, long live promotion!

What it amounts to is that such preaching is more and more determined by the pressures of the
calendar and less and less by the gospel. There is the Christian year. Then there is the year of the
church as institution. The two are not synonymous. In addition, there is the civil calendar. Put these
three together, and the cause of kerygmatic or didactic preaching is lost before it is begun.

A few years ago I jotted down a simple but incomplete list of special Sundays and weeks on the
calendar. In *January* there were New Years, Epiphany, the Universal Week of Prayer, Church and
Economic Life Week, Youth Week, *World Call* Week and YMCA Week. *February* – you would
never know it was the shortest month of the year – called for Race Relations Sunday, Brotherhood
Week, Lincoln's Birthday, Washington's Birthday, the 'Week of Compassion', Boy Scout Sunday,
the World Day of Prayer, the beginning of Lent; in addition to which it was non-resident member
month. *May*, to skip down the calendar a bit, provided Christian Family Week, Mother's Day, Rural
Life Sunday, Memorial Sunday, Be Kind to Animals Week – with a bare mention of Ascension Day
and Pentecost. May was also National Tavern Month! *October* gave us Columbus Day, World
Communion Sunday, the 'Week of the Ministry', Laymen's Sunday, World Order Sunday,
'Christian Literature Week', Convention Sunday, Reformation Sunday; in addition to which it was
Church Loyalty Month.

There simply are not enough Sundays in the year to meet the pressures of the calendar. But even
if there were, would this be Christian preaching?

This is not to say that the church does not have an institution and that the work of the institution
must not be promoted. It is to say, however, that 99 per cent of the time, the sermon is not the place
for it. If we cannot do all that needs to be done through church paper, bulletin board, and printed
announcements, what is wrong with a brief oral announcement now and then? We can simply tell
our people that the time has come for the commercial! Wherever it belongs, it does not belong in the
sermon. What is more, the necessary promotional work of the institution – if taken out of the
sermon – can be done more imaginatively and more effectively.

11. *Monologue and soliloquy.* Those who have read Reuel Howe's *Miracle of Dialogue* are aware
of the dialogical character of true preaching. Nevertheless, ministers are thought by many to be poor
listeners. If they are correct in this view, far too many sermons are monologue – one may actually
talk in one-way communication *at* passive receivers of his message. It is highly doubtful if anything
is ever received in this passive manner, but undoubtedly some speakers, ministers included, think of
themselves in a monological role. So far as they succeed, they do not even engage in monologue;
they merely engage in soliloquy. They end up talking to themselves. In an article, 'Preaching on the
Nature of Communication', later enlarged in his book, *The Empty Pulpit*, Clyde H. Reid has shown
that communication requires at least seven steps: (1) transmission, (2) contact, (3) feedback, (4)
comprehension, (5) acceptance, (6) internalization, and (7) complete communication.

Transmission means simply that the sermon is delivered so that it comes to the hearer, audibly, in
his own language. *Contact* means that it finds common ground with the hearer, presumably in some
area of ultimate concern. We used to call this 'the need step'. *Feedback* takes place when the listener asks questions, makes comments, and otherwise carries on a conversation with the audible
speaker. Some of this can be carried on inaudibly through pantomine. *Comprehension* takes place
when the hearer has clarified his understanding of what the preacher is saying. *Acceptance* is the
stage at which the hearer accepts, ignores, or rejects the message. *Internalization* is a step beyond
acceptance. Then the message becomes his own, speaks for him, becomes a part of him and begins
to influence his behavior. And thus finally we arrive at *complete communication*. 'A transfer of
shared meanings has taken place which influences conduct'.[6]

If communication is as complex as Reid indicates (and who can doubt it?) the wonder is that public speaking ever breaks out of monologue or soliloquy. The miracle of dialogue does happen, but more times than we would like to admit perhaps it does not happen at all. Perhaps a gifted speaker is really effective only to the extent that he learns how to become an even more skillful listener. At the very least, the Christian minister begins by knowing and being concerned about his people. Perhaps the formula is given in Ezekiel's example in Babylon: 'I came to the exiles at Telabib, who dwelt by the river Chebar. And I sat there overwhelmed among them seven days. And at the end of seven days, the word of the Lord came to me. . . '. (Ezek. 3:15–16).

If preaching is weak and ineffectual, arousing little expectancy in pulpit or pew, the cause may lie in one or more of the surrogates for the sermon just reviewed. To recognize these and clear them out of the way may be more than half the job of renewal, just as the wrecking and clearing away of old buildings is the first and hardest stage of an urban renewal project. Something noble, and contemporary, can be erected, once the decayed structures have been demolished. With the sermon surrogates out of the way, perhaps we can go on to genuine sermons, which, like Paul's preaching to the Thessalonians, may then come 'not in word, but also in power and in the Holy Spirit and with full conviction' (1 Thess. 1:5). We should accept nothing less.

Notes

1   John Steinbeck, *Travels With Charlie in Search of America*, New York, Viking, 1962, p. 71.

2   John Knox, *The Integrity of Preaching*, Nashville, TN, Abingdon, 1957, p. 24.

3   Dietrich Bonhoeffer, *The Cost of Discipleship*, New York, Macmillan, 1959, p. 37.

4   Harry Emerson Fosdick, *The Living of These Days: An Autobiography,* New York, Harper & Row, 1956, p. 247.

5   James M. Mathes (ed.), *Works – Elder B. W. Stone*, Cincinnati, OH, Moore, Wilstach, Keys and Company, 1859, pp. 140–2.

6   Clyde H. Reid, 'Preaching and the Nature of Communication', *Pastoral Psychology*, 14, 137, 1963.

Part 4

PERSONAL QUALITIES AND THE PREACHER

Introduction to Part 4

Thomas Troeger begins Part 4 with the argument that we need new standards by which to evaluate whether a sermon is effective or not. Classical rhetoric is losing its grip and has been revealed as laden with cultural values and theological presuppositions. Beginning not with principles but with the sermon as actually received, and making imaginative use of poetry and novels, he asks for a fresh concentration on the preacher's personal qualities. Only personal authenticity will carry theological credibility. Preachers who lack integrity or honesty, who are afraid to stay in touch with their humanity and are unwilling to reveal anything of their inner pain or their struggle with the text are likely to be seen as rationalizing or disembodied, or as sacrificing themselves to theory or dogma. 'No preacher can grab us by the entrails who is not in touch with his or her own fundamental humanity.' This is not a licence for embarrassing self-display but for 'the use of the self in order to identify the deep common core we share with other human beings'.

Thomas H. Troeger, 'Emerging New Standards in the Evaluation of Effective Preaching' is from *Worship*, 64, 4, 1990, pp. 290–307.

Preachers speak. So much so that the church often seems to want loquacious talkers more than it wants good listeners. Like Lucky in *Waiting for Godot*, preachers talk as soon as someone puts the talker's hat on their heads, but the danger for institutionalized speechifiers is that they forget who they are. The primary calling of the preacher, however, is a calling to silence. Silence discovers reality, shapes character, bestows form and meaning upon language. In 'Preaching and Silence', John Killinger's appeal for preachers to dwell in and be nourished by silence is illustrated in the story of Brother Antoninus, 'a man whose words still bore the husks of silence upon them'. The article ends with some practical suggestions about letting silence have a greater part in life.

John Killinger, 'Preaching and Silence' was first published in the *Lexington Theological Quarterly*, 19, 1984, pp. 91–101.

Alvin Rueter's article examines aspects of the preaching task that deserve ethical scrutiny. Is the appeal to self-interest always improper? Does the pulpit prophet ever 'dump' his bad temper on his hearers? Does the evangelist coerce or respect those who listen? Are loaded language, sweeping assertions or appeals to prejudice anything more than forms of lying? Should we ever borrow without acknowledging our sources or use other people's experiences without permission? He suggests that such questions are usually ignored in the homiletical literature.

Alvin C. Rueter, 'Ethics in the Pulpit' is from *Word and World*, 8, 2, 1988, pp. 173–8.

For his second article in this collection, David Day takes Jesus' temptations in the wilderness as the framework within which to explore the peculiar temptations of preachers. The opportunity to turn stones into bread is a question about the source of the preacher's life. To settle for anything less than the living word which comes from God's mouth is to risk authenticity. Jumping from the pinnacle of the temple raises questions about the nature of the preacher's relationship with God. To see God as responding when we snap our fingers is to substitute manipulation and provocation for intimacy and trust. The temptation to compromise in order to have the kingdoms of the world surfaces for the preacher in the pressure to shape the message in deference to other voices and other lords than God. But when God is not the focus of our gaze, the first casualty is our integrity.

David Day, 'The Lenten Preacher' is from *The Journal of the College of Preachers*, January 1999, pp. 29–38.

Even though the present situation is markedly different from that in which Martin Luther King preached, Richard Lischer believes that he can be a resource for contemporary preachers. After an introductory section showing that King's practice was in many respects unlike that commended by the homiletical wisdom of the time, Lischer's article highlights first his commitment to preaching whatever his personal exhaustion. Secondly, he notes King's willingness to speak in poetic terms not just as 'illustrations of abstract truth but as extensions of the biblical text' into the congregation. For King metaphor was never mere decoration. It was fundamental to God's way of caring pastorally for people. The third resource for today's preachers lies in King's performance of the Scripture with the congregation. For him word-and-response was a rehearsal for faithful performance of that word in everyday life. 'King's biblical preaching always caught the mood of the text' and always engaged with the question, 'What is God doing today?'

A more detailed exposition of Martin Luther King as preacher can be found in Lischer's book, *The Preacher King: Martin Luther King, Jr. and the Word that Moved America*, New York and Oxford, Oxford University Press, 1995.

Richard Lischer, 'Martin Luther King, Jr's Preaching as a Resource for Preachers' is from the *Journal for Preachers*, 23, 3, 2000, pp. 18–22.

12 Emerging New Standards in the Evaluation of Effective Preaching

Thomas H. Troeger

The shift from traditional homiletics

During this century our imaginative construction of the world has become more and more complex, leaving us less and less certain that the language we have inherited adequately expressed the reality we experience. Just as the general poetics of Western literature 'is distinguished by a gradual dislocation of traditional standards based on the neoclassical interpretation of Aristotle's *Poetics* and on the models of classical antiquity'[1] so also there has been a proliferation of approaches to the shape and style of sermons, calling into question the grip of traditional rhetoric upon homiletics. In part, this reflects the observation of Phillips Brooks that 'Preaching in every age follows, to a certain extent, the changes which come to all literature and life.'[2]

Recent scholarship has examined how classical rhetorical argument may lead to less effective communication because of the way television has conditioned the receptivity of people. In a detailed analysis of why former president Reagan was so effective on television, Kathleen Hall Jamieson shows how he eschewed the elevated station of traditional public speech to become more personal, narrative and graphic. One of his speech writers confesses, 'I was thinking cinematically.'[3]

To acknowledge the effectiveness of this more visual and personal style is not to say that it is the only way to preach. Nor is it to ignore the way in which personal appeal can be used to hide from dealing with hard issues and to cover heartless policies with a congenial veneer. But to understand the personal, narrative mode, particularly as it is practiced through the mass media, is essential to formulating a homiletic that can adequately address the shift in the receptive consciousness of listeners.

Peter S. Hawkins has made a study of how this shift has affected the work of three creative writers – Flannery O'Connor, Walker Percy, Iris Murdoch – who have struggled mightily 'to tell the story of transcendent experience in a period when people commonly lack the words to express it and therefore the means by which to enter it more deeply'.[4] Hawkins calls their efforts 'Strategies of Grace', a phrase that suggests the high self-consciousness about language that is part of postmodern theology. Like the writers whose work Hawkins analyses, preachers need a verbal strategy, a homiletic that takes into account how 'the whole theological frame of reference, concretely expressed in Scripture, that once provided the coherence for western culture and imagination . . . does so no longer'.[5]

Jamieson's analysis of television's rhetoric of images and Hawkins' bold statement of our cultural situation helps to explain why homiletics in recent decades has given so much attention to communications theory and the design of sermons. At their shallowest, such efforts become merely techniques, but at their best they represent an awareness of the need for 'strategies of grace' if the gospel is to be heard.

The difficulties which Peter Hawkins traces in his study of O'Connor, Percy and Mu~~r~~ also evident in the turbulent state of biblical interpretation, theology and hermeneutics. I am c~~o~~ there are more than two ways of looking at this situation, but two come immediately to mind. One ~~is~~ to assess the changes as part of the chaos of our era, the breakdown of order, yet another attack on God and the integrity of God's word.

Although I never want to be so naive as to discredit the effects of sin upon any human undertaking, including the emergence of a new homiletic, I believe another interpretation is more accurate: the contemporary shifts in theological expression are bringing to us a revelation from God. I use the word 'revelation' here in its primary meaning from the Greek, *apokaluptō*, to uncover. Theologies of liberation are uncovering the truth about people, values, social structures, and experience that our inherited way of speaking had hidden.

I am not asserting that every shift of language is a revelation from God. We human beings say a lot of foolish things, especially in the name of God, and there is no need to believe that all changes in our patterns of articulation are holy and good. Jargon comes and goes, and a lot of it is a way of hiding, not uncovering, the truth of our existence. So when I refer to shifts in language being a revelation from God, I am thinking of those transformations which have a moral resonance, which are in harmony with the spirit of the gospel so they provide 'a witness that is life-giving for women and for men . . . a witness that enables us to make choices that are authentic and good, that are faithful to the deepest needs of the human community and consonant with its noblest aspirations'.[6]

The revelation taking place through the shift in theological language is no sudden rending of the heavenly veil. It is more like a dawn that intermittently promises a day of clouds, then clear sky. For a while we see increasing brightness, then it clouds over again. But one thing we know for sure: the sun is coming up.

Because we are just beginning to glimpse what our new world will look like, our articulation of the reality is often tentative and awkward. For the time being we live with an interim homiletic, a period of learning how to speak inclusively with the grace and assurance that belonged to the older poetics that we are leaving behind. The word of God that will emerge through this process 'will never have the same monolithic uniformity for us that it has had for previous generations. We have become acutely aware of how insinuated that Word is in the criss-crossing complexity of the biblical words, of how interdependent that Word is on the conflict of images of God within Scripture. We have also become aware of our own situation-specific location in the structures of history, class, and gender.'[7]

Charting the shape of a new homiletic

Although our standards for preaching and evaluating effective sermons will not be marked by 'monolithic uniformity', certain characteristics of a new homiletic are already beginning to emerge and can help to guide us just as principles of classical rhetoric gave direction to our preaching ancestors. We need such an overview not in order to prescribe the future direction of homiletics but because, as M. H. Abrams notes in an essay on literary poetics: 'Criticism without a theoretical understructure (whether this is developed explicitly or brought in merely as occasion demands) is made up largely of desultory impressions and of unassorted concepts which are supposedly given by "common sense," but are in fact a heritage from earlier critics, in whose writings they may have implicated a whole theoretical system.'[8]

I recall a meeting of the Academy of Homiletics in which we experienced the confusion that results when there is an inadequate 'theoretical understructure' for evaluating sermons. We had all listened to a sermon that was in the classic rhetorical style, and we were now having a conversation

out his sermon. The room divided into two sections. Those sitting up front near
en impressed with the clarity and persuasiveness of the outline, while those in
muring that it would have been a fine sermon for the 1950s but not for the 1980s.
her was a guest there was a reluctance to bring out the conflict over evaluative
as present in the room. But I have not forgotten the scene. I have often seen it
rep. ave listened to the comments of colleagues in responding to various sermons in
chapel or a. vices of ordination and installation.

These experiences make clear that every judgment about a sermon is laden with cultural values and theological presuppositions. But unless we identify the basis of our judgments homiletical criticism will consist 'of desultory impressions and of unassorted concepts which are supposedly given by "common sense"'.

For teachers of homiletics, this is a major issue if not *the* major issue. They need clarity about the assumptions by which they are guiding the class response and by which they are making evaluating statements.

Our starting point: the phenomenon of the sermon as received

The development of a contemporary homiletic begins not by defining first principles but by considering the actual phenomenon of preaching as experienced by members of the congregation. This choice of starting point is a part of what it means to live in this postmodern age of ours: no accepted authority gains automatic acceptance. The authority we acknowledge is the materiality of what happens unfiltered by the bias that things ought to be this way or that way. Such a phenomenological perspective is reinforced by the belief that God does not need to be protected by our presuppositions. To believe in God means we are free to be attentive to what is. God will suffer no loss from our candid analysis of what is in fact happening to members of a congregation during the delivery of a sermon.

I identify them as members of the congregation and not just listeners because people process a sermon with all of themselves, not just their ears but with their eyes and bodies as well. If I am bored, I process the sermon through my lower back and buttocks. If I am engaged by the sermon, I am oblivious to the weakness in my back and the hardness of the pew. One definition of homiletics might be: theology processed through the body.

The British novelist Barbara Pym has a fine scene in her early novel, *Civil to Strangers*, in which she traces the way a sermon is being received by the congregation. We do not hear more than a few brief sentences of the sermon – probably about as many as a lot of our listeners hear! – but through the author's omniscient eye we see the impact of those sentences on the congregation. Pym tells us:

> The rector was pleased with the sermon he preached that Sunday. He had managed to work everything in rather well, and the central idea was most original. He began by talking about the Parable of the Talents, going on from there to the question, the challenge, almost, 'Do we make the most of our lives and opportunities.'
> 'Last week,' he said, 'I had tea with an old lady.'
> There was of course, nothing extraordinary in this. Rectors and vicars all over the country were having tea with old ladies every day. Especially, perhaps, in small country towns where old ladies are predominant.
> 'When I came upon her,' continued the rector, 'she was engaged in doing some very beautiful embroidery. Jacobean embroidery, I believe it is called, although I am not very well qualified to speak of such things,' he added deprecatingly, almost with a smile, or the nearest to a smile that was allowable in the pulpit.
> 'I remarked how beautiful her work was, how much more beautiful than any I had ever seen before.'[9]

These are the opening sentences of the chapter. Notice they describe the sermon from the preacher's perspective, and many of the classic homiletical issues are present. The outline is skillful:

'He had managed to work everything in rather well.' He has a text on which he has based his intro-duction: 'He began by talking about the Parable of the Talents'. He has named his theme: 'Do we make the most of our lives and opportunities.' He has found a choice illustration from experience that will evidently make sense to his congregation: 'Rectors and vicars all over the country were having tea with old ladies every day.' And his delivery is congruent with the established norms of pulpit decorum for this particular parish: he smiles 'the nearest to a smile that was allowable in the pulpit.'

But then the perspective shifts from the pulpit to the pew. Instead of hearing the preacher's words we begin to see the impact on the consciousness of the congregation. 'Who was this old lady? wondered some of the female members of the congregation, for they did embroidery, and the rector had not had tea with any of them last week. And yet whose work could be more beautiful than theirs? It was each one's private opinion that her work was much too good for the Parish Sale. One only did it because of the Good Cause and the dear rector.'

While the rector continues – '"Some people don't put in enough stitches," repeated the rector in a slow emphatic voice' – Pym multiplies the number of perspectives on the sermon. There is Cassandra, a beautiful young woman married to a boring writer named Adam. In the course of the sermon, she comes to realize that she is 'the old woman' the rector visited, and she is delighted with the preacher's ruse to hide her identity because it enables her to imagine life as a widow, freed at last from her husband. Meanwhile, Adam is sitting there annoyed with the preacher because he has quoted from Keats while ignoring Adam's own published work. Then there is Janie, the preacher's daughter who is 'whiling away the time by staring at Mr Paladin', the curate to whom she is considering marriage. And finally there is the newcomer in town, Mr Tilos, who is lusting for Cassandra and about whom there has been no small amount of gossip in recent weeks.

Pym's comic wit illuminates the web of meanings, fantasies and stories that holds the congregation together. What is the sermon? Is it merely the rector's words? Or is the sermon the motion of that web in response to the preacher? Or perhaps it is more accurate to speak of three sets of sermons:

1. the sermon the rector delivered
2. the sermon as responded to by each individual
3. The sermon that is defined as the conglomerate effect of all the individually heard sermons upon the corporate life of the congregation.

At the very least, a postmodern homiletic is one that tends to the complexities of the sermon as a corporate event. It is a homiletic that considers the total constellation of forces that are shaping the reception as well as the delivery of the sermon. We, therefore, find ourselves having to define more closely the transaction between preacher and congregation and what qualities of personal presentation best serve to express and awaken the living truth of God in the congregation.

Personal authenticity as the expression of theological credibility

Attention to the person or character of the preacher is not new. As Richard Lischer points out in the introduction of his anthology, *Theories of Preaching*: 'Most homiletical treatises after Augustine and through the Middle Ages (e.g., Alan of Lille and Guibert of Nogent) deal with the authority, formation, and holiness of the one who is appointed to preach. The same concerns are evident in seventeenth, eighteenth, and nineteenth century classics on the ministry, whether by Baxter, Herbert, Spener, or Schleiermacher.'[10]

Contemporary homileticians need to clarify how that traditional concern for the character of the preacher is redefined by twentieth century thought and experience. The rise of psychological culture since Freud and the atrocities perpetuated through the quasi-religious appeals of tyrants have reshaped the way we think about 'authority, formation, and holiness'. I find in myself a reluctance to employ these terms too quickly for fear of covering the sharp issues of personal integrity and group dynamics with a veneer of religiosity. Sounding religious becomes suspect when we consider the pietisms of the despotic. Recent experience with the electronic church and the scandal attached to preachers in the public eye has only served to reinforce this suspicion.

To distinguish the difference between how the character of preachers used to be judged and how it is judged now, we will compare two poems that describe pulpiteers who lack the requisite personal integrity for their calling. The first poem is from the eighteenth century by Timothy Dwight and the second is by the contemporary British poet, C. H. Sisson.

> Here stood Hypocrisy, in sober brown,
> His sabbath face all sorrow'd with a frown.
> A dismal tale he told of dismal times,
> And this sad world brimfull of saddest crimes;
> Furrowed his cheeks with tears for others' sin,
> But closed his eyelids on the hell within.
> There smiled the smooth Divine, unused to wound
> The sinner's heart with hell's alarming sound.
> No terrors on his gentle tongue attend,
> No grating truths the nicest ear offend.
> That strange 'New Birth', that methodistic 'Grace'
> Nor in his heart, nor sermons, found a place.
> Plato's fine tales he clumsily retold,
> Trite, fireside, moral see-saws, dull as old;
> His Christ and Bible placed at good remove
> Guilt hell-deserving, and forgiving love.
> 'Twas best, he said, mankind should cease to sin;
> Good fame required it; so did peace within.[11]

Even before we consider the content, we are struck by the refinements of the style, the regularity of the meter, the use of rhymed couplets, and the patrician elegance that hones to a keen edge the blade of sarcasm.

The charge against this pulpiteer, however, is much less refined than the mannered poetics: 'Here stood Hypocrisy . . . ' The poet draws his portrait from a perspective of absolute conviction about the doctrine of the gospel. There is a precise and clear standard for effective preaching: congruence between the one true theology and the speech and behavior of the preacher.

Although concern for theological integrity does not disappear when we turn to the poem by Sisson, it is expressed in a different fashion, reflecting the impact of post-Freudian, psychological culture. The poet addresses his lines to John Donne (1572–1631), famous not only for his poetry and preaching but also for the passionate loves of his youth:

> You brought body and soul to this church
> Walking there through the park alive with deer
> But now what animal has climbed into your pulpit?
> One whose pretension is that the fear
> Of God has heated him into a spirit
> An evaporated man no physical ill can hurt.
>
> Well might you hesitate at the Latin gate
> Seeing such apes denying the church of God:
> I am grateful particularly that you were not a saint
> But extravagant whether in bed or in your shroud

You would understand that in the presence of folly
I am not sanctified but angry.

Come down and speak to the men of ability
On the Sevenoaks platform and tell them
That at your Saint Nicholas the faith
Is not exclusive in the fools it chooses
That the vain, the ambitious and the highly sexed
Are the natural prey of the incarnate Christ.[12]

Not the correctness of dogma but the authenticity of the preacher's humanity becomes the measure of homiletical credibility. This shift in standards, however, is not a way of reducing theology to psychology. Instead, such authenticity is in the service of making clear the gospel: 'That the vain, the ambitious and the highly sexed/Are the natural prey of the incarnate Christ.' Notice here the economy of traditional religious language. We almost do not expect the final two words. Given our society, the sentence might have ended this way: 'The vain, the ambitious, and the highly sexed/Are the natural prey of commercial exploitation'. We all know that. But for the poet they are the 'natural prey of the incarnate Christ'. The poem ends with the center of the gospel; the incarnate Christ, and in that way it is as theologically faithful as Timothy Dwight's.

But how different the manner by which that point is achieved. For Timothy Dwight hypocrisy means replacing the gospel and its severities with a life that pleasures in the flesh. At a later point in his poem Dwight describes how the preacher 'Most daintily on pampered turkeys dined;/Nor shrunk with fasting, nor with study pined.' But for Sisson hypocrisy is denial of the flesh, the inauthenticity of the preacher who thinks himself 'An evaporated man no physical ill can hurt.' A disembodied preacher cannot credibly proclaim the incarnate Christ.

This yearning for someone in the pulpit who is fully in touch with her or his humanity represents the secularization of the holiness of the preacher. At its worst, such a homiletic results in preachers sharing inappropriately about themselves and using the pulpit to meet their own needs instead of declaring the gospel. But this distortion of a homiletic of authenticity does not invalidate what Sisson is getting at in his poem. For when such a homiletic is exercised with faith and grace, then preaching becomes nothing less than a medium of salvation.

Philip Hallie gives us a powerful example of this in his description of Pastor André Trocmé, who led his congregation into a heroic ministry of saving Jews from the Nazi holocaust. André's brother, Francis, recorded the impact of one of the preacher's sermons during the occupation: ' . . . he is a pulpit orator who is absolutely original, who surpasses in authority anyone I have ever heard speak from the *chaire*. He begins in a simple, familiar mood, starting with recent events, everyday or religious, then he raises himself, little by little, analyses his own feeling and thought, confesses his own heart with a sincerity and a perspicacity which disturb one; he uses the popular language, and sometimes crude language . . . . Is he not going to fall into trivialities? But no! See him there raising himself up . . . he climbs, climbs always higher . . . he draws us to the peaks of religious thought . . . and once we are at the summit, he makes us hover in a true ecstasy; then gently . . . he descends slowly to earth and gathers you in a feeling of peace which gives the last word "Amen" all the meaning the word has etymologically. One sits there afterwards . . . eyes clouded with tears, as if one has been listening to music that has seized you by your entrails.'[13]

No preacher can grab us by the entrails who is not in touch with his or her own fundamental humanity. That is why Sisson says earlier in his poem: 'Bring out your genitals and your theology'.[14] Unless we face the physicality of our being and its place in driving us to preach we will have a tendency to become inauthentic, to preach as though the goal for our listeners is to attain the 'evaporated' state of the parson in Sisson's poem.

A passion for defining what constitutes effective human authenticity in the pulpit illumines the homiletical studies of Hans van der Geest. Drawing on the analysis of 200 worship services as well as interviews with parishioners, he arrives at the same principle that Sisson achieves through poetic inspiration: 'I will awaken deep experiences in others to the extent that I am able to reach myself. If I overplay feelings of revenge because they are indeed terrifying, or if I rationalize a pious faith in order to agree with a theological theory, then I am closing myself off, and in the worship service I am drawing from a well which is going dry. That level of yearning and security is reached only by preachers who also seek access to their own interior, an interior which at first glance normally appears comical, childish, and not really ready to be shown in public. Preachers with compulsive tendencies become so afraid that it's painful for them to find that path to themselves'.[15]

This is not self-display, but the use of the self to identify the deep common core we share with other human beings. Again and again in preaching class I have seen these understandings of the self confused. A frequent pattern goes something like this: a student tells an unresolved, intimate story that leaves the congregation embarrassed and wondering how to care for the person in the pulpit. But in the parts of the sermon that deal explicitly with the biblical text or doctrine or theological tradition, the student's eyes grow dull and the voice becomes obsequious to the truth that 'ought to be believed'. The net effect is to leave the congregation centered on the preacher and disinterested in the text since it has been presented as an authority that cannot be questioned or challenged.

When we untangle the mixed responses of the congregation after the sermon is over, we often discover that the entire performance was a circumlocution of the preacher's unacknowledged resistance to the passage or doctrine which is supplying the theological warrant for the sermon. To use van der Geest's terms, such preachers are rationalizing 'a pious faith in order to agree with a theological theory' and thus 'closing' themselves off.

Amazing things begin to happen when we ask these preachers to tell about the process of creating the sermon. They tell how they struggled with the text, resisting and fighting it in their hearts even while they made dutiful notes and sketched an outline of the message. As the preachers speak the truth of what happened to them, the class begins to acknowledge their own ambiguities, and life is illumined. Van der Geest believes this kind of honesty is essential to the creation of contemporary sermons: 'Contact with oneself is of decisive importance while preparing a sermon. The idea for the sermon emerges only in a creative restlessness, when the preacher dares ignore those constricting thoughts acquired elsewhere, thoughts that will be needed again only when it is time to examine the ideas.'[16]

Hans van der Geest is performing an invaluable service to homiletics by getting us to look at the exposed nerve of preaching, the sermon as it is actualized through the preacher and the response of the congregation. It is from this ganglion of dynamics that the real theology of the sermon emerges.

Authenticity as shaped by gender and culture

Yet theological education has often devalued and obscured the complexities which van der Geest identifies as central to how people respond to a preacher: 'In formal training the word "objective" is quickly equated with "avoidance of existential areas". Faith can quickly be reduced to theology, and thus life to a theory, and for young theologians this often means they lose contact with the roots of their vocational choice.'[17] Now, however, that situation is changing. A homiletic of personal authenticity for the pulpit is emerging in North America through the impact of women clergy and through an increasing sense of the pluralism of the world and the church. Faced with a greater spectrum of homiletical styles we are coming to appreciate that many of our so-called objective standards are in fact the expression of our gender and the values and politics of the communities that have raised us.

I would not want to characterize any one style of preaching as exclusively male or female for fear of dishonoring individual gifts. Nevertheless, I believe that what scholars have discovered to be distinctive about women's writing is also distinctive about their preaching: 'The formulation that female identity is a process stresses the fluid and flexible aspects of women's primary identities. One reflection of this fluidity is that women's writing often does not conform to the generic prescriptions of the male canon. Recent scholars conclude that autobiographies by women tend to be less linear, unified, and chronological than men's autobiographies. . . . Because of the continual crossing of self and other, women's writing may blur the public and private and defy completion.'[18]

Before we criticize such an approach in the pulpit on the basis of an assumedly objective theology we need to ask if the true source is not our disappointment that the sermon 'does not conform to the generic prescriptions of the male canon'.

Virginia Woolf claimed that 'A woman's writing is always feminine; it cannot help being feminine; at its best it is most feminine; the only difficulty lies in defining what we mean by feminine.'[19] I believe that we are facing the same situation in homiletics. The gathering witness of women in the pulpit will disclose over time the shape of this new poetics. Meanwhile, women's preaching will in part be an expression of the continuing search 'To celebrate uniquely female powers of creativity without perpetuating destructive feminine socialization'.[20]

Recognizing the projective nature of our homiletic

Some readers may protest that preaching and the theology which feeds it should not be a search to celebrate either female or male powers of creativity. The task of the pulpit is to declare God's initiative toward us in creating and redeeming the world. But to speak of 'God's initiative' is no less a human formulation about the nature of the divine than any other. It still depends upon our language and our creative skills in employing that language.

The time has come for the church to face honestly the projective nature of all human talk about God. Such an acknowledgment does nothing to corrupt our belief in the One who braided the fibres of the brain and filled it with electric juice in such a manner that the configuration of cells would give rise to consciousness that seeks to know and adores the source of creation. When I consider the complexities of the physiological and environmental factors which would lead to such projective speech, I find myself 'lost in wonder, love and praise'.

There is, then, no need to hide from the projective nature of religious language for fear we will lose our faith in God. Besides, that strategy is no longer available to us. Third world and feminist theologies have demonstrated that the inherited imagery for God and the understandings of humanity which flow from that imagery are biased by our experience and collude with oppressive social structures. The effort to delineate an articulation of transcendence which is beyond critique keeps failing because on our multicultural globe people live in a plurality of imaginatively constructed worlds. Subsequently their expression of reality differs in profound ways. Most of us who teach homiletics find ourselves facing this diversity of expressive means in our classes, and it becomes a major factor in clarifying our standards of evaluation for effective preaching. This is more than a pedagogical issue. It takes us to theological depths, to unresolved questions about the meaning of faith and tradition in a pluralistic world. How, for example, can the church fervently proclaim the gospel while relinquishing the absolutism of universal dogmatic assurance that has been discredited by a pluralistic world?

The great Japanese writer, Shusaku Endo, demonstrates how complex this is in his novel *Silence*, which records the efforts of some Christian missionaries to Japan during the 1600s when the native rulers had decided to make the Christians retract their faith. Although the work can be read as a historical novel, the tone of the language and the conflict of cultures suggest that the author is in fact exploring the meaning of religious speech for our own age, an exploration which we homileticians undertake every time we evaluate the effectiveness of a sermon!

Father Rodrigues, the main character, is brought before a panel of samurai who question him:

> The samurai on the extreme right said in a voice charged with emotion: 'Father, we are deeply moved by the strength of your determination in coming here from thousands of miles away through all kinds of hardships. Undoubtedly you have suffered deeply.'
>
> There was a gentle tone in his words, and this very gentleness pierced the priest's heart, giving him pain. . . .
>
> 'Father, we are not disputing about the right and wrong of your doctrine. In Spain and Portugal and such countries it may be true. The reason we have outlawed Christianity in Japan is that, after deep and earnest consideration, we find its teaching of no value for the Japan of today.'
>
> The interpreter immediately came to the heart of the discussion. The old man in front with the big ears kept looking down on the priest sympathetically.
>
> 'According to our way of thinking, truth is universal,' said the priest, at last returning the smile of the old man. 'A moment ago you officials expressed sympathy for the suffering I have passed through. One of you spoke words of warm consolation for my traveling thousands of miles of sea over such a long period to come to your country. If we did not believe that truth is universal, why should so many missionaries endure these hardships? It is precisely because truth is common to all countries and all times that we call it truth. If a true doctrine were not true alike in Portugal and Japan we could not call it "true". . . . '
>
> The interpreter slowly translated the words of yet another samurai. 'A tree which flourishes in one kind of soil may wither if the soil is changed. As for the tree of Christianity, in a foreign country its leaves may grow thick and the buds may be rich, while in Japan the leaves wither and no bud appears. Father, have you never thought of the difference in the soil, the difference in the water?'
>
> . . . The priest lowering his eyes spoke quietly. 'No matter what I say I will not change your minds. And I also have no intention of altering my way of thinking.'[21]

Notice that there is a moment of human connectedness in the midst of confrontation. It comes at the point of identifying with human pain. The first samurai who speaks acknowledges how the priest has suffered and that acknowledgment brings a moment of profound human understanding: 'There was a gentle tone in his words, and this very gentleness pierced the priest's heart, giving him pain.'

But the priest a few paragraphs later refers to that pain not in order to claim their common humanity but in order to win his argument: 'If we did not believe that truth is universal, why should so many missionaries endure these hardships?' The actual universal truth – that people suffer and that the identification of our pain by another penetrates to the heart – this truth gets buried beneath the priest's urgent attempt to persuade the samurai of the truth of his case. His is a classical forensic appeal, making a claim to universal truth that can be persuasively argued.

An authentic contemporary homiletics does not clutch so fast at proving the right rational formulation. Instead, it begins at the level of human suffering and the trust and empathy awakened when our pain is recognized by another. Shusaku Endo makes it clear that it was this quality, not the classical homiletics, which first won a hearing for the gospel in Japan. Ironically, Father Rodrigues understood this at an earlier point in his career. Here is his description and analysis of why the efforts of his missionary predecessors were effective: 'I tell you the truth – for a long, long time these farmers have worked like horses and cattle; and like horses and cattle they have died. . . . For the first time they have met men who treated them like human beings. It was the human kindness and charity of the fathers that touched their hearts.'[22]

Notice the definition of truth here: the suffering of the people. The difference between this blood and sweat understanding of truth and the disembodied argument Rodrigues later has with the samurai about universal truth is the difference between a homiletic which starts with the materiality of our existence and one which works from the assumption of a superior truth that is not smudged with experience.

Imagine if Father Rodrigues were not so anxious to debate the nature of universal truth, but said what had happened to his heart when the samurai said he had suffered. Of course, it is only a novel and even in real life recognition of our common humanity through suffering is only the beginning of understanding. But it is the kind of beginning which continues in spirit the beginning of the gospel: Emmanuel, God with us, the identification with human suffering, a willingness to lay aside the prerogatives of transcendence to be fully present with a world in pain.

Our preaching must be as humble as our God. We must be willing to restrain our religious language and the historically conditioned imaginative construction of the world that it represents, so that our articulation of reality may be renewed by the source to whom we give witness. This may sound like blasphemy to those who understandably, like myself, cherish the language of faith with which we were raised. I am not talking about the abandonment of our inherited religious language but its purging and renewal through its disciplined and parsimonious use.

Throughout Endo's novel, Father Rodrigues keeps throwing against the sky his plea that God will speak and break heaven's silence in the face of the torturing of Christians. But it is only after Rodrigues himself has given up the public expression of his faith that Christ speaks to him. 'I was not silent. I suffered beside you.'[23] It is not necessary that preachers give up the public expression of their faith! But in a postmodern pluralistic homiletic, that expression will come out of the crucible of silence and suffering and an increasing openness to those expressions of truth that lie beyond the traditional articulation of our historically conditioned imaginative worlds.

Therefore, to reach toward an authentic way of evaluating sermons in our time will require far more than lists of rhetorical criteria indicating how well constructed and delivered the sermon is as a piece of oral communication. Of course, we have an obligation to tend to the technical skills of clear organization and vivid expression, but all the oratorical skill in the world will not add up to a hill of beans if our evaluation does not lead into the deeper personal, cultural and theological realities that arise from the struggle for an authentic Christian witness in our postmodern pluralistic world. I believe that if we have the courage to teach homiletics at this depth, our students will become more effective preachers because they will approach the proclamation of the gospel believing the salvation of the world depends on their efforts.

Notes

1   Alex Preminger (ed.), *Princeton Encyclopedia of Poetry and Poetics*, enlarged edition, Princeton, Princeton University Press, 1974, p. 503.

2   Phillips Brooks, 'Lectures on Preaching', in Richard Lischer (ed.), *Theories of Preaching: Selected Readings in the Homiletical Tradition*, Durham, NC, Labyrinth, 1987, p. 16.

3   Peggy Noonan, quoted in Kathleen Hall Jamieson, *Eloquence in an Electronic Age: The Transformation of Political Speechmaking*, New York, Oxford University Press, 1988, p. 162.

4   Peter S. Hawkins, *The Language of Grace,* Cambridge, MA, Cowley, 1983, p. 4.

5   Hawkins, 1983, p. 1.

6   Margaret A. Farley, 'Feminist Consciousness and the Interpretation of Scripture', in Letty M. Russell (ed.), *Feminist Interpretation of the Bible,* Philadelphia, Westminster, 1985, p. 41.

7   Mark L. Wallace, 'Theological Table-Talk: Theology Without Revelation?', *Theology Today* 45, 2, 1988, p. 213.

8   Preminger, 1974, p. 648.

9   Barbara Pym, *Civil to Strangers and Other Writings,* New York, E. P. Dutton, 1987, p. 90. All subsequent quotations from Pym are from the pages that follow in the novel.

10   Lischer, 1987, p. 3.

11   Timothy Dwight, from 'The Triumph of Infidelity' in Donald Davie (ed.), *The New Oxford Book of Christian Verse,* New York, Oxford University Press, 1981, p. 206.

12   C. H. Sisson, from 'A Letter to John Donne', in Davie, 1981, p. 285.

13   Phillip Hallie, *Lest Innocent Blood Be Shed: The Story of the Village of Le Chambon and How Goodness Happened There*, New York, Harper & Row, 1979, p. 171.

14   Davie, 1981, p. 284.

15   Hans van der Geest, 'Presence in the Pulpit', in Lischer, 1987, p. 85.

16   Van der Geest, in Lischer, 1987, p. 85.

17   Van der Geest, in Lischer, 1987, p. 83.

18   Judith Kegan Gardinar, 'On Female Identity', in Elizabeth Abel (ed.), *Writing and Sexual Difference,* Chicago, University of Chicago Press, 1982, p. 185.

19   Quoted by Elaine Showalter, 'Feminist Criticism in the Wilderness', in Abel, 1982, p. 14.

20   Susan Gubar, ' "The Blank Page" and Female Creativity', in Abel, 1982, p. 92.

21   Shusaku Endo, tr. William Johnston, *Silence*, New York, Taplinger, 1980, pp. 166ff.

22   Endo, 1980, p. 49.

23   Endo, 1980, p. 285.

13   Preaching and Silence

John Killinger

There are many dimensions to preaching – the text, the congregation, the preacher's imagination, the chemistry of the moment. But one stands above all – the speaking. The preacher may be convert, visionary, mystic, one beggar sharing bread with another. But to most people he or she is preacher, speaker, talker. If there is a speech to be given, let the preacher do it; the preacher is a talker, a *Spieler*, a spellbinder. Ministerial committees are *pulpit* committees, and they are invariably more interested in hearing a candidate preach than in listening to the story of his or her pilgrimage in the faith.

I have on my desk a letter from the parents of a former student who has been unable to find employment as a minister. He is a shy, sensitive boy who lives tremblingly in the Spirit. He was an excellent student and wrote brilliant papers. But no church has proved interested in his experience – only in the fact that he is not a hail-fellow-well-met. What can I say to his parents who are anxious for his welfare? Only that the church wants able talkers, not good listeners. Dozens of his class-mates, more loquacious than he, have had no difficulty finding positions.

The preacher as talker. Did Beckett have this person in mind when he wrote the part of Lucky in *Waiting for Godot*? Lucky is a menial, a factotum who carries suitcases and is led about on a rope. He sounds like a minister, doesn't he? And he has one unique characteristic. Every time someone puts a hat on his head, he begins to spout philosophy. Not anything coherent, really, but bits and pieces of philosophical jargon from the entire spectrum of Western thought. When someone takes his hat off, he stops. The other characters have fun putting the hat on and snatching it off. They put it on and he talks, they steal it off and he stops. Whether Beckett meant it or not, Lucky does remind you of some preachers, doesn't he? Hopefully no one too close to yourself, but someone you know. On, off. As smooth as clockwork – or Sunday morning.

It is a danger endemic in the professional ministry that we forget who we are and become talkers, speechifiers, nonstop voices inwardly despairing of their authenticity, even of their calling. Like Lucky, we become institutionalized, geared to automatic speech at a given signal – the lowering of a hat or the arrival of the 11 o'clock hour. What we say often becomes less important to us than the fact that we have something to say, can say it well, and are prepared to say it at the appointed time. In our preoccupation with ancient models of ministry who were *sent to speak*, we overlook the prior fact, that those who were sent were persons who had *seen and heard*. After twenty or thirty years spent in proliferating speech in the pulpit, we awaken with a dryness in our throats – maybe even in our souls – and realize we have been speaking without seeing and hearing.

The Gospel of Mark is especially hard on this in disciples. Again and again the author pillories those who avow discipleship yet fail to see or hear what the Master is doing in their midst. Even when he has fed multitudes in the wilderness, not once but twice, they quibble over the scarcity of bread in their midst – someone has forgotten to bring along an extra supply in the boat – and Jesus must remind them that the supplier of needs and worker of miracles is among them! And at the end

Editorial note: This paper was presented at Lexington Theological Seminary as part of the Fall Lectures, 1983.

of the Gospel, when the two women go to the tomb and find it empty, with an angel there who directs them to tell the disciples that Jesus is risen and precedes them into Galilee, they run off and tell no one, because they are afraid – because their attachment to ministry has been too shallow and they have not seen in Christ the fulfillment of the promise of victory over fear and death.

You cannot preach, Mark was saying, until you have seen and heard and felt and known for yourself the mysteries we are given to declare. There is no preaching without presence, no speaking without listening, no talking without silence.

Our calling, before anything else, is a calling to silence. Not to speak, but to be silent. To realize, as Isaiah did, that our lips are not worthy to utter the counsels of God, the secrets of life. 'Woe is me, for I am a person of unclean lips.' Before we say anything – on any Sunday or before any civic club – we must wait before God in silence. Only in this manner do we create sacred space at the center of the world. We do not do it by talking. We do it by listening.

This was the secret of the great power in Thomas Merton's life. His years of silence in the little monastery at Gethsemani, in Kentucky, fitted him with a wisdom and sensitivity rare in any age. He once described his anguish at leaving the monastery to travel into Louisville. The noise outside the monastery was deafening to him. Everywhere sound seemed to blare out and attack him, as if it were demonic and wished to destroy him. I realized, he said, that that little monastery was the linchpin holding the entire world together. If that small space of quietude were to be destroyed, the whole cosmos would be endangered.[1]

It was this, not his gift for poetry or his constantly stumbling into publicity, that equipped Merton for modern sainthood. It was the power of silence and meditation he let loose on the world. An antidote to the rapacious powers of speech gone trivial. And if we wish to be more effective ministers in the world, most of us will do well to study Merton's example. It is not better preaching we should strive for, but better presence. Not more glibness of tongue – the world is quite mad enough on that score – but more quietude of soul.

I

You see, *Silence discovers reality.* Words do too, of course; but only words formed out of silence; not words wildly ricocheting through the world in search of a target. James Dickey learned this when he followed a hunch and left his job on Madison Avenue for the chaster realms of poetry. 'I think it's absolutely absurd', he said, 'to talk about integrity when you're in something like the advertising business. There's no such thing; it's already a sell-out. The main thing is to be as profitably crooked as you can. It's essentially immoral to say things that people pay you to say.'[2] Having put the cover on his typewriter and ceased to write advertising jingles, Dickey was able to go further and say that 'business offices cut off a great many potentialities in human beings.'[3] He was talking about reality; about being open to the world around himself, open to the possibilities. The paid-for wordsmithing negated the possibilities, nixed the discoveries.

The point is, reality is palpable. It breathes in the dark, the way the *nada* or nothingness does in Hemingway's little short story 'A Clean, Well-Lighted Place'. One can feel it, brush against it, even taste it, when one is silent. But it is not amenable to noise, chatter, idle gossip, professional analysis. or cliché.

Eventually, words are necessary, so that we can 'see' what we have been listening to. But first there must be the quiet, else there is nothing to describe. Which is why Paul the preacher went into the wilderness for three years before speaking, went into eclipse before his nearly incessant verbalizing; he had to *know* what he was talking about, know it in the Hebrew sense of having sexual intercourse with it, interpenetrating it, and being penetrated.

A lay person asked me recently of people who live in monastic settlements, 'Isn't it a useless way of life?' 'Only', I replied, 'if you think of life in terms of activity, not being.' And only, I might add now, if we think of silence as a negative quality, or passive, instead of positive and dynamic.

Zen Buddhism understands this well. And so did Robert Pirsig when he wrote that lovely book *Zen and the Art of Motorcycle Maintenance*. You remember how the book began: Pirsig was discussing the difference between riding a motorcycle and traveling in a car. In the car, he said, everything one sees is framed, almost as if it were on TV. The rider is protected from immediate involvement in the scene. On a motorcycle, everything is immediate. Nothing separates the rider from his or her environment. The world rushes in, almost with suffocating force. There is no safe distance from impressions; everything is instantaneous. Those unaccustomed to Zen might suppose it to be like the experience of riding in a car – tranquil, distanced, safe. Not so. Zen is like riding the motorcycle. Meditation and awareness carry the traveler into life with immediacy, so that experiences are vivid, first-hand, even shocking.

You do understand what I'm saying, don't you? Preaching that does not begin in silence is like Dickey's advertising jingles – it is merely paid-for and immoral speech. And it is like the car ride as opposed to the motorcycle ride. It is safe, It gives people a comfortable, well-distanced view of the countryside without any immediate involvement. It is, in that sense, what the Old Testament calls 'false prophecy'. It is speech that costs nothing, demands nothing of the speaker, threatens nothing to the hearer.

II

Silence discovers reality. *It also shapes character*. Only in silence, in the space between noise, speech, and activity, is there room for a person to become focused, to achieve gravity and centeredness. Only in silence, in waiting before the mystery of existence itself, can one attain what Mary C. Richards has called 'an incorruptible instinct for wholeness'.[4] Only in silence, in brooding upon the fact that there is a world, that there is eternity, does one become endowed with true worldliness and true everlastingness.

We understand this in certain persons who have dwelled in silence and then entered the public sphere, bringing with them the aura of their quietude, trailing it like gossamer threads of being. Merton, when he emerged from Gethsemani. Camus, who grew up in the presence of a deaf mother, and later wrote that the two abiding influences on his writing were the brilliance of the Algerian sunscape and the impenetrable silence of his mother. Flannery O'Connor and her peacocks. The Yaqui soothsayer Don Juan, whose reticence is described in the Carlos Castanada books. Loren Eiseley, whose elegiac writings leapt like a triggered spring from his years of lonely abandonment on a farm near Death Valley, where he was recuperating from tuberculosis.

Max Picard, in *The World of Silence*, speaks of an actual 'substance' that people carry with them when they have lived in silence:

> A man in whom the substance of silence is still an active force carries the silence into every movement. His movements are therefore slow and measured. They do not jolt violently against each other: they are borne by the silence, they are simply the waves of silence. There is nothing vague and undefined about such a man, nothing vague about his language: the fact that his movement and his words are made individually distinct from one another by the intervening silence makes his whole personality clearer than if the silence were not there at all and the man and his words were all part of one continuous noise.[5]

This is why there is a luminousness about certain gurus – the 'substance of silence' carries over from their hours of meditation into their public appearances. It explains the weight of Moses' personality when he came down from the mountain, or Jesus' after a period of prayer. It is the secret of a modern-day prophet like Will Campbell, who lives on a cold-comfort farm in Mt Juliet, Tennessee, rocking on his front porch and playing a guitar, and comes out of retirement occasionally to deliver a bundle of pronouncements cooked up over the open fire of full concentration.

'Shy men', said Phillips Brooks, 'make the best preachers.' That is because shy persons live much in the world of silence. They are like the man described by Rilke, whose ear was closed by a god so he could hear no sound but the god's own voice, and not be led astray by 'turbid and ephemeral' noises.[6] Chattering, voluble ministers often make a botch of the gospel by treating it too glibly, too freely, too casually. Having abandoned silence, they have ceased to be formed by the eternal Word, and preach out of threadbare memories, out of mere wisps of experiences they once had but can no longer lay hold upon. Or perhaps that is the wrong way of putting it: they *can* still lay hold upon their past experiences, but the nature of experience is such that it serves reality only when we submit to it, relinquishing all self-control, not when we attempt to lay hold of it. The utilization of experience exhausts experience, sucks its being, vampirelike, and leaves it but an empty shell of itself.

Only by living in silence – by continuing to live in silence – do we continue to be shaped by the Spirit of God, so that we have mediatorial power in a world being constantly destroyed by noise.

III

As silence gives shape to human character, so also *it bestows form and meaning upon language.* Where there is no silence, words become weightless, slippery, elusive. As T. S. Eliot says, they

> slip, slide, perish,
> Decay with imprecision, will not stay in place,
> Will not stay still.[7]

There is a crisis of language in our world today. It has nothing to do with the pluralism of tongues; that, in fact, encourages silence by refusing an easy reductionism. Few things are healthier for the soul than days spent in foreign countries where one understands nothing of the language and is thrown back upon more elemental means of communication, or upon no communication at all, evoking new reverence for the immensity of life in the world. Instead, the crisis of language concerns the overuse, the overextension, of language, the constant barrage of verbiage from newspapers, magazines, television, government, school, church. The world has fallen into cliché. Cliché is the opposite of silence. It is language from which all silence has been removed.

Take the figure of the media evangelist, who has renounced silence for network coverage, for the ministry of blitz and bits, spiel and spoil. You know how little silence there is in his program, and how thin his character appears, like the patina of ions forming a picture on the tube. There is something feverish about the program, as if its makers insisted on wall-to-wall words, with no chinks of silence left, as if silence would rise up and destroy the spell of the hype, the hard-sell, the gimmicky gospel. The program is all speech and noise, and yet none of the speech is memorable, because it has been deprived of all silence. The program, far from healing the sickness of language, exacerbates its illness.

I have mentioned Samuel Beckett. As a modern poet, Beckett has been continuously engaged with the problem of language. It is interesting to recall that he began his career in Paris as an unofficial secretary and confidant to that voluble Irishman James Joyce, from whose pen words flowed with diarrheaic profligacy. Beckett has tried to restore silence to language. His plays are filled with pauses, mime, gesture. He is said to have chosen Roger Blin to direct *Waiting for Godot* because he went to a theater where Blin was directing a Strindberg play to a nearly empty house and decided that it was the proper atmosphere for his own dramatic [work].

In one play, Beckett deals forthrightly with the language crisis. The play is called *Krapp's Last Tape*. Krapp is an old man who has talked incessantly all his life, recording his thoughts for posterity on a tape recorder. He sits on the stage listening to parts of speeches from his lifetime. The words have an empty, weightless quality about them. He cannot bear to hear them any more. Impatiently, he strikes the 'fast forward' button and sends the tape speeding ahead, dipping in here and there in the attempt to locate a passage he can really bear to listen to. Only an occasional fragment holds any interest; it is usually the record of some sexual experience from his earlier years. At the end of the play, Krapp has drunk too much again, and his head falls to the table as the end of a reel of tape flaps idly on the machine. We have learned nothing at all of his life or character – and, indeed, suspect that he has no character – for his life has been all rhetoric and no silence.

What if every preacher – every media evangelist – were condemned to spend eternity auditing his or her sermons on a tape-recorder? It is a dreary, unbearable prospect, isn't it? Language is one of the great delights of the human species. Yet language deprived of silence is tormenting. It may even be demonic.

Here is what Picard says:

When language is no longer related to silence it loses its source of refreshment and renewal and therefore something of its substance. Language today seems to talk automatically, out of its own strength, and, emptying and scattering itself, it seems to be hastening to an end. There is something hard and obstinate in language today, as though it were making a great effort to remain alive in spite of its emptiness. There is also something desperate in it, as though it were expecting its emptiness to lead it to a relentless end, and it is this alternation of obstinacy and despair which makes it so restless. By taking it away from silence we have made language an orphan. The tongue we speak today is no longer a mother-tongue but rather an orphaned tongue. It sometimes seems as though man were ashamed of the language he has separated from its parent: man hardly feels he can dare to communicate his words to another. He talks more to himself and into himself, as though he wanted to crush, crumple, and destroy the words he speaks and throw them like ruins down into the emptiness of his own soul.

It is only in the language of the poets that the real word, the word connected with silence, still sometimes appears.[8]

I have felt that, haven't you? That only the poets are speaking the real word, the one connected with silence? It is what James Dickey discovered, and why he left the world of Madison Avenue. He tried for a while to live in both worlds, writing advertising copy by day and poetry by night, but learned that he could not do it, that he could not be chaste at night after being a prostitute all day. William McPheeters, a Tennessee artist, once painted a self-portrait: it was of a blind man with no hands. This was his way of suggesting the impossibility of the artist's task – to see and paint reality. And it also defines the artist's reverence for the world, that keeps him or her in touch with silence, with the power of the primordial and uncreated that gives meaning to human utterance.

It was Christina Rossetti, I believe, who once could not sleep for days because she had written the name of God on an envelope and it had been whisked away by the wind and carried madly into the crowds on the streets, whence she could not recover it.

We would do well, if we are concerned about the weight of our words as preachers, to develop a similar reticence. We talk much of the waning authority of the minister. But the real problem is not in society, it is in us. Like the speech of Simon Peter by the fire in Caiaphas' courtyard, our speech betrays us. It is naked of silence. The husks of quietness have long been shorn from its sides, which are now as slippery-smooth as stones washed by the restless sea. We need, if we are to be restored to efficacy, to be struck dumb the way Zechariah was before the word of the coming of the herald of Christ; then, when we do speak, people will be amazed at our words, as they were at his.

I cannot forget a portrait of a preacher I read years ago in *The Christian Century*. It was in an article by Richard L. Stanger, the chaplain of MacMurray College in Illinois, about the visit to MacMurray of San Francisco poet William Emerson, known as Brother Antoninus. The visit was such a success that Brother Antoninus was prevailed upon to speak in chapel on a Friday night. People poured into the chapel sanctuary despite the usual competition of Friday night events. Every seat was taken, and guests sat in the aisles and around the chancel. When the moment arrived for the sermon, what people beheld was a tall, middle-aged Dominican standing quietly in the chancel area, waiting for a voice. The words came slowly, awkwardly. He began to pace the chancel like a great bear, his white robe flowing behind him as he groped for speech. He read some of his poems, reflected on the untidy impressions and occurrences of his life. Again and again he bolted across the chancel, as if trying to seize some phrase or sentence taking wing and eluding his grasp. The audience was electrified. When it was over, they didn't want to leave. One girl even came forward to the altar, though there had been no altar call. Stanger said the event made all his upbeat liturgies and sermons seem pallid and empty by comparison. Why? What was there about Brother Antoninus's appearance that should have produced this effect? 'I think', said Stanger,

> it was the 'becoming' quality of the man and the event. Brother Antoninus had little idea where the evening would go. Certainly he had some intention, emerging from his vocational commitment, to risk a radical openness with his audience that some might be led to an awareness of the living God who moves amid the 'horrors' of the human heart. But the outcome was not laid out in advance. Nor was his life! One had the sense that here was an unfinished product – a life still writhing, still struggling, still becoming.[9]

The man's words still bore the husks of silence upon them. They still trailed gossamer threads of being. They were the words of a poet, wrung courageously from the heart of reality, and shared like fresh-picked fruit with a spirit-hungry audience.

IV

Please do not misunderstand. I am not suggesting, even for a moment, that we cease to prepare the prayers and sermon for Sunday morning. This is no white-paper for slovenly performance. What I *am* suggesting is that both we and our speech need more of the character that was evident in Brother Antoninus' performance – a character born only of daily struggling with the holy mysteries surrounding our existence. There need not be glaring hiatuses in our speech on Sunday morning – pausings and hiccupings of the Spirit. But the words should easily betray the silence in which they were wrought, what Antonin Artaud in his work with drama called 'updraughts and downdraughts' and 'temptations' of the soul.[10] There should still be husks of silence clinging to them, making us occasionally clear our throats and recall, along with our congregations, that this Sunday morning speech, for all its simplicity and commonness of vocabulary, is not ordinary speech. It is words derived from and expressing *the* Word itself, and becoming the Word again in the lives of those who hear.

To that end, there are some very practical things we can do. We can become, if we are not already, persons of prayer and meditation, setting aside precious minutes every day when we become all ears, and listen to the silence of God. I do not mean talking to God. We can do that at other times, when we are busy about our daily routines. I mean listening – waiting in the void – lying open to the Spirit like a fresh-plowed field to the gentle rains of winter. Not spring, but winter; for it is not always easy.

We can read – and listen to – the poets. Wordcrafters. Hewers of speech, who know from their practice of silence the heft and breadth and width of words. They work in language as other persons work in bricks or boards, making things tangible. The husks still cling to their words. The blank spaces on their pages are as viable as the print – sometimes more so. They can teach us to speak slowly, carefully, quietly, that we not disturb the mystery we are describing.

Then, too, we can take vacations from speaking, for a day at a time, or a week, if the malady of speech is too much upon us. There are wonderfully nourishing things to do: a 'silent trip', visiting art galleries, churches, parks, and public buildings in one's area without uttering a word on the entire pilgrimage; a speechless journey to a state park or retreat center for a couple of days; a few days' meditation in some nearby convent or monastery, where architecture and nature and monastic rule conspire to hush the restless tongue; or even, in the normally resounding space of one's home or office, a resolve not to utter speech for an entire day, aided and abetted by a sympathetic spouse or secretary who fends off intruding phone calls or demands for personal attention.

Corita Kent – the former Sister Corita – understands. Once, when I wrote to invite her to lead a series of worship services at our university, she replied with a single sentence on a postcard. 'Dear —', she said, 'I am trying to be quiet.' It is the only antidote to being like Lucky, who spoke whenever a hat was thrust on his head, or Krapp, who despaired of all his life's speeches, or John or Jane Q. Minister, who would hate to be condemned to listening to his or her past sermons. 'Trying to be quiet' – so that the word we speak is the real Word, the creative Word, the living Word, the word with husks of silence on it.

Now, Lord, forgive me for having spoken, for I am a man of unclean lips.   Amen.

Notes

1   Thomas Merton, *The Secular Journal of Thomas Merton,* New York, Dell, 1960, pp. 153–73.

2   James Dickey, *Self-Interviews*, New York, Dell, 1970, p. 44.

3   Ibid., p. 45.

4   Mary C. Richards, *Centering in Pottery, Poetry and the Person,* Middletown, CT, Wesleyan University Press, 1969, p. 6.

5   Max Picard, *The World of Silence*, tr. Stanley Godman, Chicago, Henry Regnery, 1952, p. 51.

6   Rainer Maria Rilke, *The Notebooks of Malte Laurids Brigge*, tr. M.D. Herter Norton, New York, Capricorn Books, 1958, pp. 70–1.

7   T. S. Eliot, 'Burnt Norton', V, in *The Complete Poems and Plays, 1909–1950*, New York, Harcourt, Brace and Co., 1952, p. 121.

8   Picard, 1952, pp. 26–7

9   Richard L. Stanger, 'All There Was Was a Man – Struggling', *Christian Century*, 1969, pp. 1248–9.

10   Antonin Artaud, *The Theater and Its Double*, tr. Mary C. Richards, New York, Grove, 1958, pp. 82–3.

14   Ethics in the Pulpit

Alvin C. Rueter

In some Protestant churches there is the 'children's sermon'. The pastor invites all youngsters to the chancel for conversation. One Sunday the preacher began the children's sermon asking, 'What has four legs and a bushy tail and runs up and down trees and gathers acorns?' No answer. Again, 'What has four legs and a bushy tail and runs up and down trees and gathers acorns?' Still no answer. A third time, 'What has four legs and a bushy tail and runs up and down trees and gathers acorns?' At last one tot volunteered, 'Sounds to me like a squirrel, but I'm sure the answer must be Jesus.'

Hearing unpredictable answers from precocious tykes is one reason grownups enjoy the children's sermon. As a practitioner, I was delighted with these surprises. I found it easy to 'milk' the darlings for laughs and gratify my desire to be an entertaining performer in the chancel. I could *use* the children – a question of ethics.

The appeal to self-interest

Kenneth Burke, who has done an encyclopedic study of geniuses in the history of speechmaking, discovered that their common secret was in *identification*, which he explained like this: 'It is so clearly a matter of rhetoric to persuade a man by identifying your cause with his interests.'[1] Some preachers in the electronic church are aware of this, making capital out of claiming the more we give them, the more we'll prosper.

Karl Barth warns against making preaching 'a service performed for clients'.[2] Grady Davis in his widely-used homiletics textbook cautions:

> Any successful appeal to selfish motives, however 'religious' the form it takes, leads my victim away from the lordship of Christ.[3]

With my Lutheran spectacles I have looked at Kenneth Burke's prescription to identify with one's hearer's interests in terms of a 'theology of glory' versus a 'theology of the cross'. It was out of self-interest that James and John asked for the two most prominent positions in Jesus' cabinet in the coming kingdom. It was not in Peter's self-interest that the Messiah should be crucified. A 'theology of the cross' does not seem to be congruent with a theology of self-interest.

As a parish pastor, I found myself exegeting texts on *agape*, selflessness, all the while I was learning about the attention~holding power of *identification*, self-interest. One week I encountered Matthew's conclusion to the Sermon on the Mount about the wise person who built his house upon a rock, enabling his structure to withstand all manner of calamity. It came to me: Jesus was appealing to my self-interest. If I hear his words and do them, I'll be prudent and survive. And what

This paper is condensed by the author from seven longer essays published in Emphasis (April–October, 1986).

are these words? They are about *agape*: turning the other cheek, going the second mile, and loving my enemies. Was Matthew portraying Jesus as appealing to my self-interest in order to move me to be selfless?

Then it struck me that the Beatitudes promise that if I'm poor in spirit, or mourn, or am meek, or hunger and thirst for righteousness, or show mercy, or am pure in heart, or make peace, or am persecuted, I'll be happy. In time I began to see the appeal to self-interest in other accounts of Jesus' teaching: that the truth sets us free (John 8:32–35), that he came to give us the abundant life (John 10:10), and that he wants our joy to be full (John 15:11). Certainly the promise of eternal life identifies with my self-interest.

Although skeptics scorn such motivations as 'pie-in-the-sky', the devout take them seriously. I saw that, from time to time, I had already been identifying with my people's self-interest, although not consciously. I asked, 'Why not do it on purpose?'

Then I had this text from Luke 14 about my ego. Jesus says that when I'm invited to a marriage feast, it is in my self-interest not to elbow my way to the best place at the table because someone is bound to come along who outranks me, and then with shame I shall have to move down. Rather I should start at the lowest place, and then the host is bound to come and say, 'Friend, go up higher.' At that point I'll gain approving looks from everyone present. But then comes the punchline (which I see as nothing else than legitimate self-interest): 'For everyone who exalts himself will be humbled, and he who humbles himself will be exalted' (14:11).

Motivating people by showing what's in it for them – it's risky. Yet in my view it's all over the Bible, in Deuteronomy, in the Psalms, in Jesus, and in Paul. If it's scriptural but risky, how do we know when we're using it ethically? So far I haven't been able to develop any formula – just guidelines, testing my appeals by the Golden Rule, the 'theology of the cross', and asking, 'Am I being as wise as a serpent and harmless as a dove?'

Although the risk of abuse is always there, I wonder if we aren't sometimes at fault in the other direction. If we expect people to 'listen up' just because we stand in the pulpit, giving them no reasons for believing and obeying, aren't we treating them as objects? We give all credit to Karl Barth for rescuing a large segment of the church from nineteenth-century rationalism by insisting that, 'since God wills to utter his own truth, his Word, the preacher must not adulterate that truth by adding his own knowledge or art.'[4] But in his zeal to protect the Word from human artifice, Barth may have overstepped on the side of disregarding the personhood of those before him. F. L. Herzog has observed:

> It is well known that according to Barth, revelation creates its own point of contact. An understandable objection to this view asks whether this does not mean to throw the Biblical message at man like a stone.[5]

To assume that everyone wants to grow in spirituality, to love the neighbor, or to support social justice is not realistic. To ignore mind, will, and emotions without showing the advantages of believing and obeying in the midst of our miseries – that may not be ethical either. It's risky to appeal to self-interest; it's risky not to do so.

The ethics of the preacher's attitude

A certain pastor boasts of graduating from college with a double major *magna cum laude*. Another who has been to the Holy Land doesn't let the people forget it. Still another who knows some important people just happens to find ways to drop a big name now and then.

A superiority complex does not improve communication. One theorist defines persuasion as the art of reducing the distance between Sender and Receiver. Arrogance hardly supports that strategy. Exalting ourselves while proclaiming him 'who did not count equality with God a thing to be grasped' – this has moral implications.

One would think that we heralds of *agape* – of all people – would be protected from a lack of humility. But there are some things built into our vocation – good things – that create the temptation, and those good things are that we are called to be prophets, evangelists, and priests.

1. *Our Attitude as Prophets.* Responsibility weighs heavily on those who stand watch on the walls of Zion. But therein lies the snare – to assume that we are beyond contradiction. And so it has been said concerning the preacher's message:

> The truth or virtue of it we are to accept without proof. . . . The choice for the addressee boils down to whether he will say 'amen' or throw bricks.[6]

This comes from a rhetorician who seems to have chosen to throw bricks. Perhaps one might react to him as I first did when I said, 'This man is anti-clerical. After all, we can't help we're called to proclaim, "Thus says the Lord." '

As I've wrestled with this, however, I have come to see that it's my attitude that's the issue. If I'm 'dumping' on the people, then the verdict of this rhetorician is just. But if I recognize that 'Thus says the Lord' applies also to me, that gives it another tone.

After all, not all the gifts belong to us. The Holy Spirit 'apportions to each one individually as he wills' (1 Cor 12:11). It has been said that in matters of justice, the Bible gives us clear directives on the *what*; but since we're now living in a different culture, it can not define the *how*. In the age of Deuteronomy it worked well to leave the corners of the field unreaped for the benefit of the poor, but that system can not apply in our economy. So we preachers need the insights of other members of the body of Christ on the *how*. Herbert Farmer allows the preacher to speak with authority but also observes: '*Deus cognitus, deus nullus.* A theology that knows every mortal thing is a sham.'[7]

2. *Our Attitude as Evangelists.* During the 1960s I became acquainted with some writings of Harry Golden. In one of his pieces he wrote:

> I consider Billy Graham a great Christian and an eminent gentleman. He is an evangelical minister of the Gospel who never tries to evangelize me.[8]

Before commenting on that, let me bring in something else. Some rhetoricians claim that monologue is unethical, since the monologist – speaking from the top downward as the dispenser of truth – apparently assumes that he or she is superior to the listener. Rather, the speaker should be in dialogue, communing with the souls of the audience, aware of their self-interest. One rhetorician writes:

> Although the speaker in dialogue may offer advice or express disagreement, he does not aim to psychologically coerce an audience into accepting his view. The speaker's aim is one of assisting the audience in making independent, self-determined decisions.[9]

The word that leaps out is *coerce*. The man has a point; the ethical speaker respects the personhood of the listeners. That brings to mind the picture drawn in Revelation 3:20: 'Behold, I stand at the door and knock.' Even the omnipotent Lord won't force his way into any heart.

Now I go back again to Harry Golden's remark about Billy Graham who 'never tries to evangelize me'. At first that would seem hard to believe. Yet, since Billy Graham understands *agape*, it isn't hard at all. We know about the salesperson who is friendly because he or she has a house to unload. We recognize that in our zeal to share the gospel we shall not negate the gospel. Billy

Graham, even while yearning for the conversion of a person like Harry Golden, can still love that person without making conversion a condition of that love.

Gabriel Marcel describes our dilemma this way:

> The Christian in fact cannot in any way think of himself as possessing either a power or even an advantage which has been denied to the unbeliever. There we have one of the most paradoxical aspects of his situation, for in another sense, he is obliged to recognise that grace has been bestowed upon him. This, however, only remains true on condition that the grace should inhabit him, not only as a radiance, but as humility. From the moment that he begins to be proud of it as a possession it changes its nature, and I should be tempted to say it becomes a malediction.[10]

Evangelism in the pulpit? Of course. One of the New Testament words for preaching is *euangelizō*. That is not a matter of trying to coerce people with glittering generalities, but making the Good News accessible to them, showing how it fits their need and brings them the blessings they want, 'assisting the audience in making independent, self-determined decisions'. Or in the imagery of Revelation 3:20, it is letting them open the door from the inside.

3. *Our Attitude as Priests.* There is a tale about a colonial Puritan preacher who was against a certain women's hair style known as the 'Top Knot'. He preached on the text, 'Top Knot, Go Down'. Challenged to produce chapter and verse, he pointed to Mark 13:15: 'Let him who is on the housetop not go down.'

Is this a parable of the temptation that comes to us as priests? Is the cause so noble that anything goes, since we know what's best for our people?

What happens sometimes? Social issues might raise the emotions and beguile us into using loaded words and making sweeping judgments about welfare cheaters or Bible-thumping rednecks. Or there could be appeals to prejudice or unsupported assertions. In one denomination where there is a dispute about historical criticism, a befuddled lay person was heard to exclaim, 'I don't understand what it's all about; all I know is, I love the Word of God', suggesting that this person has heard speakers oversimplifying the issue. I have been on both sides of this question. I can testify from my own experience that love for the Word of God is common ground between the opponents.

No matter how noble our aim, the use of loaded language, the making of sweeping assertions, and appealing to prejudices are forms of lying.

What about plagiarism in the pulpit?

I can not pretend that I have questions about plagiarism because I have such a noble character. It is rather by providential accident. About the time that I was first reading C. S. Lewis and Dietrich Bonhoeffer, there came into our congregation a young Ph.D. in mathematics who was also reading them. Before long he offered to teach a high school class, and – wouldn't you know it? – it turned out to be a course on C. S. Lewis and Dietrich Bonhoeffer. It would have been folly for me to have taken from these writers and not to have acknowledged them. So I quoted them directly, usually taking their books into the pulpit. I had the sensation that it gave more credibility to my own material when I freely admitted that lines were from someone else. I had the same experience when I paraphrased someone's idea and gave him or her the credit.

Should we acknowledge our sources? I think so. But this can be carried to a fault. There may be preachers who read a lot and cite every author, so that their messages are one quotation after another. I like their honesty, but I'd rather not preach that way. And which sources should we mention? Do we give an oral bibliography, including Nestle's Greek text? There is a stylistic problem of clutter. Common good sense will tell us when we should cite our sources and when it would be pointless.

What about borrowing from others when we're out of time? Preaching from Sunday to Sunday is hard enough, but then there's Christmas and Easter, Advent and Lent. I marvel at the incredible schedule of preaching that Roman Catholic priests have with their daily masses. The people in the pews probably have small appreciation of the effort required. Doesn't the exigency excuse us from the ordinary rules of honesty as we serve the Lord so diligently?

When we are caught like this, and the only way out is to use someone else's homily, why not just take the book into the pulpit, acknowledge whose work it is, and read it? I have done that. On each occasion a good number of people gave me positive feedback. Not that it didn't take time; I rehearsed the reading out loud several times.

Using other people's experiences without permission?

'Let me tell you about a person who came to see me in my office last week. . . . ' The preacher senses a rising tide of attention and the coughing subsides.

But let's put ourselves into the skins of the people. Some are hurting. We say, 'Well, they should come and see us.' They're saying, 'Yes, and then become the subject matter of another juicy sermon illustration?'

We could counter, 'Of course I never reveal anything that goes on in my present parish.' Or, 'You must understand that I'm serving an area where no one knows anyone.' The people are still objecting, 'Whether now or twenty years from now, whether people know me or not, I still don't want my secret life blabbed about in public. So I don't trust you as a pastor.'

Some Protestant preachers mine a lode of illustrations from their family life. People are usually delighted to hear of the antics of the baby and the toddler. I find no fault with that. But the toddler soon becomes acquainted with the language and aware of the self. What then? We might explain, 'Well, I only report the good things my child does.' But don't 'preacher's kids' have enough to contend with already? Why embarrass them?

What to do? The gospel shall be proclaimed. We have evidence of its life-changing power from personal observation. And we're denied this resource? Not altogether. When the good Lord has brought solace, reconciliation, or freedom, the person, couple, or family may be willing to celebrate that victory in the communion of saints. Why not ask permission to share it? If given, we protect ourselves by explaining that we relate this incident only with consent.

The legitimate appeal to self-interest, the preacher's attitude toward the people in light of the calling as prophet, priest, and evangelist, the heavy schedule that tempts one to borrow without attribution, the desire to enliven the sermon by using others' stories without permission – I haven't found much in the homiletical literature on these matters, but I believe they deserve attention.

Notes

1   Kenneth Burke, *A Grammar of Motives and a Rhetoric of Motives,* Cleveland, World, 1962, p. 579.

2   Karl Barth, *The Preaching of the Gospel*, Philadelphia, Westminster, 1959, p. 136.

3   H. Grady Davis, *Design For Preaching,* Philadelphia, Muhlenberg, 1958, p. 136.

4   Barth, 1959, p. 13.

5   Frederick L. Herzog, 'Theologian of the Word of God', *Theology Today*, 13, 1956, p. 326.

6   Huntington Brown, *Prose Styles: Five Primary Types*, Minneapolis, University of Minnesota, 1966, p. 71.

7   Herbert Farmer, *The Servant of the Word,* Philadelphia, Fortress, 1964, p. 63.

8   Harry Golden, *You're Entitled,* New York, Fawcett, 1963, p. 125.

9   Richard L. Johannesen, 'Attitude of Speaker toward Audience: A Significant Concept for Contemporary Rhetorical Theory and Criticism', *Central States Speech Journal*, 25, 2, 1974, p. 96.

10 Gabriel Marcel, *Homo Viator: Introduction to a Metaphysic of Hope*, London, Victor Gollanz, 1951, p. 159.

15   The Lenten Preacher

David Day

It is tempting to address the topic of the Lenten Preacher as if it were about preaching the Lenten themes. How am I to preach on sin, judgment, repentance, temptation, justice . . . ? Despite the attractiveness of that route, I do not wish to follow it. I take the Lenten Preacher to be as much about the Lent which the preacher must carry about in the heart, as the content of what a preacher ought to say during Lent. Therefore, my thoughts turn first not to, 'What shall I say to the congregation?' but, 'What shall I say to myself?' A traditional focus in Lent has been the temptations of Jesus. Since the gospel narrative is about Jesus' awareness that he is the son of God, I want to explore the idea of the preacher as one who stands in the presence of God, is called to speak in the name of God, and to be God's mouthpiece. 'The Lenten preacher' is then less about the content of the preacher's message as about his or her person and the quality of the relationship with God. The voice of the tempter which I must learn to recognise is the voice that says, 'If you really are the herald, the messenger, the mouthpiece of God then . . . '

The temptation to turn stones into bread

The choice, stones or bread, is about the source of my life as a preacher. It presses the question, 'Where do I go for sustenance?' and therefore, 'Where do I go for the source of my sermons?' Jesus' answer distinguishes between feeding on literal bread and being nourished by every word which proceeds from the mouth of God. Behind the answer lies the question, 'As a preacher, what is it that nourishes me?' and the temptation to seek food in the wrong place.

Dressed in borrowed clothes

The temptation might appear first in a desperate desire to rush to the commentaries, sermon outlines, joke books or other people's sermons (an abomination to the Lord) as opposed to listening in silence and being prepared patiently to wait for God to speak. Here, as in so many places, Fred Craddock gives sound advice: Never begin with the commentaries. 'They suppress and intimidate the preacher. After all, who is going to venture a thought or an interpretation when at the very same desk are six internationally known Bible scholars? . . . Some preachers who spend much time in study have confessed to having preached texts which they had not even read in the process of preparation.'[1] I remember hearing a well respected teacher of homiletics in the USA complain that he would wander through the college library and find students surrounded by books, 'getting up a sermon'. But on being questioned, the majority confessed that they had not grappled with the passage for themselves. He observed, 'My students don't read the text, they read books about the text.'

The fast-food sermon

A second way in which this temptation shows itself is in seizing upon an idea and preaching on that rather than working hard at what the text really says. It is tempting to 'use' Mark's account of Jesus and the leper in Mark 1:40–45 as an excuse to parade some interesting thoughts about Jesus' healing ministry and ours. But the distinctive thrust of the text is then lost, swallowed up in generalities. There is much more in this passage than an opportunity to discuss my views on healing. Most of us could knock up a passable sermon on the prodigal son. We let the words escape from the mouth but do not need to engage the brain. A mere glance at the Call of Isaiah will provoke a pop up sermon on the Vision of God, sense of Sin, Forgiveness and the Call to Witness.

But the feel of the passage is something else, and a more patient reading will pick up the terror, the pain and the burden of the prophet's experience. The hymn says, 'Bright the vision that delighted once the sight of Judah's seer'. I question if the man who wrote that had ever read Isaiah's call.

These are ways of stuffing ourselves full of fast-food sermons rather than turning faithfully to the source of our life. Listening in silence is an act of trust in the love of God and his call to me to preach his word for this occasion. It requires me to believe that he will not betray me. He will feed me. I don't have to force stones into bread, even on a Saturday evening.

Shuffling the cards

Sermons cannot be detached from the people who preach them. Where is the source of my life when I am not being a preacher? When my sermon does not reflect my life, the congregation will often sense that sermon and self are not quite in tune. I can easily drink from a well that is running dry. Lent is the perfect time for what W. E. Sangster called *A Spiritual Checkup*. Where should I go when I want a life-giving word to preach? To the life-giver.

Unfortunately, it is easy to do no more in the pulpit than shuffle a well-worn pack of cards, laying them out in different sequences and arranging them in pretty patterns. Resisting this temptation calls for reality in the pulpit. Sermons are real when there is genuine engagement with the problems of life, when the preacher speaks out of his or her own experience of God and the struggles of the life of faith, without disparaging either. One preacher said that the finest compliment he had ever received was from someone who said, 'You cut the crap.' When the sermon touches reality, when it deals with deeply felt emotions and when it opens up the spiritual dimension of our existence, then people not only get the sense that God is real for the preacher but also that he is real for them and is speaking to them. The play acting is over and the action has begun. Charades are fun but no substitute for real living.

These three examples illustrate the truth that the preacher lives not by bread but by the living word which comes from God's mouth. If we fall victim to the temptation to settle for anything less, then the first casualty is our authenticity.

The pinnacle of the temple

The pinnacle of the temple is about the nature of my relationship with God. The background to the temptation is a question taken from the murmuring tradition of the Exodus wanderings. Israel asked, 'Is the Lord among us or not?' with the underlying complaint, 'We don't think he is. Let us violently test the relationship.' From this act of rebellion arose the complaints and the ungrateful murmurings which came to be called, 'The day of provocation'. Israel's behaviour was essentially manipulative. It was an attempt to force God's hand.

For Jesus, the setting of the temptation is particularly significant because the temple is the place above all where God is to be found. And, uniquely for the temptation story, the scriptures are themselves the basis of the test. It is often said that Satan misquotes Scripture for his purpose. I cannot see this. In context, the words which are cited from Psalm 91:11–12 do invite an attitude of trust and confidence in God's willingness to catch you lest you dash your foot against a stone. It is precisely because Satan quotes accurately and in context that there is a temptation to be resisted.

The leap of faith and the leap of provocation

To the observer there is no visible difference between a leap of trust and a leap of provocation. Jumping from the pinnacle might be an instance of trusting God but might be provoking him. And no one outside your head will ever know; only you and God will know the inside story. From within, of course, trusting God has a different feel about it. It involves waiting on him, being summoned, and obeying in some fear and reluctance. There is all the difference in the world between being brought by God to the pinnacle and called in the name of Scripture to risk leaping into the abyss in blind trust – and jumping in order to force him to bend to your desires.

There are instructive parallels with preaching in that, as a preacher, I find it easy to take God for granted and use him for my purposes. He will come when I snap my fingers. He is a slot-machine God. I am not humbly standing beneath the word or at the foot of the cross but proudly calculating and independent. I am six feet above contradiction. This is a long way to fall, but I'm not bothered, because he will catch me and bail me out.

At the heart of the temptation lies the question, 'Will I treat God as truly my friend, my intimate? Or do I use him and abuse his commitment to me?' Calvin said, dauntingly: 'Voila the pulpit, the throne of God'. We stand in the holy place and yet know that it is possible to abuse the relationship. The first casualty then is love and intimacy. The friendship is damaged when we take it for granted. What might be the homiletical examples?

Back of an envelope

I know of a minister who told his congregation, 'What I'm to say to you this morning God only knows'. They were not impressed with this casual sauntering up to the pulpit. It represented a lack of care, a dereliction of duty, a failure to listen and pray. He was altogether too much 'at ease in Zion'. Presuming on God, taking him for granted in this way, is very different from the cry of Moses: 'If your presence does not go with us, do not send us up from here' (Exodus 33:15). This is the cry of the man to whom God would speak face to face, 'as a man speaks with his friend'. This is the man who came away from God's presence with his face shining. Unfortunately, the shining face cannot be kept in a jar by the door. It comes from fasting and waiting, looking and listening. Back of an envelope sermons, ill-prepared and casually thrown together, betray the friendship. We provoke God, pushing the relationship to the limit. The wonder of it all is that very often, in his grace God catches us, even when we don't deserve it.

Pulpit performance

Though clearly preaching is a craft, a cunningly devised piece of persuasion, which aims to produce an effect, it is still possible to become rather too good at it. Then we can perform superbly and at the same time prostitute our calling. We end up doing it just because we're good at it. Lancelot Andrewes, aware of the peril, prayed, 'Lord, inform my gestures.' In one of those unlikely stories which may yet be true, a world famous Italian tenor moved an audience to tears while secretly managing to put a sausage into the tiny, frozen hand of the female lead. Most preaching has a performance element to it but it can never be just a performance – at least, not without the loss of something irreplaceable.

Preaching by numbers

The mechanically constructed sermon will work. That is precisely the problem. We can learn to preach by numbers. An illustration goes in here; here I shout loudly because the argument is weak; I need a joke at the beginning, relevant or not doesn't matter; I tell this anecdote as if it happened to me even when I know it didn't; this sentimental story will move the hearers; I shall not pursue this aspect of the text or this facet of Christian experience because they are messy and complex but I shall move swiftly on to safer ground. Inside your head you know how empty the sermon is.

Convinced by one's own dogma

One of the great expository preachers of the post-war period told a meeting of ministers towards the end of his career: 'If I had my time again I would say what it is really like.' It is possible to preach a message which carries you away by its own rhetoric. Fred Dawson speaks of 'going beyond the terra firma where faith is actually located' and quotes Charles Causley's description of 'a person convinced by his own dogma'. There is a proper tension between the great affirmations of the faith, which do take your breath away, and the need to say what it is really like, refusing to distort reality in the interests of an ideology. Life is often more grey and less black-and-white than our preaching suggests. Dawson continues, 'Going beyond my brief, I feel hollow and negative, at a lower ebb than almost at any other time. The only response is humble silence before God. And God says, "This is not the way it is between us."'[2]

The ego-trip

Two of the contemporary gurus of homiletics have fastened on the abuse of preaching to feed the ego of the preacher. Craddock notes the tendency of preachers to gravitate 'towards the best seats in the text'. We need to guard against this possibility. 'If this step is not taken deliberately, it is very likely that the sermon will be prepared and delivered from the choice places in the texts. The congregation will hear loud and clear what is not stated but implied: today our preacher is Jesus and we are the Pharisees; today our preacher is Paul and we are the Corinthians. Today our preacher is the loving father and we are the older son pouting on the back porch.'[3]

Richard Lischer identifies 'preaching out of need-love' as another way of feeding up self-esteem: 'Those who preach out of need-love never get enough of preaching. Why? Because they can never get enough of the stroking that denies or temporarily controls those terrifying aspects of the self that has not yet been recognised or transcended in Christ. So it is when the sermon is finished, depending on audience response, such preachers either go on a high of exhilaration or crash in utter despondency. This exaggerated need for self-affirmation of the self turns preaching into therapy – not for the congregation but for the preacher.'[4]

All this from the pulpit, out of the scriptures and in the name of God. The observer may never suspect that anything is wrong, but we know that somewhere along the way something infinitely precious, the intimate friendship with God, has been put under strain.

The kingdoms of the world

The final temptation is about the focus and direction of my gaze. The Old Testament passage which is evoked by Christ's quotation is about divided loyalty. In the desert Israel is warned that, once they enter the land, they will be tempted to serve other gods. God predicts, 'You will try to share me with other gods.' For Christ the panoramic vision of all the kingdoms of the world represents authority, success and infinite possibility but only *at a price*. That price is compromise. However, the story portrays Christ as one who will not divide his devotion between God and anything else. As the Gospels reveal, Christ will serve the kingdoms of the world and will win them, but only by undivided obedience to God and by following his methods.

The preacher undergoes a similar test. It is tempting to shape what I have to say by reference not to God but to other voices and other lords. It is easy, for example, to preach a 'smooth' word which offends no one and reinforces what people want to hear. The smooth word sounds like the gospel, but in fact represents an accommodation to the power and authority of the congregation. Jeremiah complains: 'They heal the wound of my people lightly.' It was the false prophets who proclaimed the false gospel of a false promise, 'Of course we shall go free in a year or two.'

This tension between true word and capitulation to what is expected has been entertainingly analysed by Walter Moberly in a study of Micaiah ben Imlah in I Kings 22:5.[5] Micaiah is aware of the pressure brought to bear on him by the unanimous confidence of the court prophets. The stakes are high. But the king knows a man of integrity when he hears one: 'He never prophesies anything good about me.' Micaiah's message to Ahab is a mixture of mockery ('Go up and conquer'), of tragic vision ('I saw all Israel scattered') and a homiletical tour de force which tries desperately to touch the heart of the king ('God says, "How can I deceive Ahab? I'll send a lying spirit to deceive him"'). In all this Micaiah is moved by the determination to be true to the word God has given him. He refuses to serve the king with flattery, even on pain of death. 'Here I stand. I can do no other.' He is a model to all preachers.

Reframing the truth

Marsha Witten's book, *All is forgiven*, gives numerous examples of how congregations shape the preacher's preaching.[6] Under the impulse of a variety of rhetorical devices the concept of sin is attenuated; it is deflected away from the listening audience and projected on to specific groups of outsiders. The instances of sin used in sermons carry the message that other people are the ones who sin, whether they are children, adolescents in rebellion, or members of a diseased secular world, caught up in drug abuse, alcoholism, compulsive gambling, murder and prostitution. Sometimes sin is reframed with reference to a social science perspective. Sin is a flaw in a family system or naivete or immaturity. With dispassionate analysis Witten makes the case that many American preachers are engaged in a process of making their message palatable to their listeners and conformed to the values and behaviour of secularity.

Properly insulated prophecy

A traditional Ash Wednesday reading from Isaiah 58 calls the preacher to proclaim justice. This theme is a particularly slippery one. It is easy to preach 'prophetically' but run no risk at all of being driven from the building and taken to the brow of a hill by an angry mob. The most common move, for example, is to discourse on safe topics: disarmament, conservation, third world debt, industrial peace, ethical investment. In the recent past, South Africa and apartheid used to be a popular evil against which to inveigh. There is no chance of being misunderstood or attacked. You might as well preach against marrying your wife's father's mother.

Much the same result is obtained by keeping the treatment general and safe. After all, we might think, ethical and justice issues are so complex. But then, the sermon might as well be taken from the broadsheets or *Frost on Sunday*. The mark of the word that is difficult but necessary, dangerous yet needing to be said, is often its specificity. When the preacher deals with specific and local issues he or she runs the risk of offending the listeners. Amos's remarks about 'Cows of Bashan' went down badly with the women of Bashan, however much others enjoyed them. Often general comments are the refuge of the scoundrel or the coward. Fred Dawson comments wryly on the showdown between Amos the prophet and Amaziah the priest and observes, 'We build an Amos perspective into the task of shrine management.'[7] None of this is to be understood as a licence for being bad-tempered in the pulpit, of course, but it does remind us how difficult it is to keep our eyes fixed on God when we prepare a sermon and how quickly integrity disappears under the cold scrutiny of a disapproving congregation.

These dire warnings may imply an unnecessarily bleak view of the preacher and the preacher's task. That is not their intention. The Lenten themes offer preachers wonderful opportunities to castigate congregations and give full rein to personal prejudices and private niggles. There is no better way to settle old scores. Concentrating on the Lent which the preacher carries around inside is a necessary corrective. It is the homiletical equivalent of Jesus' story about the mote and the beam.

Notes

1   Fred B. Craddock, *Preaching,* Nashville, TN, Abingdon, 1985, p. 106.

2   Fred Dawson, 'Preached to Death', *New Fire*, 8, 1984–5, pp. 485–9.

3   Craddock, 1985, p. 120.

4   Richard Lischer, *A Theology of Preaching,* Durham, NC, The Labyrinth Press, 1992, p. 68.

5   Walter Moberly, 'To Speak for God: the Story of Micaiah ben Imlah', *Anvil*, 14, 4, 1997, pp. 243–53.

6   Marsha G. Witten, *All is Forgiven: The Secular Message of American Protestantism*, Princeton NJ, Princeton University Press, 1993, and 'Preaching about Sin in Contemporary Protestantism', *Theology Today*, 50, 1993–4, pp. 243–53.

7   Dawson, 1984–5, p. 488.

16   Martin Luther King, Jr's Preaching as a Resource for Preachers

Richard Lischer

I

Every year we hear the voice on the crackly tape cry, 'I have a dream', and preachers sigh and wish that they could preach like that. Yet the man who once said, 'In the quiet recesses of my heart, I am fundamentally a clergyman, a Baptist preacher', is rarely studied in homiletics classes or given scholarly consideration by homileticians. Although he continues to inspire imitation among young African-American preachers, the preacher, Martin Luther King, Jr, has pretty much been relegated to the realm of historical research.[1]

Perhaps this is because King's peculiar talent and the even more peculiar historical moment that summoned it cannot be duplicated. The further we get from the turbulent 1960s the more outrageously unrepeatable they appear. The epoch-defining causes of the sixties that mobilized King's passionate eloquence have given way to a new set of less-definable concerns. Today's social ills are more likely to be dealt with by piecemeal economic engineering than by public demonstrations, moral crusades, or biblical oratory. This is true the world over. If Tony Blair walked into the House of Commons and promised blood, sweat, toil, and tears, there would be polite tittering from the back benches. Likewise, if the most famous of King's 'sermons', 'I Have a Dream', was preached by a new leader in the techno-reliant atmosphere of the new millennium, it might evoke a very different response: 'We don't want dreams. We want computer training and economic parity.'

Although King continues to inspire preachers, his actual homiletical practices did not resemble current theories of preaching, at least the ones practiced in communities with which I am most familiar: middle-class, largely-white, Protestant churches.

For example, King was not much of a story teller or humorist in the pulpit. He had a few stock stories and one or two jokes which he inserted into many of his sermons, but he was in no sense a narrative preacher, preferring instead to organize his sermons around a few universal themes. The themes, such as the destiny of 'man', the importance of love, or the greatness of God, appeared in his sermons throughout his career. He developed these *topoi* (conventional 'places' or repositories for arguments) differently as he grew older and the fortunes of the Movement changed.

In a deeper sense, however, King was a profoundly narrative preacher. The story of the Exodus underlay and informed nearly everything he said on the subject of race, freedom, and justice. Even when he did not cite the Exodus-event explicitly, his sermons were marked by an emotional and rhetorical *breaking through* from suffering, anger, and struggle to freedom and joy. One can not listen to a King sermon and miss the exaltation of *release*.

When it came to humor, King didn't exclude it from his sermons because he was a humorless person. On the contrary, intimates recall how thoroughly at home he was in the back-slapping, fraternity-culture of preachers, in the guarded privacy of which he kept his friends in stitches with jokes and impressions of his fellow preachers.

In the pulpit, however, he never settled for humor's payoff, which is basically ironic: the pleasurable recognition of a discrepancy. The aims of humor roughly correspond to ancient rhetoric's goal of delighting an audience. King's oratory was no stranger to delight, but he always strove for rhetoric's higher goal, which is to *move* the listener to a profound change of heart and behavior.

Unlike contemporary preachers, King rarely talked about himself or bared his soul in the pulpit. When he did include a reference to himself, it was always as a part of a larger story in which he figured as an observer or minor player. With the exception of his late sermons in which he appears to have been suffering from depression, the point of his first-person references was never to share his feelings with an audience or to disclose what sort of person he was. Of necessity he did speak of himself but almost always from behind a public persona of great dignity and reserve. He knew his experiences were ingredients in the history of the Movement but not essential to it.

In place of personal opinions, impressions, and self-revelations, King offered arguments on behalf of freedom. These he abstracted from Christian doctrines and biblical texts as well as from non-Christian sources such as the Declaration of Independence. Although he spoke from the heart of a specific church, or perhaps *because* he did so, he felt free, especially in the early years of the struggle, to presuppose a broad partnership of Christian truths and civic aspirations. King's own liberal practice of civic religion infused his sermons with a universality and a generous love of humanity that is foreign to much of contemporary preaching.

Although King was a creature of the media of his day, he spoke in an era that had not yet reduced oratory to cyber-town meetings, soundbites, or lip-biting sincerity. Like most speakers, he understood the need for identification with his audience, and, indeed, no one could create empathy with audiences as King did. But he was also the product of a rhetorical tradition that stressed the intellectual and moral *difference* between speaker and audience. He therefore didn't bother with the conversational approach to preaching but fully invested himself in the risky, all-or-nothing style of oratory in which the preacher soars higher and higher toward the sun and dares his hearers to come along. In the best of his sermons, he and his listeners burnt up the church. If his hearers were not bold enough to go with him, that was their problem. It is not the prophet's job to hold back.

A final difference between King and many contemporary preachers has to do with his method of interpreting the Bible. Early in his ministry he abandoned the historical-critical theories he had learned in seminary and reverted to the older techniques of typology and allegory, not because he was particularly interested in a christocentric reading of the Old Testament, but because allegory allowed his hearers a greater opportunity to identify their struggles with those portrayed in the Bible. Like a man in a black hat and silk cape, he discovered civil rights on the Jericho Road and the despair of Vietnam in the Far Country. He did not subscribe to the typical Enlightenment step *back* from the Bible in order to assess its historical reliability; rather, he followed the Negro church's practice of stepping *into* the Bible, where on its storied pages the church continues to find its own true life fully displayed. Ironically, King's Boston Ph.D. changed the modern world by reviving techniques of interpretation that scholars had already dismissed as antiquated.

II

Given the several factors that distinguish King's preaching from our own, how does his example serve as a resource for contemporary preachers? It is not necessarily helpful to invoke the musical range of his voice, the vividness of his imagery, or even his prophetic courage and then to add, 'Go and do likewise'. There's more to it than that. Martin Luther King, Jr is a resource to all who preach because he fully and unreservedly embraced God's word in its spoken form as his vocation and allowed it to shape his ministry in the world.

Some years ago, when I was doing research on King, I spent many afternoons at the King Center and other repositories, listening to cassette and unedited reel-to-reel tapes of church services in which King was the preacher. Although I never met him or saw him in person, I felt I had been to Ebenezer and worshiped with him many times. During the course of these sessions, several realizations about my own preaching, pallid as it is by comparison with his, began to dawn.

The first thing you pick up from the tapes is how bone-tired the man was. I am not referring to the affectedly ponderous beginning of many black sermons, but something real in the preacher. *Tired.* The listener can't help but wonder if he's going to get through to the end. Why does he force himself to preach, even at Ebenezer, where surely everyone would have understood if he took the day off?

King apparently subscribed to the theory that it is the preacher's job to show up on Sunday morning, no matter what. A Pentecostal colleague once told me that he only preaches when the Spirit moves him to do so. I said that if I followed that rule, I wouldn't preach very often. And neither would have King.

He stood up to preach after all-night negotiating sessions, bombings, and the kinds of problems that would lead many of us to phone in the Sunday sermon. He did so doggedly out of duty, perhaps, as he kept on keeping on, but he also stuck with it because the act of interpreting the Bible and expounding it to a congregation never failed to revive his spirit and sustain him in his ministry. He began his career with the preacher's stigmatic belief in the power of the word of God to melt hearts of stone. That world will either redeem the soul of America or damn it to hell, just as it did on a smaller scale every Sunday in his father's church. Even when he began to doubt that the word was going to work its black-church magic on American society, he never doubted it would work for *him*. What he once said of marching (at a low point in Chicago) he might have said of preaching:

> Yes, I'm tired of going to jail;
> I'm tired of all the surging murmur
>   of life's restless sea,
> But I'll tell anybody,
> I'm willing to stop marching.
> I don't march 'cause I like it;
> I march because I must
> And because I'm a man
> And because I'm a child of God.[2]

Preachers may disagree with one another in matters of theological emphasis, but none of us should underestimate the health available to those who routinely, like ancient navigators, read the Bible and chart the coordinates between Scripture, church, soul, and world.

That King persisted in preaching and saved his own soul in the doing of it, was my first discovery. The second was how high and beautiful an art he pursued, even when he was away from the public glare speaking to his own congregation in Atlanta. One would imagine that familiarity with one's audience breeds laziness or dereliction of poetic duty but not so for King. He knew how to follow the curve of a religious idea as it takes possession of a congregation, and he did so with joy Sunday after Sunday.

The poet possesses the gift of seeing one thing in terms of another or of uncovering hidden realities beneath the squalor of everyday life. This faculty was the truest mark of King's genius as a preacher and a prophet. He discerned the transformation of history taking place in, of all places, Montgomery, Alabama, and saw, really *saw*, the dignity of the human race in striking sanitation workers in Memphis. He invoked 'the iron feet of oppression', 'the Pharaohs of the South', 'gigantic buildings [that] kiss the skies', 'sunlit paths of inner peace', and, of course, 'the Dream' for his congregations because, unlike so many talented preachers, he understood the linkage between prophetic vision and the pastoral care of oppressed people. Metaphoric language does not merely decorate some of our better ideas; it is fundamental to God's manner of touching and changing human beings.

His sermons were therefore expressions and extensions of the life of actual communities. Today, many of our model preachers are writers, seminary professors, or free-lance religious personalities. They have much to teach us, but they can not offer the complete homiletical package because God designed the word to be the beating heart of real churches like Ebenezer Baptist, with street addresses, parking lots, and red-inked budgets.

The sermon does not elevate itself above the embarrassment of local attempts to practice the ordinary Christian virtues of hospitality, friendship, mercy, and justice. It participates in these practices and learns from them. In King's ministry the word even shaped itself to a messily political and sometimes disorganized struggle for human rights carried out by ambitious leaders and fallible human organizations. The preacher King taught us to ground the word in the suffering and joy of the community at hand. In this regard, perhaps it is helpful to think of the vivid language, examples, and narratives of our sermons not as *illustrations* of an abstract truth but as *extensions* of the biblical text into our churches and neighbors.

Finally, King was not afraid to claim this partnership with God and his people and to act upon it. He and his audiences performed the Scripture no less than an actor *does* Lear or a pianist vivifies a Brahms concerto. King's first inclination, born of many Sundays in black congregations, was to locate the word of God wherever people were responding verbally to the sermon. He later came to understand word-and-response as a dress rehearsal for the community's performance of the word in its daily life. To be word of God, the sermon must move people to new expressions of courage and discipleship. He altered his definition of preaching by subtly shifting the criterion of its authenticity from brilliance of effect to faithfulness of commitment. If the sermon is promoting the kinds of love and liberation that God sponsored in the ministry, death, and resurrection of Jesus, and if it is opposing the kinds of injustice God has always hated, then we've got the word of God in our church.

The lessons of King's preaching for the next generation of preachers are not simple or direct, but the notion of 'performance' suggests several implications. Preachers can be so devoted to the analytic 'step back' from the text or so desperate for illustrations of biblical concepts that they overlook the ancient techniques that enhance participation *in* the text. The big question is not What did the text mean? or What's a good translation of sin? but What is God doing today?

Preaching-as-performance encourages the preacher to examine his or her own language to determine the extent to which it reflects the religious lecture-form rather than the riches of biblical expression. Every modality of language has its own beauty and therefore its own potential for expressing the joy of the gospel. Within the boundaries of the congregations' own traditions, let the sermon boldly voice the liberative *mood* of the Exodus, the pathos or anger of prophecy, the vision of hope, or the vulnerability of love. King's biblical preaching, though not so exegetically careful, always caught the voice of the text.

Performance is not some new technique for the already-burdened preacher to master, but a series of reliable perspectives – poetic, pastoral, hermeneutic – by which the Baptist preacher, Martin Luther King, Jr, continues to instruct and encourage a new generation of witnesses.

Notes

1   Edited cassette tapes of some of King's sermons are now available with the collection *A Knock at Midnight*, by Clayborne Carson and Peter Holloran (eds), New York, Warner Books, 1998.

2   'Why I Must March', Chicago, August 18,1966, quoted and poetically arranged in Richard Lischer, *The Preacher King: Martin Luther King, Jr and the Word that Moved America*, New York, Oxford, 1995, p. 264.

Part 5

STORY, PARABLE AND IMAGINATION

Introduction to Part 5

Jolyon Mitchell argues that, in a media-saturated society, preachers must learn to engage critically with the communicative environment. Television has not irrevocably undermined people's ability to listen, but it has changed the way they listen and the expectations they bring with them. Listeners are accustomed to an increasingly conversational form of discourse. Moreover, they do not come into church like a passive clean slate waiting for words to be written on to them, but as an 'active audience' with a range of images, stories and experiences already engaging their attention, many of which will have been drawn from the mass media. Rather than constituting a threat to preaching, however, this situation offers new opportunities. Mitchell advocates a move from 'single camera' to 'multi-camera' discourse, from proclamatory to conversational discourse, and from visual to multi-sensorial discourse. Preaching can reframe, re-imagine and redescribe the world so as to offer a counter-narrative to that rendered by secular culture.

Jolyon Mitchell, 'Preaching Pictures' is a revised and expanded version of 'Preaching in an Audio-Visual culture', *Anvil*, 14, 4, 1997, pp. 262–72.

In the second piece in Part 5, David Buttrick sketches the history of the understanding of parables – as allegories, as moral tales after Jülicher, and as stories of crisis and eschatology following Dodd and Jeremias. He notes the surreal element in many parables and the fact that they are plotted so as to exhibit movement rather than a 'single point'. Sermons which follow earlier understandings of parables distort their nature either by making points, domesticating their capacity to disrupt or forcing them into a preordered framework. By contrast, Buttrick illustrates his own homiletic, based on movement, intention, language modules ('moves'), point of view and theological field. At the end of the article he raises questions about the way parables both assert and deny analogy, and about the power of parables to speak to our condition once preachers free themselves from an excessive concern with original meaning.

David G. Buttrick, 'On Preaching a Parable: the Problem of Homiletic Method' was originally published in *Reformed Liturgy and Music*, 17, 1983, pp. 16–22.

Richard Eslinger's article mounts a timely corrective to much of the current orthodoxy about the role of story in sermon illustration. First-person narratives, far from demonstrating solidarity with the congregation, will often only serve to distance the preacher from the hearers. Extended or elephantine story illustrations become so dominant that they need to be 'illustrated' by the biblical material rather than vice versa. Sermons which run biblical and contemporary stories in parallel will invite comparison and competition between them, usually to the detriment of the biblical story. By contrast, images or brief stories will do a better job of illustration. They do not need to be developed into full-blown narratives. Eslinger demonstrates his standpoint by means of an analysis of a sermon on the raising of Lazarus. In each movement images carry the illustrative power but none is expanded into a narrative. The only story is that of Lazarus and the congregation.

Eslinger's books, *Narrative and Imagination* (Minneapolis, MN, Fortress, 1995), and *Pitfalls in Preaching* (Grand Rapids, MI, Eerdmans, 1996), both carry extended discussions of the advantages and dangers of stories.

Richard L. Eslinger, 'Story and Image in Sermon Illustration' was first published in *Journal for Preachers*, 9, 1986, pp. 19–23.

Richard Lischer believes that imagination is sidelined in homiletics teaching. In 'Imagining a Sermon' he argues that, rightly understood, imagination is involved at every stage of preparation. The article examines the different roles of imagination – theological, historical-literary, hermeneutical and homiletical. He counsels against cheap evasions of imagination: art for art's sake in the pulpit, 'let's pretend' as an exercise in historical imagination, newspaper preaching, 'how I felt when I read this text'. What is arresting is not exotic imagery or farfetched stories but the strangeness of 'the gospel in human vesture'. A final section on 'slogging it out' examines how imagination works in sermon preparation and delivery. Imaginative leaps seldom short-circuit the normal processes of thinking. The key ingredient is commitment to the cause of communicating the gospel. Preachers succeed in their task 'not by special processes but by special purpose'.

Richard Lischer, 'Imagining a Sermon' is from *Word and World*, 5, 3, 1985, pp. 279–86.

17   Preaching Pictures

Jolyon Mitchell

Introduction

Preachers today face a highly competitive communicative environment.[1] Many of their congregation on Sundays will already have glanced at a weekend paper, listened to the radio, or caught sight of an advertising hoarding before entering church. Some of their listeners will have spent several hours the evening before relaxing in front of Saturday night television, some will have snuggled down to view one of over 7 million videos rented each week in the UK. Others will have passed into the world of celluloid dreams, gazing at digitally formed images, while immersed in quadraphonic surround-sound at the local cinema or multiplex. An increasing proportion will have been exploring the universe of computer games, or surfing the World Wide Web. Given these diverse and often rich media experiences, it is not surprising that listening to one voice, while seated on a wooden church pew or plastic chair, can compare unfavourably. Not only visitors, but also the regular attendees, may find that a pulpit monologue is hard to concentrate upon. Even in churches renowned for their preaching ministries, it is not uncommon to hear the sermon described as 'frustrating', 'tedious' or 'irrelevant'.[2]

The central contention of this paper is that if preachers want to be heard today, they need to take seriously their communicative environment. This environment is described by some scholars as a 'visual culture' and by others as an 'audio-visual culture'.[3] Behind these terms lies the belief that our context has been significantly shaped by a series of revolutions in communications. Given the development of many media technologies it is probably accurate to describe this history not solely in terms of revolution, but also in terms of the evolution of communications. The advent of the printing press, the telegraph, the wireless, the cinema, the television and the computer have brought both radical, revolutionary changes and also gradual, imperceptible shifts in how we communicate.[4] Whether historians of communication employ evolutionary or revolutionary metaphors in their accounts, they frequently point out that we now speak and listen, work and relax in a 'media saturated' society.[5]

The rapidly evolving communicative setting has serious implications for anyone hoping to communicate orally and effectively. The mass media represents a central element of this setting and few preachers now totally ignore this vital aspect of their listeners' context. Thor Hall argued in the early 1970s that: 'The study of communications media belongs inextricably within the ecology of homiletics.'[6] Stewart Hoover asserted in the early 1980s that for those involved in developing expertise in teaching, ministry or counselling: 'media awareness is no longer a luxury, an affectation or a hobby.'[7] With the rapid development, expansion and convergence of communication technologies in the late 1990s and so called 'noughties' (2000–2010), many preachers are learning to engage critically with their communicative environment.

This chapter is divided into two main sections. First, I set out some of the reasons why preachers should take seriously the implications of working within an audio-visual culture. Secondly, I suggest that a number of developments in homiletics have much to teach preachers who are competing with a whole range of audio-visual stimuli for their congregation's attention. On this basis, I conclude that this highly competitive communicative context necessitates a renewed approach to preaching.

Why it matters?

Our audio-visual culture is like a wall of video monitors simultaneously playing out many different scenes, it has many faces. This section focuses primarily on one face of our mediated audio-visual culture: television. On average the British adult watches well over 20 hours of television a week. The precise psychological and social effects of such regular television viewing is an area of considerable scholarly debate. Television clearly has the *potential* to nurture beliefs, influence opinions and subtly transform our understanding of the world we live in. The question addressed here is: How have writers about preaching described and analysed the impact of television?

Listening capacities reduced?

A common refrain is that television has undermined our ability to listen. Leander Keck, for example, argues that television has 'eroded the place of the sermon' because it has made it 'more difficult for people to attend carefully to merely verbal communication'.[8] On this side of the Atlantic, Simon Vibert articulates the view that 'television provides a threat to serious preaching' as it 'has taught us to expect a frequent change in style of presentation – of presenter, scenery, topic – and this is to be accompanied by a rapid succession of visual images. Preaching, it is presumed, is too long and too dull in a TV age.'[9]

Unsurprisingly, John Stott, one of the twentieth century's well-known British preachers, does not support this presumption, but he does assert that 'preachers have to reckon with a TV-conditioned congregation':

> We have a colossal task on our hands if we hope to counteract the baneful tendencies of much modern television. We can no longer assume that people either want to listen to sermons, or indeed are able to listen. When they are accustomed to the swiftly moving images of the screen, how can we expect them to give their attention to one person talking, no frills, no light relief and nothing else to look at?[10]

It is fair to assert, with Stott, that we cannot assume that congregations will listen. In a televisual age, preachers certainly need to contend for 'people's attention'.

According to Bernard Reymond, a French Professor of Practical Theology, a further factor contributing towards the crisis in the way we listen to preaching is our increased reliance upon the 'zapper' or remote channel control, '"Zapping" has become part of normal behaviour; in front of the TV, the average viewer switches from one channel to another immediately they feel bored; faced with a sermon from the pulpit, they still zapp around in their minds, letting it wander wherever it will.'[11] Reymond argues for a 'revised rhetoric' and a 'video orality' which will help distracted listeners to concentrate more easily on the sermon.

Like Keck and Vibert, Stott and Reymond make a persuasive case. At the heart of these arguments is the belief that television has reduced the churchgoer's capacity to listen. Many of their conclusions about the impact of television on listening, however, they leave comparatively unsubstantiated. Their assumptions about television and listening may not appear unreasonable, but they use little empirical data to support their claims. The danger with such an approach is that it can too easily slide into an over-simplistic 'direct effects' approach to television's influence.[12]

It is necessary to develop a more sophisticated understanding of how our audio-visually saturated environment, and television in particular, cultivate audiences into particular habits of attending, viewing and listening.[13] Such an approach would recognise that 'exposure to television programmes [and other media] will, over time, have a cumulative influence on viewers' perceptions of the world and their place in it'.[14] The cumulative influence of the form and content of the electronic media may indeed influence how congregations now listen, and also how audiences use these media to weave meaning around their own lives.[15]

Of course, one week's viewing will hardly alter the way people listen; nor do specific genres of television necessarily change attention habits. Nevertheless, repeated exposure to this 'audio-visual tapestry',[16] of which television is but one part, undoubtedly has a cumulative influence on how congregations attend. In other words, I do not disagree with the basic conclusions of scholars such as Reymond in this area, I simply question the way in which they have been reached and the breadth of their analysis.[17] A highly significant theme is ignored by each of these authors: Listeners to sermons use television and other media in a range of fashions. They inhabit different, partly self-constructed media-scapes, depending on the media that they choose to consume. Or to put it another way, listeners have multiple media intelligences and practices, which reflect and shape their world views and their patterns of listening.

On this basis it is possible to agree with the author's discussed above that television has *not* irrevocably undermined the ability *to listen*, but it has changed *how people listen*. This transformation has made the task of the preacher a harder one. Whichever approach is used to argue that television, and other electronic audio-visual stimuli, have changed and weakened congregations' ability to listen to the sermon, the sheer frequency with which this view has been asserted points towards a second significant issue: expectations about sermons.

Listening expectations changed?

Television, amongst many other media, has also contributed towards a change in how we expect to be spoken to in the public sphere. The language of television is markedly different from the language of the Victorian pulpit. It has also influenced expectations about the length, style and content of public discourse.

First, a point which connects with the previous section: length. In the 1890s it was not uncommon to hear an impassioned political speech lasting over sixty minutes. In the 1990s some commentators claimed that the average electioneering sound-bite on American television news programmes was down to under ten seconds. British networks may claim to give interviewees or speech-makers more time, but the tendency in news reports is towards short clips of under 30 seconds. The reductionist, selective and fragmentary tendencies of television have contributed to the abbreviation of public discourse.

Secondly, style: a growing number of communication scholars and linguists argue that television has transformed the style in which we expect to be addressed in the public sphere. We do not expect to be spoken at or down to, rather we expect to be spoken with. Kathleen Hall Jamieson, for example, in her fascinating book on *Eloquence in an Electronic Age* argues that:

> Television has changed public discourse dramatically. Increasingly, eloquence is visual, not verbal. Where once we expected messages laced with impassioned appeals, now we respond positively to a cooler, more conversational art; where once audiences expected to be conquered by an art bent on battle, today's television viewer expects instead an intimate rhetoric of conciliation.[18]

Even if the change in public discourse is not as radical as Jamieson suggests, and eloquence is only gradually becoming more visual and conversational, this 'democratisation'[19] of discourse also has serious implications for preachers. Other writers argue that in addition there is a sense in which a more colloquial and spontaneous style of orality is now expected from speakers.[20]

If this analysis is accurate, then it is significant for preaching methodology. A sermon which is constructed as a written text may display literary lucidity, but may lack the apparent spontaneity or colloquialisms necessary for effective oral communication. This shift towards conversational discourse serves as a warning to preachers who are constricted by their reliance on a written text which would be better 'read, silently, by the eye', than 'heard by the ear'.[21] The shift towards a more conversational form of public discourse on television, therefore, has contributed significantly to the changed expectations of listeners.

A third changed expectation is centred on content. Few writers on preaching have seriously engaged with the fact that television has the potential to raise profound theological questions among viewers. The all-too-often repeated images of the two planes exploding into the Twin Towers, for example, led to the preaching of many sermons wrestling with the question of why God allowed this tragedy to happen.[22] Consider, also, Michael Buerk's reports in October 1984 from Korem on the Ethiopian famines. These historic and powerful broadcasts, which spoke of a biblical famine and showed images of children dying of starvation, were the catalyst for BandAid and a huge international relief effort.[23] Like many news reports of tragedy it served as an awakener to issues beyond our physical localities. For many people it raised significant theological questions, such as: Where was God in all this? This is not to suggest that television news, or other television genres, should set the agenda for the preacher, rather they offer a natural bridge into the imaginative world of many listeners. The task of the preacher may be to reframe some of the news imagery offered to the viewer.

Paradoxically, the increased coverage of such suffering has also led to a weariness with such stories, journalistically described as compassion fatigue.[24] Television can transport us right into faraway worlds and yet at the same time can distance us from them. The TV screen image which can herald tragedies, or raise questions of theodicy, can also *screen* us from the reality of suffering. A disaster can often be the lead story for a few hours or days, only then to be dropped to be replaced by the latest 'spectacular' news. While tragedy is rarely transitory for those who experience it first hand, television news may endue real tragedies with an unreal ephemeral quality. This process can turn us into forgetful voyeurs and so anaesthetise us to these images of pain. But it raises a twofold challenge for preachers: to be awakeners and to be interpreters.

The simple reminder being made here is that listeners will have many issues, questions and dilemmas raised by television, and other media, in their minds each Sunday. I am not arguing for a topically-based approach to preaching which always relies upon a news story for its starting point. Unlike Barth who regretted mentioning the First World War in his sermons,[25] I am suggesting that an exposition of biblical texts which entirely ignores the underlying questions or memorable images raised by major stories of the week, will either fail to connect with listeners who are immersed in an audio-visual environment, or will become an act of collusion with those who would prefer we spent our resources on new commodities, rather than alleviating suffering.

In this section I have outlined various reasons why some preachers take seriously the implications of working within an audio-visual culture. First, I have suggested that television has not irrevocably undermined the ability *to listen*, but it has changed *the way people listen* and the expectations they bring with them. On this basis, I have secondly drawn attention to the fact that listeners are accustomed to an increasingly conversational form of discourse. Thirdly, listeners do not come into church like a passive clean slate waiting for words to be written on to them. They come instead as an 'active audience', who have a whole range of images, stories and experiences already engaging their attention. Many of these will have been drawn from the mass media. These three reasons are not intended to be a comprehensive list, rather a reminder that wise preachers engage critically with our communicative context, and so develop an understanding of how listeners are likely to receive their sermons.

How to respond to our communicative context?

In an age where some writers on preaching believe that 'television and motion pictures have shaped a visually orientated generation',[26] it remains important to underline the competitive nature of the communicative environment in which preachers are now operating. The preacher today is normally only an amateur in a world of professional communicators and no longer the only educated voice in the village or town. The preacher's voice is now but one amongst a multitude of others. Preachers are competing for the attention of congregations who are confronted by a kaleidoscopic choice of audio-visual media.

The advent of electronic audio-visual stimuli could be feared as dealing a fatal blow to preaching. One response to such an analysis is to withdraw from preaching, and concentrate on pastoral care, small discussion groups or liturgical and musical excellence. A second more traditionalist response would be simply to highlight the areas where biblical preaching is experiencing a renaissance and argue that these are successful and faithful models worth imitating. A third response, and the one taken here, is to argue that our communicative context raises not only challenges, but also new opportunities for preachers. The contention of this chapter is that our changed context does not toll the death-bell for the sermon. Rather, it provides new challenges and opportunities for preachers who are willing to adapt and to engage critically with the way we communicate today. This second-half of the chapter will therefore explore the ways in which certain writers have attempted to adapt their approaches to our rapidly evolving communicative environment.

From single-camera to multi-camera discourse

David Buttrick's seminal work on how to make 'moves' in sermons is pertinent to this discussion. He frequently draws cinematic or photographic analogies to illustrate his case. In *Homiletic*, for example, he argues that:

> In an earlier era, movie directors worked with a fixed-location camera and moved actors around in front of the lens. Once upon a time the procedure was considered reality, but now when we view old films on late-night TV, they seem stilted and quite unreal. Today directors use a camera on a moving boom so that camera angles change, lenses widen or narrow, distances vary, imitating the actual way we perceive reality. . . . Twentieth-century consciousness views the world from many different standpoints.[27]

On the basis of this change in perception Buttrick argues for a similar development in approaches to making moves within preaching. His point is that a speaker whose set discourse adopts a single, static or fixed point of view, like one of the earliest cameras, may seem slow and turgid to an audience more used to rapid shifts in viewing angles.[28]

Significantly, however, Buttrick does not uncritically adopt and translate cinematic techniques in his methodology for movement in sermons. He argues that speakers to large groups wishing to effect successful moves need to take time with their transitions: 'Group consciousness simply cannot handle rapid shifts in subject matter. To move along from subject to subject every few sentences would "freak out" an audience; the effect would be similar to watching a movie film that has been speeded up many times the normal frames per minute. Minds will wander when pace is intense.'[29] So Buttrick may draw upon film analogies to support his case, but he does not go so far as to argue that preachers should mimic cinematic devices such as rapid camera movement and swift point-of-view moves in their oral discourse. It is plain from this that he has a clear understanding of the distinction between oral and audio-visual forms of communication. This can also be seen by the way in which he draws extensively upon the image of a photographic camera to consider point-of-view in moves, and how to vary 'focal field, lens depth and focal depth'[30] in preaching. Buttrick's use of cinematic and photographic analogies in *Homiletic* demonstrates a sensitivity to his communicative context. He is aware that listeners are used to a range of electronic communication. While these modern media appear to have influenced the development of some of his homiletical theories, it is clear that he is cautious and critical in the lessons he applies from visual media to oral communication.

David Buttrick is a good example of a leading writer on preaching who has attempted to integrate developments in communication with his homiletical method. A good test of his approach is to reflect on how his methodology might work out in practice. Consider, for example, the tale of the Good Samaritan (Luke 10:25–37), where the story can be told from a variety of angles. Inviting the congregation to stand with the questioning lawyer, to walk with the religious professionals or to lie in the ditch with the mugged traveller, may help the listeners to experience the story more fully.[31] Shifting the viewpoint runs the risk, of course, of being taken to ridiculous extremes, with expressions of what the donkey saw or the bird in the nearby tree spied. Furthermore there is a danger that too many viewpoints or idiosyncratic perspectives might distract from the original direction of the parable. As long as these qualifications are born in mind, then, 'shifts in character point of view, as with the parable of the good Samaritan, are rich with potential for new insight and even new hearings of the biblical narrative.'[32]

Such shifts from one point-of-view to another are by no means a new homiletical technique. Preachers have long employed such a multi-angled approach. A common rhetorical device is to lead listeners to different viewpoints at the crucifixion. The perspective of the gambling soldiers, mocking religious leaders, weeping women or cowardly disciples enables the preacher to explore contrasting responses to Jesus' death. Similarly, in terms of preaching on parables, the power lies in enabling listeners to see the story from a variety of angles and so catch new glimpses of the familiar. The goal is that it will draw listeners into viewing their lives and the world in alternative ways. The danger, however, of being locked into one viewpoint remains. On the basis of Buttrick's argument, this could be described as a single fixed-camera approach, which merely allows the characters to pass across the screen of the imagination, or simply views the entire story from one perspective. This will also limit the story's potential power for multi-angle conditioned listeners. A different form could be described as a multi-camera approach. If sensitively handled, this could lead listeners into and through a story and so allow them to experience its movement and its depth.

For Buttrick the power lies not in discovering and making a single point in three different ways, but rather in enabling listeners to move through the story itself and so encounter its original force afresh. This multi-camera approach appears to have the potential to engage, even empower, listeners who are used to frequent changes of points of view in the cinema or on the small screen.

It has been implied in this section that Buttrick's argument, characterised as the move from a single fixed-camera form of preaching to a multi-camera approach to preaching, is robust, especially when it is recognised that cinematographic developments have ensured that listeners are now used to viewing from a number of perspectives. If this is the case, then a form of orality that offers a variety of perspectives is more likely to hold listeners' attention.

From proclamatory to conversational discourse

It was suggested in the first section of this chapter that we have become accustomed to a more conversational form of discourse. Think for example of a BBC Radio 1 DJ or Radio 4 *Today* presenter, who speak as if they were friends in your front room. Such conversationalised discourse means that for many listeners the single voice attempting to speak authoritatively from the pulpit has lost much of its power. In our transformed preaching situation the sermon delivered as a closed monologue may fail to connect with listeners.

A range of writers have identified the real danger of alienating or at least distancing listeners by relying on the traditional monological style of preaching. Henry Eggold, for example, suggests in *Preaching is Dialogue* that: 'One of the exciting and hopeful developments in preaching today is the accent on preaching as dialogue. It is an attempt to think of the sermon as a dialogue between preacher and listener instead of as the dreary monologue that it so often is.'[33] Note here how Eggold is arguing not so much for a termination of it as a single-voiced communicative practice, but rather as a reconceptualisation of preaching as dialogue. Eggold is by no means a lone voice in this understanding of preaching as dialogue.

Other writers have moved on from the image of preaching as dialogue to that of preaching as conversation or interaction. David Schlafer suggests that 'preaching is more of a community interaction than an individual monologue.' He develops this point, suggesting that:

> Preaching is more than speaking *to* a congregation, however sensitively, it is speaking *for* and *with* a congregation as well. Preaching attempts to articulate the concerns, questions, commitments, and celebrations of the whole faith community. . . . The sermon is not a monologue, but an unfolding conversation of the people of God – a conversation about and with God, and about their struggles to know and be faithful to God.[34]

At the heart of Schlafer's argument for conversational preaching is the strongly stated belief that preachers should listen to a whole range of voices before speaking.

At this stage it is valuable to see how certain writers have attempted to develop a more dialogical or conversational mode of preaching. Many draw upon Fred Craddock's work on preaching. Craddock identifies the problem of the monological approach which treats listeners like vessels for pouring information into. He suggests that 'sermons which begin with conclusions and general truths arrived at by the minister in the privacy of a study tend to oppress and treat as less than fully faithful and capable a listening congregation. Today, this is often called the banking method of communicating; that is, the speaker simply makes deposits of information in the mind of the listener.'[35] Craddock is explaining how he came to prefer an inductive approach over a deductive approach for preaching. He suggests inductive movement is from the 'particulars to the general', and deductive is from 'the general to particulars'. The inductive approach attempts to turn the sermon from a closed monologue into a conversation between 'the congregation and the biblical text'.[36]

In the parable of the Good Samaritan (Luke 10:25–37), for example, a deductive approach might begin with the general statement: 'Love your neighbour as yourself'(v.27). The parable would be used as a tool to support this imperative. An inductive approach might invite the listeners to reflect on the characters portrayed in this story. How do they act? What do they say? How is it pertinent today? These could be questions raised to consider by a speaker preparing to preach on this story. In short, Craddock's approach to inductive preaching is an attempt to move the authority from the preacher to the text. The congregation is invited to explore it with the help of the speaker, rather than have the answers thrust upon them.

Some have gone further than Craddock's inductive model[37] and argued that preachers should use an 'interactive' or a 'collaborative' form of preaching. Interactive preaching involves listeners in the actual preaching event by encouraging responses to questions, while collaborative preaching encourages listeners to participate in the sermon preparation and feedback process. In both *Interactive Preaching*[38] and *The Roundtable Pulpit*,[39] it is clear that the authors are keen to move away from the monological or 'sovereign' approach which often finds its theological support in a Barthian understanding of preaching. This move raises a foundational issue: 'Since preaching is essentially monological, how best can principles and practices of truly participative dialogue be incorporated?'[40] Such a question lies behind Eggold's, Schlafer's and McClure's discussions of preaching as dialogue, conversation and collaboration.

In this section I have demonstrated how there has been an attempt by certain writers and preachers to move away from seeing preaching as a monologue to a more interactive model, which involves the listeners participating more actively in the process of preaching. Underlying these attempts is the recognition that there has been a crisis of confidence in the authority of the preacher, partially brought about by the multiplicity of voices communicated through the electronic media. To be heard in such an environment many preachers are now attempting to involve listeners more in the communication process. This 'truly participative' form of discourse is rooted in inductive, dialogical, conversational and collaborative preaching practices.

From visual to multi-sensory discourse

There are forms of discourse which are appropriate to our competitive communicative environment. One theme touched upon in the first half of this chapter is the move from verbal forms to visual forms of communication. A range of writers have attempted to explore how to communicate effectively in this apparently image-saturated culture. Our new preaching situation, where television and film as electronic storytellers and image creators dominate, led Paul Scott Wilson to argue that: 'What Barth told preachers needs updating: Have the Bible in one hand, the newspaper in the other, and the TV on in the background'.[41] Wilson has added the TV to the famous Barthian dictum.

A frequent refrain in Paul Scott Wilson's text-book, *The Practice of Preaching*, is the 'need for preachers to make a movie with words'.[42] Wilson develops this theme in *The Four Pages of the Sermon*, where he describes the preacher as someone who is filming both trouble and grace in the Bible and the world.[43] Imagine, for example, what decisions you would have to make if you were filming the paralysed man being lowered through a roof to Jesus. One of the strengths of this approach is that it liberates preachers from thinking of creating a sermon as similar to the act of writing an essay. There are obviously significant differences between the craft of cinematography and craft of preaching, becoming a 'movie director' with words demands that the preacher develop skills for helping listeners experience imaginatively the world of the scriptural text. In *Visually Speaking* I suggest that the craft of radio broadcasting, perhaps even more than film-making, has much to teach preachers.[44]

Some writers' advice in this area resonates with an Ignatian approach to biblical texts. Charles Rice, for example, suggests that, 'if we have an experience of the text, allow ourselves to be led deeply into its images – in our mind's eye to see its people, places, and things – to experience its language as a new dawning, there is every likelihood that the resulting sermon will in form and content, rely upon and awaken the imagination.'[45]

One of the great strengths of re-imagining the world of the text is that it unleashes a stream of concrete and 'vivid language',[46] with which the preacher can create images on the screens of listeners' imaginations.

The best preachers go beyond engaging the visual imagination. They use 'words which you can see, smell, touch, taste, hear and feel'.[47] As I suggest in *Visually Speaking* one of the strengths of such multi-sensory language is that it can work on many different levels, feeding different parts of the listeners' imaginations. Behind many of these calls for the development of pictorial or multi-sensory language is a serious attempt to generate effective oral communication and so engage the listener more actively in the communicative act. This kind of preaching is a more interactive form of discourse. This part of the discussion began with a call for preachers to act like movie directors, and has ended with an encouragement to develop a discursive style which engages all the senses.

From reframing to reimagining

Television news creates frames around particular events, which help to concentrate the audience's attention upon particular images or stories. Inevitably this selective process not only includes, but also excludes vital information. The Second Gulf War, for example, dominated the news frames of the West, while the ongoing war in the Congo, which claimed over 3 million lives in the last decade, was usually entirely excluded. The picture of the toppling of Saddam Hussein's statue in Baghdad was frequently framed as an iconic symbol of victory, relegating images such as the small Iraqi boy, Ali, who lost his arms and legs in American bombing to one of the previous day's pictures. The way a particular news story is framed also contributes to our understanding of the actual situation.[48] Preaching at its best also involves the reframing of world events in the light of the good news of God's redemptive involvement in the world.

While Jesus' parables reframed reality in unexpected ways, they also encouraged the listener to reimagine the world in new ways. Biblical scholar Walter Brueggemann describes preaching as an act of 'reimagination'. He sees the preacher as offering an 'image through which perception, experience, and finally faith can be reorganised in alternative ways'. This is ultimately like an invitation to 'abandon the script in which one has had confidence and to enter a different script that imaginatively tells one's life differently'. For Brueggemann nobody 'can switch worlds unless an alternative world is made richly available with great artistry, care and boldness'.[49] The listener is encouraged not only to reframe the world differently, but to reimagine her or his place in that world. In some circumstances, such reframing and reimagining will help the listener to laugh at themselves and their experience of the world.[50]

Conclusion: preaching as re-description[51]

Many of the craftspeople who work in producing films, news or other television programmes are highly skilled at describing the world. They often do it with 'artistry, care and boldness', assisted by extensive resources to support their endeavours. Many of these descriptions in the West reflect an agnostic or atheistic understanding of reality. They may not be intentionally secular, but they tend to slide towards such a world view. In this context the preacher is called to help the listener reframe news and reimagine reality through acts of verbal re-description. This may go beyond what Mary Hilkert describes as 'naming grace' in the world,[52] and provide a counter narrative which invites listeners to participate in God's redemptive love for the world. Participation in the life, death and resurrection of Jesus Christ is a central foundation for listeners and preachers seeking to redescribe some of the media's 'realities'. Regular worshippers may well already have a deep reservoir from the Christian tradition to draw upon as they collaborate with the preacher in developing practices of resistance, celebration or reintepretation of the media.

This theological grounding is more significant than the fact that as a face-to-face medium, in which a single voice relies primarily on verbal communication, preaching is a rare species in our audio-visual jungle. Preaching's communicative idiosyncrasy may actually help preachers be heard as they seek to redescribe the world in the light of God's grace. When compared to other forms of communication habitually used today, preaching stands out, almost alone, as a set piece of public discourse. This strangeness may be a strength in a context where electronically mediated communication appears to dominate. Nevertheless, even if preaching is *sui generis*, preachers cannot afford to ignore our audio-visual context, nor should they acquiesce entirely in its more seductive images. Preaching has reached a transitional period where both its theory and practice are at last beginning to adapt to an environment where many congregations are becoming more used to interactive and audio-visually based communication.

Preachers who wish to be effective communicators of the *evangelion* today cannot yearn for or mimic styles from 'the golden age of pulpit princes', nor can they continue without making at least some concessions to the more dialogical forms of public discourse that listeners are accustomed to hearing. Voices from the new homiletic movement which point towards shifts in how we speak and listen are starting to be heeded. Preachers who seek to point distracted congregations towards a Galilean who adapted his discourse to challenge his listeners, need to adapt likewise to and critically engage with our highly competitive communicative environment. He was skilled at preaching pictures and telling stories that helped listeners reinterpret their own lives in the light of the good news of the Kingdom of God.

Notes

1 This article is an updated, revised and expanded version of 'Preaching in an Audio-Visual Culture', *Anvil*, 14, 4, 1997, pp. 262–72.

2 See Mark Green, 'Is Anybody Listening?', *Anvil*, 14, 4, 1997, pp. 283–94.

3 See: Chris Jenks (ed.), *Visual Culture*, London, Routledge, 1995, and Henk Hoekstra and Marjeet Verbeek, 'Possibilities of Audiovisual Narrative', in Philip J. Rossi and Paul A. Soukup (eds), *Mass Media and the Moral Imagination*, Kansas City, Sheed and Ward, 1994. They argue that the 'audiovisual culture' represents 'the culture of the masses' (p. 215).

4 See, for example, David Crowley and Paul Heyer (eds), *Communication in History: Technology, Culture, Society*, New York, Longman, 2002.

5 Wesley Carr, *Ministry and the Media*, London, SPCK, 1990, p. 58, 'one point is indisputable, we live in a media saturated environment.'

6 Thor Hall, *The Future Shape of Preaching*, Philadelphia, Fortress, 1971, p. 4.

7 Stewart Hoover, *The Electronic Giant*, Illinois, Brethren Press, 1982, p. 155.

8 Leander E. Keck, *The Bible in the Pulpit: The Renewal of Biblical Preaching*, Nashville, Abingdon, 1978, p. 40.

9 Simon Vibert, 'The Church in the Age of the TV Image: Dare We Still Preach?', *Orthos*, 12, Northwich, Cheshire, Fellowship of Word and Spirit, 1993, p. 19.

10 John Stott, *I Believe in Preaching*, London, Hodder & Stoughton, 1982, p. 75. Stott had earlier argued pessimistically that 'TV has the tendency to make audiences physically lazy, intellectually uncritical, emotionally insensitive, psychologically confused, and morally disorientated' (pp. 70–2). See also Michael Rogness, *Preaching to a TV Generation: The Sermon in the Electronic Age*, Lima, Ohio, CSS Publishing, 1994, p. 29: 'One of the results of passive listening is superficial listening'; and Derek Weber, *Preaching To Be Heard in a Television Age*, unpublished PhD thesis, University of Edinburgh, 1993.

11 Bernard Reymond, 'Preaching and the New Media', *Modern Churchman*, XXXIV, 5, 1993, pp. 19–29. He believes that 'people are becoming trained by TV to share out their attention in quite new ways', p. 24.

12 There is a huge literature on media effects research, a good introductory text is: Denis McQuail, *Mass Communication Theory: An Introduction*, London, Sage, 1994.

13 'Cultivation analysis looks at [television's] messages as an environment within which people live, define themselves and others, and develop and maintain their beliefs and assumptions about reality'. 'Cultivation Analysis: Conceptualization and Methodology', in Nancy Signorielli and Michael Morgan (eds), *Cultivation Analysis: New Directions in Media Effects Research*, Newbury Park, California, Sage, 1990, p. 18.

14 David Gauntlett, *Moving Experiences: Understanding Television's Influences and Effects*, Acamedia Research Monograph 13, London, John Libbey, 1995, p. 97.

15   See, for example, Lynn Schofield Clark, 'The 'Funky' Side of Religion: An Ethnographic Study of Adolescent Religious Identity and the Media', in Jolyon Mitchell and Sophia Marriage (eds), *Mediating Religion: Conversations in Media, Religion and Culture*, London, T. &T. Clark/Continuum, 2003, pp. 21–32.

16   Gordon L. Berry and Joy Keiko Asamen, *Children and Television: Images in a Changing Sociocultural World*, London, Sage, 1993, p. 1. Television is described as an 'audiovisual tapestry on which is being woven a complex and ever-changing national and international set of images that are hung on the small screen for all to see'.

17   My critique is based primarily upon the methodologies of homileticians such as Reymond, Vibert and Stott, who appear to rely too heavily on a hypodermic needle model of communication. This is 'a mechanistic and unsophisticated model of media-audience relationship, which sees the media as "injecting" values, ideas and information into each individual in a passive and atomised audience, thereby producing a direct and unmediated effect'. Tim O'Sullivan, John Hartley, Danny Saunders and John Fiske, *Key Concepts in Communication*, London, Routledge, 1983, p. 105.

18   Kathleen Hall Jamieson, *Eloquence in an Electronic Age: The Transformation of Political Speechmaking*, Oxford, Oxford University Press, 1988, p. 44.

19   See Norman Fairclough, *Media Discourse*, London, Edward Arnold, 1995, on 'Democratisation' of media discourse, pp. 148–9.

20   See Alyce M. McKenzie, *Preaching Proverbs – Wisdom for the Pulpit*, Louisville, Kentucky, Westminster/John Knox, 1996, p. xix.

21   G. Robert Jacks, *Just Say the Word! Writing for the Ear*, Grand Rapids, MI, Eerdmans, 1996, p. 1.

22   For examples of sermons following 9/11, see William H. Willimon (ed.), *The Sunday After Tuesday: College Pulpits Respond to 9/11*, Nashville, Abingdon, 2002; Forrest Church (ed.), *Restoring Faith: America's Religious Leaders Answer Terror with Hope*, New York, Walker and Company, 2001; David P. Polk (ed.), *Shaken Foundations: Sermons from America's Pulpits after the Terrorist Attacks*, St Louis, MO, Chalice Press, 2001; and Martha Simmons and Frank A. Thomas (eds), *9.11.01: African American Leaders Respond to an American Tragedy*, Valley Forge, Judson Press, 2001.

23   For extensive discussion of this coverage, see Greg Philo, 'From Buerk to Band Aid: The Media and the 1984 Ethiopian famine', in John Eldridge (ed.), *Getting the Message: News, Truth and Power*, London, Routledge, 1993, pp. 104–25.

24   For an analysis of how the American media threatens our ability to understand the world around us, see Susan D. Moeller, *Compassion Fatigue: How the Media Sell, Disease, Famine, War and Death*, London, Routledge, 1999.

25   See David Buttrick's foreword to Karl Barth, *Homiletics*, Louisville, Westminister/John Knox, 1991, p. 9.

26   Patricia Wilson-Kastner, *Imagery for Preaching*, Minneapolis, Fortress, 1989, p. 21.

27   David G Buttrick, *Homiletic: Moves and Structures*, London, SCM, 1987, p. 55; see also his 'Preaching to the "Faith" of America', in Leonard I. Sweet (ed.), *Communication and Change in American Religious History*, Grand Rapids, MI, Eerdmans, 1993, p. 316.

28   David G. Buttrick, *Homiletic: Moves and Structures*, London, SCM, 1987: 'Preaching that talks objectively about everything, as if from a third-person observational position, will not only seem archaic but may have an aura of unreality' (p. 56).

29   David G. Buttrick, 1987, p. 25.

30   'Alterations in focal field, lens depth, and focal depth can be managed with ease. Thus we can widen or narrow focus without much difficulty, although we cannot include more than one such alteration in any single move'. David G. Buttrick, 1987, p. 63.

31   See: Robert W. Funk, *Parables and Presence: Forms of the New Testament Tradition*, Philadelphia, Fortress, 1982, pp. 29–34. Funk argues that this parable should be interpreted from the perspective of the victim and not the Good Samaritan.

32 Richard L. Eslinger, *Narrative and Imagination: Preaching the Worlds that Shape Us*, Minneapolis, Fortress, 1995, p. 145.

33 Henry J. Eggold, *Preaching is Dialogue: A Concise Introduction to Homiletics*, Grand Rapids, MI, Baker Book House, 1980, p. 11.

34 Henry J. Eggold, 1980, p. 24.

35 Fred Craddock, 'Inductive Preaching', unpublished paper for the Societas Homiletica, Stetson University, August 20–23, 1990, p. 8.

36 Fred Craddock, 1990, pp. 10 and 12.

37 See Paul Scott Wilson, *The Practice of Preaching*, Nashville, Abingdon, 1995, p. 214. Wilson makes an incisive critique on the use of inductive and deductive categories to describe the form of a sermon. He argues: 'Inductive and deductive categories may work to describe styles of preaching, but they do not work when each is attached to a particular form of sermon. . . . Preaching can be authoritarian in any form.'

38 D. Stephenson Bond, *Interactive Preaching*, Missouri, St Louis, CBP, 1991.

39 John S. McClure, *The Roundtable Pulpit: Where Leadership and Preaching Meet*, Nashville, Abingdon, 1995. See especially Chapter 2: 'Towards a Collaborative Homiletic' and Chapter 3: 'Collaborative Preaching'.

40 John S. McClure, *The Roundtable Pulpit*, p. 47.

41 Paul Scott Wilson, *The Practice of Preaching*, Nashville, Abingdon, 1995, p 279. He continues: 'The lives of our congregation's members are shaped by media. How they think is affected by media. What they talk about is in part provided by media.'

42 Paul Scott Wilson, 1995, pp. 255 and 112. 'We become like movie directors.' See also pp. 183 and 132.

43 Paul Scott Wilson, *The Four Pages of the Sermon: A Guide to Biblical Preaching*, Nashville, Abingdon, 1999.

44 Jolyon P. Mitchell, *Visually Speaking: Radio and the Renaissance of Preaching*, Edinburgh, T. & T. Clark, 1999.

45 Charles Rice, 'Shaping Sermons by the interplay of Text and Metaphor', in Don M. Wardlaw (ed.), *Preaching Biblically*, Philadelphia, Westminster, 1983, p. 104. Also cited by Richard Eslinger in *A New Hearing*, p. 22.

46 Sidney Greidanus, *The Modern Preacher and the Ancient Text: Interpreting and Preaching Biblical Literature*, Grand Rapids, MI, Eerdmans, 1988, p. 186. Greidanus emphasises the importance of 'using concrete, vivid language'.

47 Edward F. Markquart, *Quest for Better Preaching*, Minneapolis, Augsburg, 1984.

48 For a more extensive discussion of reframing news, see *Media and Christian Ethics*, Cambridge University Press, forthcoming.

49 Walter Brueggemann, 'Preaching as Reimagination', in *Theology Today*, 52, 2, 1995, pp. 313–29, see especially pp. 323 and 327. (Chapter 2 of this volume.)

50 See David Day, *A Preaching Workbook*, London, Lynx, 1998, pp. 65–70 and *passim*.

51 I am indebted to Nick Adams and Ben Quash for encouraging me to think about redescription.

52 Mary Catherine Hilkert, *Naming Grace: Preaching and the Sacramental Imagination*, New York, Continuum, 1998. Writing from a Catholic perspective, Hilkert sets out both the foundations for, and way in which preachers can name grace in the life of their listeners, even if broken by suffering and tragedy.

18   On Preaching a Parable: The Problem of Homiletic Method

David G. Buttrick

A *nouveau riche* mid-westerner took his wife to dinner at a posh French restaurant. Seeking to impress, he grabbed what he thought was the menu and, mispronouncing, rattled off an order. Unfortunately, he had picked up the Wine List so he ordered two bottles of wine as an appetizer, six bottles of wine as an entreé, and instead of after-dinner coffee, two more bottles of wine. 'Monsieur', said the waiter as he replaced the Wine List with a Menu, 'It helps to know what you are reading!' Good advice for preachers pondering a text; it *does* help to know what we read. What are the parables? Are they allegory, simple first century 'sermon illustrations', mysterious metaphors extended into stories? Our understanding of *what* we preach will usually determine *how* we preach. So, the question: What is a parable?

What is a parable?

For eighteen centuries the answer was easy: Parables were allegories. From early fathers of the faith to mid-nineteenth century, from Origen to Trench, parables were read and preached allegorically.[1] Oh, the Reformers protested, but Luther was known to lapse and allegorize from the pulpit.[2] Of course, it was scripture itself that got the notion of allegory established. Does not the Gospel of Mark follow the little parable of the sower with a labored 'allegory of the soils' and, what's more, attribute the allegory to Jesus himself? The same Gospel cites an odd justification for allegory in words that sound strangely like the stuff of Mystery Cults:

> To you has been given the secret of the Kingdom of God, but for those outside everything is in parables, so that they may indeed see but not perceive, and may indeed hear but not understand; lest they turn again, and be forgiven. (Mk 4:11–12)

Certainly the words seem to add up to an elitist understanding of parables; abstruse language for an in-group to encode by faith, while those on the 'out' stand excluded, unable to crack the code. So no wonder interpreters read into parables all kinds of exotic allusion. For example, every detail of the prodigal son story was unraveled with care: the robe = Adam's original innocence; the ring = baptism; the feasting = Eucharist; and 'the fatted calf' was surely Christ himself, presumably a calf fatted 'from the foundation of the world!'[3] Other old favorites suffered a similar fate. Would you believe that in the nineteenth century an Anglican rector (better nameless) insisted that in the story of the 'Good Samaritan' when Christ mentioned Inn and Innkeeper he actually had in mind the Established Church and her Victorian Archbishop; or that in our twentieth century a Presbyterian (also better nameless) in an affluent congregation praised the innkeeper as an honest entrepreneur, symbol of Christ's holy enthusiasm for the American free enterprise system?

The big break-away from allegory is usually associated with the name of Adolf Jülicher whose two volume work on the parables, published in the 1890s, inaugurated a new age of interpretation.[4] Two of Jülicher's conclusions have received widespread endorsement: (a) Parables are stories of everyday life in first century Palestine, and (b) Parables are simple comparisons with a single focus or meaning. Jülicher saw Jesus as a wise preacher drawing sermon illustrations from the stuff of everyday, illustrations that could be grasped easily and immediately by his audience. The two notions are, of course, antithetical to allegorical interpretation for they undercut esoteric reference and multiple meaning, the stuff of allegory since the time of Cicero.

While Jülicher's contribution to parable study is well-known and still much admired, the simple 'meanings' he found in many parables sound suspiciously like the general religious 'truths' of turn-of-the-century theological liberalism; they border on banality. Jülicher read the story of the talents and observed, 'A reward is only earned by performance.' He unpacked the Parable of the Unjust Steward and summed it up, saying, 'Wise use of the present is the condition of a happy future.'[5] His interpretations are as unexceptional as the rhetoric of a Rotary convention! If allegory is theologically objectionable – Would a God who wants to reveal himself to a loved world talk in code?; Jülicher's summary statements seem equally improbable – Would the high and holy God of Israel wrap his glory in a Whitman's Sampler? Jesus' teachings reduced to conventional wisdom sound so utterly bland that his cross is inexplicable; the only reason to execute such a bumbling fool would be to end boredom! All biblical interpretation is a product of historical consciousness and therefore a reading by particular theologies no matter how cautious a scholar: Jülicher looked at parables through Ritschlian glasses.

Since the turn of the century, and particularly since Albert Schweitzer's *Quest* ended up in eschatology,[6] scholars have chucked Jülicher's 'liberal' interpretations. C.H. Dodd working from a 'realized eschatology', denied Jülicher's somewhat moralistic interpretations in favor of the thesis that parables are best understood in relation to the crisis of Jesus' ministry.[7] J. Jeremias, adopting a 'progressive eschatology', set parables in the mind of an expectant church, looking toward the future of God.[8] Bultmann, Dodd, Jeremias, and others elaborated methodology, refined classifications, rewrote interpretation with an eye toward New Testament eschatology; but nevertheless, Jülicher's basic 'axioms' – *stories of everyday, simple single meaning* – stood for more than half a century.

Some new questions

About 1960, some new questions began to be raised.[9] Nowadays both of Jülicher's basic convictions appear to be in trouble. Oh, the change of mind signals no return to allegorical interpretation, but contemporary scholarship does sense that parable form is more mysterious than supposed and that a rhetoric of parable may be intricate indeed.

Are parables stories of everyday life in first century Palestine? Rather than finding reflections of common life in parables, some scholars have spotted odd details in many (*not* all). Is it likely that a woman would spend all day looking for lost small change and then throw an expensive bash in the middle of the night to celebrate her finding? Is it probable that when Jesus asks, 'Which of you having a hundred sheep and losing one will not leave the ninety-nine ... ', local sheep herders would agree? Is it sane to suppose that a man owing a four billion dollar loan would say in effect, 'Just give me a little more time and I'll pay it off?' Would farmers sowing seed toss most into thorn bushes, rock piles, and down the center stripe of highways?[10] While not every parable contains a surreal detail, a touch of the bizarre, a breach of reality, a *verfremdungeffect* ('alienation effect'), many, many do.[11]

Years ago a surrealist artist painted a picture of a desert. There was flat sand, a flat horizon line, a flat sunset sky, and rubble from an old adobe house. In the middle of the painting, however, was a large, limp pocket watch. The effect was troubling. Without the big-as-a-house watch, viewers could assemble details of the picture into a consistent 'world' of meaning, but the pocket watch could not, would not be assembled; it didn't fit in and so threatened a viewer's 'world construct'. So with some parables: At first we enter their world with ease because, after all, parables are startlingly clichéd having stock plots, stock characters, and usually stock 'world constructs'. But a sudden intrusion of the surreal tends to threaten our stock world – laborers are paid the same for one hour's work as for twelve; mustard seeds replace triumphalist cedars; a *woman* bakes dozens of 'temple loaves' in a bread-box-sized semitic oven.[12] The stock 'world' of conventional wisdom is suddenly dissolved, and we are distanced by the bizarre.

Now modern parable research has challenged traditional assumptions in still another way. The hallowed notion of a simple, single meaning which Jülicher ventured (from his reading of Aristotle),[13] now seems less than sure. Parables have structure and by their structured 'plots' produce a traveling action in consciousness. We seem to be dealing with a language that, by moving in the mind, transforms or converts. What we do not meet in parables is *a* teaching, *a* single 'point', *a* religious value or theological proposition. To take a simple example, study the little parable in Luke 17:7–10. The parable begins by placing listeners in a position of mastery: 'Which of you having a slave will . . . ?' The arrogance of mastery is reinforced by, 'Does he thank the slave for doing what was commanded?' Suddenly in the last verse, the parable substitutes a different 'model': '*We* are unworthy slaves. . . ' Yes, preachers could distill a 'topic', e.g. 'servanthood', and proceed to elaborate on the topic with 'points', but the radical shift in 'models' would thereby be lost, the power to transform overlooked. Most parables are much more sophisticated, but no less action in consciousness. To reduce parables to a single 'point' turns them into static propositional truths, frustrating their intentional power.

What parables may do is to let us enter them on *our* terms, to find at the outset our own rather stock understandings of self, world, and God; then, suddenly, to disrupt our world so that in the end we find ourselves translated into a mysterious new world, dimly grasped, forced to change – to rethink our lives before The Mystery.[14] Some parables remind you of Lewis Carrolls's *Through the Looking Glass*'.[15] At the beginning of the story, Alice is playing with her kitten in a secure Victorian parlor. Suddenly a mirror over the mantle turns milky. She investigates and unexpectedly tumbles into a strange other world where she senses that somehow she must change herself. Such a pattern lurks in the Parables of the Workers and Hours. At first the world is recognizably *our* world; a world of hours, cash, and farm workers. Then, without warning, all workers are paid the same. We listeners are incensed, and at once identify with the all-day worker's 'Grievance Committee', only to hear the Boss address us, saying, 'Take yours and go!' Baffled, we begin to make sense of the rebuff when the Boss adds, 'Didn't I pay you what *you* bargained for?'[16] Good heavens, all along we've been living life as a religious bargain; no wonder we've resented free grace for neighbors! Finally we are left standing in a free-grace Kingdom forced to decide which world to live in. How can such traveling action in consciousness be reduced to a 'topic?' Modern parable study seems to have annihilated the notion of a 'single point'.

Preaching and parables

Take a look at homiletic theory. In seminary, most of us were taught some particular way of putting sermons together. A few popular systems may be singled out and described.

'*Point-making' Sermons*: Many preachers read a text and, with congregation in mind, distill from the text a topic on which to preach. A number of points are then made about the text, often categorically. Notice that 'points' do seem to *point at* aspects of the topic from what might be described as a 'third person' rational point-of-view. How does such a method fare with parables? Not well. We have remarked that parables can no longer be boiled down to a single truth or teaching because they contain moving 'plot-lines' that structure dynamically in consciousness. When preachers pick out 'something to preach on' from texts, they select a static subject matter which tends to frustrate the unfolding action of parables. More, 'point-making' involves an objective looking *at* and talking *about* which turns parables into a subject of discussion rather than a language designed to interact in consciousness.

Situational Sermons: Ever since Harry Emerson Fosdick, some preachers have begun sermons with the delineation of human concern, a real problem troubling people in 'the living of these days'. Scripture is then imported into the sermon as a 'resource' offering insight or, sometimes, an answer. Because 'raw' scripture seldom seems to address actual situations without interpretation, preachers select and read scripture in light of the particular problem they have chosen to describe. How do parables function in Situational Preaching? Parables are forced to fit into our world, to adjust to our definition of *our* problems. Thus parables are scaled down to problem-solving. They are domesticated, and the disruptive power of the 'surreal' is tamed. Because parables are forced to address a particular reading of a particular human situation, they become over-focused and their 'world' trans-forming power is negated. In a word, parables are *used*.

Conversionist Sermons: In the American revivalist tradition, preachers seem to assume that all scripture intends conversion, and that conversion has a proper sequence, a set *Ordo Salutis* ('Order of Salvation'). As a result, conversionist preachers will force texts to fit a sermon sequence such as Conviction of Sin, Good News of Grace, Call to Repentence. The notion that parables may convert is not far-fetched; we have noted that parables may challenge conventional 'models' and, by their traveling action, change us. However, a fixed *Ordo Salutis* cannot be found in all parables. Thus, any attempt to impose a conversionist pattern will deform parables. For example, while many scholars have read conversion in the story of the Prodigal Son, suppose, hypothetically, that there are actually *no* conversions in the parable. The younger son's 'conversion' looks suspiciously like soup-kitchen calculation, while the older brother shows no inclination to turn and join a party in progress. Were such an interpretation valid, we would be left with nothing more (or less) than a free-grace 'Father' with no interest in required repentence. Notice that if we begin with a conversionist eye, we cannot even conceive the option.

Add it up: Traditional 'Enlightenment' homiletics cannot cope with parables. If, as many scholars suppose, parables are in some sense prototypical words of Jesus, then Christ's own preaching judges our homiletic procedures inadequate. Somehow or other, we must search out a new way to speak.

What to do?

Let me step into the foreground to write autobiographically; personal narrative may clarify. None of us two-legged types is terribly original. We do not manufacture 'new' ideas; they come visiting. Language, by changing, threads new ideas in our minds, so that at any cultural moment 'new thought' may be weaving into the fabric of an age.[17] So, I would not pretend originality, but perhaps I can gesture toward some culturally-at-hand ideas that have nudged my mind.

About two decades ago, though conventional homiletics seemed to be working well enough and even packing churches (What didn't during the halcyon fifties?), I became disaffected. Yes, I preached regularly and my preaching seemed appreciated, but I was uneasy. (Taught by Tillich, my early sermons tended to correlate existential probing with Christian understandings. Looking back now, they seem incredibly 'personalist'.) Disillusioned with a British-American preaching tradition often either pretentious or trivial, I groped for some other way of speaking. Homiletic texts were, sad to say, of little help. Eventually, my search sent me scurrying about in poetics, hermeneutics, the Black narrative preaching tradition, phenomenologies of language (after flirting with analytic philosophy and its first cousin communication theory).

At the outset, I chucked conventional 'sermon topics' often built on a single verse text. After all, there were biblical passages to choose, pericopes which may have evolved from original homiletic material. Long-enough biblical passages at least offered something substantial to grapple with. So I asked, Could sermons be faithful to the structural content of a passage and, to some degree, match form for form? (Concern for fidelity may have been prompted by a determined ploughing through Barth's *Church Dogmatics*, while preoccupation with form probably resulted from an early collision with the 'new hermeneutic', particularly as pushed by Amos Wilder.) My initial homiletic experiments were clumsy, compulsively biblical, and something of a disaster (My poor students!), but from these experiments I salvaged two notions which now seem indispensable: (a) The idea of *movement* in language led me to examine the 'logics' by which different pericopes traveled (a semi-structural preoccupation); and (b) the idea of *intention* (*not* authorial, but in and of the language) piqued the suspicion that sermonic speech should be designed 'to do' in congregational consciousness. Ever since I have been tinkering with a homiletic based on 'movement' and 'intention'.

At the same time as I chased down theoretical questions, I was able to launch a series of semi-empirical studies aimed at determining how *in fact* language did function in communal consciousness. Again and again, findings seemed to contradict conventional homiletic advice – all the technical stuff put forth in 'How-to-Preach' books about structure, syntax, illustration, introductions, conclusions, and the like. Either homiletic texts were wrong or, if once correct, were no longer applicable to an emerging, quite different cultural 'mind'. Gradually, piece by piece, I began to assemble a substantial new repetoire of homiletic ways and means to teach. One finding seemed to suggest that nowadays it may take as long as three minutes to 'fix' a simple idea in congregational consciousness while, at the same time, attention span for a given conceptual may be brief – not much more than three minutes! As a result, I began to design sermons as a sequence of language modules, 'moves'. Sermon outlines took on a new look, resembling 'scenarios' more than the usual I, II, III, A, B, C, sort of schemas. While traditional homiletics arranged 'points' categorically, or according to well-worn rhetorical strategies (e.g. Thesis, Antithesis, Synthesis; Not X, Not Y, but Z, and so forth), I grew curious as to how human consciousness actually did conjoin ideas. The result was a journeying system of 'moves' assembled by various 'logics'. When preached, such sermons did seem to heighten attention and retention in surprising ways. More, a mobile system offered freedom to fulfill intention, to alter models in consciousness, in a word to *change* minds.

To the basic idea of 'movement', I stirred in insights drawn from literary theory. (During the early sixties, I was reading biblical form critics while taking courses in contemporary literary criticism.) I was gripped by a simple distinction first found in E. M. Forster, the distinction between 'plot' and 'story' (history). I began to realize that the bible did not offer history so much as a series of 'plots'. Thus, preaching could be liberated from an over-zealous biblical historicism and begin to pay attention to 'plots', trying to get at the hermeneutic consciousness that once upon a time conceived them. As I probed 'the rhetoric of fiction', I learned that 'plots' in their particular sequential logic were acts of interpretation, and that pericopes could be *replotted* freely into sermons for a more modern age without losing track of the Gospel. Gradually, I began designing sermons as *plotted* movements of moduled language.

From study of how poems 'worked' came further insight. I wondered how 'meaning' was formed by poems when poems were often only an assemblage of image and metaphor with little conceptual language. Obviously much of the bible is image and metaphor if only because God-talk is analogical. Kenneth Burke and many others tuned my understanding of how image and structure interrelate to create astonishingly precise 'meanings' in consciousness. I sensed that poets could teach preachers a wisdom seldom found in homiletic texts. Could an inter-relating 'grid' of images be created to function with sermon 'plots'? More important, could such strategies be taught prospective preachers?

Another literary notion, 'Point-of-View', proved even more exciting. Point-of-view is perspective in consciousness – attitudinal, temporal, spatial, psychological, etc. – expressed in language.[18] For the better part of a year, I sifted through centuries of Christian preaching to discover that while perspectual shifts could be found in most sermons, no homiletic text had ever studied point-of-view or specified 'ground-rules'. (There are such!) Preachers do have astonishing control over the perspectual shifts that occur in congregational consciousness. Thus, modules in a sermon, 'moves', can be plotted with different points-of-view so that preaching will *imitate the angled modes of perspectual human consciousness.* As a result, people will not so much hear sermons talked at them, as have preaching move through their minds with the immediacy of their own imaged thought processes. Point-of-view I realized was more than a literary device, it was native to human consciousness in the Twentieth Century.

Problems arose. There was the troubling problem of rhetorical unity. While a traveling, plotted language did permit sudden shifts in thought as well as movement 'from-to', it could easily pull apart rather than coming together to form some sort of shaped understanding in consciousness – a serious problem indeed. Traditionally, the unity of sermons was guaranteed by 'topic', often phrased in a clear propositional statement, or so most homiletic texts proposed. But, long before, I had abandoned a topical approach. Hermeneutic literature (Ricoeur and others) led me to guess that biblical 'plots' had unity as they played in some sort of hermeneutic-theological 'field'. The notion of 'field' might be likened to a spotlight on stage in which dancers dance, and without which dancing might dissolve into helter-skelter. The idea of a theological field was large enough to allow freedom of movement while offering deep cohesion to sermons.

Problems, many problems, still multiply and answers come slowly (Some of us are slow learners!), but gradually I seem to be patching together the fabric of a rather different homiletic for our strange new world-a-forming, a homiletic which might be labelled 'phenomenological'.

So much for a semi-autobiographical excursis and, with it, a broad barn-paint sketch of a homiletic theory.

A test of method

When we glance at parables, our theory seems apt. In parables we are dealing with plotted language that travels through consciousness. Even so-called similitudes of the Kingdom usually contain some kind of sequential 'plot'. For example, the Parable of the Treasure moves from the surprise of free-finding (contra reward-at-the-end-finding), to joy of discovery, to a determination to possess (buy the field), to outright laughter at the mere idea of possession (in Jewish law, treasure did not normally go with a field, but could revert to a previous owner).[19] Note that, in a single sentence, we have 'movement' with astonishing twists and turns. While the twists are in the structure of the sentence, surely they produce action in an attendant consciousness. We are dealing then with a system characterized by 'movement' and 'intention' that begs a mobile, plotted homiletic.

Of course, the particular sequence of a passage need not be reproduced in sermon design. Sequence may be replotted, amplified, reduced, or rearranged with altered logic. For example, a preacher might reorder the structure of the Treasure Parable by starting out with desire for the Kingdom (treasure), move to a willingness to sacrifice (liquidate and buy), then to discovery that God's Kingdom cannot be possessed, returning to the idea of free-gift finding, before finally ending with joy. While the original parable worked from free-finding to an eventual 'frustration of expecta-tion',[20] the sermon, still faithful to the structural 'theology' of the passage, could move through frustration to an affirmation of free-finding as glad gift of God. Though the parable has been rearranged, and a rather different 'logic of movement' developed, it still fulfills 'intention', and still plays in the same 'theological field'. Arrangement of homiletic sequence is never capricious, a random re-shuffling of episodes or ideas – homiletic strategy and theo-logic govern plotting. Thus, original sequence of a scriptural passage is *not* binding; intentional fidelity *is*. Some sermons may well travel much the same route as scripture, while others will be replotted to function in different twentieth century consciousness. What matters is that sermons do work with a clear 'logic of move-ment', are characterized by 'intentional obedience' (that they *do* what wants to be done), and that they have unity within a theological field of meaning.

Now, stop and consider: Is it possible that *all* biblical language 'moves' by some logic through a discernible theological field? Answer: More than likely. We could analyse different kinds of biblical rhetoric – e.g. controversy-pronouncement stories, resurrection accounts, types of Prophetic dis-course, Johannine 'signs' or 'mystery dialogues', mythic stories from the first few chapters of Genesis, and others, asking how they 'move' and what they 'intend' in attentive consciousness. If a rhetoric of parables can be developed, other biblical rhetorics may be ventured as well. Further, it may be possible to develop rhetorical-theological norms drawn from passages to guide the selection and employment of images, metaphors, illustrations and the like. If *all*, or virtually all, biblical lan-guage travels intentionally by different kinds of 'logic', then we may end by designing different kinds of sermons with variable homiletic strategies to fulfill different intentions. The advantage of a mobile system, with a variety of 'points-of-view' built in, is that it permits freedom of structure allowing the biblical word to be fulfilled in proclamation.

Post-scripts

Now a few odd post-scripts on parable:

Maybe parables happen on the boundary line between analogy and denial of analogy. We are familiar, most of us, with the peculiar nature of theological language; while it necessarily employs analogy, at the same time it counters analogy in order to affirm God's 'otherness'. God-talk is incur-ably analogical because, in a finite world, we can speak of an infinite God only by grasping analo-gies – 'God is like. ... '[21] Once ventured, however, analogies must be countered cautiously by dialectical denials ('God is *not* like ...) so as to guard the transcendence of God, whose ways are not our ways. In a sense parables, particularly Kingdom parables, may function the same way. The phrase, 'The Kingdom of God is *like* ... ', plunges us into analogy, by which the realm of God is likened to some stock image of our world. Yet distortions in parables, what we have termed the 'surreal', may serve to shatter analogy. The action of analogy clearly makes a God-like-us and Kingdom like our 'world', so the action of anti-analogy could leave us 'worldless' as well as without a 'God-like-us'. Thus, anti-analogy in parables might drive us to a kind of mystic silence, standing mute amidst a negation of images. But parables do not leave us in mystic silence. Instead they seem to lead us into hermeneutic consciousness where 'our world' is judged by The Mystery, but where dim outlines of the shape of Mystery may be traced by ways in which it shatters our 'world'. So parables *do* not give us *statable teachings*, rather they stand us before The Mystery of a Kingdom-contra-our-world. Preachers who themselves may lust for clear propositional truths must offer none when preaching parables. Sermons on parables may not domesticate The Mystery, but should be designed to place listeners in the paradox of analogy and anti-analogy and let faith-consciousness try to discern the nebulous shape of grace.

Another idle thought: For the past few decades parable study seems to have been torn between C. H. Dodd's brilliant 'realized eschatology', which interprets parables as referring to the Kingdom come near in Christ Jesus, and the 'progressive eschatology' of J. Jeremias, for whom parables address an eschatologically expectant church. Thus preachers have tended to refer parables either to the past tense of Jesus Christ or to the future tense of churchly expectation in Christ. When it comes to interpreting the strange, self-evident 'present tense' power of the parables, many preachers seem less than sure. As action in consciousness, the parables of Jesus do seem to function *now*; now, right now, they stand us before the present tense Presence of Mystery. Perhaps our problem is that we can't let go of the notion of 'original meaning'. As long as we search for an original meaning we are bound to end up with either Dodd or Jeremias, with either a Jesus come or a Christ yet to come. But, as *intentional language*, parables might lead us in another direction – to a 'second stage' christology, a christology celebrating Risen Christ, which may have been the hermeneutic that transmitted the parables.[22] Perhaps the only place where parables can 'live' is in consciousness that confesses risen Christ, for if there is King, then there is Kingdom *now*, though robed in swirls of Mystery.

Notes

1 For brief summaries of the history of parable interpretation, see A. M. Hunter, *Interpreting the Parables,* Philadelphia, Westminster, 1960; D. M. Granskou, *Preaching on the Parables*, Philadelphia, Fortress, 1972; G. V. Jones, *The Art and the Truth of the Parables,* London, SPCK, 1964. For extensive bibliography plus a history of interpretation, see W. S. Kissinger, *The Parables of Jesus: A History of Interpretation and Bibliography*, ATLA Bibliography Series 4, Metuchen, NJ, Scarecrow, 1979.

2 A. M. Hunter cites Luther's sermons on The Great Supper and The Good Samaritan as examples of allegorization (*Interpreting the Parables*, Philadelphia, Westminster, 1960, p. 32).

3 Ibid., p. 24. The example is from Tertullian, *On Modesty*, chapter 9. Tertullian's interpretation was picked up and elaborated by R. C. Trench, *Notes on the Parables of our Lord,* New York, Fleming H. Revell, n.d., pp. 298–323.

4 A. Jülicher, *Die Gleichnisreden Jesu, Zwei Teile in einem Band,* Darmstadt, 1969. First ed. 1896; second ed. 1899.

5 Hunter, 1960, p. 38. From Jülicher, 1969, II, p. 188 and II, p. 511.

6 A. Schweitzer, *The Quest of the Historical Jesus,* tr. W. Montgomery, London, A & C Black, 1911.

7 C. H. Dodd, *The Parables of the Kingdom,* New York, Charles Scribner's Sons, 1961.

8 J. Jeremias, *The Parables of Jesus,* rev. ed., New York, Charles Scribner's Sons, 1963.

9 See N. Perrin, *Jesus and the Language of the Kingdom,* Philadelphia, Fortress, 1976, chapter 3.

10 See my article, 'The Seed Parable: From Text to Homily', *Kairos*, 2, 1/2, St. Meinrad School of Theology, pp. 2–19.

11 For *verfremdungeffekt* theory, see *Brecht on Theatre*, trans. J. Willet, New York, Hill and Wang, 1964. Brecht saw the intrusion of 'surreal' as a way of distancing, of preventing catharsis inducing identifications that could rob drama of revolutionary impact. I am indebted to Brecht for some understanding of the 'surreal' in parables. Mary Ann Tolbert, *Perspectives on the Parables*, Philadelphia, Fortress, 1979, p. 17, writes, 'At first glance the parables appear to present a realistic picture; however, the realism is just as often exploded by an extravagance in detail and description.'

12 See Robert Funk, *Jesus as Precursor,* Philadelphia, Fortress, 1975, for interpretations of the Mustard Seed and the Leaven.

13 Jülicher, following Aristotle, grabbed the word 'like' in the parables as a indication of simile. To him, 'like' functioned simply, as in 'A is *like* B', to indicate a single comparison. For criticism of Jülicher's

'rhetoric' see Robert Funk, *Language, Hermeneutic, and Word of God,* New York, Harper & Row, 1966, pp. 124–62.

14   I am indebted to my friend Bernard Brandon Scott, *Jesus, Symbol Maker for the Kingdom,* Philadelphia, Fortress, 1981, for an understanding of how parables may function. He should not be held responsible for my misunderstandings.

15   Lewis Carroll, *Through the Looking Glass and What Alice Found There,* New York, Random House, 1946, chapter 11.

16   Greek *symphonasas* in v. 2, translated 'agreeing' by the RSV, probably implies agreement *after* negotiations, i.e., bargaining.

17   See Owen Barfield, *Speaker's Meaning*, Middletown, CT, Wesleyan University Press, 1967.

18   On 'point-of-view' see Boris Uspensky, *A Poetics of Composition,* tr. V. Zavarin and S. Wittig, Los Angeles, University of California Press, 1973. Also Wayne C. Booth, *The Rhetoric of Fiction*, Chicago, University of Chicago Press, 1961. Initially, I thought Point-of-View to be an occasional homiletic device, but now I view it as integral, indeed crucial to sermon design.

19   I am indebted to J. D. Crossan, *Finding is the First Act,* Philadelphia, Fortress, 1979, for insight into the sequence of the Treasure Parable. However, I follow a suggestion from B. B. Scott on the ending. For law governing treasure finds, see J. D. M. Derrett, *Law in the New Testament,* London, Darton, Longman & Todd, 1970, pp. 1–16. Notice a similar sequence in *The Wisdom of Solomon*: in v. 7:14 we are urged to acquire wisdom ('treasure'), but in v. 8:21 reminded that we cannot gain possession of wisdom except as God gives.

20   The phrase 'frustration of expectation' is suggested by W. Iser, *The Implied Reader,* Baltimore, MD, John Hopkins, 1974, p. 279: ' . . . literary texts are full of unexpected twists and turns, and frustration of expectations.'

21   See G. F. Woods, *Theological Explanation*, Welwyn, Nisbet, 1958, chapters 12 and 13.

22   See the second set of diagrams in R. H. Fuller, *The Foundations of New Testament Christology*, New York, Charles Scribner's Sons, 1965, p. 245. The stages usually noted are (1) a christology of the primitive Palestinian church which stressed the historical Jesus and his parousia; (2) a christology of hellenistic-judaism which added to the simple structure (because of delay of parousia) emphasis on the exalted, regnant Christ; (3) a developed christology which adds a notion of pre-existence, thus of descent and ascent. See also, J. Knox, *The Humanity and Divinity of Christ*, Cambridge, Cambridge University Press, 1967, for a similar diagrammatic structure.

19   Story and Image in Sermon Illustration

Richard L. Eslinger

Story telling is widely seen as the homiletic new wave ... a movement in preaching with a dynamism and vitality which may finally supplant topical preaching's three points and a poem. Its advocates point to the many advantages of the narrative sermon, ranging from foundational support in narrative theology and hermeneutics to the shift toward a new 'personalism' in the pulpit.[1] When the preacher begins a story on Sunday morning, ears are unstopped and scales fall from the eyes. If for no other reason, preachers are turning to a more frequent use of stories because their congregations become more alert and interested when [discursive] speech gives way to the narrative.

In a number of cases, sermons have clearly moved to some sort of full narrative structure,[2] but it remains the case that most use of story in preaching relates to the task of illustrating conceptually developed ideas. Here, too, may be detected some important shifts in the traditional conventions as to story illustrations. At this point, there seems to be good news and bad news. The good news is that the old style 'war horse' illustration finally seems to be on the wane. These grand old stories of the (largely male and Victorian) heroes of the faith sound increasingly quaint in late twentieth century preaching. As these old friends visit sermons less frequently, the hearers are no longer asked to adopt a previous era's culture and values in order to be persons of faith. The bad news is that a new breed of story illustration has exploded on the scene with its own ambiance and implied value system. Conveyed largely through the commercial homily services, these latter day canned illustrations more often trade in 'warm fuzzy' pop psychology and tales of the underdogs. Presumably the purpose here is to evoke congregational guilt while soothing it somewhat before the benediction. Given both the old and new sermon illustration, perhaps it is time to assess the limits of story when employed as an illustrative system and to suggest another option which may not involve as many potential liabilities. The limitations of story illustrations are proposed through the following theses:

1. *Most first person stories do not serve their intended purposes of demonstrating solidarity with the congregation and providing an immediacy to the 'point'.* Ironically, the typical first-person story served up by the preacher distances him or her from the people by either introducing homiletically extraneous issues or by connoting a pulpit posture of hero or victim. These self-disclosures intended as examples of common experience in many cases serve to highlight and set the preacher apart. Moreover, it is almost impossible for such stories to get their point across; they will typically serve to illustrate the preacher rather than the sermon.[3] The exception here may be in the Black church where the preacher is invested with a much stronger communal identity and his or her story is more readily 'our story'.[4]

2. *Extended story illustrations are problematic with regard to any homiletical intent.* Under the banner of preaching as storytelling the proportions of story illustrations have swollen noticeably. These rather elephantine stories circulate with some rapidity from pulpit to pulpit, being traded among preachers like baseball cards. Their purpose, seen especially when they are used as an introduction, is not so much to illustrate as to serve as quasi-scripture. The authority for a sermon's

message, as well as the organization and message itself are all derived from the extended non-biblical story. Ironically, the biblical material present within the body of the sermon may actually be serving to 'illustrate' the dominating story's purposes.[5]

Among the many difficulties with this misuse of story, two overriding concerns must be noted, one methodological and the other theological. With regard to the former, the preacher who utilizes such extended story illustrations runs the risk of leaving the hearers stranded in the story. For better and for worse, the more extended a story in the sermon, the more difficult it becomes to remove the congregation from its narrative 'world' and refocus its attention elsewhere. This difficulty in extrication is compounded if the material which follows an extensive story is devoted to a conceptually-oriented explanation of the story's intended meaning. Such material is almost never heard by the congregation; they will remain within the story and assign their own meanings to it. The preacher's options become, then, to expand the story further into an exclusively narrative sermon,[6] or to employ story illustrations which are considerably more economical and even terse. Turning to the latter concern, the question becomes that of the theological 'fit' of these big stories with the biblical witness. Unfortunately, most of these vast illustrations romanticize and moralize on the faith. Only the rare extended sermonic narrative is crafted in such a fashion as to be theologically congruent with the specific pericope. And almost none of the larger stories in current circulation reflect such congruence or fit with regard to any specific portion of biblical material.

3. *Sermonic structures involving parallel development of biblical and contemporary stories will not integrate in the consciousness of the hearers.* Instead of a creative fusion of the biblical and contemporary, the two narrative systems will present themselves as competing worlds within which the congregation is asked to live. Almost unconsciously, the hearers will choose the narrative context which is most concrete, detailed as to characterization and setting, and aligned with lived experience. That narrative context which will 'form' in the consciousness of the hearers will, with few exceptions, be that of the contemporary story. The other half of the doublet will not be able to unify itself with the more dominant story nor actually be remembered by itself. For congregations with a vividly presented contemporary story, a more distantly presented Bible story will fade from consciousness as it is being told.

In spite of the identifications of certain questionable uses of story within a sermon, it remains the case that well-focused, brief stories can be effectively employed for illustrative purposes. In many cases, however, the preacher does not need to elaborate the illustration into a full narrative system; rather, a clearly focused image can be equally effective in forming the thought in the consciousness of the hearers. These images all come to awareness within the context of some story or other, some lived experience, but they gain an independent life in our memory and lurk in our subconscious. Because of their concreteness, images are considerably more determinative for personal and communal identity than conceptual definitions. In fact, Christian ethicists have argued recently that images of self and world orient not only how we see reality, but what we see as well.

> What it is profitable to will depends upon the identity of the self that wills. A sense of identity is the result of a process of imaging; it is simply a cluster of images that inform the consciousness of the self, bringing specificity to its volition and liberty, and counseling it to pursue something rather than everything.[7]

This image-formed vision of self and world largely determines volition and specific behavior. Consciousness can be reached only by the preacher through the images that narratives project and that consciousness retains. Consequently, it is not just the case that images *may be used* within illustrative systems in preaching, they may well *have to* be employed if the sermon is to communicate meaning and value.

By way of example, the imagery employed in a recently preached sermon[8] will be identified and interpreted with reference to its function and interplay. This sermon, dealing with the raising of Lazarus (John 11:1–44) was shaped with references to the plotting of the biblical narrative.[9] The four component sections or 'movements' of the sermon were:

I.   In the midst of life's dyings, we ask: 'Jesus, where were you when we needed you?'
II. And Jesus responds, 'I am the resurrection and the life.'
Ill. But what does this do to the world's definitions of life and death?
IV. The question then comes: 'Do you believe this?'
Conclusion: 'Come out!'

Given these four elements of the structure of the sermon, the images within each will be explicated and discussed as to their intended function. It should be noted that in none of these illustrations is it necessary to move to a narrative system; the only full 'story' is the biblical story of Lazarus.

Movement I. What is sought here are images which express our longing for the Lord in the midst of the 'deaths' we experience in life. These are times when we want to say with Martha, 'Lord, if you had been here', this loss would not have happened. Three types of 'dyings' in the midst of life are explicated here – the dyings of our loves (the lost relationships), the dyings of our worth (rejection by others), and the dyings of death (the death of family or friends). Since these categories are still expressed in rather conceptual language, much more specific imagery is needed in order that this entire movement not be lost in its hearing. Therefore, 'the dyings of loves' is imaged by a marital (or other) separation in which 'the old rituals are still continued for a while, yet the one we loved now feels strange even to touch'. 'The dyings of our worth' is imaged through rejection, because of what we stand for, or our race or sex. Knowing this rejection, the old spiritual, 'I've been 'buked, I've been scorned', does a solemn dance in our mind. Finally, 'the dyings of death' are established by the images of the funeral of a loved one where we gaze at the green of the plastic grass and smell 'the cut, used flowers'. Within this first movement, images are chosen which span across sensory experience – touch, hearing (an 'internal' kind), sight, and smell. Following each image, a perspective is then established which will persist as the 'place' of the hearer until near the end of the sermon. 'And we, too, join in the dying . . . the grave clothes are wrapped around us, the tomb door slams shut, and we are alone.'

Movement II. Since a perspective has been established of the hearer in the tomb, this next movement must take into account this point of view or intentionally redirect it. The logic of the text calls for this shift, however, only at the end of the sermon and the hearers, then, must remain in the tomb. Jesus as the resurrection and the life is imaged by the Te Deum, sung at the Wedding Banquet of the Lamb which is joined by the saints at 'Mt. Bethel Church, who are having their homecoming this weekend with dinner in the grounds'. We hear this triumphant song of all the saints rather muffled, 'from behind the thick, tomb door'.

Movement III. The world's understanding of life and death is imaged through its technology. 'Almost every week we watch a hospital show on T.V., and the patient is hooked up to a heart monitor. The rhythm looks normal for a while, but then there is a crisis and we see only a straight line.' This conventional definition of life and death, though, is upset by the Johannine theology of eternal life in Christ. The confession that Jesus is resurrection and life is not reserved to only those saints who 'from their labor rest'; in the midst of this life, with its death and its dyings, eternal life is given in Christ Jesus. This reversal is given through a reversal of the image system – 'What if the guy driving the BMW with the gold American Express card and all the golf course memberships is "flat line" and the little grandmother who volunteers for work in Old First's soup kitchen is a bouncing, picture of life? What if the world's categories are all backwards? Life in the midst of our dyings, eternal life now . . . ? What if the world has it all wrong?'

Movement IV. The issue now becomes the nature of our response to this lifegiving confession. Jesus asks Martha regarding the affirmation concerning resurrection and life, 'Do you believe this?' But while belief in the Johannine sense does involve rational assent, 'belief in', something more is at stake. Commitment to, sharing in, and worship of are also components of Johannine belief. The image presented here is of a man and woman who do believe in each other though much more is involved. 'The two join hands and the man says to the woman, "I take you to be my wife" and the woman says to the man, "I take you to be my husband." Rings are exchanged and the church rejoices in this union, this covenanting, this wedding.' Not only does this marriage imagery expand the usual definition of 'beliefs' but it also implicitly links this question of belief in Christ to the confession of Christ as resurrection and life (the *Te Deum* was sung in Movement II at the Wedding Banquet of the Lamb). There is no attempt to explicitly link these image systems – to be obvious here would be to detract from the power of this interplay of images. Almost subconsciously the relationship is established, and such interaction of images, as David Buttrick observes, may have 'awesome power'.[10]

Conclusion. The perspective established within the first movement is brought to immediacy once more. 'The stone is rolled away, our name is called, and we are summoned out of our tomb. We blink in the brightness of this new day and the obsolete grave clothes are unwound and thrown away.' (In Movement I, it was the funeral flowers which were thrown away.) The conclusion ends with this gift of new life raising the same question for us as it did for Lazarus – 'So now, what do we do?'

What is important to note, in summary, is that while each of the component parts of the sermon are illustrated, those illustrative systems are all essential to the meaning of the respective movements. Furthermore, these systems are comprised of imagery developed to interplay with each other and designed with a point of view in mind. In no case, however, was it necessary to elaborate in illustrative image into a narrative; the only 'story' in the sermon is the biblical story of the raising of Lazarus, . . . and of ourselves.

Notes

1   Charles Rice, 'The Expressive Style in Preaching', *The Princeton Seminary Review*, 54, 1, 1971, p. 188.

2   See Charles Rice, 'Shaping Sermons by the Interplay of Text and Metaphor', in Don M. Wardlaw (ed.), *Preaching Biblically: Creating Sermons in the Shape of Scripture*, Philadelphia, Westminster, 1983, pp. 101ff for a discussion of these alternative narrative structures.

3   I am indebted to David Buttrick for this insight.

4   See Henry H. Mitchell, *Black Preaching*, New York, Harper & Row, 1979.

5   Innumerable 'stewardship sermons', based on stories such as the familiar 'Desert Pete' tale, inevitably display this tendency. If scripture is present within such a sermon at all – the biblical witness being rather optional within this approach – it can only serve to illustrate a message of works righteousness derived from the big tale.

6   See Rice, 1983, pp. 106–9.

7   David Bailey Harned, *Images for Self-Recognition: The Christian as Player, Sufferer and Vandal*, New York, Seabury, 1977, p. 2. See also Stanley Hauerwas, *Vision and Virtue*, Notre Dame, IN, Fides, 1974.

8   'The Raising of Lazarus', preached on All Saint's Day, 1985, at York Chapel, Durham, NC, Duke University Divinity School.

9   See David G. Buttrick, 'Interpretation and Preaching', *Interpretation*, 25, 1, 1981, pp. 46–58 for an explication of this 'phenomenological' approach to the plotting of a pericope's movement and structure.

10   David G. Buttrick, 'Intensive Seminar on Biblical Preaching', sponsored by the Board of Discipleship, United Methodist Church, 1981.

20   Imagining a Sermon

Richard Lischer

The phase of sermon preparation that preachers find most excruciating and for which they find themselves least prepared is the one seminaries don't teach and, many would say, cannot teach. Exegesis, with its many criticisms, is standard equipment for students and pastors, and many are conversant with the sophisticated hermeneutical theories of Bultmann, Ebeling, Fuchs, Gadamer, and Ricoeur. Sermon design has always been the mainstay of homiletics, with new patterns and forms for sermons emerging with some regularity. Even the delivery of sermons, nurtured by the rhetorical arts of memory and elocution, though rarely taught, is believed to be teachable and learnable. But the role of the imagination in preaching eludes us. Like most teachers of preaching, I have prepared a list of activities that students should check off on the way toward the Sunday sermon. The list begins and ends in prayer and touches on most everything in between, from establishing the text to expunging split infinitives. But, like the question of the place of the Holy Spirit in preaching, where on this list does one insert the imagination? Dare we speak of exegesis and even hermeneutics as technical proficiencies to which must be added the charism of the imagination as it manifests itself in a clever sermon illustration or an inspirational verse? I want to argue in this article that the imagination is at work at every stage of sermon preparation and, later, try to sketch some of the specific operations of the imagination in preaching.

The theological imagination

Notice the title, 'Imagining a Sermon', is a gerund rather than a substantive noun. This is to indicate that imagination is an activity and not a compartment of the brain, nor a physical image impressed upon the brain in perception. Imagination is an activity of thinking as that thinking is influenced by the realities of living and the exigencies of communication. It always involves a crossover from one realm of life to another or from one world of discourse to another, so that one dimension is seen in terms of another and with such clarity as to possess a revelatory quality. But to have said this is already to have strayed into the language of theology, for the one-in-another principle pervades all religious communication, including the Christian: 'If I have told you earthly things and you do not believe, how can you believe if I tell you heavenly things?' (John 3:12) is representative of the Christian mind-set but is alien to those who seek a clearer illumination of the thing itself without reference to other realities.

Before pursuing this principle of analogy, let me defend the association of theology and imagination. This is not to imply that theists carry a sixth sense, a third eye, or any other special equipment that makes them more imaginative or creative than others. Indeed, when it comes to preaching, the opposite may be true on theological grounds. Theological imagination belongs to all whose art or communication is infused by or reflective of the divine spirit. Theopoesis, as Amos Wilder names it, is characteristic of those who create out of a sense of the immanence and the transcendence of God, for whom the act of creation is both a partnership with God and an interminable quest after him. The theological imagination is greater than the sum of individual believers who acknowledge God when thinking creatively. It is a legacy from Plato and Paul to western thinking and is embedded in the persistently religious imagination of the modern and postmodern age.

When we come to the exercise of the imagination in Christian preaching, the picture becomes more focused. Here we discover specific occasions for liberation as well as constraints and responsibilities. For the Christian imagination, if we may call it that, is not only concerned with a divine being but with the particularities of Israel and the Bible, the mystery of Jesus, the foolishness of the cross, with the arena of the church, the character of the poet (preacher), and the needs of an audience (congregation). Under such conditions it becomes more difficult to speak of Christian *poesis* in a way that would satisfy Shelley or Pound. Wilder reminds us that the New Testament is common in its language. He calls it not *Hochliteratur* but *Kleinliteratur*, a kind of folk art.[1] Since much of the New Testament is a testimony or sermon about Jesus, preaching that is faithful to the New Testament will also be a folk art, something for the people. The notion of art for art's sake is as foreign to preaching as it is to the New Testament. Homiletics should be nervous about putting on airs as an art form and hobnobbing with drama, literature, poetry, dance, or autobiography. These exercises of the imagination are born in the freedom of the human spirit and elaborate their own expressive forms. The only constraints they obey are formal. Preaching, on the other hand, is as indifferent to form as the New Testament, both abounding with a mixed multitude of forms, but the *matter* of Christian proclamation is so welded to Jesus Christ that a neutral observer might mistake preaching for ideology.

Imagination's threefold role

Preaching is an exercise of the imagination, in that the gospel is faith seeking expression. The truest and most effective preaching does not separate the message from its form, but asks, What is it about this facet of the gospel that necessitates this particular form of expression? In the whole process of preparation, the role of the imagination is threefold, that of the historical-literary imagination, the hermeneutical imagination, and the homiletical imagination.

Historical-literary Imagination. The preacher's use of imagination does not begin by establishing the reality of God. It begins with the witness to that reality in the Bible. Scripture is basecamp for the preacher because it is the Word of God. Because the Bible is a document of another age and people, it does not freely dispense its treasures without historical and literary prying. It may be well and good to ask how Abraham must have felt when he set off for the Promised Land, but it also helps to know the location of Ur, the literary form of the covenant, and the relation of the Abraham story to the first eleven chapters of Genesis. Similarly, Paul's controversy with the Corinthians has a deeper meaning to one who knows something of gnosticism. Mark's theology of the cross makes more sense to one acquainted with the predicament of his addressees, etc., etc. Of course, the first stage in historical-literary study is to know as much as possible about the situation, audience, purpose, shape, and function of the biblical text. The evidence is usually not unambiguous, and the preacher does not have the student's luxury of listing and footnoting options without making choices. The point is, often the scholarly choice is something other than a weighing of Bultmann versus Dodd versus Jeremias versus Brown, but rather the result of a theologically informed intuition, perhaps an intuition sparked by the preacher's imagination of how the text might have been preached.

A historical and literary study of the Parable of the Marriage Feast in Matthew 21:1–14 will yield more than moralistic admonitions about excuse-making and a perfunctory mention of the puzzling tag-end parable of the man without a garment. Certainly the preacher wants to know the *Heilsgeschichte* as well as the recent local history that lies behind Matthew's version of the parable. The interpreter also wants to see how Matthew's theological purpose differs from Luke's, and how allegory differs from true parable. But the interpreter also wants to appreciate the literary and dramatic quality of the parable. The preacher may retell the story by casting it into acts leading to the climactic appearance of the king in a silent and stunned banquet hall. If the preacher knows how parable as a genre works, he or she will not be too hasty to make a theological point of the final few verses. Not only the reversal, but the inexplicable and perverse reversal of expectations, is a feature of other parables, e.g., the parables of Kafka. In Kafka such a parable is an exemplar of an alien and lost world whose inhabitants are penalized for wanting what they can't have. In retelling the biblical story will the preacher's words and tone betray anything of the bafflement of the modern world? If not, the preacher has missed something in the story itself.

The second, most common – and most abused – stage of the historical imagination is the preacher's imaginary flight into the first century. True historical imagination, which often entails hard choices on soft data, is exchanged for a game of Let's Pretend. Let's pretend we are with Peter in the courtyard or with Mary in the garden. Imagine that Jesus has invited *you* to walk on the water with him. The trouble with this approach is at least threefold: First, it skips historical and literary study and moves directly to psychologizing or spiritualizing of texts. Second, it is exceedingly hard for even the most devout Christians to imagine that they are first-century Palestinians. Too much has come in between! Third, effective preaching does not bus twentieth-century Christians into the first century, but enables the events of long ago to live again in a new and different setting. Proclamation always looks ahead,

Historical imagination is necessary because no document can say everything necessary about an event. And what is presented is not so much a photograph as it is a lush and colorful impressionistic painting. The historical imagination does indeed relive the events recorded in the Scripture, but not in the psychological game alluded to above nor in the sense that R. G. Collingwood suggests, namely, in the mind of the individual historian. Preaching emerges from a matrix of liturgy and tradition in which the sacred events are being relived, interpreted, and transmitted from one generation to the next. The corporateness of the historical imagination leads to a discussion of hermeneutics.

Hermeneutical Imagination. The most distinctive element in the Christian imagination is the necessary role of hermeneutics in it. Just as Hermes was the messenger of the gods, the imagination is the mediating activity that links and confronts different orders of reality, worlds of experience, and modes of discourse. Ray Hart compares the imagination to canal locks capable of joining two different levels of water.[2] This linkage is the whole mission of the gospel and therefore necessitates the hermeneutical imagination. The hermeneut's basecamp is the Bible; the destination is the experience of the contemporary listener. But how to make the trip without playing games of Let's Pretend or using other devices that either leave the preacher mired in the land of the Jebusites or the congregation adrift in current affairs? The first mistake merely repeats what the Bible says; the second replaces what the Bible says with other stuff.

The resolution of the dilemma depends on an understanding of the thing investigated. For the great Romantic theorists of the imagination, Wordsworth and Coleridge, the world was not an object on which the poet impressed his personality. The world was already alive and coming out to meet the poet. Likewise the Bible is no inert object under investigation. If it is a basecamp, as we have said, it is one that sends out messages to us the messengers. Or, to change the image, the Bible is 'oratorical' (Northrop Frye); it 'wants' to address others and be heard. When the preacher opens the Bible, he or she encounters the living God and a community that includes the interpreter.

Thus hermeneutics encompasses more than the rules for interpreting Bible passages. It seeks understanding, which is the translation – not the repetition nor the replacement – of the biblical message in an idiom appropriate to the deepest levels of contemporary experience. Not long ago I asked my daughter what she knew about Anne Frank. She said she knew what she read of her *Diary*. 'Well then', I asked, 'do you feel that you understand her?' 'Yes', she replied. 'You mean you understand what it is to be a Jewish girl in Europe during the time of Hitler?' My daughter was embarrassed to go on with the dialogue, for she knew that she did not in fact *understand* in any way commensurate with the terror and the pathos experienced by Anne Frank. She knew that to under-stand means more than to have grasped an explanation. But instinctively she had claimed 'under-standing' because, despite the vast differences in the girls, there were similarities: both teenagers, both lovers of books, and both mature beyond their years. It is the hermeneutical imagination's business to sort through the points of contact and the divergencies and, where possible, to see how the biblical text is at work in this world.

Hermeneutics and rhetoric work together, for the rhetorical shape of the sermon depends on the hermeneutical insight. The sermon finds its climax when the intent of the gospel is unfolded with the utmost intensity and clarity in terms of the hearer's situation in life. The Word works again. I think that is what Joseph Sittler means when he defines imagination as 'the process by which there is reenacted in the reader the salvatory immediacy of the Word of God as this Word is witnessed to by the speaker'.[3]

Hermeneutics seeks to exegete both the text and the destination of the text. In the latter case, this means the several worlds of the preacher. There is the big world of national and global events, the little world of the parish and local community, and the preacher's own world, his or her own heart. Faulkner once said, 'The only thing worth writing about is the human heart in conflict with itself.' This is too narrow a subject for the preacher but not too narrow a field. Certainly the congregation deserves more than the first-person, 'How-I-felt-when-I-read-this-text' genre of a sermon, but the gospel is intended for the human heart, and the first available heart for testing is the preacher's own. The hermeneutical imagination, then, at this stage of the sermon's development, imagines an audi-ence. It is an audience of human hearts just like the preacher's, but also an audience through which all the hope and suffering of the world are present.

Homiletical Imagination. Coleridge made the distinction between the fancy and the imagination. The former is the juxtaposition of unlikely entities; the latter is a fusion or reconciliation of unlike qualities. Too much preaching corresponds to fancy – propositions sandwiched between stories and illustrations crammed into the sermon not because they help unfold the burden of the text, but merely to add some color or human interest.

We have already considered the need for historical imagination as opposed to simple repetition of Bible texts or lengthy and learned 'backgrounds' for congregations. It was Fosdick who reminded us that only the preacher comes to church with a burning interest in the Jebusites. The other leg of the hermeneutical arch is anchored in the real world. But the real world doesn't yield sermonic material any more readily than the world of the Bible. Many preachers believe that merely by men-tioning the real world they have made the message relevant and even imaginative. 'Newspaper preaching', for example, documents the biblical teaching on sin and evil by reeling off a list of current hotspots on the planet: Northern Ireland, South Africa, Afghanistan, Lebanon; or: hunger, drugs, unemployment, sex. 'Television preaching', to take another example, relates the gospel not to real life but to life as it is falsified on situation comedies and soap operas, as though the whole con-gregation should participate in the inanities of this make-believe life. The homiletical imagination does not content itself with the crude imprinting of images on the unsuspecting brains of people subjected to tabloids, Harlequin Romances, and sitcoms. Indeed, this is the older and mechanistic view of the imagination – the imprinting of images on a passive brain. Just as parents admonish children, 'Why don't you turn off the T.V. and use your imagination', so the preacher will try to overcome his or her own passivity to world events and stimuli and resurrect the active, creative, synthesizing imagination – the homiletical imagination. When parents say 'Use your imagination', they mean for the child to comb its experience and memory as a base from which to fabricate new roles and relations in the world. Moreover, if I am not reading too much into parental exasperation, I think they mean for the child to use its observation of the world as both a source and a test for new forms of play. Young preachers sometimes mistakenly think that if they have not had certain experiences, they can't legitimately speak about them from the pulpit. But this is to understand the imagination in literalistic and passive terms as an image imprinted by a specific experience, whereas the homiletical imagination aggressively synthesizes scriptual image, theological truth, memory, experience, and general knowledge.

The homiletical link between the Bible and raw stuff of contemporary experience is metaphor. It effects the reconciliation Coleridge sought by fusing text and experience at a new and higher level of unity. One ingredient in metaphor is imitation. Preaching should be realistic enough to effect what Fred Craddock calls 'the nod of recognition'. 'Yes', says the hearer, 'I can take part in this sermon without having to suspend my humanity.' The imitation may be generic rather than photographic, as Aristotle might have said it today. That is, it need not describe 'the thing that has happened but a kind of thing that might happen' (*Poetics*, 9). In tragedy, he continues, the audience is moved with pity not merely by the suffering of another person, but by the undeserved misfortune of *one like ourselves* (13). Nothing is neutral in the sermon, neither biblical background nor current allusion, but all has import as it is accessible to and apprehensible by people like ourselves.

The second ingredient in metaphor is contrast. 'How like a podium is this pulpit' is a bit too imitative to be effective. But 'how like a prow is this pulpit' captures physical and functional likeness in two very different objects. When Flannery O'Connor stuns the reader with this figure: 'The Sun was a huge red ball like an elevated Host drenched in blood . . . ' she is not 'describing' a sunset, but integrating nature and grace at an imaginative level.[4] It goes without saying that preachers cannot literalistically borrow such metaphors from the artist, but they can observe the artist's way of interpreting the continuities and discontinuities in the world.

C. H. Dodd's definition of parable is justly famous. It is 'a metaphor or simile drawn from nature or common life, arresting the hearer by its vividness or strangeness, and leaving the mind in sufficient doubt about its precise application to tease it into active thought'.[5] What Dodd says about a literary form might with modification be applied to the homiletical imagination itself. What is most arresting to hearers of a sermon is not its exotic imagery or farfetched stories, nor the finality with which it nails down familiar points. What is arresting is the 'vividness or strangeness' of the gospel in human vesture. No one knew this and implemented it better than Luther. The watchword for his colorful and imaginative use of narrative, for example, was not the distance of the otherworldly but the depth of the truly human.[6] He knew that the homiletical imagination has no other task than to pronounce the gospel of God in language most expressive of the deepest yet most common realities of human life. Metaphor is the life's work of the preacher for two reasons: God became a man, and God is not a man. Likeness and contrast: one thing embedded in another and yet only heretically and idolatrously identified with the other – this is the theological theater of the Christian imagination. If the pulpit can get all that right, no one in the churches will mistake the imagination for mere fancies.

Slogging it out

But how does the imagination *work* in sermon preparation and delivery? It is difficult to say. Many who live by their imaginations, including preachers, tend to throw up a romantic fog around their acts of creation. Coleridge was a notorious liar about his own creative energies that went into the production of *Kubla Khan*. Many preachers, too, may be rational in their work descriptions until it comes to sermon preparation. Then it is a matter of each man (and it usually *is* a man) going to the Jabbok alone to wrestle with his angel. This sort of heroic nonsense not only robs the congregation of its role in sermon preparation, but it perpetuates a misunderstanding of preaching itself. Too many congregations have the idea that the preacher gets sermons from a few inspirational, mountain-top experiences during the week. They consequently fail to appreciate the bone-crushing work involved in the researching and formulation of the sermon.

The imagination is hard work. Perhaps that is the most sobering thing to be said about imagining a sermon. D. N. Perkins in his book, *The Mind's Best Work*, makes the same point and along the way dispels several myths about the imagination. One is the myth of Still Waters that pictures critical imaginative leaps as occurring in the subconscious or during extended periods of incubation. Although it may be true that some problems need to be put aside and returned to at a later time, their solution occurs as a result of mental engagement, not disengagement. A second myth is the Blitzkrieg theory of the imagination. Perkins' studies indicate that while insight does not actually occur in incubation, neither does it happen in a flash or in any way that shortcircuits the normal processes of reasoning.[7] The fluency that is so often associated with artistic creativity and great preaching is usually more apparent than real. In most cases fluency in the creative process is inferred from the fluency of the product, in our case, the natural and dynamic qualities of the sermon. The most important component of the imagination is what Perkins calls teleology by which he means nothing other than purpose. They are more likely to succeed who have committed themselves to the cause. Those who have grasped the intent of the gospel and devote themselves to its communication will accomplish their task – not by special processes but special purpose. The artistic triumph, scientific breakthrough, or brilliant sermon is the result of arduous preparation. As Pasteur said, 'Chance favors the prepared mind'.[8] In this respect, the preacher must slog it out with the poets, scientists, and all others who by the exercise of the imagination are driven toward things unseen.

Notes

1   Amos N. Wilder, *Early Christian Rhetoric*, Cambridge, MA, Harvard, 1971, p. 28.

2   Ray L. Hart, *Unfinished Man and the Imagination*, New York, Herder and Herder, 1968, p. 323.

3   Joseph Sittler, *The Ecology of Faith*, Philadelphia, Fortress, 1961, p. 56.

4   'A Temple of the Holy Ghost', in *Three by Flannery O'Conner*, New York, New American Library, 1953, p. 194.

5   C. H. Dodd, *The Parables of the Kingdom*, rev. ed., New York, Scribner's, 1961, p. 5.

6   See Richard Lischer, 'Luther and Contemporary Preaching: Narrative and Anthropology', *Scottish Journal of Theology*, 36, 1983, p. 487–501.

7   D. N. Perkins, *The Mind's Best Work*, Cambridge, MA, Harvard, 1981, pp. 49–66 and 164–9.

8   Ibid., pp. 100–101.

Part 6

PREACHING AND WORSHIP

Introduction to Part 6

In a search for clarity over the terms preaching and worship, David Buttrick's paper examines three models – religious, Hebrew corporate-historical and Christian – and spells out the kinds of worship and preaching which are characteristic of each. Focusing more narrowly on the interplay of preaching and worship as it is seen in the Eucharist, he notes that this is primarily a ritual meal with an enormous range of meanings for the Christian community. It is thus a tensive rather than a steno-symbol and is 'crammed with the whole import of the whole gospel'. The task of preaching at the Eucharist is not so much to rehearse the 'meal pericopes' again and again but to tell the whole story of God-with-us. A final section looks at the interaction of word, sacrament and praise. In an ideal situation the church is the embodiment or sacrament of the word. Given the defects of the actual community, however, the Eucharist functions between word and church to express the gospel and challenge the church to embody it in eucharistic living in the world. When word, Eucharist and community combine then Christ is known doxologically – in praise and obedience.

David G. Buttrick, 'A Sketchbook: Preaching and Worship', is from *Reformed Liturgy and Music*, 16, 1982, pp. 33–7.

The African-American pulpit tradition has evidenced power, relevance, vividness of imagery and a phenomenal memory for Scripture. Over many years it has demonstrated the capacity to support and heal an oppressed people. Henry Mitchell's article suggests that it has much to offer the whole church. Black preaching has its roots in African culture and stresses involvement of the whole human being and not just the rational consciousness. It expects experiential encounter and corporate participation. It invites celebration or 'ecstatic reinforcement' towards the end of the sermon. Mitchell lists six features of black preaching which are increasingly playing a part in forming a homiletic common to black and white cultures: faith comes in an experience; it is a gift of God; it is fed through folk practices of singing, praying and preaching; the heart of preaching is the skilful telling of the story with the help of the Spirit; the focused story draws hearers into vicarious experience; the rules of focus are relatively simple and are directed towards building identification. In Mitchell's view the area of greatest divergence between black and mainstream churches, that of emotional expression, is also the area of greatest potential for growth.

Henry H. Mitchell, 'African-American Preaching: The Future of a Rich Tradition' originally appeared in *Interpretation*, 51, 4, 1997, pp. 371–83.

John Melloh's article poses the question whether the address at a funeral service should take the form of a homily or a eulogy. Those who favour the eulogy argue that preaching must celebrate the deceased as a way of consoling those who mourn. On the other hand Roman Catholic liturgical documents explicitly exclude the eulogy. Paradoxically, the supposedly more personal eulogy may be as impersonal as a résumé, consisting of a conventional listing of family, education, moral qualities, and so on. But the deceased is never the 'object' of the rite since all liturgy glorifies God. By contrast, the homily should offer consolation and strength through the 'proclamation of the mystery of God's love and Jesus' victory present in the life and the death of the deceased as well as in the lives of family and friends'. Preachers contemplating a funeral homily should ask themselves what is the dominant 'emotion' of the funeral and what has given rise to it. They should then ask how God's word speaks to this emotion and to what new relationship with God the congregation is being called.

John Allyn Melloh, 'Homily or Eulogy? The Dilemma of Funeral Preaching' was first published in the *College of Preachers Fellowship Paper 105*, June 1998, pp. 45–50.

21   A Sketchbook: Preaching and Worship

David G. Buttrick

The topic, 'Preaching and Worship', is puzzling. It is difficult to handle because [the] words 'preaching' and 'worship' are fuzzy: they all but defy definition. James White growls that '"worship" itself is an exasperatingly difficult word to pin down.'[1] The word 'preaching' is no less difficult. Every book on homiletics seems to stumble on a new definition; from the clichéd idiocy of 'Truth through Personality' (Liberalism) to the clichéd obscurantism of 'Proclaiming the Word' (Orthodoxy). So, at the outset, we are stymied.

I

Underlying the problem of definition lies a deeper issue: 'Models'. We can psyche out sets of assumptions which seem to lurk in the several definitions. There are definitions (a) which stress *benefit*. In such schemes, worship is 'therapy' or 'motivation' or even 'catharsis' and, therefore, preaching is 'insight' or 'inspiration' or a 'climax' in worship. Other systems seem (b) to feature *content*, viewing worship as either dramatic enactment of 'Holy History', or as a didactic moment in which tablets of law tumble down. In such schemes, preaching is 'recital' or 'revelation'. Finally, there appear to be (c) definitions which are *relational* in which preaching and worship are *Wort* and *Antwort*. Of course, schemes may be intermixed or confounded by various understandings of God and of Church.

The problem with the categories we have set up is that phenomenological examination will reveal that the Church's liturgy contains elements from all our 'models'. To some extent, worship recapitulates the story of God-with-us (*anamnesis*), does involve instruction, seems to confer benefit, and is said to involve real relating to a real God. So, to spot 'models' does not clear up ambiguity, it simply increases our befuddlement. Perhaps our safest option is to throw up our theological hands and admit defeat: we can worship and we can preach, foregoing delights of definition.

II

Is there any way to reconstruct 'models' and probe for clarity?

(1) *A Religious Model*: Folk have argued that human being is an innate worshipper, just as *Homo loquens* is a natural born talker. Since Augustine, it has been vogue to argue that human desires outstrip earthy satisfactions, that the heart is restless, that the self automatically chases an 'ultimate concern', etc. I confess chronic reluctance when it comes to crediting restless hearts as [the] origin for worship.

However, we can admit that human beings in their finitude bump into mysteries, and that such bumping may be the stuff out of which notions of a transcendent 'other' arise.[2] Non-historical religion views human being as boxed by mysteries – death, birth, providential sustenance, social order – mysteries which serve to signal both finitude and something or 'other' up-against finitude.[3] The model might be sketched thus:

In the perennial religious model there is a lone figure because any idea of universal experience posits a universal self (so, oddly enough, does analysis of existential experience). By ignorance or impotency, the Self finds 'limits', and in limitation a 'threat' to being. So, for example, we may think of being born as 'givenness', but also as the possibility of non-being. We can face death as

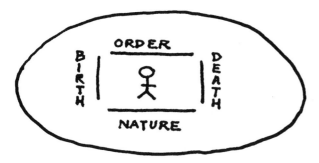

'release' (if I am conscious of having to die, does not my consciousness extend beyond death), or as 'threat' of annihilation. While our lives are sustained is there not something chancy about agricultural 'grace'? We could be cut off. There may be useful social order, even justice, but also 'threat' of both Law and chaos. In bumping 'limits', human being construes either a bulging 'grace' or *nihil*.

What is worship/preaching in the religious model? They involve either the warding off of 'threat' or the acquiring of benefit. In the religious model, worship is static, vertically defined and celebrates either subjective pathos or patterned recurrence. Preaching in the model, if it happens, is either gnostic disclosure, perennial philosophy for imprisoned souls, or something like apocalyptic revivalism, a winning of benefit through salvific alignment with the 'other', a getting-right-with-God so as to escape threat and ensure benefit. Because the model trades in mystery, it is the usual wisdom of Mystery Cults and, God knows, we have those around aplenty, even in our Churches.

In the diagram, I have drawn a circle around the boxed Self. While primitive religions may posit many gods beyond the facets of 'limitedness' – gods of Law, gods of Nature, creation and demolition gods; so-called 'higher' religions may identify the 'other' in monotheistic terms. The model will then feature a Self and an 'other', and so embrace static notions of *analogia entis* in both worship and preaching.

(2) *A Hebrew Corporate-Historical Model*: If we poke about in the origins of Israel's worship, we will stumble on the religious model – human being confronted by mysteries of birth, death, social order, and nature, for after all Israel's feasts were agricultural or legal before being historicized.[4] Nevertheless, students of Israel's worship, though often at a loss to explain, do notice a shift in the model. Two changes stand out: (a) The solitary Self of the religious model is displaced by Community because, long before George Herbert Mead, Israel knew of no such thing as a solitary Self before God; (b) The model is set in motion by a sense of narrative history. So, movement nudges the non-historical religious model and Community disrupts its soulful solipsism. We may sketch the changes as follows:

In the Hebrew Historical Model, God is not a surrounding fixity whose attributes may be ticked off by *analogia entis*. Of course, dialectical thinking does occur – We perish; God is eternal, we are dumb; God is wisdom, etc., and a sense of mystery still lingers: God's name (YHWH) cannot be spoken and even to spy his hindquarters is an off-chance bet. In the Hebrew Historical Model, God is moving teleological purpose and his people are on the go with him. Notice: the model is not vertical (in spite of all that 1930's nonsense about Isaiah in the Temple) and salvation is scarcely alignment; rather getting-right-with-God is now a matter of going along with him. Remember the Ark of the Covenant: it travelled!

In such a model, memory and hope function. God is remembered in connection with Israel's story (or is it vice versa?). If Israel were asked, 'Where is your God?', they would not reply, 'In the mirror of my religious affections', but would be apt to answer, 'Well, the darndest thing happened to us on the way out of Egypt!' On the basis of communal memory (the dotted lines in our diagram) of past experiences, Israel not only affirmed God's covenant-fidelity, but hoped toward the future of God's promises.

What about preaching/worship in the Hebrew model? Quite obviously Hebrew worship and preaching involved *anamnesis*, ritual enactments of the past (*not* I think as understood by re-presentational theologies) and recitations, which often included liturgical material (linguistic crystallizations flung up by paradigmatic events of Israel's checkered past with YHWH). Preaching was story and naming: a telling of the narrative of God-with-Israel, a protending of God's promises, and a naming of Presence with Israel on the basis of faith. Certainly preaching was no gnostic insight for prisoned selves, but was speaking out of YHWH's faithful track record with Israel.[5]

Please note: in spite of supra-Barthian denials, the framework of the religious model survived in Israel (try to get rid of it), so that while Israel's feasts were historicized, they were still seasonal and often included hoopla celebrations of Creation. More, the sense of mystery intrinsic to the religious model was enlarged, cosmically.

(3) *A Christian Model*: Is Christian worship unique as the Gospel of John (4:20–24) supposes? Does it demand radical alteration of the Hebrew model? Not at all: the model is still communal, still historical, still based on memory and hope. What *is* unique in the Christian model is (a) Jesus Christ, and (b) *his* Messianic Spirit with Community. So, we will alter our picture slightly:

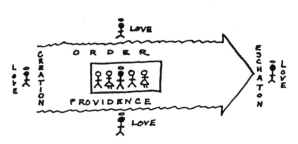

The figure of Christ (in [sic] black with halo!), joined to us in community, alters the model, particularly the residual religious model. In Christ we dare name the Mystery 'grace'. For Christ, his life and death and resurrection, puts a face on the Mystery (though it is still emphatically mysterious). Does not Christ's astonishing birth narrative testify to the 'grace' in being born? Do not resurrection stories declare 'grace' in, through, and beyond dying?[6] Surely his Love-law redefines order as 'grace', and his care-less trust ('Do not be anxious ...' 'Foxes have holes, but the Son of Man ...') demonstrate confidence in the 'grace' of Providence.

What is preaching/worship in the Christian model? The model is still historical-teleological and therefore the Church still recalls and anticipates in Community. But now the Spirit of trusting Sonship, the Spirit that impudently bawls 'Abba' at Mystery, is with Community. So, the pattern of worship and preaching is now words about God that become word *of* God, and words about God that become word *to* God in the trusting Spirit of Christ who has named Mystery the 'grace' of Abba! Worship and preaching involve thankful response in grace to grace for, as K. Barth was wont to say, everything is Grace!

III

Now let us turn to chase down the interplay between preaching and worship, glancing at essentials: Word and Sacrament – specifically Eucharist. Again, we will be fooling around with 'models' if only because drawing pictures is such fun.

Begin with a question: Phenomenologically, what is Eucharist? If nothing else, and in spite of past Papal demurrers, Eucharist is *meal*: we call it Lord's *Supper*. Now admittedly we Christian types have done almost anything possible to obscure the *meal*ness of Eucharist. We've pressed bread into tablets or dice-cubes, served wine in sanitary thimbles, sat around in studied silence to the tune of 'Beneath the Cross of Jesus', avoiding looking or talking festively to others, etc. But, at least for first century folk, the Lord's Supper was *supper*. Of course, we must be quick to agree that the supper was no casual pick-me-up, a TV dinner at the fag end of faith. The campus minister a few years ago who urged T-shirts, jeans, coffee and donuts deserved to flunk his course in sacraments: the Lord's Supper is a formal, celebrational banquet. Eucharist celebrates in memory, *anamnesis*, much as Israel celebrated liberation from Egypt or in covenant feasts recalled their election at Sinai. Nevertheless, phenomenologically Eucharist is a ritual *meal*.

A second question: How did the Lord's Supper function in the hermeneutic consciousness of the first disciples? What were mental associations by which they grasped the significance of the meal? Obviously, a meal will be understood by recalling previous prototype meals. The list is astonishing. As good Jews, the disciples would have recalled Passover (though I doubt the Last Supper was in fact a Passover meal), remembered Covenant ritual, dreamed the Messianic Banquet bash promised on Mt Zion. More, as disciples surely they would remember past eating and drinking with Jesus (check through the many N.T. pericopes with eucharistic overtones), thought of his feasts with sinners, perhaps the glut of wine at Cana, the feeding of a hungry five thousand with borrowed loaves and fishes, the solemn bread breaking on the eve of his death, resurrection parties (as O. Cullman has noticed), the sayings so full of Kingdom banquet talk. All of these images must have overlapped in consciousness. What an odd sketch we will have to make:

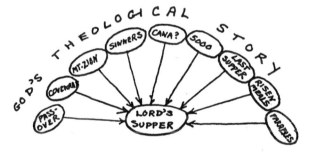

Anyone who has plowed through Sacramental theology in almost any tradition will have discovered that the Lord's Supper is not a 'steno-symbol', but a 'tensive' symbol. Interpreters speak of the many, many meanings of Eucharist and then, in a kind of dumb helplessness, tick off a list. The reason for a list of meanings should be obvious when we catch sight of the spread of prototype meals that must have collided in consciousness as baffled disciples took stock of the Lord's Supper.

Let's skip further into the matter of meanings. Each of the remembered meals involved God-with-us and, therefore, was plump with theological meaning: Passover = God the Liberator; Covenant = God the Elector; Messianic Banquet = God the Promise; With Sinners = God of Mercy who enjoys joining sinners; Cana = God the New Life Giver; The '5000' = God whose Grace is sufficient; Last Supper = God who saves by sacrifice; Resurrection = God whose fidelity makes Light of death; Kingdom Parables = God whose Victory is for the bums of the world. The list suggests that we are not dealing with the story of Israel or stories of Jesus alone, but with a come-together Story of God-with-us. Eucharist gathers the time and space of God-with-us, is crammed with the whole import of the *whole* Gospel. 'Tensive Symbol' may be too mild a term!

Preaching tells The Story which fills the sacrament with 'tensive' meaning: God-with us. Oh, we don't imply that sermons will rehearse the meal pericopes again and again, any more than with Baptism we would suggest telling Noah's flood or the Red Sea escape over and over. Israel remembered paradigmatic events about which other events clustered in mind ('In the time of the exodus . . . ', 'In the time of the exile . . . '), and these events do associate with a sequence of theological affirmations as we have noticed. Preaching tells the *whole* story (a reason why lectionaries are useful) and, juxtaposed with Eucharist, articulates the different meanings of the Sacrament. Clergy need not be concerned to build a mood-bridge from Sermon to Sacrament, or to preach eucharistic meditations whenever the Supper is served: the word of Christ preached will call to the event of Christ sacramentally without our contrivance.

IV

What about patterns between Sacrament and Sermon and the communal voice of Praise – all the basic stuff of worship? What pictures can we sketch? We will package ideas from E. Schillebeeckx (tricky to pronounce and spell) and J. Calvin (the Reformed tradition's founding Whiz Kid).[7] Obviously distinctions of form (show vs. tell) and similarities of 'gift' (Christ himself) have been much debated and, all in all, are not much help. So, our question, what is the pattern among word, sacrament and the people's praise?

Ideally, the true sacrament of Word would be Community. The Church herself ought to demonstrate and even validate the Gospel message. Of course, in one sense, mere *existence* of the Church does testify to the truth of the Gospel. If for example someone tells you the fanciful story of John Birch, you may find his heroics overdrawn and, in a word, improbable. But, note, the mere fact that there *is* a John Birch Society lends the story credence (after all, there are few if any Purple Heffalump Societies). More, insofar as the Birch Society uses liturgical texts drawn from their story, e.g., 'Pinko', 'Commie', etc., credibility is increased. If the Society seems to perpetuate John Birch's values and to continue his mission, your willingness to believe the Birch message is enhanced. So, though our analogy to the Birch Society is hopefully inappropriate, the *mere fact* of the Church – liturgy, Spirit, mission – does tend to give credibility to the story of God-with-us, the Gospel message. We can begin by sketching a simple 'model', one espoused by many protestant communities, particularly those of the 'Holiness' tradition:

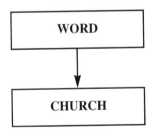

Can we admit that the simple 'model' puts an awesome burden on the Church? Yes, to be sure, Christian communities should embody the Gospel but, to be blunt, the Church's living of the Gospel is not always self-evident. The Good News may announce that 'there is neither slave nor free', but the Brooklyn Dodgers baseball team was integrated long before many American protestant Churches. The Gospel may declare 'Peace on Earth', but in wartime, Bishops have been known to anoint battleships. At best, the Church is a cloudy sign of the Gospel. What's more, whenever the Church over-strives to embody the Gospel she often ends in legalism which, of course, emphatically contradicts the Good News of grace. So, quick, let's venture another sketch:

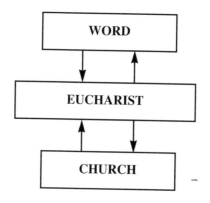

Eucharist functions between Gospel and Church for, if nothing else, the Lord's Supper enacts the Gospel on the one hand, and discloses the hiddenness of Church on the other. So, the whole action of reconciliation (The Kiss of Peace); mutual acknowledgment and mutual serving – should show the shape of the Gospel, and in doing so be a 'disclosure model' for the Presence of God-with-us.[8] Likewise, not only should the supper display the true nature of the Church as Body of Christ, but at the same time, should call the Church to enact herself sacramentally in the world. Of course, if a Church is facetious and filled with self-concern, folk may 'eat and drink judgment' on themselves because they can no longer discern the Body, that is the Body of Christ, in their common life. But, insofar as the Church with the Spirit in brokenness displays Christ then Word, Sacrament, and Community coordinate to call forth faith, and faith's doxological cry!

Now we come to a series of sticky statements. The Catholic 'heresy', inasmuch as there is still some neglect of the preached Word, is 'superstition' – Eucharist without story can do no more than to react with Community, risking loss of full significance as well as prophetic edge. However, the Protestant 'heresy' (and old John Calvin railed against it to his death), neglect of the Eucharist, results in doubt and/or legalism. While Gospel may be preached, faith may not grasp its reality, or Community understand true Community (as Body of Christ and not a bag of believers!). No wonder that Liturgical Renewal, Catholic and Protestant alike, calls for a *regular* conjoining of Word and Sacrament so that Christ may be for faith.

What of doxology? When Word and Eucharist collide in Community, there is Presence for faith. Faith understands Jesus Christ 'in a new way', which, I take it, is to know him doxologically. We know Christ not as an object of historical inquiry or as vague eschatological hope, but *in* praise and obedience – the only *real* ways he can be known.

V

Could we draw more pictures? Sure. Perhaps we could design a composition to draw our multiple 'models' together.[9] Happily restrictions on space prevent the attempt (Whew!). Better to let 'models' dance in our minds bumping clumsily or actually bending with grace toward one another. After all, this paper – an of-the-weekend, slap-dash special – is intended as nothing more than a conversation piece or, better, pages from a sketchbook.

Notes

1   James F. White, *Introduction to Christian Worship*, Nashville, TN, Abingdon, 1980, p. 15.

2   In my thinking I am indebted to Gordon D. Kaufman, *God the Problem*, Cambridge MA, Harvard, 1972, see particularly pp. 41–146.

3   The model was suggested to me by reading Edward Farley, *The Transcendence of God*, Philadelphia, Westminster, 1958, and by a brilliant article by Farley, 'Jesus Christ in Historical and Non-Historical

Schemes', *Perspective*, IX, 1968. However, Dr Farley should not be blamed for directions in which I have ventured.

4   See for example Walter Harrelson, *From Fertility Cult to Worship*, New York, Anchor, 1970, although the best support for the statement may be Hans-Joachim Kraus, *Worship in Israel*, Richmond, John Knox, 1966.

5   See my patchwork phenomenology, 'Story and Naming', Cassette, The College of Wooster, 1977.

6   David G. Buttrick, 'Preaching on the Resurrection', *Religion in Life*, 1976, pp. 278–95.

7   E. Schillebeeckx, OP, *Christ: The Sacrament of the Encounter with God*, New York, Sheed & Ward, 1963. For Calvin's eucharistic doctrine, the finest study I have found is K. McDonnell, *John Calvin, the Church, and the Eucharist*, Princeton, Princeton University Press, 1967.

8   The phrase 'disclosure model' is Ian Ramsey's (*Models and Mystery*, New York, Oxford, 1964), and Ramsey means by the phrase that the 'model' bears the reality it discloses.

9   I have attempted a coordination of some of the understandings in this paper in an unpublished Pitcairn Crabbe Foundation Lecture, 'Functions of the Word', n.d.

22 African-American Preaching: The Future of a Rich Tradition

Henry H. Mitchell

African-American preaching has been of interest to America's white majority ever since the days of 'Black Harry' Hoosier, the 'guide, servant and assistant preacher' to Methodist bishops Francis Asbury and Thomas Coke. Coke wrote the following report on November 29, 1784: 'I have now had the pleasure of hearing Harry preach several times. I sometimes give notice, immediately after preaching, that in a little time he will preach to the blacks; but the whites always stay [to] hear him.'[1] The nineteenth-century Methodist historian W. H. Daniels remarked: 'At different times (Black Harry) acted as driver for the carriage of Asbury, Coke, Whatcoat, and Garrettson; but he excelled all of his masters in popularity as a preacher.'[2] Bishop Coke and many others said essentially the same thing, even though Harry Hoosier could not read or write. And there were others. Henry Evans preached with power and founded the first Methodist church (white) in Fayetteville, North Carolina.[3] Joseph Willis was well known in Mississippi and Louisiana; in 1837 he organized the Louisiana Baptist Association, a primarily white association.[4]

In the South, many African-American preachers were silenced or forced to flee to the North, largely due to the politics of slavery, but there was a time before the widespread establishment of theological education when much of the best preaching done was by blacks. In the absence of formal training, the tools of African traditional communication served black preachers remarkably well. One cannot help wondering how much was lost to the cause of Christ when God-given genius and pulpit power were expelled or crushed on purely racial grounds, but the question is moot and fruitless to pursue. It is important, however, to identify the source of the power of traditional black communication. This essay will also suggest that the survival of the church might be assisted by the recovery of this rich preaching tradition.

At the outset one needs to clarify what is meant historically by the black pulpit tradition. Victim for more than a century of many stereotypically negative characterizations in the media, the black tradition at its best has yet to be carefully defined or widely understood. Books, plays, and television presentations abound that disparage the black church and its preachers and pulpit tradition. Even now, it is all too common to hear Gardner C. Taylor referred to as 'Dean of the Black Pulpit', rather than 'Prince of the *American* pulpit'. He merits that title along with the likes of George Arthur Buttrick and Harry Emerson Fosdick.

Stereotypical images of the black pulpit are all the more harmful because they are partly true, and because they make great humor and get great audience response. This appeal translates into money in the world of entertainment, and one fails to consider the destructive side effects. The fact that black entertainers and pseudo-intellectuals join the chorus of critics could be constructive, if only the positive images were given equal time. As it is, the most fruitful preacher of them all, Martin Luther King, Jr, is seldom remembered as the primarily pastoral and preaching figure that he was. His 'I Have a Dream' is seen as an address, when it had done duty as a sermon many times. African-American sermons, by popular misunderstanding, are not supposed to have such world-shaking impact.

The stereotypes span two extremes. One is the idea that the common characteristics of African-American folk preaching are the product of failed attempts to meet Western culture's pulpit standards. Throw in some intentional gimmicks known to slay black audiences, and you have the popular image. Almost nobody – white or black – is aware that this folk preaching style is evidently the descendant of public discourse in African traditional religion. This includes the feature called 'whooping', which preserves the tonality of African languages, though without maintaining the tones' capacity to communicate full meaning without words. The tone is no less valid than that of European plainsong; black tonality has greater dramatic power and appeal, partly because of its function as a nostalgic ethnic marker and affirmer of identity.

The latter attribute points in the direction of spiritual nourishment, which completes the explanation of the stubborn determination of this folk preaching style to stay alive. It has met people's needs. Whatever disrespect this folk style may have suffered in the wider world, it has been so supportive and healing of oppressed people that they cling to it, even when many unfortunately suspect that the Western way is proper, or 'white is right'.

The stereotype at the other extreme couples pious respect and sincere ignorance on the part of white would-be doers of good and builders of bridges. They admire black folk culture, preaching, and religion, but they have no clue as to its depth and meaning. They wish they could replicate the ecstasy in their own spiritual lives, without the loss of dignity. A few such pious souls will go so far as to join a black congregation, but most simply marvel from afar.

There is good reason to suspect that these bridge-builders possess subtly seeking hearts that would welcome a 'proper' infusion of life-giving warmth and power in their own pulpits. Nobody possessing the blessing of the African-American pulpit tradition at its best should hesitate one moment to share it, maintaining the authenticity of the gift and the dignity of those who receive it.

Which African-American tradition?

The reader may already have noted the use of the phrase 'at its best' in relation to the African-American pulpit tradition. This is because the images of black preaching most widely circulated are not the best. But there is no value in saving the down side of any tradition. People preserve their best, not their worst. The category of 'best', however, encompasses a variety of types. There is the historic best, the genius of the sincere slave, crafting sermons from a phenomenal memory of scripture and a culturally enriched imagination, and guided by the Holy Spirit. The quality of some of the few recorded sermons is so good that I use them as models in homiletics classes. They may not have used the dialect of the people in power, better known as standard English. They may not have exhibited the polish and verbal virtuosity common in the pulpits of the sophisticated, but their capacity for vividness of imagery and communication from the depths is unsurpassed. They also had a knack for relevance that would be hard to match.

A case in point would be Uncle Pompey's eulogy at the funeral of Uncle Wash, who had been unjustly convicted because he was too independent. Friends and kinfolk undoubtedly wondered how much correlation there was between the unjust white system and the judgment bar of God. Could Uncle Wash get into heaven with a criminal record? '[Uncle Pompey] told what a good-hearted man Uncle Wash was, and then he 'llowed as how his goin' to jail didn't necessarily mean he didn't go to heaven. He declared it wasn't eternally against a church member to get put in jail. If it hadda been, Paul and Silas wouldn't 'a' made it to heaven, and he *knowed* they was there. . . .'. During a vivid description of the 'dyin' thief' welcoming Uncle Wash to heaven, Uncle Pompey had them sing 'There Is a Fountain'. An ex-slave recalling the scene said that '. . . when they got to singin' 'bout the dyin' thief in heaven, an' when they seen the 'surance of grace that was in it, they like to never quit praisin' God'. It is hard to imagine a more powerful gospel, or one as relevant to real need.[5]

This level of homiletic genius would not have been heard every Sunday. The benefits of black folk preaching as a whole, however, were an important part of the psychic survival kit that helped keep folk alive and creative for nearly 250 years of slavery, and through oppression continuing even today. The tradition includes many levels of less-than-astounding quality, less-than-wholehearted effort, and less-than-complete sincerity. As is true everywhere else, there are times when people are blessed in spite of the preacher, and not because of him or her. The very wrath of human beings shall praise God, and the labors of self-centered preachers of a manipulative gospel fall in the same category. But I dare to believe that we have survived as well as we have because the vast majority of black folk-preaching was sincere and blessed.

Despite the manifest power of this tradition, there is a genre of black preaching that is consciously dedicated to getting away from black culture. This type of preaching is most common in churches of predominantly white denominations, but there are 'high church' Baptists and African Methodists as well. This commitment to Western as opposed to African cultural roots was once a sign of determination to be progressive. It held, thus, a modicum of spiritual health. Modern blacks are generally not attracted to such preaching because it is unlikely to nourish and satisfy the spirit.

The preaching tradition affirmed in this essay *is not* the tradition of these preachers who seek to escape black tradition. Yet I would be careful not to condemn their efforts to follow their consciences in the pulpit. I can only work and pray for the day when they will appreciate the best of black tradition, forsaking a path now manifestly suicidal to whole congregations. One cannot truly love and serve God and yet hate the ethnic identity assigned at birth by God.

It must also be understood that many of the most militant laborers for liberation are members of predominantly white church bodies. Presbyterians, Episcopalians, Roman Catholics, and Methodists all have fellowships of preachers and laity who are more committed to black liberation than are many who are committed to the black preaching tradition. One of the strongest black churches in commitment to the spiritual strengths of indigenous culture is the huge and active Trinity Congregational Church (UCC) of Chicago.

A hybrid of the strengths of these two extremes has been evolving for two centuries. There have always been a few who used both the best of Western education and the best of the black pulpit tradition, whether consciously or not. And that number has swelled impressively in the past twenty-five years. It is a result of the fact that Western theological education has at last affirmed black culture and other minority cultures, to the point of helping students train for practice within their own cultures.

The blessings have accrued to all concerned. History has come full circle, and whites once again recognize the value of the black pulpit tradition, not only for others, but for themselves as well. The powerful influence of African-American models in athletics and music (both secular and sacred) may yet be paralleled in the pulpit. Of what might such eclectic models consist? We begin with the African roots of the black pulpit tradition.

The African roots of black preaching tradition

Authentic African-American preaching is just that: first African, and not intended to imitate the preaching of any other group. Those who would suggest that black Christianity is a simple product of missionary activity by slaveowners are mistaken. This is most evident in preaching. The contrast with Western preaching starts with the African worldview, which makes no division between sacred and secular. Thus religious observance, including preaching, involves the whole human being, not just the rational consciousness. Hearing a sermon is a holistic experience, not just an affair of the intellect or 'spirit'. The sermon is designed, therefore, to appeal to the entirety of human consciousness – intuitive, emotive, *and* cognitive,

By contrast, the Western preaching tradition has tended until recent years to focus only on the cognitive. Sermon preparation has been essentially directed to ideological content. The formula of three points and a poem appealed to the cognitive, and so did other variations on the rational essay. Even much of what has been called narrative theology has still been about meaning and not about experiential encounter with the Word and its Lord.

In African culture we find evidence that the abstract is best communicated with imagery of the concrete. Children's prodigious recall of African traditional proverbs came from stories and pictures, songs and dances, all of them concrete but laden with unforgettable meaning. The whole person was enlisted in the recall, because the whole body, mind, and spirit had been engaged in the presentation of the tradition.

Ritual communication in African traditional religion knows no spectators; all are participants. The often mentioned call-and-response phenomenon is no isolated feature; it is at the heart of the whole African process. Educators know that children learn what they do, not what they hear, and this doing is what makes African children in traditional villages seem to be so gifted in memory. What child could forget a proverb danced with maneuvers such as no-hand flips? It is the reason they did not need a system of reading and writing to preserve their faith. Such holistic encounter is also the reason the Bible flourished among slaves in America, who were legally prohibited from learning to read, but not from vividly envisioning the biblical story.

Another factor contributed immensely both to the retention of sacred wisdom and to the way it influenced behavior: in Africa the tradition was regularly revisited in a context of joyous celebration. Stories, songs, and dances combined great pleasure and sacred substance. In America, the celebration factor was adapted into the sermon conclusion. People 'got happy' and shouted near the end of a well-timed sermon. I have called this 'ecstatic reinforcement'.

So the African-American sermon has traceable African roots. It obviously depended on European culture for the language used, and this inevitably influenced sermon form. But the major characteristics are of African origin. I was especially impressed with this fact when leading the Martin Luther King Fellows (Colgate Rochester Divinity School) on an intensive study tour in search of our roots. Time and time again, the comment was, 'We are far more African than we are European in the black church. I had no idea we were so African.' African-American preaching is on a continuum that starts in West Africa, not Western Europe.

Much of the influence of this African heritage has been integrated into the American Christian pulpit, through southern churches, para-Pentecostal television ministries, and a growing number of homileticians at accredited seminaries. Other African-American influences parallel elements generated independently in Western culture. The 'crossover' in both directions, together with the things already held in common, makes it less and less possible to speak of any contemporary group's homiletic as unique.

An emerging homiletic common to black and white cultures

While cultural diversity is likely to characterize the pulpits of America for decades to come, it is already true that important homiletical principles and patterns are followed across cultural, denominational, and theological lines. The way principles are applied in a given culture may vary in tone of voice and loudness, in pace of delivery, and in the images used, The point, nevertheless, is that the body of homiletical theories and supporting principles is rapidly approaching a working unanimity.

(1) African-American tradition has no universally agreed definition of faith, but the folkways suggest that faith is not the fruit of intellectual effort. The old folks said, 'If you didn't feel nothing, you ain't got nothing.' In other words, faith, as opposed to intellectual assent, comes in an *experience*.

Western culture has tended to treat faith as data, and sermons as primarily informative. But Euro-American thinking has never been completely committed to such an approach. The French philosopher Blaise Pascal (1623–1662) wrote that 'the heart has reasons which reason does not know.'[6] Pascal, also a mathematician, was known to speak of faith in terms of probability. Faith is betting everything that God is. In a word, he saw faith residing in the intuitive; it comes without the direct benefit of any intellectual effort. It arrives through an experience given by God.

John Wesley's founding of the Methodist church tradition was based not on his Oxford education or any books he read. 'About a quarter before nine, while he was describing the change which God works in the heart through faith in Christ, I felt my heart strangely warmed. I felt I did trust in Christ, Christ alone. . .'[7] The whole course of his life and of Protestant history was changed on the basis of this experience of his heart being strangely warmed.

So the two streams of tradition meet; as my old folks would say, 'If you are truly saved and receive the gift of faith, you will feel something deep down inside.' This emphasis on experience means that sermons for all cultures must be crafted to assist the Holy Spirit in the bottom line of an experiential encounter, not just an idea or a fact.

(2) The folk theology of African-American tradition has no official dogma, but it is always assumed that the Holy Spirit gives the gift of faith, to which one clings as best one can. Western analytical explanations of all this come from depth psychology, which would concede that faith is not fact, and therefore does not reside in cognition. Faith, by the providence of God, resides in a sector of consciousness for which we can take no credit, and is thus gift. So faith is a gift of God, not a work, not even an intellectual work, of human beings.

(3) The question then arises as to what agency God uses to generate the experiences that feed and nourish intuition's supply of faith. African-American tradition would not ask such a question, perhaps, but it does have some answers. These answers are found in folk practices of singing, praying, and, preeminently, preaching, as used by the Holy Spirit. The most important unspoken assumption is that worship, especially the sermon, is under the control of the Holy Spirit, which is how the gift is given and not earned. One prepares services of worship in most black churches today, but that does not mean that the pastor or congregation retains control. God uses the preparation of worship as a concert pianist uses the work of the piano tuner. One must stay within the limits of the diatonic scale, but there is no music until the master plays.

At this point Western tradition has the least in common with African-American tradition. When one defines worship as the gospel *properly preached* and the sacraments *properly administered*, the elements of human, definition, propriety and control, loom large. The prospect of closer and closer cultural commonality is great, however, as new generations move away from the rigidities of class culture and clamor for a spirit of spontaneity, thus making room for the gift that human beings cannot plan.

(4) There is a definite place for skill in the African-American tradition. A typical African-American deacon seeking an effective pastor for his church used to ask, and often still asks, 'Can the prospective pastor tell the story?' So far as the deacon is concerned, that sums it up. He wants to be blessed by vivid, eyewitness biblical narratives. And anybody can tell the story with the help of the Holy Spirit if they have engaged in serious and skillful preparation. The preacher must be an artist, a raconteur, a person the Holy Spirit uses to make the Bible come alive.

Of course, this is more than marvelously entertaining biblical tale-telling, but there is no perceived need to define the 'more' that goes beyond entertainment, and no need to explain why this is so important. If the deacon were questioned in this regard, he would probably answer that God uses these stories to save people. That answer is altogether correct as far as it goes, but the psychological wisdom available to both cultures makes it possible for us to cooperate with and be used by the Holy Spirit to enhance the power of the story.

(5) The most the African-American folk tradition would say about skills might be: 'The preacher ought to stick close to the sermon text.' This is probably more a conscious matter of authority in the mind of the deacon, but there are intuitive, unspoken demands that sermon art be coherent and focused. Black audiences are known to vote with their feet when a preacher wanders about aimlessly in a sermon. This criterion of focus has more than the need for biblical authority and the artistic requirement for coherence to support it. The insights of psychology tell us that the well-told story is focused to draw hearers into meaningful identification with the story. This vicarious experience enhances intuition and increases faith, trust, and obedience.

A weakness of those who just tell the story is that they often fail to focus it. Even many folk preachers who skillfully focus their stories are prone to do it by intuition. We now know, however, how to discipline the way the story is shaped, to accomplish in the hearer a particular behavioral progress toward the new person in Christ. This kind of wisdom can be a great benefit to folk preachers, as well as those with professional training.

Homileticians who oppose Bible storytelling in the pulpit are likely unaware of this way of making narration so pointedly fruitful. They may also be unaware that stories teach more effectively than abstractions. This is why Jesus told parables. The problem is that they see being entertaining as the opposite of being instructive. The opposite of 'entertaining' is not 'educational' but boring. Unless the gospel is engaging, it is hardly heard, much less remembered. Great preachers are not those who project the pose of a scholar; they are the ones who act like a peasant who stood by the road and remembered all that was seen.

(6) The rules of focus are relatively simple; any resistance to the rules suggested here is likely born of fixed habit, not ignorance.

First, choose a biblical text – preferably brief – that supplies or implies not only truths but a *behavioral goal* in the hearer. No truth is significant that has no obvious counterpart in human action or attitudes. Second, choose a framework by which the text and its literary context may be formed in consciousness, or *experienced*. The most common such vehicle of vicarious experience is the narrative, the same thing. He had his preaching students read their pericopes and list every physical detail they could find. The story becomes vivid when there are concrete details the hearer can envision, and almost anyone can make a hearer see it, having first seen the story oneself. So preachers must *see* the story to understand it and retell it. They must skim for stories and images, not abstract ideas, before they can communicate meaningfully. For the most part people remember pictures better than they remember words.

(7) The seventh and final factor in focused communication is *feeling*. Just as preachers read for physical detail, they must become sensitive to emotional detail. The most powerful identification with biblical characters is with their emotions. People instantly identify with the psalmist's cry, 'My God, my God, why have you forsaken me?' (Ps 22:1). It should come as no surprise that black preaching is most effective in this area. But two of my most vivid recollections of the feeling tones of a biblical character are of preaching by white pastor-professors. The best of two cultures' traditions converge here.

Harry Emerson Fosdick, in a midweek Bible study, read in Paul's letters a list of people to be greeted, and helped us reminisce with Paul about experiences with each of them. It was as if we were there, and the deep feelings transferred and transformed us. And Gene Bartlett, at an American Baptist Convention, set the last judgment in Matthew 25 before our very faces. The emotion was surprise, and the vivid portrayal was of people who were so helpful without any hint of self-consciousness. 'When in the world did I see you hungry and give you something to eat? Nice of you to speak so kindly of me, but I think you must have the wrong person.' My spirit still responds to my vivid memory of Bartlett's crescendo, 'Inasmuch as ye did it unto the least of these . . '. I would love to have heard him do that at a black convention; it was such a powerful evidence of the universal appeal of vivid biblical narration. Preaching is most effective when it transcends culture and conforms to criteria that generate experiential encounters with God and the Word. It is in this area of emergent commonality that the highest growth takes place in all cultures.

The point of greatest divergence

It is unfortunate that after the celebration of commonality there should have to be a candid address of the issue of greatest divergence, the role of emotion. One could omit this subject and keep the peace, but herein lies the greatest potential for growth. While the African-American pulpit tradition is stereotyped as excessively emotional, mainstream middle class America is noted for quite the opposite. Apart from a few mostly independent mega-churches and television ministries, Americans maintain a carefully controlled environment of worship, spurning overt and spontaneous emotional expression.

One reading of mainstream preaching as dull appears in William F. Fore's report on the response to an article he had written on the electronic church: 'The perception of many mainline churches as dry, unfriendly, and moribund is not just a religious problem, for the vacuum that is created has spawned a crisis in society as a whole.'[9] In an era when the dualism of flesh and spirit has been discredited in philosophy and in the healing disciplines, the ethnic majority's churches still act as if emotion is something to be avoided. Mainline churches tend to prefer that sermons be 'moving', but not evoke deep emotion. If preachers appeal to deep feeling, they are accused of 'getting emotional on us', as if that were audience manipulation. Yet faith, hope, and love are strongly emotional. Everybody knows that fear is an emotion, but so is its opposite, trust. Likewise with hate and love, despair and hope. The sermon that fails to reach the emotions fails to reach the very heart of faith.

Meanwhile, African traditional religion held that possession by the spirits of various sub-deities was the zenith of cultic observance. Human control of worship was an abomination. This view of possession was baptized into the black church tradition, and appears today in shouting, a practice especially welcomed in folk black churches. God is known by a trinity of manifestations, of which one is the Holy Spirit. Thus, a form of possession lost from European Christianity, perhaps in the Middle Ages or earlier, was resurrected in America in part because of African cultural influence.

The first Great Awakening burst forth with shouting of its own, under no less worthy a preacher than Jonathan Edwards – though he was wary of it at first. The shouting really burst forth under Whitefield and the Tennents. Thus, in discussing emotion, if one goes back as far as the first and second Great Awakenings, one finds the streams merged even here. In a letter to George Whitefield, Gilbert Tennent wrote in 1741: 'Multitudes were awakened, and several had received the great Consolation, especially among the young People, Children and Negroes.'[10] An ex-slave named Gustavus Vassa, in his autobiographical slave narrative, tells how greatly he was impressed by the 'fervor and earnestness' of George Whitefield.[11]

The Methodist church, known in the Awakenings as 'The Shouting Methodists',[12] was growing at a phenomenal rate. Starting from zero, Methodists became the largest denomination in the United States by 1820. Today, Methodism and all the other mainline denominations are losing ground rapidly. It makes sense, then, to suggest serious consideration of the best of the black pulpit's approach to emotion – incorporating into the emerging commonality the emotion that was lost to white churches during the late nineteenth or early twentieth century.

There are other reasons for resistance to emotional expression in religion. The extremes of the Billy Sunday revivals and the malpractice of emotional televangelists have caused many thinking people to reject this vital component of religion. The African-American pulpit tradition is just as opposed to manipulative emotionalism as any thinking group or cultural tradition. But the extremes of emotionalism so widely stereotyped are not to be confused with the lofty and intense emotion in the best of African and African-American tradition.

In West Africa and Haiti I have seen possession rites that were astoundingly intense, but never allowed to endanger the psychic or physical wellbeing of the one possessed. The *houngan* (priest) of authentic Voodoo (African traditional religion) guides the possession to healing results. Sincere believers within the black church in this country are quick to spot people and practices that are not of the Holy Spirit. The most strenuous movements of sincere shouters are somehow protected from doing harm. There are culturally built-in safeguards. Psychiatrists say a subsection of the rational ego sits in the corner of the psyche, as it were, and pushes the red button if there is any danger or nonsense. I have seen audiences freeze almost instantly when a usually well received preacher took liberties with the Bible. After that, the only shouter was the preacher's wife. We all have cultural expectations buried deep in the psyche, and it requires no thought to follow those safeguards. One can stay 'in the Spirit' and 'happy' without fear, knowing that God has placed in the depths a monitor to keep one safe.

On the positive side, the invitation to rejoin African Americans in the stream of spiritual surrender, allowing the Spirit free rein, has much to offer that is worthy of trust. There is the possibility of being used by the power of the Holy Spirit to bless lives with the Word. Sermons are transformed, even after careful preparation, and one preaches and views, sometimes in utter surprise, the very handiwork of God.

The most important thing to be said in this regard is that the celebration at the end of the sermon serves as ecstatic reinforcement, the last blow of the hammer to drive in the nail. The preacher does not 'use' emotion; holy emotion uses the preacher. She or he is used by the Holy Spirit to achieve the transformation of the hearer in the direction of the text and the behavioral purpose of the sermon. The celebration has been called the 'gravy', and dismissed as manipulation.[13] To stick with the metaphor, I would suggest that real gravy is made from the substance of the meat, and is a valid way to conclude a sermon. Celebration is gladness about the text, and people remember what they get glad about. This is focused, intentional, and productive emotion. Without it, the sermon may be easily forgotten, and ignored as an influence on behavior. With a celebration, as opposed to a paste-on conclusion, the experience becomes etched in the heart and mind, and impossible to forget.

Granted that faith is a high emotion, and that emotion is not influenced unless deep calls unto deep, the question is not 'Will white middle class preaching begin to accept more fully the emotional resources offered by the Holy Spirit?' Rather it should be, 'How can we begin to train congregations to accept and enjoy and be blessed by holy emotion? How can we move them to seek and not just tolerate the life-giving power of the Spirit of God, who is able to save the churches from certain death? And how can we assure them that the bizarre behaviors seen on television are the least of their worries?'

So it may be that even this divergence can be ended, and the churches saved. It may yet be that the best of the African-American church's pulpit tradition can be disciplined, focused, and shared. The very prospect has already moved many seminaries to seek African-American instructors in homiletics. These new experts will need to research seriously into the depths of their tradition, and not just teach what they were taught.

The sharing has already taken place in the enrichment of American popular entertainment. Desirable features of African-American culture are received with a remarkable lack of inhibition. The churches of America's majority-for-now should accept the invitation to the feast of the black church. And the African-American pulpit should adhere to the very best of its own tradition.

Notes

1   Holland N. McTyeire, *A History of Methodism*, Nashville, TN, Southern Methodist Publishing, 1887, pp. 346–7.

2   John W. Coleman, 'Heroic Black Figures of Early Methodism', in William B. McClain (ed.), *Black People in the Methodist Church*, Cambridge, Schenkman, 1984, p. 41.

3   There are numerous references to Evans's fearless preaching in the face of brutal opposition. See John W. Coleman, 'Henry Evans: Church Organizer', in McClain (ed.), 1984, pp. 51–4; Carter G. Woodson, *The History of the Negro Chruch*, Washington, DC, Associated Publishers, 1921, pp. 47–8.

4   Ibid., p. 74.

5   Quoted in Henry H. Mitchell, *Black Preaching: The Recovery of a Powerful Art*, Nashville, TN, Abingdon, 1990, p. 35.

6   Samuel Enoch Stumpf, *Socrates to Sartre: A History of Philosophy*, New York, McGraw-Hill, 1966, p. 217.

7   Kenneth Scott Latourette, *A History of Christianity, Vol. 2: A.D. 1500–A.D. 1975*, New York, Harper & Row, 1975, p. 1025.

8   Henry H. Mitchell, *Celebration and Experience in Preaching*, Nashville, TN, Abingdon, 1990, Chaps 2, 5–10.

9   William F. Fore, *Television and Religion: The Shaping of Faith, Values, and Culture*, Minneapolis, Augsburg, 1987, pp. 99–100, quoted in Richard F. Ward, 'Beyond Televangelism: Preaching on the Pathway to Re-Formation', in Martha J. Simmons (ed.) *Preaching on the Brink: The Future of Homiletics*, Nashville, TN, Abingdon, 1996, p. 122.

10 Stephen Nissenbaum, *The Great Awakening at Yale College*, Belmont, Wadsworth, 1972, p. 26.

11 Gustavus Vassa, 'The Life of Gustavus Vassa, the African', in Arna Bontemps (ed.), *Great Slave Narratives*, Boston, Beacon, 1969, p. 99.

12 Withrop S. Hudson, 'Shouting Methodists', *Encounter*, 29, 1, 1968.

13 The most common sin of the black pulpit is the use of the stock celebration, known to slay audiences. It is remembered for its emotional intensity, but erases from consciousness the substance preceding it. It is therefore guilty of manipulation. Often this sin is committed in utter sincerity and ignorance of homiletic principle.

23   Homily or Eulogy? The Dilemma of Funeral Preaching

John Allyn Melloh

I still remember the words spoken to me some ten years ago, after I had preached at the wake of a Catholic man married to a Jewish woman. 'Father John', began the father in law of the deceased, 'I want to thank you so much for not giving a eulogy. A eulogy would have ripped our hearts out, but what you said gave us all hope.' I had done nothing more than follow the prescription of the 1969 *Ordo Exsequiarum*: 'A brief homily should be given after the gospel, but without any kind of funeral eulogy.' Our different faith traditions, I mused later, could have prompted his gracious remark. A homily was what this service required; a homily, not a eulogy, is what the wake service demands.

More recently, however, I have become acutely aware of the tension between homily and eulogy in Roman Catholic circles. Some preaching students and workshop participants have adamantly disagreed with my approach to funeral preaching, strongly defending the eulogy; colleagues who teach preaching have met similar vigorous resistance. Those who favour the eulogy advance the argument that preaching must be personal. Preaching needs to celebrate the deceased, especially by rehearsing significant moments in that person's life. Providing insight into the deceased or offering a final chance to come to know the person better, they state, offers consolation to the bereaved. Although I do not find the arguments for the eulogy persuasive, they do couch an important principle, namely, that the preached word is not antiseptic or platitudinous. It must refer to the death of this particular person.

Real tension exists between the eulogy and the homily. The liturgical documents are explicit. The 1969 prohibition against the eulogy is reiterated even more pointedly in the 1986 *Order of Christian Funerals*: 'There is never to be a eulogy.' Yet many people feel a need for the eulogy and many eulogies are regularly preached at funerals. This article will discuss the funeral homily, supporting the assertion that a eulogy should not replace the liturgical homily. I explore three different areas to elucidate current directives: (1) the funeral as an occasional rite; (2) the function of the Word in the funeral, and (3) there classical Greek funeral oration model. A final section provides a model for preparing the funeral homily.

The funeral as occasional rite

What is often neglected in considering funeral preaching is the context in which it occurs, namely, the liturgy. The various funeral rites are occasional rites, celebrations 'occasioned' by some event. Just as serious sickness occasions rites for anointing, and the pledging of mutual love calls for the marriage rite, death in the Christian community occasions the complexus of funeral rites. Liturgy, however, celebrates God in a corporate act whose subject is the Church. In the funeral celebration the deceased is not the 'object' of the rite, since the sacramental rites occasioned by death, as in all liturgies, glorify God, sanctify people and build up the ecclesial body.

If occasional rites have tended to focus on individuals as objects of special ministrations, so too has the preaching at these rites. For example, the wedding homily can become an 'instruction' to bride and groom. The funeral homily, a word addressed to the congregation in a context of prayer, must have as its goal the goal of the liturgy itself. Contemporary eulogistic patterns, concentrating on the deceased, tend to involve the assembly primarily in inner-directed personal consolation and sympathy. If not at odds with the purposes of worship, these forms ill accord with the goals of liturgy.

The function of word in the funeral celebration

If occasional rites focus on being the Church in Christ, so too does preaching. While the 1986 *Order of Christian Funerals* is clear about the matter of preaching, the document, importantly, takes a holistic view of the liturgy itself. Since worship involves the whole person, attention to all that affects the senses is required: readings and prayers, music, ritual gestures, actions, postures, liturgical signs and symbols. Meaning in the celebration is communicated, therefore, by more than simply the Word proclaimed and preached. Nonetheless, the document asserts that the Church attaches great importance to the proclamation of the Word of God. The readings not only proclaim the Paschal Mystery, but also convey hope of being gathered in God's reign; they teach remembrance of the dead and encourage Christian witness. Over all the proclamation of the Word manifests God's design: that suffering and death will not triumph over God's people.

The homily is given primacy of place. 'A brief homily based on the readings is always given after the gospel reading at the funeral liturgy and may also be given after the readings at the vigil service, but there is never to be a eulogy.' The preacher is admonished to be attentive to grief: planning the liturgy should be done with an eye towards the spiritual and psychological needs of the family. Consolation and strength are to be offered, especially through the proclamation of the mystery of God's love and Jesus' victory present in the life and in the death of the deceased as well as in the lives of family and friends. That the document mentions themes of Christian witness, and dying and rising with Jesus, as part of the congregation's own experience, strongly suggests that the homily goes beyond the parameters of the eulogy.

The commendation, a final farewell that 'acknowledges the reality of separation and affirms that the community and the deceased, baptised into one Body, share the same destiny, resurrection on the last day', entrusts the deceased to God. New to the funeral rite is this addition: 'A member or a friend of the family may speak in remembrance of the deceased before the final commendation begins.' This rubric, a logical consequence of the document's expansive view of ministries, is consonant with the prohibition of the post-gospel eulogy. Even these memorial words should not be equated with a eulogy; the rhythm of the liturgy and its contextualizing prayers eschew a 'time out' for praise of the deceased. The Order of Christian Funerals, in sum, sees the entire act of worship as communicating meaning. This liturgy supports faith and offers consolation, but not through eulogising the deceased.

How are these directives of the *Order of Christian Funerals* to be understood? Specifically, what does, 'The Church attaches great importance to the reading of the Word of God' mean? The way in which the Word functions within the funeral celebration will shed light on the subject.

Consider the Sunday Eucharist. The proclaimed Word is the variable part of an otherwise rather invariable liturgy. As such it is what differentiates, for example, the 10th from the 11th Sunday of Ordinary Time. The Sunday readings, additionally, are determined by a fixed cycle of lections. The funeral, however, is different. First of all, it is occasioned by an event, rather than by a calendar. Secondly, the readings are not fixed by a lectionary, but chosen from suggested options so as to meet the spiritual and psychological needs of the assembly. The Word, therefore, functions differently within the funeral celebration. The Word itself is determined, even dominated, by the event. Thus, the first hermeneutical decision to be made is the selection of texts, which is usually determined on a pre-critical basis, that is, with a kind of intuition that these texts will speak to the congregation under these specific circumstances. The lessons proclaimed differentiate this particular celebration from another, but they tend to melt into the background and become part of the collage of liturgical symbols and actions. The readings do not carry the meaning of the rite in isolation. Thus, 'A careful selection and use of readings from Scripture for the funeral rites will provide the family and the community with an opportunity to hear God speak to them in their needs, sorrow, fears and hopes.' Whereas on an ordinary Sunday the lectionary texts nuance the mystery celebrated, in the funeral service it is the reverse. The event of death, not calendar, makes claims on the text. Word is in service to the event.

Effective funeral preaching is more mystagogical than purely biblical: it is a preaching of the mystery celebrated, a breaking open of the symbolic with an invitation into the mystery. Yes, the biblical readings do serve as a way into that mystery, but they are not the only entry point. Liturgical prayers, gestures and rites also speak the mystery. Mystagogical preaching interprets the event of death through the liturgical symbols as an actualisation of the Paschal Mystery, not just on the part of the deceased, but of the congregation as well. The funeral liturgy confronts the congregation with the reality of death, but proclaims symbolically that death is the beginning of eternal life with God, begun in baptism. The baptismal motif, clearest in the sprinkling with holy water and the placing of the pall, reminds the assembly of all Christians' baptismal living. Thus, the passage of the deceased, ritualised in worship, speaks to the on-going mystery of Christian living, namely, dying to sin and rising in new life, and sharing a common destiny. It is through the liturgy, especially, that the faithful are enabled to express in their lives and manifest to others the mystery of Christ.

Classical Greek rhetoric

Although the liturgical directives forbid the eulogy to replace the liturgical homily, eulogising the deceased still finds its way into current funeral celebrations. A preacher's lack of familiarity with the classical Greek funeral oration does not imply that this model is not still in use. Its liturgical suitability, however, needs to be questioned. It does not actually meet the felt need for 'personal' preaching.

Both the Greek and Latin funeral orations of pre-Christian times had a monotonous similarity. While rhetorical flourish stood out, a marked philosophical chilliness persisted throughout. Even 'consolation' was expressed by using maxims (for example, 'All are mortal.' 'To have lived virtuously, rather than long, is of prime importance'), or by appealing to widely-held beliefs, such as that death frees from the ravages of disease or the evils of old age. An important shift occurred when the classical model was adapted for Christian usage. Although the classical structure and subjects remained the same, the Christian faith, especially resurrection hope, furnished an 'incomparably superior means of consolation'. Moving away from a litany of humanistic platitudes signalled a new development.

The Christian funeral oration was generally not given at a liturgical celebration, but preached well after the burial of the person. It aimed both at reinforcing an opinion of the deceased through praise and at consoling the bereaved. The purpose of the modern funeral homily is not exactly the same. Rather, it offers consolation through the proclamation of resurrection faith and aims at the renewal of Christian living among the assembly. The classical model is less than liturgically suitable. As practised in today's Church, eulogistic preaching generally follows the ancient rhetorical patterns, with the subjects of family, education, moral qualities, and so on, forming the nucleus of preaching. The recital of biographical entries, however, does not insure a 'personal' quality of preaching. It is as personal and impersonal as a resume: 'personal' data is standardised and resumed in 'impersonal' categories. The eulogy, thus, does not really meet the need for a personal word.

Homily or eulogy?

It is the liturgical homily which deserves the premier place as the preached word. Interpreting the mystery of death, it proclaims good news in Word, just as the rest of the liturgy proclaims good news in deed. Further and more importantly, the homily invites all into renewed living of the Paschal Mystery. Conversely, the eulogy either stops at a rehearsal of biographical details or continues with the addition of consolatory material. The deceased Christian deserves better and the community needs more.

A mystagogical homily, however, captures the 'spirit' of the deceased and reverences that spirit by pronouncing a word of faith. Imbued with the 'presence' and the 'ethos' of the deceased, the homily pulsates with the life of the deceased. It does that modestly, with perhaps the simplest of references to the deceased – a phrase, a word, an incident – but one strong enough to bear that precious freight. Mystagogical characterises not only the homily, but also the personal word at the final commendation. During a recent funeral, the youngest son spoke in remembrance of his mother. He had composed a letter, as though written by his mother, which said in essence: 'What has always held this family together is love, in times good and bad. It is that same love that holds us together now and in the future.' A more eloquent testimony could not have been spoken. No biographical details or incidents were mentioned, but the living spirit of one who had died was present.

'It is not sufficiently considered', said Dr Johnson, 'that men more frequently require to be reminded than informed.' Let the personal word in the rite of commendation remind us, rather than inform us about the deceased.

Conclusion

The preacher should ponder the following questions in preparing the homiletic word. First, what is the 'emotion' that surrounds this celebration? A commonly shared feeling, even if negative, needs to be identified specifically. More importantly, however, the preacher should name the deeper and more permanently abiding 'affection' below the emotional surface. Second, what has shaped this attitude? For example, a sense of relief that long painful suffering has ended may give rise to thankfulness. Joy may be the attitude: a peaceful death brought a ripe old age to an end. The tragedy of early or violent death may surface anger. Third, how does the liturgy and the proclaimed word speak to the event and to the attitude? For example, God's word may confirm our attitude, but it may challenge or even repudiate it. Fourth, what new relationship between God and God's people obtains through this celebration? For example, God's word in face of a tragedy may call us to solidarity and corporate hope. Pondering these questions can lead to biblical preaching 'through the text', preaching directed to the community at prayer. It will orient the community's own passage rite, geared toward re-integration, and will accord well with the purposes of faithful worship.

Part 7

THE WOMAN AS PREACHER

Introduction to Part 7

Cheryl Sanders asks if we hear the feminine voice of God when women preach and, if so, how it may differ from the masculine. She analyses 36 written sermons by black preachers, both male and female, categorizing them by sermon form, biblical text, central theme, use of inclusive language and homiletical purpose. The bulk of the article consists of illustrations of the different homiletical tasks attempted by the sermons and draws exclusively from the women's sermons. At the end she concludes that women and men differ slightly in their choices of themes and tasks, hardly at all in form and texts, but markedly in their preference for inclusive language. In their sermons men and women preach the same word but 'women tend to emphasize the personal and men the prophetic.'

Cheryl J. Sanders, 'The Woman as Preacher' is from *The Journal of Religious Thought*, 43, 1, 1986, pp. 6–23.

The next article, 'Gender and the Aesthetic of Preaching', explores the difficulties that traditional pulpit design may raise for the woman preacher through the author's interview with an Episcopal priest called 'Sue'. The architecture of the pulpit sets up expectations that may be at odds with women's voice, gesture, appearance and manner. It may constrain her preferred choice of content, subject matter and rhetoric. The lofty pulpit symbolizes a division between preacher and congregation and reinforces a particular kind of authority, objectivity, almost 'an assault on the world'. By contrast, Sue wanted to access 'her inner life' when preparing to preach. The article explores gendered contrasts like 'male' and 'female', 'inner' and 'outer', 'experience' and 'exegesis', preaching as 'who I am' and as 'what I do', searching for 'truth in a text' and 'opening horizons'. With a description of Sue's recent setting for ministry the article commends the vitality of a new aesthetic which acknowledges God in our midst.

Virginia Purvis-Smith, 'Gender and the Aesthetic of Preaching' was first published in the *Journal of Women and Religion*, 11, 1992, pp. 74–83.

The final article in Part 7 is a study of white rural Pentecostal congregations. Elaine Lawless explores the stories told by women who declare that they have a divine call to preach in a culture which in the name of Scripture explicitly denies that possibility. Women preachers describe their call in spiritual life stories, a pastiche of personal experience and traditional expectations, which 'affirm identity in the act of telling'. These stories become models by which other women can live their lives. 'Life accounts may or may not reflect historical fact', but they serve to legitimate the alternative lifestyle which the women have chosen. The stories disrupt the status quo and illustrate some of the ways in which women can take control of their lives. They are thus stories of liberation. At the same time, it is possible to discern in the stories an element of denial, decisions for the 'acceptable' against the 'actual', and shaping reality to fit group expectations.

Elaine J. Lawless, 'Rescripting their Lives and Narratives: Spiritual Stories of Pentecostal Women Preachers' is from the *Journal of Feminist Studies in Religion*, 7, 1991, pp. 53–71.

24   The Woman as Preacher

Cheryl J. Sanders

Introduction

When the Reverend Suzan Johnson was installed last year as pastor of Mariners' Temple Baptist Church in New York, a 'first' for black women within the American Baptist Church, *USA Today* reported the event with the comment that 'Johnson hopes to bring the "feminine voice" of God to her parishioners.'[1] That quote echoes the central concern of this lecture – do we hear the feminine voice of God when women preach? If so, how does the feminine voice of God differ from the masculine voice of God? In other words, what are the distinctive characteristics of the preaching of women as compared with the preaching of men?

I have sought to answer these questions by conducting a comparative analysis of women's and men's sermons taken from three sermon anthologies: *Black Preaching: Select Sermons in the Presbyterian Tradition*, edited by Robert T. Newbold, Jr; *Outstanding Black Sermons* by J. Alfred Smith, Sr; and *Those Preachin' Women*, by Ella Pearson Mitchell. My sample includes thirty-six sermons: eighteen by women and eighteen by men. I have used all fourteen women's sermons in Mitchell's collection, three from Newbold, and the one sermon by a woman judged to be outstanding by Smith. The eighteen men's sermons have been selected at random from Newbold and Smith. For ease of comparison, I have only studied sermons preached within the black tradition. However, a broad variety of denominations is represented within the sample, including Baptists, Presbyterians, United Methodists, the African Methodist Episcopal Church, the United Church of Christ, and several independent groups. Most of these preachers are pastors, but the sample also includes lay preachers, professors, and those who are employed by agencies or denominational headquarters. Because written sermons only lend themselves to analysis in terms of content, no attempt will be made here to compare women's and men's preaching on the basis of style or delivery.

The purpose of this analysis is not to promote stereotypes or caricatures of women preachers. In a recent article entitled 'Black Women Preachers: A Literary View', Betty Overton addresses the question of the distinctiveness of black women preachers from the rather negative vantage point of black literature:

> Are black women preachers any different from their male counterparts? Probably not. What one does garner from the few women ministers in black literature is a half view, a view characterized by an attitude that women do not belong in the pulpit and that they earn their suffering and problems by their daring to take on this role. For the most part they are not admirable characters but stereotypes of the worst that is in religious ministry.[2]

Although Overton's conclusion that in real life black women preachers are probably not different from their male counterparts is a reasonable one, her statement reminds us that negative stereotypes from literature or other sources can produce a biased 'half view' of women's preaching. Indeed, actual sermons preached by black women constitute the best resource for a realistic examination of the question of the uniqueness of the feminine in the tradition of preaching.

Analytical procedure

I have analysed and compared sermons preached by women and men in terms of five key categories: (1) sermon form, (2) biblical texts, (3) central themes, (4) the use of inclusive language with reference to God and persons, and (5) homiletical tasks. First, I identified each sermon with one of four basic sermon forms: expository, narrative, textual, or topical. Next, I categorized the principal biblical text chosen by the preacher by literary type and by Testament. In cases where multiple texts were cited, the one text that appeared to have the greatest relevance to the central concerns of the sermon was singled out for analysis. The literary types include narrative, prophecy, or poetry for Old Testament texts, and narrative, prophecy (i.e., apocalyptic), or epistle for New Testament texts. I also noted whether or not the text chosen deals specifically with women. As a third step, I examined the content of each sermon in an effort to discern its central theme, which was often, but not always, conveyed by the title of the sermon. The fourth category I took into consideration was whether the preacher used inclusive language or exclusively masculine terms when referring to God or to persons. The fifth and final step was to take account of the range of homiletical tasks the sermon was designed to perform, that is, to ask what the preacher was trying to accomplish in and by the sermon.

Sermon form

The four basic sermon forms applied in this analysis are described and illustrated by James Earl Massey, who concludes that the most popular and traditional sermon form is the *topical*:

> This design highlights the truth or importance of a topic or theme, letting the logical points or facets of that topic control the sequence of treatment and timing of the application. The topic can be chosen from any one of a number of sources, but it is usually backed or supported by a related scriptural text.[3]

Ranking second in 'popularity' is the *textual* sermon form, in which the sermon is designed to follow the divisions or sequences of thought in the scriptural text. Thirdly, the *expositional* sermon form addresses an extended passage of Scripture, centering attention upon some one emphasis in that passage, 'purposefully treating a teaching, an insight, a promise, a hope, a warning, a character, an experience, a meaning, a prophecy, a virtue, a key word, and so on'.[4] For the purposes of this study, the expositional form is distinguished from the textual form based upon the length of the scriptural text and the manner in which it is treated; a textual sermon focuses attention on the message contained within a short passage of Scripture, while the exposition takes a more extended passage and draws from it some particular aspect or application. A fourth sermon form is the *narrative*, which treats some biblical story with particular concern for atmosphere, character, plot, tone, and movement.[5] Both in content and in form, the narrative sermon is centered upon the telling of a story.

There appears not to be much difference between women and men in the selection of sermon form. In accord with Massey's description of the topical form as the most popular among preachers, the majority of sermons preached by both the women and men in the sample followed the topical form. In fact, the proportions were identical; 67 percent (about two-thirds) of the women's sermons and 67 percent of the men's sermons were topical sermons. Second in popularity among the women was the narrative form; 22 percent of the women's sermons were narrative sermons. The remaining 11 percent of the women's sermons were in the textual form, and none of the women preached expository sermons. On the other hand, the one-third of the men's sermons that were not topical in form were evenly distributed among the three other types – 11 percent were narrative, 11 percent textual, and 11 percent expository.

Biblical texts

The women and men in the sample appeared to be more alike than different in the selection of biblical texts for their sermons. Thirty-nine percent of the women preached from the Old Testament, and 61 percent from the New Testament, whereas 44 percent of the men preached from the Old Testament, and 56 percent from the New Testament. In terms of actual numbers, only one more of the women's sermons was preached from the New Testament than was preached from the New Testament by the men. There was more variation between women and men in terms of literary type. Forty-four percent of the women preached from narrative texts, in comparison with 61 percent of the men. The second most favored literary type among the women preachers was the epistle, and 33 percent of their sermon texts were taken from the epistles, primarily of Paul. By contrast, only 11 percent of the men took texts from the epistles. Seventeen percent of the women's sermons were preached from biblical prophecy, and an identical proportion of the men preached from prophetic texts. The Psalms and Proverbs were used as texts for only 5 percent of the women's sermons and 11 percent of the men's sermons, representing one and two sermons, respectively. Only two of the men's sermons (11 percent) and three of the women's sermons (5 percent) were based upon texts that made specific reference to women.

Sermon themes

An effort was made to organize the central themes of these sermons into several general categories. Three themes were common to the preaching of both women and men: the church and its mission, Christian virtues, and racial identity. Twice as many men (six) as women (three) preached on the church and its mission, four of the women's sermons and three of the men's were preached on Christian virtues, and equal numbers of women and men (three each) chose racial identity as a central sermon theme. However, no one theme was the dominant choice of women or men. The most popular theme, the church and its mission, was chosen by only 25 percent of all the preachers. The second most widely used theme, Christian virtues, was actually preached by 19 percent of the preachers. Only 17 percent of the women and men preached on the racial identity theme.

Three sermon themes peculiar to the women's preaching included survival, healing, and ministry. Two themes, preaching and the nature of God and/or Christ, were exclusively preached by men.

Inclusive language for God and persons

The fourth analytical category applied to the sermon sample was the use of inclusive language. As might be expected, the men were far more likely than the women to use words like *he*, *his*, and *father* with reference to God, and to speak of people in general as man or mankind in their sermons. In fact, the majority of the women and a minority of the men used inclusive language in both cases. Twice as many women as men referred to persons using inclusive terms; 89 percent of the women as compared with 44 percent of the men. With reference to God, 61 percent of the women consistently used other than masculine terms, in comparison with 39 percent of the men.

Homiletical tasks

Homiletics is the art of preaching as a subject of theological study. Etymologically speaking, the term *homiletics* translates from the Greek as the 'art of conversing' or 'a conversation with the crowd'.[6] Thus the expression 'homiletical tasks', as used here, connotes the particular functions and objectives the preacher undertakes in the course of carrying on a conversation with the crowd. The homiletical tasks represent what the sermon has been designed to accomplish, which is perhaps the single most critical dimension of preaching.

I have identified seventeen homiletical tasks that the preachers in the sample have undertaken in their sermons. They are: (1) affirming; (2) celebrating; (3) criticizing the church; (4) criticizing the society; (5) exegeting Scripture; (6) exhorting; (7) interpreting Scripture; (8) inviting the hearers to Christian commitment; (9) observing a liturgical event; (10) proclaiming an eschatological vision; (11) quoting lyrics of hymns; (12) quoting lyrics of Negro spirituals; (13) quoting poetry or drama; (14) story-telling; (15) teaching; (16) testifying; (17) translating Scripture into the vernacular. It is possible that this list omits some homiletical tasks that would be germane to other types of sermons and preaching traditions. However, my intention has been to account for the specific homiletical tasks undertaken in the sermons selected for the present analysis. Each of the seventeen homiletical tasks will be defined and illustrated with examples taken from the eighteen women's sermons. I will use my discussion of these homiletical tasks as an opportunity to provide a sampling of the power and beauty and diversity of black women's preaching.

Affirming

Affirming is the task of speaking in positive, encouraging terms to an individual or group, usually with reference to a declaration of belief or commitment in solidarity with others. This homiletical task can also be understood to mean affirmation of the promises of God as appropriated from Scripture and applied to personal experience. An example is found in 'Beyond Ourselves', a sermon preached by Barbara Campbell to the members of Pioneer Church, a small, struggling congregation:

> I think Pioneer Church has a proving ground right here in this community. You have already made a good start in extending yourselves beyond the boundaries of your church. You are already in the field, helping those in your community to help themselves no matter what faith they may be.
>   I say to you that progress is often slow and the race is not always won by the swift, but by the diligent. I marvel in your desire to minister to your community. I ask God to give you renewed vigor when you are tired, so that you will continue to go forward. I feel confident that you dedicated Christians will not let Pioneer Church die.[7]

Celebrating

Celebrating is the task of calling attention to the joy of worshiping and praising God. Mary Ann Bellinger incorporates celebration and praise into her sermon 'Upright but *Not* Uptight', which deals with the healing of the woman who suffered from a spirit of infirmity:

> I entitled my sermon 'Upright but *Not* Uptight' because all too often when we 'get religion', we figure that no one else has it like we do. We become so goody-goody that we can't praise God. And if by chance we do praise God, we want to make sure the right people are there so they can see how holy we are!
>   Look at this woman once again. When Jesus called her, she went forward and received healing. When she was healed, she didn't hold onto her joy selfishly but immediately began to minister to those around her in

the synagogue. Praise God! She sang! Praise God! She encouraged!
What did you do when God did something in your life?[8]

Criticizing the church

This is the task of pointing out the problems and shortcomings of a particular body of Christians, or of the church at large. Deborah McGill-Jackson offers such a critique in her sermon 'To Set at Liberty', based upon Luke's account of how Jesus read and interpreted the prophecy of Isaiah in the synagogue at Nazareth:

> We in the church cannot afford to reject the gospel that convicts us in our comfort. The church must loosen the shackles by which it is bound – the shackles of tradition, the irons of prejudice, the bars of isolation and suburban escapism – lest church people and their ecclesiastical palaces deteriorate in their own captivity, which is due to the sin of alienation.[9]

Criticizing the society

This is the task of pointing out the problems and shortcomings of the society, and especially the unjust social structures and systems. In her sermon 'Jesus Christ, the Same Yesterday, Today – Forever', Thelma Davidson Adair compares the problem of the oppression of women with the fight for civil rights and the abolition of slavery:

> Many women of the Third World spend their lives in the fields, suffer malnutrition and cruel treatment, and have no access to education. The concerns of women in the United States and in the Third World are massively different, but the underlying thrust is the same. It is the quest for fulfillment, the recognition of personhood, and a consistent wish for self-development. . . .
> Our church must constantly seek to support this thrust. The church must again, as it did during the fight for civil rights, actively seek the disorder, the drastic social change which some social scientists predict will come from restructuring our society. Some Americans feared the social chaos which they were certain would follow the disruption of a highly profitable societal and economic slave structure. But with Jesus as the stabilizer, the constant in the changing world, the institution of slavery was overthrown. Today we rejoice in that event. With regard to women's rights, not just in the Western world, but around the globe, we will rejoice to see women free at last.[10]

Exegeting Scripture

To exegete Scripture is to perform a critical analysis or examination of the text. Although exegesis normally connotes interpretation, in the present investigation interpretation is treated as a separate homiletical task in itself. Thus, for our purposes, the exegetical task is understood to be the analysis and examination of Scripture in an effort to present the text in its proper historical and literary context. Ellen Sandimanie offers a brief exegesis of I Corinthians 4:2, the text of her sermon 'On Being Faithful Stewards':

> Paul's letter to the church at Corinth was written for the purpose of correcting disorders that had arisen in the church and setting before the early Christians a standard of Christian conduct.
> The theme of this epistle is 'Christian Conduct' in relation to the church, the home, and the world. . . .
> Paul had completed his formal warnings against the parties in the church at Corinth. Now he turns to the responsibilities of those who are to teach. They are servants of Christ, not subject to the whims of anyone.[11]

Exhorting

To exhort is to admonish the hearers to act or to exhibit some virtue. The task of exhorting differs from the task of affirming. Exhortation challenges while affirmation congratulates, and it carries an implicit critique that is absent from the affirming statement. Katie Cannon concludes her sermon 'On Remembering Who We Are' by challenging the hearers to identify with the biblical character Hagar and to do what the sermon title suggests:

> If we know of a sister or a brother – wandering around lost unto herself or himself – who doesn't know which way to turn or where to go, who is bent on self-destruction and cut off from the joy of living because she or he has been cast out into the wilderness of life, then let us open ourselves to the Spirit of God so that we can help provide the spiritual water that that sister or brother needs to come back home. Let us open ourselves to the grace of God and share the many blessings that God has bestowed upon us. . . .
>
> In closing I challenge you to go forth remembering who you are. You are persons created in God's own image. You are sisters of Hagar. And, when in doubt, simply recall the word *WHO* – *W* for willingness, *H* for humility and *O* for openmindedness – and the God that we serve, the true and living God, has promised to hear your prayers. Amen.[12]

Interpreting Scripture

To interpret Scripture is to expound the significance of a particular text with an emphasis upon application. Occasionally a preacher will interpret or apply Scripture without providing an exegetical basis for analyzing or understanding it. Marjorie Leeper Booker interprets and applies her text, Philippians 2:5–9, as 'A Prescription For Humility', the title of her sermon:

> We have discussed the three ingredients that are required for true humility as set forth by Jesus Christ: the emptying of self, humility, and true obedience. Paul set forth these virtues, which Jesus had portrayed in his saving act. With this prescription one can acquire the mind of Christ.
>
> How will the mind of Christ benefit us? With the mind of Christ we will be able to live the life we talk about. We will be able to overcome the temptation to glorify and gratify ourselves. We will be able to hear the cries of the needy and the deprived and be sensitive to their needs. We will be able to deny ourselves and put the interest of others before our own. We will be able to pick up our crosses daily and follow Christ. We will be able to obey God and do God's will, saying, like Jesus, 'Not my will but thine be done.' With the mind of Christ, we will be able to rise up and speak out against injustice, wherever and whenever it may be found. With the mind of Christ we will be able to look at all God's children as sisters and brothers in Christ. We will be able to play together, grow together, live together, love together, and serve God together.[13]

Inviting hearers to Christian commitment

The invitation to Christian commitment is an appeal to the hearers to accept Jesus Christ as Savior and Lord. Typically it is presented at the conclusion of the sermon and designed to lead into an altar call. The task of invitation differs from exhortation in its sense of urgency; it is an exhortation to immediate response and action. Peggy Scott offers an invitation at the close of a sermon that is directed specifically to foster children and parents. This invitation calls the hearers to inner healing as a prerequisite to effective Christian commitment. Five steps to inner healing are outlined in her sermon, 'God Has a Master Plan for Your Life':

> God has a master plan for our lives. If we, children or adults, are to become effective Christians, we must receive an inner healing for all our hurts, pains, resentments, feelings of rejection, and other negative emotions. God wants to heal us; God cares about us. We can be healed today and begin to realize that God has a plan for us. But how can we be healed?

There are five steps in receiving inner healing. (1) *Believe and confess* –'If thou shalt confess with thy mouth the Lord Jesus, and shalt believe in thine heart that God has raised him from the dead, thou shalt be saved' (Romans 10:9). (2) *Acknowledge that you are a new creature* – 'Therefore, if any man be in Christ, he is a new creature: old things are passed away; behold, all things are become new' (2 Corinthians 5:17). (3) *Acknowledge that your name is in heaven* – '. . . but rather rejoice, because your names are written in heaven' (Luke 10:20). (4) *Acknowledge God as your true mother and father* – 'When my father and mother forsake me, then the LORD will take me up (as his own)' (Psalm 27:10). (5) Forgive – '. . . forgive, and ye shall be forgiven. . . . Love ye your enemies, and do good, and lend, hoping for nothing again; and your reward shall be great, and ye shall be the children of the Highest' (Luke 6:37, 35).

Accept your family's circumstances; do not let them interfere with your relationship to God and with your spiritual growth. It is not so much what has happened to you as how you react to what has happened that matters.

If your situation is too painful, too much of a burden, too heavy a load to carry, then ask for forgiveness, and yield to Jesus. Allow the love of Jesus and the indwelling of the Holy Spirit to heal you today. 'King Jesus will roll all burdens away'.[14]

Observing a liturgical event

This task involves citing the significance of a special liturgical event, such as the Lord's Supper or Pentecost Sunday. The sermon theme and texts are directly related to the occasion. Nan Brown's sermon, 'The Mind of the Insecure', highlights the significance of Advent:

When Herod sent the wise men to Bethlehem to search diligently for the Christ child, he had no thought of worshiping him. Herod was intent on murdering him. I trust that in the Advent season we all remember whose birthday we are celebrating and give gifts to him who deserves them, worshipping him who gave us life.[15]

Proclaiming an eschatological vision

An eschatological vision is one that looks to the ultimate or last things. As a homiletical task, to proclaim an eschatological vision is to announce what the future holds in an ultimate sense, usually with reference to heaven or to some notion of the reign of God. The eschatological vision proclaimed by Effie Clark in her sermon, 'How a People Make History', is a vision of black nationalism. She quotes the militant imagery of Margaret Walker's poem, 'For My People', to illustrate this vision:

Let a new earth rise. Let another world be born. Let a bloody peace be written in the sky. Let a second generation full of courage issue forth, let a people loving freedom come to growth. Let a beauty full of healing and a strength of final clenching be the pulsing in our spirits and our blood. Let the martial songs be written, let the dirges disappear. Let a race of men now rise and take control.[16]

Quoting lyrics of hymns

Preachers sometimes quote the lyrics of hymns in order to create a certain effect or to convey a particular mood in keeping with the sermon's message. Usually the hymn is familiar to the hearers, as is sometimes the hymn-writer. These lyrics may function as authoritative sources or summaries of sermon content. Clara Mills-Morton quotes a hymn to dramatize an important point in her sermon 'The Blessings and Burdens of the Divinely Chosen':

The preacher preaches, and souls are saved. The teacher teaches, and learning and growth take place. The philanthropist gives resources, and vital improvements are made possible. The physician administers the proper care and treatment, and healing occurs. Yet they all realize that their resources are given by God and that the results are made possible because of the blessings of God. Beatrice Brown expressed this with tremendous clarity when she wrote, 'Without God, I can do nothing; without God I would fail; without God my life would be rugged, like a ship without a sail.'[17]

Quoting lyrics of Negro Spirituals

The lyrics of the so-called 'Negro Spirituals' are sometimes quoted to illustrate and reinforce sermon themes. These songs serve as a repository of the sacred history and tradition of Christians who suffered as slaves in the United States. In a sermon entitled 'Singing the Lord's Song', Yvonne Delk quotes spirituals to illustrate her central theme and text (Psalm 137) with reference to the black experience of slavery and injustice:

> Black people know about singing God's song in a strange and foreign land because Black Americans' spirituality was born in the context of the struggle for justice. We sang our songs on boats called *Jesus* that brought us to America. We sang our songs on auction blocks – 'Over my head I hear music in the air; there must be a God somewhere', We sang our songs on plantations – 'Walk together children, don't you get weary; there is a camp meeting in the promised land.'[18]

Quoting poetry or drama

Some sermons make use of quotations from the works of great poets and playwrights that capture the essence of the thought being communicated. Carolyn Ann Knight begins her sermon 'The Survival of the Unfit' by expounding upon a familiar quotation from the play *Hamlet* by William Shakespeare:

> 'To be or not to be, that is the question'. What was an existential question for Shakespeare's Hamlet as he stood at the crossroads of his life is, for us today, an ontological question as well. Hamlet's plight of survival is a universal one. In a society that is disgruntled by the contrary winds of desolation and degradation, in a world that is scorched by the burning suns of trials and pestilence, in a civilization that is bombarded by the falling rocks of mutilated humanity, we too must grapple with the question 'to be or not to be'. With each new day that dawns, we stand on the brink of nonexistence.[19]

Story-telling

The story-telling task has rich biblical antecedents, most notably in the gospels where Jesus tells stories in the course of preaching and teaching. In many sermons, and especially in the sermons that follow the narrative form, stories from the Bible or from human experience are told to make the sermon's message 'come alive'. Laura Sinclair offers an exciting rendition of the familiar story of Ezekiel in the valley of dry bones in her sermon 'Can Your Bones Live?':

> Ezekiel was in a valley that had nothing but dry bones all around. An arm here, a leg there, just dry bones everywhere. God looked at these bones and asked Ezekiel, 'Can these bones live?' Now I'm sure that Ezekiel wanted to say no, for he knew how these bones became dry. He knew that their dryness was an indictment on Israel for specific sins that the nation had committed. These sins included cultic abuse, such as profaning of the sabbath, and ethical crimes, such as bloodshed, adultery, extortion, dishonor of parents, and the violation of the rights of orphans, widows, and sojourners. But Ezekiel also knew that the God he served was merciful and compassionate and that anything was possible with God. So he said, 'O Lord, thou

knowest.' And sure enough, the mercy and compassion of God came forth. God told Ezekiel to preach to the bones, to tell them to hear the word of the Lord, and he, God, would cause them to live.

Ezekiel was obedient to God, and he preached to the bones. He saw something happen that I am sure astounded him. Many times the Lord will give his servant a directive, and the servant will look at it and say, 'I'll do it, but I know that it will only be an exercise because I know that nothing will happen.'

Well, to Ezekiel's surprise, as he preached, he heard noise and saw the bones shaking; he saw them coming together. He saw toe bones connected to foot bones, foot bones connected to ankle bones, ankle bones connected to leg bones, leg bones connected to knee bones, knee bones connected to thigh bones, thigh bones connected to hip bones, hip bones connected to back bones, back bones connected to chest bones, chest bones connected to shoulder bones, shoulder bones connected to arm bones, arm bones connected to hand bones, back bones connected to neck bones, neck bones connected to head bones. All the bones were connected. He saw sinews come upon them, and he saw skin cover them. But they were not breathing; they still were not living.

I'm sure Ezekiel must have looked up to God in puzzlement. But God didn't keep him puzzled for long. God told Ezekiel to preach to the wind, and he did. Ezekiel told the four winds to breathe upon the bones so that they might live. And as he preached, the breath came into those dry bones that had come together and been covered with sinew, and men stood upon their feet as a great army.[20]

Teaching

As a homiletical task, to teach is to set forth a structured presentation of information within the sermon. Typically, three points of information are offered, but the actual number of points is less important than the quantity and quality of content being conveyed. In her sermon 'Our Spiritual Account', Margrie Lewter-Simmons presents her teaching on the subject of spiritual self-examination in four points, as summarized here:

(1) Let's look at some methods of bookkeeping that might help with the audit of our lives. Look over your records. Turn your pages in the ledger of life back to a year ago. Have you hurt anybody? . . .
(2) Still another category in good bookkeeping is found in Matthew 5, where Jesus speaks of a selected audit. Blessed are the meek. Have you been meek or have you been running off at the mouth, bragging and offending people? Blessed are the peacemakers. Did you keep the peace or disturb the peace? Blessed are you when you shall be 'buked and scorned', reviled and persecuted, talked about and yet unwilling to fight back. These things happened for the Lord's sake. Blessed. Blessed – your books are in good shape.
(3) One other means of *adjusting* your spiritual account can be found in Paul's letter to the Galatians, chapter 5. There he talks about a special kind of bookkeeping called the 'fruit system'. If you go through the books and see what has been produced, then you get your account settled and straight with a good running balance. . . .
(4) One final concept is your *balance*, the previous balance. Peter said that if you come to the end of the record year and you have less than the previous year, you're in big trouble. 'But grow in grace and in the knowledge of our Lord and Saviour Jesus Christ' (2 Peter 3:18). So, however good your balance sheet looks, if you haven't grown in grace, if you haven't grown in the joy of the Spirit, if you haven't grown in your capacity to forgive, if your faith cannot be measured as being deeper and more abiding than before, then you're in serious trouble. You're in deficit.[21]

Testifying

The task of testifying offers a personal word of witness to the self-disclosure of God, usually with reference to conversion. Here testifying is distinguished from story-telling in that it is based strictly upon personal experience. Sharon Williams incorporates personal testimony into the dramatic climax of her sermon 'Studying War Some More', which is based on Paul's description of the weapons of spiritual warfare in Ephesians chapter 6:

You see, Jesus puts out this fantastic helmet. It took him three whole days to make it up just for me. He began forging the metal one Friday in the scorching noonday sun. And he didn't finish it until Sunday morning in the cool darkness of a rich man's tomb. When the stone was rolled away, out came Jesus, carrying my helmet of salvation. . . .

And while Jesus was working on my helmet, he fashioned a sword, which he called the Holy Ghost. He didn't issue it with the helmet. That sword came special delivery to a crowded upper room some fifty days later. The sword came just as he had promised. I can't go to war without my sword.

And I can't go to war without the Word. I've got my Bible, and I've got my helmet. I've got some faith, and my new shoes feel good on my feet. My breastplate is strapped on and my loins are girded round about.

I'm waging war by forgiving all enemies.

I'm waging war by practicing gentleness.

I'm waging war by giving up jealousy and backbiting.

I'm waging war by walking in a meek and lowly way.

I'm waging war by telling the truth, even when I am threatened by violent liars.

I'm waging war by bringing peace.

I'm waging war by feeding the hungry.

I'm waging war by supplying the poor with what they need.

I'm waging war by healing the sick,

I'm waging war by having patience and reconciliation.

I'm waging war by having a contrite and broken spirit.

I'm waging war by a will surrendered to God.

I'm waging war.[22]

Beverly Shamana offers a more pensive testimony in her sermon, 'Letting Go', as she reflects upon the disappointment of failing to receive what she felt God had promised:

Like many of you, I've gone through surgery. What an ordeal! Yet even after the bright prognosis and a clean bill of health, I felt a great sense of 'But you promised': My body should have worked. My arm, my liver, my kidney, my uterus – it should have worked, according to the medical journals and books. And if not, why couldn't I go to a doctor and get it fixed? To remove it was so final. Now it will never work because it's gone. Anger. Guilt. Blame. Sadness. And, finally, goodbye. What a long journey it was from a tight-fisted grudge match to an open hand! What an arduous journey it was from the former things to the new thing!

God indeed created something new. I've developed greater appreciation for these bones, this skin, this muscle, this chamber that I now have. I've found that I can even soar to new heights. For one thing, my body is lighter! I have surrendered the excess baggage of weight.[23]

Translating Scripture into the vernacular

In general, the term *vernacular* refers to the standard language of a particular locality. The task of translating Scripture into the vernacular means making use of idiom, jargon, and/or slang, to convey the meaning of biblical texts and ideas in terms that would be familiar to a particular audience. An example of this task is found in a sermon by Suzan Johnson entitled 'God's Woman', based upon the story of Esther:

Now, in our story the Persian king was looking for a new wife to replace Queen Vashti, whom he had cut loose because she refused to dance nude in front of him and his friends. So he sent a search team to look throughout all the land for a new queen. I imagine that as all the women gathered, the scene was something like the Miss America pageant that we see today – the most 'beautiful' women on parade. And of all the women that the king saw, the one he chose as his new wife was Esther, this Jew who was living in Persia.[24]

Results

I have evaluated the entire sample of thirty-six sermons preached by women and men with regard to the seventeen homiletical tasks, although all the examples cited here were drawn from the women's sermons. The task analysis highlights some interesting distinctions between women's and men's preaching. The typical woman's sermon involved an average of seven homiletical tasks, listed here in order of frequency of occurrence: (1) interpreting Scripture, which was done in 100 percent of the women's sermons; (2) exhorting, 78 percent; (3) exegeting, 72 percent; (4) teaching, 67 percent; (5) affirming, 56 percent; (6) story-telling, 50 percent; and (7) testimony, 44 percent. The typical man's sermon encompassed an average of six homiletical tasks: (1) interpreting Scripture, 89 percent; (2) teaching, 78 percent; (3) criticizing the society, 61 percent; (4) exhorting, 56 percent; (5) affirming, 44 percent; and (6) exegeting, 39 percent. Judging by frequency of occurrence alone, it is clear that the single most important homiletical task in the preaching of both women and men is the interpretation of Scripture. Other tasks that are important to both groups, listed in descending order of frequency, include teaching, exhorting, exegeting, and affirming. Thus, based upon a comparison of women's and men's sermons in terms of those homiletical tasks deemed most important by both groups, we can conclude that, in general, women and men seek to accomplish the same things in their preaching.

However, it would be appropriate at this juncture to ask whether these results signify even a slight distinctiveness in women's preaching. When the typical woman's sermon, comprising seven homiletical tasks, and the typical man's sermon, comprising six such tasks, are compared, several subtle distinctions emerge. First, the difference in the average number of tasks can be seen as an indication that the women sought to accomplish a greater variety of tasks than the men did in their preaching. Next, it appears that story-telling and testifying were generally more important to the women preachers than to the men, while criticizing the society seemed more important to the men than to the women. This is not to suggest that women's preaching is all story-telling and testimony while men's preaching is all social criticism. The point is that more men (61 percent) criticized the society than women (39 percent), and more women (50 percent) told stories as a key component of their sermons than men (33 percent). Testifying was the one homiletical task which showed the greatest discrepancy between men and women; only one man out of eighteen offered personal testimony in his sermon, yet eight out of eighteen women did so in theirs.

This last finding suggests that it might be useful to compare women's and men's preaching based upon those homiletical tasks that occurred with the least degree of frequency. There were four homiletical tasks that appeared less than 20 percent of the time in the women's sermons: only 11 percent of the women criticized the church, while 17 percent engaged in the tasks of celebrating, quoting poetry or drama, or observing a liturgical event. A somewhat different set of four homiletical tasks was of least importance in the men's sermons: only 5 percent of the men included testifying, inviting the hearers to Christian commitment, or observing a liturgical event in their preaching, and 11 percent gave attention to celebrating. Thus there seems to have been a consensus among both women and men preachers not to lend great importance either to celebration or to liturgical concerns. However, it is interesting to note how the women and men differed with regard to the other least popular homiletical tasks: the women were reluctant to criticize the church and to quote poetry or drama, while the men shunned the tasks of testifying and inviting hearers to Christian commitment.

Final conclusions

By way of summary, we have observed that women and men preach the same types of sermons, from the biblical texts, but differ slightly in their choices of themes and tasks, and differ greatly in their talk about God and persons in inclusive terms. Perhaps we can say that women and men preach the same Word but with distinctive *accents* – women tend to emphasize the personal and men the prophetic. If this assessment is accurate, it reflects that ubiquitous false dichotomy between the spiritual and the social that has plagued the Christian church for centuries. Yet, it may be that this small discrepancy between women's and men's preaching holds the key to a possible resolution of this dichotomy in our own age of rapid social and cultural change. Women's preaching calls for men to incorporate into their homiletical, theological, and christological themes such basic and practical issues as survival, healing, and the hardships of ministry. Women's use of inclusive language challenges men to demonstrate genuine appreciation of the presence and participation of women by adjusting their talk to address he and she, God the Father and God the Mother, instead of just talking to and about 'man' all the time. Women's sermons can teach men to temper social criticism with compassion. At the same time, women can learn from men how to sharpen their own testimonies and calls for Christian commitment with the cutting edge of prophetic indignation.

What shall we say then? Does God indeed speak with a feminine voice? If so, how does the feminine voice of God differ from the masculine voice of God? My conclusion is that God speaks with a feminine voice and with a masculine voice. God speaks to women and to men in their particularity, and in their commonality as well. After all, preaching is the telling, interpretation, and application of God's story. It is more than proclamation alone – it is 'a conversation with the crowd' that is consummated when that crowd hears and bears witness to that proclamation. And as long as that crowd includes both women and men, there will be a need for God's story to be proclaimed in ways that embrace the experience of both genders.

Some serious theological implications emerge from our comparative analysis of women's and men's preaching. In an article entitled 'Preaching in the Black Tradition', the Reverend Leontine Kelly offers an insightful description of some key assumptions concerning the nature of God that are borne out by black women's preaching:

> The black woman preacher does battle sexism, but she draws upon the spiritual confidence traditional in her culture. She is theologically and experientially grounded in a God who is Creator and Sustainer of the universe, actively holding the 'whole world in his/her hands'. She draws her understanding of a father/mother God from the traditional expression of the spiritual of her people, 'He's my father, he's my mother, my sister and my brother, he's everything to me.'[25]

If we confess that God is creator and sustainer of the universe, and Father and Mother of us all, then we must also accept the masculine and feminine voices and the masculine and feminine vessels that God has ordained to equip the church to perform a truly inclusive and wholistic ministry in the world.

As I close, I am reminded of the Old Testament prophet Elijah, who, having run for his life from a woman named Jezebel, sought desperately to hear a Word from the Lord. And the Bible says:

> behold, the Lord passed by, and a great and strong wind rent the mountains, and brake in pieces the rocks before the Lord; but the Lord was not in the wind: and after the wind an earthquake; but the Lord was not in the earthquake: And after the earthquake a fire; but the Lord was not in the fire: and after the fire a still small voice (I Kings 19:11–12).

Sometimes the voice of God thunders, and at other times God whispers. If the Creator of the wind and the earthquake and the fire can choose to speak in a 'still small voice', then that same God can surely give utterance in the voices of women as often as in the voices of men. For God calls daughters and God calls sons, some with the accent of testimony and others with the accent of critique, to be heralds of the same living Word of truth.

Notes

1   'Baptist Group Names Black Woman Pastor', *USA Today*, March 5, 1984, p. 2A.

2   Betty J. Overton, 'Black Women Preachers: A Literary View', *The Southern Quarterly* 23, 3, 1985, p. 165.

3   James Earl Massey, *Designing the Sermon*, Nashville, TN, Abingdon, 1980, p. 21.

4   Ibid., p. 23.

5   Ibid., pp. 35–7.

6   See definition of 'homiletics' in *The American Heritage Dictionary*, New York, American Heritage Publishing Co., 1975.

7   Barbara Campbell, 'Beyond Ourselves', in Robert T. Newbold, Jr (ed.), *Black Preaching*, Philadelphia, Geneva Press, 1977, p. 51.

8   Mary Ann Bellinger, 'Upright but *Not* Uptight', in Ella Pearson Mitchell (ed.), *Those Preachin' Women*, Valley Forge, Judson, 1985, p. 75.

9   Deborah McGill-Jackson, 'To Set at Liberty', in Mitchell, 1985, p. 39.

10   Thelma Davidson Adair, 'Jesus Christ, the Same Yesterday, Today – Forever', in Newbold, 1977, pp. 16–17.

11   Ellen Sandimanie, 'On Being Faithful Stewards', in Newbold, 1977, p. 36.

12   Katie G. Cannon, 'On Remembering Who We Are', in Mitchell, 1985, p. 50.

13   Marjorie Leeper Booker, 'A Prescription for Humility', in Mitchell, 1985, pp. 90–91.

14   Peggy R. Scott, 'God Has A Master Plan for Your Life', in Mitchell, 1985, pp. 110–11.

15   Nan M. Brown, 'The Mind of the Insecure', in Mitchell, 1985, p. 66.

16   Effie M. Clark, 'How a People Make History', in J. Alfred Smith (ed.), *Outstanding Black Sermons*, Valley Forge, Judson, 1976, pp. 31–2.

17   Clara Mills-Morton, 'The Blessings and Burdens of the Divinely Chosen', in Mitchell, 1985, p. 97.

18   Yvonne V. Delk., 'Singing the Lord's Song', in Mitchell, 1985, p. 58.

19   Carolyn Ann Knight, 'The Survival of the Unfit', in Mitchell, 1985, pp. 27–28.

20   Laura Sinclair, 'Can Your Bones Live?' in Mitchell, 1985, pp. 21–2.

21   Margrie Lewter-Simmons, 'Our Spiritual Account', in Mitchell, 1985, pp. 115–17.

22   Sharon E. Williams, 'Studying War Some More', in Mitchell, 1985, pp. 82–3.

23   Beverly J. Shamana, ' Letting Go', in Mitchell, 1985, p. 105.

24   Suzan D. Johnson, 'God's Woman', in Mitchell, 1985, p. 121.

25   Leontine T. C. Kelly, 'Preaching in the Black Tradition', in Judith L. Weidman (ed.), *Women Ministers*, San Francisco, Harper & Row, 1981, p. 72.

25   Gender and the Aesthetic of Preaching

Virginia Purvis-Smith

When a clergywoman preaches from a pulpit, she enters a space which has particular aesthetic value, for this space has been occupied and its character defined by male presence for centuries. She faces the double challenge of establishing her personal style and of confronting any number of aesthetic expectations which are associated with the pulpit. These expectations do not necessarily complement characteristics which are associated with her gender, characteristics such as voice, gesture, appearance, and demeanor. These characteristics also include matters of rhetorical strategy, such as word choice, subject matter, and organization of material.

My research with women who preach discloses that even though we are authorized by virtue of ordination to speak, the aesthetic of preaching – in particular, aspects of architecture, the rhetorical form of the sermon, and liturgy – is often at odds with our purposes. This disjunction between aesthetic and purpose has been particularly apparent in the experience of an Episcopal priest whom I call Sue. Moreover, as Sue has confronted the challenges posed by the disjunction, she has transformed the aesthetic of preaching.[1]

My interview with Sue two years ago had begun with as simple and open-ended a statement as I could devise: 'Tell me about your experiences as a woman who preaches.' She responded by tracing them for the prior fourteen years, that is, since her days in her seminary field placement position. Sue described her early days in these terms:

> I guess I had some ideal in my head that had something to do with the men I'd heard preaching. I remember vividly my rector [in the field placement position] saying, 'Sue, this is the way you need to go about preaching.' He swaggered as he stood up in the pulpit and started to talk. He was a great big, big man of sixty-five and I was a little woman, I'm only 5' 2", of thirty-five. They used to put Coca-Cola cases in the pulpit for me to stand on so I could be seen. I have enough sense of myself now that I wouldn't need the extra elevation, but the pulpit was very large and I felt dwarfed by it then.

When Sue described the swaggering man in the large pulpit, I visualized him elevated and remote from the congregation, an image reminiscent of Herman Melville's pulpit in *Moby Dick*. It shares a design basic to that of many twentieth-century pulpits; its distinction lies only in the exaggerated aspects of its architecture. His preacher attains its 'lofty height', not by stairs, but by a rope ladder. Once the height is gained, he pulls the ladder in after him, 'leaving him impregnable in his little Quebec'. The pulpit design is that of a ship's bow:

> What could be more full of meaning? – for the pulpit is ever this earth's foremost part; all the rest comes in its rear; the pulpit leads the world . . . Yes, the world's a ship on its passage out, and not a voyage complete; and the pulpit is its prow (chapter 8).

This architectural design symbolizes the pulpit's meaning – protruding and intrusive as it slices through the waters and leads the rest of the ship.

Sue's description of the large, remote pulpit, occupied as it was by the swaggering rector, communicates a similar meaning, but it also implies a particular configuration of the universe. This structure is well-developed in another literary source, Dante's *Divine Comedy*. Dante's universe revolves around a vertical axis, with the circles of hell at the bottom and those of purgatory and paradise above, in ascending order. In order to reach paradise, Dante must traverse this hierarchical arrangement. He has several guides for his journey through the universe: the poet Virgil and, as he travels through the circles of paradise in order to reach the Center, the virtuous and beautiful Beatrice. Virgil cannot enter paradise with Dante because he is, of course, not a Christian.

The inhabitants of Dante's universe are consigned to prescribed spaces. Similarly, each participant in Sue's field placement sanctuary was consigned to her or his prescribed space and role. The congregation was 'down' in the sanctuary, close to the mundane, material world and positioned as a group of listeners passively waiting to receive God's word, the preacher was lifted up, closer to paradise, serving as the conduit to and from the holy. These literary images are not necessarily in the minds of people in worship, but Dante and Melville's characterizations reflect six hundred years of Western Christian culture, and the pulpit Sue describes architecturally reinforces that mindset and interpretation of the preacher's task.

These representations are not only evident in church architecture; they are reinforced by liturgical phrases such as, 'Let us go to God in prayer.' This language seemingly exhorts those in worship to leave their present location and go ... where? I have to suppress a giggle when I hear this phrase, because I imagine a congregation will someday be listening to the words and will get up and leave. Perhaps the words direct those in worship to scale the heights to something resembling Dante's paradise, where God, in 'His resplendence', declares, '*I am*' ('Paradise', canto XXIX). This liturgical language complements the architecture which consigns people to particular spaces. Although the congregation is not clear about what space God occupies, they are led to believe it is somewhere they are not. Sue felt physically inadequate to bear the responsibility of occupying such a pulpit without the additional elevation, that is, authority, of a Coca-Cola case. And apparently Sue's rector was as uncomfortable as she was with her demeanor in that pulpit. She describes him as being 'embarrassed' to the point of urging she visit a speech teacher regularly. Sue remembers his discomfort was shared by a member of the parish:

A man came up to the rector after one service when I preached what I thought was an adequate sermon. 'These women are so dramatic. They shouldn't be gesturing like that from the pulpit.' That made him uncomfortable because usually the men would put their hands on the pulpit and 'tell us the way it was'. I think my style was a departure. You know what that's like, that kind of looking to see if you are good as measured by certain standards and not realizing that it's possible to be good by being oneself. That's really what we've been up against for a long time: the need to be competent and the need to be able to do what they do in order to prove ourselves in their world.

The design of the pulpit and its implied expectations communicated to Sue that it belonged to 'their world', and whatever that meant at the time to Sue and that congregation, it was clearly not a space she comfortably inhabited from either her perspective or theirs. The pulpit's influence even colored the way Sue thought of her sermons in that it externally buttressed the authority of the words she expounded from it. She consistently talked about each aspect of her preaching in terms of their 'inner' and 'outer', or external, aspects. For example, when she started preaching, she located the value of her sermons outside of herself, in the manuscript, as though it, too, was a form into which she must fit. She describes how that perspective began to change when she went to the speech teacher:

At one point the teacher said, 'Get up. I want you to preach your sermon from last Sunday.' Then she took my notes away from me. I said, 'I can't do that.' She said, 'Go ahead and talk to me.' That started me realizing that I could get up and talk to people about what I was wanting to communicate. The value wasn't in the manuscript. There was something coming out of me that was of value as well.

As she talked about her more recent process of sermon preparation, she said she simply no longer molded herself to fit 'their world'. She emphasized that she took a long while to step outside that mold, but she had reached the point of feeling secure enough to assert, 'It's my world, too!' The shift from a manuscript that is read to 'something coming out of me that was of value as well' had continued so that the locus of the agency had clearly changed. She had clearly begun to rely on a sense of her 'inner value' rather than on 'their' external markers of authority and competence.

For Sue, sermon preparation is a learning process, and when she wants to learn something, she begins with her 'inner life'. She determines what she needs to learn and 'goes out' to seek it.

I start with 'Who am I' and 'Where am I' and 'What do I know about this?' Then I go out and find answers to my questions. That's what information is out there for. My inner life is very real to me.

As she talked about her strategy, she reflected that, from her observations, this is a 'female' approach. 'I think we females are much more inclined to start with our own experience'. She contrasted this with the learning and sermon preparation approach she has experienced with the faculty at the diocesan school:

I notice in Bible study, the men always want to start by doing exegesis, or what they think is exegesis. Very seldom do we get down to 'How does this relate to you?' I think that kind of process is a very male process. That is, there's all that reality out there and now I'm going to try to see where I fit into it. I listen to the men struggle over exegesis, trying to figure out things that we will never know – the exact context and intentions of the author. It's a kind of literalism that is not appropriate to the situation. I think a lot of what we're trying to do with our learning is to remember that it is ancient, that it came out of a different context, but we've lost the possibility to communicate in the present if we do too much of that. I think the way of teaching in seminary is masculine: Let's try to find out what this is really all about and then we'll preach the truth.

Sue's characterizations of her early experiences construct the image of a swaggering man, high and lifted up in a pulpit which leads the assault on the world, who attempts to capture an objective truth by this approach to exegesis. This man gives the impression that he has found the truth and that he can confidently rest his hands on the pulpit and declare, 'This is the way it is.'

As Sue talked about her struggle to redefine preaching for herself, she continued to do so in terms of gendered contrasts between 'male' and 'female' approaches.

By retelling her story, I do not mean to imply that I am trying to identify a 'woman's way' of preaching. I do mean to highlight how some women experience the milieu of the pulpit as uncongenial because it has been a masculine-defined space for so long. In order to feel at home there, women have to imprint not only their personal style, but also their gender.

Sue's gendered contrasts paralleled her application of the categories of 'inner' and 'outer' to the various aspects of preaching. She goes 'out' to seek information, and brings 'back' what she learns. She talked about this process as one in which she needs to keep the material 'close' and 'fresh'.

Preaching is really a strange kind of process. Somehow I'm not always sure how I get the sermon. I read the propers [lectionary] early in the week and then pay attention. I listen very carefully to what's going on around me and rely on something coming up that will help to make this scripture and faith make sense to people. I probably won't write down anything until Saturday night and will revise it Sunday morning. That makes it very fresh for me. My sermon is something out there and I try to get it inside. It's coming from out of me. It has to be very close to me. The thing is in process for me always. It's sort of like having a baby.

When I asked Sue to clarify the comparison she was making between sermon formation and pregnancy, she said she was comparing the two processes of delivery – not being sure you're 'there' yet. I still didn't quite understand, so I asked her if she meant that the process itself takes over.

Yes. I've always felt it was somewhat mysterious, and, while I think I do a pretty good job at preaching, I feel somewhat modest about that because I really do feel it's the Holy Spirit which helps me to make the connections.

Sue appealed again to the metaphor of giving birth when she described a sermon which she preached about her sense of vocation. She had told the congregation:

A vocation comes on one. It's there. It's a feminine experience of a being inside you and you can't get rid of it. You're going to have to give birth to it even though you may have all kinds of feelings about it: bad feelings, mixed feelings, or happy feelings, or frightened feelings.

When I asked how she would assess her strengths as a woman who preaches, her response integrated the gender and 'inner/outer' categories. She commented that 'Preaching is now more who I am than what I do'. She explained:

For a long time I tried to figure out how to be like that field placement rector in the pulpit, how to be like the man. Finally, I realized that part of my gift was my femininity, however that gets used. It's very important to realize that who we are physically enables us to do some things quite easily.

I think the person of the preacher is part of the message. I'm relaxed, I have fun with it, and I love it. But the value is not in my performance, although I get a big kick out of performing well. It's not as task-oriented as that, and I think that's another difference between male and female. It's much more relational. I may not have the most finely crafted sermons all the time, but if I've touched somebody's life and helped them in some way, that's the measure of my sermon.

Sue had gradually transformed her approach to preaching and her concept of herself as a preacher since those field placement sermons, and the setting in which she preached (the architecture) had changed as well. At the time of our first interview, she was serving as the vicar of a very small, suburban congregation in addition to her full-time administrative and teaching responsibilities in the diocese. The membership of the congregation was declining, and Sue had been appointed to assist it as it made difficult decisions about its future.

The interior of the sanctuary was designed with the focus on the altar. It occupied the center with a wide aisle all the way around it, which was, in turn, encircled by concentric rows of pews. The pulpit stood off to one side, by the edge of the sanctuary closest to the organ. The choir (of three to five members) sat to the other side of the organ, in the concentric pews which were broken only for the space occupied by the organ, pulpit, and several aisles leading away from the altar like the spokes of a wheel. Therefore, the choir and the acolytes sat as members of the congregation, as did Sue. Congregation and worship leadership sat in the pews, on the same plane.

Each time I worshipped in this sanctuary, Sue stepped out from behind the pulpit when she preached and moved, with animation and energy, to different points in the aisle around the altar. During the sermon she would, from time to time, address questions to the congregation in expectation of response, and the members did respond. In Sue's congregation, those at worship did not sit passively! Sue's evolving approach and her preaching space were complementary.

So I have an artistic sense about the sermon. I try not to give answers. All the time I think, 'How can I help this be an experience for the listener?' There's something besides just telling that person everything I know. How can I set up the sermon in such a way that it opens up the horizons for somebody else?

The circular sanctuary and Sue's words, which describe preaching as a process of opening horizons, contrast with the preacher who searches for 'truth' in a text and mediates that truth from his impregnable 'little Quebec'. Melville's austere imagery and mood are foreign to Sue's description of preaching, as is his characterization of the person of the preacher. His representation visually gathers nineteenth-century American cultural norms which provide a model for twentieth-century, mainline Protestant pulpits. From Melville's pulpit, 'the storm of God's quick wrath is first descried . . . and the God of breezes fair or foul is first invoked for favourable winds'. His characterization of the task of preaching is also much different from the one Sue offers:

> Preaching is inviting the congregation to play with the text, inviting them to be in relationship, inviting them to be in relationship with me, the text, and one another. We're all at this party of eucharist and sermon, and we're all doing this together. I don't just preach from the pulpit. I preach from everywhere. In a circular setting all of it's the same. You can preach anywhere.

The architecture of the sanctuary and her transformation of the rhetorical form of the sermon are complementary; however, since the aesthetic of preaching involves rhetoric, architecture and liturgy, liturgy also needs to be reconceived. For example, the liturgical phrase, 'Let us go to God in prayer', is incongruous in a space where the congregation's vital presence has shaped the sermon's formation and its delivery, where the 'pulpit', the authoritative location for speaking, is diffused throughout the circle.

This diffused image of authority calls for a reconfiguration of Dante's universe. This new structure is developed in a novel, *Across the Acheron*, by the French feminist writer Monique Wittig, which repatterns every aspect of Dante's *Divine Comedy*. Hell, purgatory and paradise are not vertically arranged. Wittig levels Dante's topos, just as Sue's sanctuary leveled the multi-tiered architecture of that field placement church. Whereas Dante differentiates places and freezes time along the vertical axis of eternity, Wittig's places seem to be simultaneous matrices which take shape as her perspective alters. Her place and her time are 'here' and 'now'.

More specifically, Wittig's route to hell is a desert, and it is flat. In fact, the desert is on the same plane as hell, purgatory, and paradise. Each simply appears to occupy a different dimension on the plane of the earth's surface. The only 'lower' dimension seems to be that of the abyss of forgetfulness, into which the river Acheron empties. That would be a void, without words, without relationship.

The victims and their victimizers are together in Wittig's hell. The situations of the victims are desperate and escape is nearly impossible, but hell is not so rigid that escape is out of the question. In fact, she and Manastabal, her guide, will assist any of the damned souls in their release if they think the rescue has a chance. Wittig and her guide have moral responsibility to work for the rescue of these souls. And Wittig's providence is distinguished by engagement with the mundane and material, a providence identified by her deeds of kindness, not by her remoteness and inaccessibility, as is Dante's resplendent '*I am.*'

A liturgical phrase which more adequately represents Wittig's universe and Sue's circular preaching space is not the injunction to 'go' to God; it is a descriptive phrase: 'We gather to acknowledge God in our midst.' Rather than having to leave our present location and scale the heights to paradise, we have only to call attention to the divine matrix which comes into being through the words and spirit among us. A circle acknowledges that people occupy the same plane. At any given time, some may feel closer to heaven, others to hell, and the same person may feel tossed between the two in any single worship experience. Moreover, the face-to-face setting of a circle gives opportunity for engaging one another in relationship.

Since our first interview, the church building has been sold, but the members have covenanted to become a community of ministry. This means meeting for worship, for mission, for study, and for discernment of what shape their individual and corporate ministries will take. The community meets in a variety of locations throughout its sprawling urban area: in members' homes, shelters for the homeless, soup kitchens. Different members have responsibility for leading the discussion prior to the celebration of eucharist, and, so far, no one has yet raised the question of who should 'preach'.

Sue says she asks herself what she should do about preaching. 'When should I take the leadership for speaking? But right now, we're feeling our way.' Perhaps in a circle, preaching can happen anywhere, by any one of the people, and often as conversation.

A recent experience illustrates the vitality of this new aesthetic, one which acknowledges God in our midst. A member with multiple sclerosis has found it impossible to host the service in her apartment or to attend when they meet in other locations. One Sunday, someone brought a speaker telephone so those who came could hear and be heard by their apartment-bound member. Sue says the dynamic of the woman present through her voice gives a whole different feeling and meaning to 'presence':

> It emphasizes the importance of voice, of being present to one another through our conversation. It has shown me that there are a lot of ways to be present to people. And it's had an impact on the way I think of God's presence. When we moved into the dining room for eucharist, we carried her with us and put her on the altar, on the dining room table. The effect of meeting in our homes, of her presence through her voice, and the phone on the table has changed the meaning of the symbols in worship for me. Their meaning is now much more internal.

For Sue, and for the covenanted community, preaching is more who they are than what they do.

Sue's path for the past sixteen years has led to a transformation of the aesthetic of preaching which involves more than a modification of the external forms of pulpit, rhetoric, and liturgy. Her transformation of these forms has led to an aesthetic of presence. This aesthetic is much more difficult to identify and solidify into form because it emerges in relationship, that is, in attention to the words, spirit, and ministries of service of a covenant community.

Note

1   My analysis of Sue's story is phenomenological. The emphasis in phenomenological analysis is the interpretation of experience, in this case Sue's experience. This type of analysis does not claim that what Sue has experienced can necessarily be generalized to the experience of other women or men who preach. It does, however, invite readers to see potential connections between Sue's experience and their own. While I have chosen phenomenological analysis in contrast to other approaches, which draw on external authority to make theoretical points or to substantiate particular arguments, and while I associate much of what Sue says with the thought of a number of theorists, I have not made reference to any of this body of literature in order to focus on the meaning of Sue's experience and to maintain its integrity.

Works cited

Dante Alighieri, *The Divine Comedy*, trans. Charles Eliot Norton, Great Books of the Western World 21, Chicago, Encyclopaedia Britannica, 1952.

Melville, Herman, *Moby Dick: or, The Whale*, Great Books of the Western World 48, Chicago, Encyclopaedia Britannica, 1952.

Wittig, Monique, *Across the Acheron*, trans. David Levay, London, Peter Owen, 1987.

26 Rescripting their Lives and Narratives: Spiritual Life Stories of Pentecostal Women Preachers

Elaine J. Lawless

Pentecostalism is a twentieth-century, fundamentalist, charismatic religion, which draws on the Holiness tradition of early Methodism,[1] especially religious injunctions concerning Christian behavior and dress,[2] and which stresses the importance of spirit-led and spirit-filled religious services. Personal salvific encounters with the Holy Spirit include public exhibitions of glossolalia, or speaking in tongues as evidence of possession by the spirit. Since 1978, I have been researching and writing about the role of women in this extraordinarily patriarchal religion as it is practiced in southern Indiana and southern Missouri in white, rural congregations.[3] In this rural, regional context, in the home and in the church, Pentecostal males claim complete power, control, and authority over women and children; this dominant position for men is supported by a Pentecostal interpretation of Paul's writing in the New Testament, especially passages that explicitly deny women authority and a religious voice: 'But I suffer not a woman to teach, nor to usurp authority over the man, but to be in silence' (1 Tim. 2:12) and 'Let your women keep silence in the churches: for it is not permitted unto them to speak' (1 Cor. 12:34).

Within this religious context, women who have become preachers and who seek access to the pulpit or seek to maintain that access tell stories about their calling. In long testimonies, sometimes in prayers, in 'witnessing' to others, in private conversations, and in their sermons, women tell their life stories. And, in the course of my research, they told their stories to me. This paper, then, is an examination of the stories Pentecostal women preachers tell. It is about how limiting our notions of 'life stories' really have been, and it is a reexamination of how life stories can become strategies for female liberation in sociocultural/religious contexts which openly work toward female subjection and submission to males. It will, finally, point to the fact that while the rescripted lives liberate in one sense, they deny women the right to their *own* stories at the same time.

Field research and methodology

My fieldwork with Pentecostal women began in 1978. I lived five miles south of Bloomington, Indiana, in the limestone quarry region. Nearby Bedford claims to be 'The Limestone Capitol of the World', yet a drive through the countryside provides evidence of an industry that no longer thrives and has left the land looking used and abandoned. Strip mining has rendered the hills stark, with no vegetation replanted to cover the scars of years of abuse. Pieces of heavy machinery quietly stand rusting next to deep and mysterious quarries now filled with clear, blue water. In truth, the limestone industry provides little work for the people in this region these days. What work there is is seasonal, for the limestone cannot be cut in the cold winter months. Workers then must seek government assistance to feed their families and heat their homes. Most of the small towns in this area suggest great poverty and need. In the rural areas, many families live in older, poorly heated houses or in weather-beaten mobile homes. The school system is poor and many children quit school at the age of sixteen. Women generally do not work, although some have been forced by the economic situation to seek financial help for the family. Some of them babysit for other women in the area; some have found work in Bedford at fast-food places or discount stores. These jobs offer them minimum wage only and do little to better their financial situation.

My fieldwork in this region focused primarily on the rural-based Pentecostal churches which dot the landscape. Pentecostals that have remained independent and autonomous and have not associated themselves with the larger United Pentecostal Church or the Assemblies of God maintain their small churches in this area. Sometimes two, three, or even four different churches can be found on one single country road, for splinter groups are common when congregation members disagree on biblical interpretations or on proper decorum and/or dress. Ministers in these independent Pentecostal churches are never seminary trained. In fact, it is a point of pride that if one is 'called by God', seminary training is unnecessary, for the minister can always count on God giving the 'message' to the people through the minister, who serves only as a mouthpiece for the divine. Occasionally, a minister will take a correspondence course in order to be licensed. In order to marry and bury people, most of them must be registered with the county as licensed ministers, but this is not difficult to do. None of the ministers here are paid for their services. They usually hold regular jobs in addition to their duties as pastor. Only occasionally is a house provided for them.

The services in these small churches are lively and loud and, to the newcomer, appear to be unstructured. The notion that God will spontaneously provide a sermon for the minister while she/he is in the pulpit guides the services, which have no set schedule. Members in these churches decry the use of a printed bulletin, claiming that mere humans should not determine 'where a service will go', and prefer to go to church unprepared and 'see where the spirit leads'. In keeping with my training as a folklorist, my focus has generally been on the oral genres that are still a vibrant part of this Pentecostal religious tradition: prayers, testimonies, sermons, healings, songs and choruses, and speaking in tongues are all delivered in a spontaneous, extemporaneous style, which marks the Pentecostal service as an arena for oral tradition and expression. All of these oral genres are firmly framed in traditional patterns formed and protected over time and which dictate structure, content, style, language and delivery; that is, prayers must always sound like prayers, testimonies like testimonies, tongues like tongues – at least in terms of the expectations of each particular group.[4] Visitors to Pentecostal services often comment on what appears to be chaos and lack of structure in the spirit-led services; yet an understanding of the oral, traditional constructs and the belief in a constant direction from God, which frame and inform the service, makes it clear how the members of the group shape religious experience, practice, and ritual.

My field research from 1978 until 1982, when I left the state, consisted of regularly attending services in several of these rural churches. Over time, I gained permission to tape-record all services and I was allowed to take photographs. My in-depth interviews with several women in these congregations focused on their testimonies, their religious experiences, and the role of religion in their lives. I also interviewed some of the men in the congregations, primarily the male pastors. These interviews were all tape recorded. When folklorist Elizabeth Peterson and I wanted to make a film on the Pentecostal religions experience in southern Indiana, however, we were met with strict and unmoving opposition. Following an injunction against television and movies, these rural congregations never consented to our filming or videotaping their services.[5]

Field research which resulted in my first book, *God's Peculiar People: Women's Voices and Folk Tradition in a Pentecostal Church* (see note 1), revealed that, surprisingly, the Pentecostal religious services I was observing provided a forum for women's verbal expression: women sang, prayed, testified, 'shouted', and spoke in tongues. The Pentecostal perception of women as more spiritual and more in tune with the supernatural set the stage for their active spiritual involvement, even leadership, in the various religious genres available in a religious service.[6] *Testifying*, the act of standing in the pew and declaring in a rather ritualized presentation what God has done for you that week, was an especially fruitful arena for female verbal expression. Testimonies often became long, elaborate narratives, set within the appropriate 'testimony frame'. If skillfully delivered, these testimonies could, in fact, become so long that if several women testified at length in one particular service, the male preacher would not have time to give his sermon. Of course, this power to disrupt the service and usurp the authority of the males was never openly acknowledged by the women, although they often matter-of-factly recounted stories about services where the women just 'testified and testified' deep into the night. The men I interviewed were clearly disturbed by this pattern and were frustrated when their time in the pulpit was cut short or eliminated. I have argued that the women understood their subtle power within this religious context and exploited it to their benefit.[7]

Occasionally, during my field research in Indiana I would hear a Pentecostal woman preach. Given Paul's injunction against women speaking in church and the Pentecostal affinity for Paul's directives, I was astounded to find women actually gaining access to the pulpit in these small, extremely conservative churches. In the early 1980s, determined to learn more about how these women came to the pulpit, I turned my field research to women preachers in central and southern Missouri. That work resulted in *Handmaidens of the Lord: Pentecostal Women Preachers and Traditional Religion*.[8] The women I encountered were either itinerant ministers, traveling from town to town conducting revivals and camp meetings, or pastors in very small, rural-based Pentecostal churches.

The small towns and rural areas where I conducted fieldwork for *Handmaidens* have been hit hard by the farm crisis. Portions of central and southwestern Missouri kiss the foothills of the Ozarks and continue to evidence the lower-class, country existence that has been the hallmark, and the stereotype, of hill-folk in this region. People here are quite poor, salaries are extremely low, the standard of living ranks far below that of even northern Missouri, and certainly of the fertile fields of Iowa. Fundamentalist religion thrives in a region still proud to claim Jimmy Bakker. Ministers here, as in Indiana, are not seminary trained. And the male or female minister's right to the pulpit hinges upon their call from God to preach the word. As I intend to illustrate, the legitimacy and authenticity of that call from God, as evidenced in the calculated construction of the women's narratives, take on an exaggerated importance when it is *women* claiming the pulpit.

Personal experience and life stories as folklore

As early as 1977, folklorist Sandra Stahl argued for the traditional roots of personal experience narratives, suggesting they were appropriate to the study of folklore because the actual, personal experience and the shared, group tradition (that is, in terms of form, content, structure, language) fused in these stories which, if closely examined, often sounded remarkably similar from one narrator to another.[9] Jeff Titon's important article, 'The Life Story', published three years later, examined life stories and life histories as traditional 'fictions', understood within the context in which they exist.[10] Similarly, the study of life histories and life stories has come to the attention of sociologists, anthropologists, literary scholars and theorists, feminist scholars and historians. The literary connections between autobiography and life stories, particularly in terms of women's stories, inform the recent works of Joy Barbre and the women in the Personal Narrative Group at the University of Minnesota in their book *Interpreting Women's Lives*, that of Bella Brodzki and Celeste Schenck's *Life/Lines: Theorizing Women's Autobiography*, and includes what Germaine Bree termed *autogynography* in James Olney's new collection *Studies in Autobiography*.[11]

Spiritual life stories of Pentecostal women preachers

Examples of what I have chosen to label *spiritual life stories* are representative of the kinds of stories Pentecostal women preachers tell about their lives.[12] There has been a fairly longstanding concern among anthropologists and folklorists about the differentiations that ought to be made among *life story*, *personal history*, [oral] *autobiography*, and *life history*. I am calling the accounts given to me by women preachers *spiritual life stories*, for I hear the recollections to a very large degree as 'fictions' which draw on an understanding of *facio*, not a lie but a 'making'. The stories are creations; they cannot be viewed as *pure history* (although that term itself is suspect). I prefer the term *life stories* (plural) because I am skeptical of the notion of the existence of a constructed oral life story or life history (singular) that is formulated and delivered in chronological order and somehow fits our epic notions of oral autobiography. *Spiritual life stories* enables us to assume that these very specific life stories about women in religion are, in fact, not perfected entities, but rather each is a collection, a pastiche of stories, many of them based on both personal experience and traditional expectations at the same time. Like epic songs, the life story is, in fact, a series of smaller components, vignettes, each developed into a concrete story that follows the rules of traditional religions folk narrative. Most important to this present study is Titon's suggestion that 'the life story's singular achievement is that it affirms the identity of the storyteller in the act of telling. The life story tells who one thinks one is and how one thinks one came to be that way.'[13]

The narratives of the women in this study clearly embody both unique life experiences and folk (shared, group traditions) narrative elements. While the stories are certainly related as personal experience stories, their archetypal structure cannot be ignored. Joseph Campbell's monomythic heroic pattern begins, in fact, with a call and a refusal to obey.[14] First, the women relate that they believe they have been called by God to preach. Then, they relate their horror at such a fantastic notion – their horror, of course, reflects their awareness of the general opinion of their religious group about such an idea. The testing of God to validate the calling is a standard motif and the style of narrating such an incident remains identifiable from one corpus of stories to another. The following illustrates such a 'testing' of God and presents the preferred dialogic style of storytelling, which further authenticates the incident as 'real':

> I didn't know if this was of God or of the devil or of myself, so I said, 'God, if this is of you then tomorrow morning at exactly 8:00, Brother Simmons is going to call me and he's going to say, "Anna, would you consider coming to be our pastor?"' And, Elaine, the very next morning at exactly 8:00, Brother Simmons called me and he said the very words that I told God. He said, 'Anna, would you consider coming to be our pastor?' And it nearly knocked the breath out of me.[15]

Sister Anna Walters loves to tell this story, and she has recounted it on many occasions and in many different contexts, including my interview with her. It has the flavor of a story told often and with conviction. Her account has analogues in nearly every interview I have conducted. Sister Mabel Adams recounts how she felt the call, then resisted:

> I felt like, no, I can't do that. So I began to pray, 'Now, Lord, if you really have called me to preach and you want me to preach, you have her call on me tomorrow in church to preach'. That was my point of contact, you know, for certainty. And every time the Lord would give me a dream the night before, and in the dream he would give me the message, the Scriptures and everything, and then the very next morning, on Sunday, she would call on me to preach, see, and then I knew.

This motif – the testing of God for validation – is typical in the women's narratives and illustrates how so much of what they are doing is, of necessity, couched in terms of what *God* has called them to do. The stories always validate the calling and illustrate for the listener the woman's proper reluctance to accept the call; the 'test' embedded in the story dramatizes for both the woman and her audience the authenticity of the call.

That many of the vignettes embedded within these women's life stories are identifiable, either in structure or in content, as traditional ones (belonging to the group) can be illustrated with examples taken from different states. The explanation for clear analogues collected in places over five hundred miles apart depends on understanding the role of oral tradition in these religious contexts. Although the Pentecostal women in Missouri may never have sat in the same church as the women from Indiana, their experiences have been similar, and women who have visited in one area attend meetings where women from another area speak, and then they bring those narratives home with them. Large camp meetings and revivals, where women testify and tell their stories provide a forum for exchange not only of performance structure and style, but content as well. Both in the pan-Pentecostal religious arena, as well as in the local churches, there is clearly community collaboration on the 'authentic' story, its structure, its components and its performed delivery.

The spiritual life stories of women preachers illustrate the collaborative aspects of community-shared narrative. Early in my interviews with many different preachers, I became aware that their life stories certainly followed a pattern. Pivotal points of their narratives included: the experiences of being saved, being baptized in water, being baptized in the Spirit, and getting the call to preach. At first, it seemed remarkable that the women I interviewed so often structured the story of their personal life in this sequence with little or no attention to their home life, their family, or any female adolescent concerns they might have had. While fully acknowledging that my presence as an interviewer collecting the life stories of women preachers biased the material from the start, I was, nevertheless, unprepared for the consistency of the narratives. I have come to understand that this patterning has shaped their identities – these events, these experiences do make sense of their lives, individually and within the religious community. These patterns further confirm the woman's identity, first as a good Christian woman, and second as a woman preacher. The women both hear these stories and tell them within a common community and before a 'critical' audience which serves to authenticate and validate the experience as 'from God'. If it proves *not* from God, then the woman will not gain access to the pulpit.

Women who wish to become ministers must rescript their lives to fit the acceptable 'woman preacher' life script. These acceptable narratives follow some of the same inclinations most personal-experience stories share and which Stahl and others argue place them in the world of 'folklore' – that is, the components of a 'good' or expected story come to replace or accompany 'pure truth', while specifics, especially dialogue, often become formularized or crystallized, so that the story comes to 'say' what the narrator wants it to say. It is, after all, a story delivered to make some point or to entertain a certain audience. It will, therefore, have a focus. History will be modified, melded, pushed, and molded to create a story that is based on truth, but is, in fact, a created story; there is a pact between the narrator and the listener that disallows scrutiny and allows a measure of fantasy, within mutually agreed bounds. The context determines the flexibility of the boundaries. Religion happens to be one area in which the range for creativity in personal-experience fictions is quite broad, largely because the narrator takes refuge in the fantastic world of the supernatural and/or the divine. Here we find a strong pact that allows for stories of visions, possessions, and healings that, delivered in any other context, might be met with scorn, disbelief, or hilarity.

In the religious woman's construction of her life stories, selection is critical. Which events, what themes will emerge as most important? What will be developed, what excluded? The key appears to be just how concisely the narratives affirm the identity of the storyteller in the act of the storytelling. I would argue that the degree to which a life story has been formulated, honed, and developed will be in direct proportion to how secure the narrator's sense of identity actually is. In the case of

Pentecostal women preachers, there is a clear relationship between the elaborated life story, complete with its crystallized, most important components (specific vignettes that are utilized in various contexts), and the degree of positive self-identification. Women who have 'made it' as preachers – as pastors, especially – have much better developed stories than those who have not. When we read/hear the orally delivered stories of women preachers, then, we need to listen for what identifies them as individuals and what identifies them as traditional storytellers.

In the hostile, antifemale world of conservative Pentecostalism, women are denied their rights. They are required to be submissive to the men in their lives – their fathers, brothers, husbands, and male pastors. In the home, in the community, and in the church, they are denied their independence and their rights even over their own bodies. While the women of this study must decry the feminist movement and deny that they have chosen a strong, feminist stance against the dictums of their world, it is undeniable that they have clearly chosen for themselves an alternative lifestyle, even against the wishes of husbands, family, and friends. Feminist scholarship that deals with narrative strategies in literature can aid us in understanding how these midwestern women have had to rescript their lives. I am interested, then, in how these new scripts become available to women as acceptable scripts and how the scripts then become the models for lived lives. Carolyn Heilbrun, in *Writing a Woman's Life* offers this provocative statement: 'What matters is that lives do not serve as models: only stories do that. And it is a hard thing to make up stories to live by. We can only retell and live by the stories we have read or heared. We live our lives through texts.'[16]

Rescripting as narrative strategy

In her discussion of twentieth-century women writers, Rachel Blau DuPlessis has suggested that, unlike nineteenth-century women writers whose characters basically could choose only between marriage and death (because that was the reality of women's lives at the time as well), contemporary women writers are 'writing beyond' those restrictive endings for women's stories.[17] DuPlessis has suggested that the mythic quest (or *Bildung*) was unavailable to women characters (and women) in nineteenth-century fiction (and reality), that the only acceptable social script available to them was that of the 'helpmeet'. To become a 'heroine', the woman character had to embrace the roles of wife and mother, or die, largely because the nineteenth-century novel had to obey the 'structuring dialectics' of the social and economic limits of middle-class women as a group. But DuPlessis sees twentieth-century women writers as inventing alternate resolutions for the lives of women characters, a new set of choices. These alternative narrative patterns help to locate ways to 'neutralize the power of the standard socio-cultural script'. Simply by virtue of rescripting, the author is commenting upon the status quo, calling it into question, dissenting from it.

In my attempt to understand both the lives of women preachers and their narrated life stories, I should like to rely on such an understanding of narrative strategies. It will be constructive for us to view the reconstructions, or rescriptions of women's lives in the form of life stories, as narrative strategies that reinforce and validate the identity sought in the living script. The ability to create elaborations of reality may stem from what Patricia Spacks has termed the 'female imagination', or the 'power that penetrates the inner meaning of reality but also a power that creates substitutes for reality'.[18] The task of the folklorist here is not to determine where truth leaves off in these autobiographies and where imagination begins; rather, it is most productive for us to view the narratives as we do other oral, traditional genres – as stories with identifiable characteristics, structure, and content; stories that are dynamic and change with the context and the audience; stories that embody a shared understanding of the world and transmit that world view to others within the group. The life accounts may or may not actually reflect historical fact, but for the women who develop and recount them, they become very real indeed. As real, in fact, as the alternative lifestyle they have chosen.

Like nineteenth-century women, women in this regional context know that their prescribed role is in the home. The only totally appropriate script is that of housewife and mother. To be an 'old maid' is to live a sad and pitied life, cared for by no one. What better example, then, of the woman rescripting her life and refusing to accept the stance of female as muted than the woman preacher? Yet, the woman who chooses this vocation – and she does *choose* it, all refutation aside – must work to make certain her independence and outspokenness do not appear as a denial of the traditional female role of good wife and mother. Most especially, her credibility must not be shaken by any suggestion that she is a feminist or that she is in any way a threat to the status quo or that she is making a statement about women's rights. Within the conservative, Pentecostal religious context, the only acceptable premise for her behavior is the assertion that God has called her to preach; luckily, this claim helps to keep resistance from others at bay, although it certainly will not eliminate criticism. Since no one can be quite certain how God works, it remains dangerous to question his[19] motives, although a certain amount of grumbling about the woman in question is inevitable. If we follow DuPlessis's thinking, these women *are* feminists, in fact, simply by the act of rescripting – both in life and in the narrative reconstructions of life. The rescripting itself is a comment upon the status quo. Ritual disclaimers such as 'I'm not for ERA . . .' or 'Don't get me wrong, I'm not a women's libber' insulate the speakers from acknowledging the sagacity of their life strategies, while their narrative reconstructions reinvent the strategies and validate them for others.

The stories embody some of what the women actually did in their lives, which alone represents an astounding feat given the circumstances; they illustrate what the women perhaps wished they had done and said; and they present the women's interpretation of what has happened to them in their lives. Both the women's lives and their fictive reconstructions of their lives serve as alternative narrative strategies for women in this region.

The women's stories

The identifiable components of these traditional narratives of life experiences remain surprisingly consistent from narrator to narrator. The elements that nearly always figure in the narratives, in addition to those structural markers already mentioned, include: a clear perception of difference from other young people; an often severe conviction of a sinful nature; an attraction for the religious revival and/or missionary work; a concrete recounting of the conversion and the call to preach; and a construction of an alternative life strategy.

Virtually every one of the Pentecostal women who has related her story to me has remarked that she was born into a very poor family. Almost all were raised in rural counties and grew up on farms or in very small towns in rural areas. Nearly all of them belonged to large fundamentalist families, usually of Baptist or Holiness background. Indiana and Missouri are largely Bible-belt states of rural thinking, staunch conservatism and traditional values. Notions of the importance of the nuclear family, monogamy, female/male sex roles, and the importance of religion prevail and direct the daily lives of the people who live here. I stress this traditional milieu and value system because it bears directly upon the single most unusual aspect of these women's perceptions of themselves, supported by their lives and reinforced in their narratives, and that is their perception of themselves as *different* and their strength to act upon that perception in such a way as to reinforce and validate that difference. Most of these women were born into ordinary farming families with several, often many, children. The accepted roles of girls in this region were and continue to be clearly defined and inherently restricting.

Yet the life stories of women preachers hinge upon the fact that even as very young girls, they *felt* different or knew that they *were* different from other girls, from the other children in the family. Most tell that the most visible mark of their difference was their inclination toward the church, toward God, toward things religious. Importantly, this point in a reconstructed life story must be recognized as part of the narrative structure and strategy; that is, whether or not this is an actual historical point, it has become an important ingredient of the script that is created to validate the woman as different, different enough to be a preacher. And the women find dynamic ways to illustrate their difference. One woman tells an elaborate story of how she was ridiculed in primary school for her conservative clothing and her long, unadorned hair, which are required dress for Pentecostal girls and women. Her response to her difference was to ask the principal of the school if she could conduct prayer meetings in the cafeteria during recess. 'And, you know', she said with pride, 'they allowed it. And we had prayer meeting during our recess. And I led those services.' This story embodies much that Sister Mary wishes to convey about herself. It is a crafted story, told as true and intended to convince. The incident occurred nearly fifty years ago, yet details in the story, such as precisely remembered dialogue, will surprise us unless we understand that it is a created fiction – a recreation of an event. The girl speaks with authority, conviction; we have to applaud her strength, and, of course, that is the point of this story. It is one of the important vignettes in her life story; it sets the stage for the subsequent acts of pure impudence she will commit.

The stories of other women preachers strongly parallel this woman's story, in effect if not always in content. Sister Anna loves to recall that even while still in her mother's womb she was 'marked', when her mother was frightened by a snake and stumbled. Anna's family folklore supports her belief that she is different, that she was 'marked'. A favorite uncle started a story when she was only two that her insistent babbling was actually her premature inclination toward speaking in tongues and the world of the spiritual.

Many of the women emphasize their family's poverty and lack of worldly amenities; most tell of walking great distances alone to attend church services, more inclined toward things religious than even their religious families. The women speak of being fascinated with the church and the religious services, acutely tuned to the spiritual aspects. Almost all, too, associate their gravitation to the church with their own conviction of their sinful nature. Many relate tearful experiences when they feared they might not make it into heaven, or as one woman expressed it as a response to a song which suggested some would make it into heaven and others would have the door closed in their face: 'I'll never forget, they sang a song and here I was, just small, but I have used this as an illustration many times in my messages, that they sang this old song "Standing Outside the door – Oh, what an awful picture, left standing outside." That made such an imprint upon my mind, that I think that's why I can preach with vividness heaven as a real place.'[20]

Nearly all of the women interviewed stated that their first stirrings toward a religious life began in revivals. I think there is a good reason for this. Revivals were like carnivals come to town. In isolated rural areas, the church was and still is often the focal point of activity, at least of activity that could include all members of the family. Men and boys could certainly visit and hang around the local granges, the grain elevators, cotton gins, and even the taverns. And the children went to school as much as possible. But the church was an arena for all members of the family to participate. The strict religious standards did not allow for exploring new places or possibilities – with the exception of the revival and camp-meeting circuit. For young girls in this context, there were all too few role models – their mothers, female schoolteachers, and the occasional woman preacher. Clearly, women preachers and religious leaders made an impression on many young women. Importantly, religious life provided the opportunity for young girls to leave home and travel. No doubt the life of a missionary or an itinerant preacher was an appealing one for girls who doubted that they would, in any other way, be able to be independent and actually leave home before marriage.[21]

Missionaries brought excitement and glamour from faraway places, but the revivals held in the local areas certainly provided a more tangible kind of lure for young girls. Weeks, sometimes months before a revival was scheduled to begin, flyers would be posted on fences, at the grain elevator, on the church and grocery doors. The face of a traveling evangelist would smile down on the readers' eager faces, promising exciting meetings, singing fests, and religious fervor. Just like the carnival, the revivals and camp meetings were often set up on the edge of town; men, wielding huge hammers, set up enormous tents that would put a circus to shame, or, in some areas, constructed temporary 'brush arbors', large, open-air constructions with roofs made of brush and tree limbs. Benches, logs, and chairs were lined up inside, a makeshift altar prepared, a pulpit tacked together, sawdust was dumped on the floor, and sometimes a piano was brought out. Services could last anywhere from three days to three weeks. Many women relate their religious conversions to these religious extravaganzas. Almost all remember a most significant revival when a woman came to preach.

Like Dinah in George Eliot's *Adam Bede*, the traveling woman preacher was a sight to behold – bold in her independence, calm in her assurance of herself, captivating with her religious message.[22] It was so easy to become enthralled, to respond to the calls to repent, to dedicate, to exhibit the zeal of the Lord. And respond they did. Historical accounts of revivalism always note the enthusiastic female participation in these meetings, and my own work attests to the consistency of women's enthusiasm.[23] The messages took on a very personal appeal for these girls: they wept; they saw themselves as blatant, stained sinners; they went to the altar and prayed fervently; and some of them promised God they would live in his service – and that promise meant the possibility of an alternate life, a new life-script. To be a revival preacher meant daily doses of new faces, travel, independence, and status. In fact, it just may have represented the most outrageous break with tradition available without castigation – offering much more mobility than school-teaching, for example. And, to make it even more appealing, if the call could be authenticated as from God and not of the girl herself, then the decision gained divine validation. But none of this is to suggest that just because there were women preachers that preaching was a condoned activity for women. It was not, and still is not, in most Pentecostal contexts; at best it is tolerated only because of the respect for and belief in divine intercession. God's call, then, becomes the single most important component in the rescripting. The girl's story must relate the moment when she believes she is being called to do and to be something special.

Because of the inherent danger of announcing this belief that God has called them, most of the women's stories have embedded in them a ritual disclaimer of sorts – a message that either clearly states or implies, 'Look, I didn't ask for this. God called me. What could I do but obey? I tried to resist, but you really ought not try to resist God.' Implied is the message that the young women did not actually wish to be called. Importantly, in the oral re-creation of the life story a degree of hesitancy must be in evidence; no greediness, no rushing toward this life in the center stage is allowable.

> . . . the Lord just spoke to me, you know, let me know that he had called me and wanted me to preach. And I just rebelled, I really did. I didn't feel like, you know, that I could. I just felt like, well Lord, surely you could find somebody that could do a better job than I can. But he said, you know, 'YOU!' [Mabel Adams, Hooperton, Missouri][24]

Resistance is important, for personal intent would discredit the woman's legitimate claim to the pulpit. While the woman must disclaim any personal desires, her stories must prove that she has, in fact, been selected by God and that she will be effective in the capacity of preacher. Sister Anna says:

I've had to prove all of these years that a woman can be called into the ministry. And I've kept loving the people even when they've criticized me and I tell them, 'Look, this wasn't my choice.' I've stood in front of the mirror lots of times and said, 'God, are you sure you know what you're doing? I'm a wife; I'm a mother. I didn't come into this on my own.'[25]

Compare this narrative with the following story which exemplifies the hesitancy, the reluctance, and the power of God in one woman's call-to-preach narrative:

Well, the call of God first come into my life when I was seventeen years of age, it like to scared me to death and I said, 'Lord, I'll do what I can to help others, but leave me alone'. And which he did for a while. I would try to get away from it you know. I would rather not have went to preach. I would rather have set in the pews. But God slayed me under his power and I saw a vision. I saw it seemed like the earth opened and a big river of water come pouring in and in this I saw a bunch of sheep coming out through that water and I said, 'Lord, what does this mean?' And he said, 'This river of water is the river of life that I'm willing to give unto the people that is ready and needing it.' Then I saw a big field of people in this same vision. A large field and my brother who was a minister running back and forth trying to preach to all them people. And I said, 'God, what does this mean?' And he said, 'That he has got more to reach than he can possibly reach and I have called you to go and help him and my calling is without repentance.' [Leah Moberly, West Park, Missouri][26]

Compare Sister Mary's concern when she felt in the woods that God had given her, a mere sixteen-year-old girl, the sermon for that evening's revival service:

And I never will forget that place because there was a big old grapevine, it was just about this big around. And when I – it just seemed like God just almost slew me, cause I got down on my back, flat on that ground and I couldn't get up. And I started praying and God started dealing with my heart and the Lord started saying, it just seemed like – not in an audible voice – but I could just hear the Lord speaking in a still, small voice, saying, 'Will you go where I want you to go? And will you do what I want you to do?' And, you know, it was hard for me because I thought, now, is this *me*? Because I had admired this other girl that preaches *so much*, I'd always all my life, you know, I'd always thought, oh, I would like to be an evangelist, but the thoughts came to me, how can *I* preach? How can I do anything? But the Lord just kept dealing with me and I couldn't get up and finally I said, 'Lord, whatever you want me to do, even though I within myself, I'm not, I know I'm not worthy of this calling, but I'll do anything you want me to do because I know that it's in your power to speak through me.' And then I could get up.[27]

The biblical nature of the language of these narratives further serves to authenticate them. These young, rural American women adopt a stilted prose style in their stories, one which is generally incongruent with their everyday language, as they talk of 'God slaying them in the spirit' and 'dealing with their heart' and 'speaking in a still, small voice'. They tell their audience that they have agreed to serve God against their own desires and better judgment, openly acknowledging they are not 'worthy of this call'. God speaks to them as he spoke to his disciples, 'Will you go where I want you to go? Will you do what I want you to do?' And the women finally acquiesce and answer, 'I'll go where you want me to go; I'll do what you want me to do'. Mary cinches the argument by recounting that she agreed to follow God's directive because, she says, 'I know that it's in your power to speak through me.' No person in this religious context is able to argue with that definitive statement. They would *all* have to agree that God has the ability, the power, to speak through *anyone*, even a woman.

A striking number of these young women called to preach actually did have female models to follow, usually within the context of the tent revival or the religious camp meeting. And that is where they heard other women recount their stories. In many cases, in fact, the pivotal point of their decision to undertake the ministry revolves around an important encounter with a woman preacher. Over and over, the turning point in the story is a reference to how a woman preacher helped her to make the decision to follow God's call. By this female association and perhaps even more impor- tantly through the stories of other women's lives, the call to preach was received in a context of pos- sibility, if not probability, that what they sought to do was not queer or absurd, for other women had done it. Sometimes these influences came from total strangers or from the stories of total strangers, but sometimes the influences were very close to home. Experiences in their own families were the ones that would assure the young girl that she could act on her calling, that a rescripting of the 'normal' female life strategy did not necessitate a rejection of home and family, but it would require the adoption of new life strategies for both women and men.

> My grandmother was a minister for many, many years. She was Church of God-Holiness – and so she wasn't pastoring but she was an evangelist for many years and she had five children. And my grandmother was holding a revival down at a little old schoolhouse way down south and my mother was about middle ways in the family and I've heard my mother say, course she had long hair, and that Grandpa's hands were so rough, so she always hated it when Grandma was gone to revivals because Grandpa had to braid her hair. But, then, when Grandma'd come home, and instead of money – about all they could give her were squirrels and rabbits or deer meat, because that's all they could give her, but she'd be so thrilled because she could bring that home – course that wasn't what she was in it for. But this is really where I got my background. [Sister Anna Walters][28]

Sister Walters is speaking about the early years of [the twentieth] century in central and southern Missouri, and, given the cultural milieu, it is an amazing narrative. The force of the narrative is not so much the discomfort the girl experiences when her mother is gone as it is the matter-of-fact way in which the mother's occupation and traveling, her leaving five children in the care of the father, is depicted – her leaving to preach is a given. Religion makes women brave; God's business is not to be scoffed at by any person. Yet, neither is the woman's place in the family and in the home to be neglected or ignored. Many stories clearly embed images of home and children, making the rescripting more palatable. Sister Anna, when offered the pastorship of a small church two hundred miles from her husband and family, tells how she begged God for answers as she 'agonized, slumped over a basket of clothes'. The women are careful not to suggest that theirs is a life in the public eye, that they seek the world over the home.

After a Pentecostal woman has entered the world of the ministry, and either taken the position of itinerant preacher or church pastor, her life does not necessarily get any easier. She continues to encounter opposition to her right to the pulpit. People stop her in the grocery store or in the parking lot to quote Scripture that 'proves' women should not be preachers. Some women preachers say they receive threatening and harassing letters and books that damn women preachers. Their stories about life in the ministry, then, accentuate their position, its inherent dangers, and their strategies for dealing with opposition. As one woman so aptly put it: 'I've been told folks don't believe in women preachers. I've told them they didn't hire me and they sure couldn't fire me. *God* called me and I'll be here!'

Conclusion

The oral narratives, the spiritual life stories, of Pentecostal women preachers serve as model life scripts for women entering the ministry; the scripts of women who have come before them in this strange and demanding world serve as scripts not only for their lives but for their own narratives; and, in turn, the narratives serve to dictate the structure of other women's lives – as much as texts are able to influence life experiences. Life experiences are interpreted within the constructs recog- nized as the appropriate components of a narrative life script, a text that serves as a rescripting for an actual life.

This delicate interweaving of text and life experience, script and rescripting, serves, on the one hand, to illustrate the power of language and narrative to validate and authenticate the lived life. It suggests how women's stories serve to disrupt the status quo, call it into question, and provide the means to weaken male power and authority and deflect religious injunctions intended to silence women's voices. It is indicative of the ways women take control of their lives and their voices, subvert the dictates of a male hierarchy, and violate man-made codes which restrict them. The story of the Pentecostal woman preacher can be read as a strong statement about strong women who defy restrictions about what they can do and say; it can be interpreted as a story they tell about themselves – a story of liberation.

On the other hand, a critical feminist reading of these texts and their utility for the women who tell them suggests that the stories may not, in fact, authenticate, validate, or honor the actual 'lived life'. The life lived by the individual woman may be subverted in the telling of these rescriptings prescribed by the group. She may feel, in fact, that she must abandon her *actual* story in favor of the *acceptable* story. The 'rescripting' DuPlessis has suggested for female characters in literature constitutes an actual move toward liberation for women, while these new scripts for women preachers may not have the same liberating effect. DuPlessis speaks of new and better choices for women, alternatives to the 'marry or die' constructs that constrict their narratives and their lives. We see some of the characters in the literary stories *and* some real women actually altering the status quo, changing the rules of the game, and we hope, eventually, coming to enjoy a variety of life choices without castigation, repression, or reprisals.

A feminist reading of the women preachers' rescripting of their lives suggests also a level of denial, however. On the one hand, rescripting one's life to fit the expectations of the group and 'authenticate' the call from God to preach is certainly a calculated narrative strategy that ought to be applauded, for it certainly works to provide a way for women to gain access to the pulpit. On the other hand, we must acknowledge the discomforting effect of having to structure one's life narrative to fit an acceptable pattern (and in the process abandon the reality of what actually happened). Furthermore, in the oral, community-based context in which these stories are related, heard, and retold, they come to serve not only as acceptable scripts for life narratives, but also as scripts for lived lives. That is, the power of the structure of the narrative comes to be superimposed upon the lives of young women who believe they should be preachers. The rescripting, then, may become the blueprint for experience, or how experience will be interpreted and articulated to others. Is this construction, then, liberating for women? Yes and no.

Within the Pentecostal context, rescripting does afford a modicum of independence, a space in which to move as a female minister. It does not allow women, however, the truth and vibrance of their own stories; it may not validate and authenticate a woman's own, individual, unique narrative. In some ways it perpetuates the status quo and molds itself to the constraints of the religious context in which the women live. But in other equally real ways it provides the means for new and different life scripts – and the women are, in fact, involved in the process of the rescripting, of both their stories and their lives. That in itself is liberating.

Notes

1   Histories of Pentecostalism and its roots in both white and black American religious traditions include: Vinson Synan, *The Holiness-Pentecostal Movement in the United States*, Grand Rapids, MI, W.M. Eerdmans, 1971; Melvin Dieter, *The Holiness Revival of the Nineteenth Century*, Metuchen, NJ, Scarecrow, 1980; Nils Block-Hoell, *The Pentecostal Movement*, Oslo, Norway, Unversitetsforlaget, 1964; W.J. Hollenweger, *The Pentecostals*, Minneapolis, Augsberg, 1972; Robert Mapes Anderson, *Vision of the Disinherited*, New York, Oxford University Press, 1979; Elaine J. Lawless, *God's Peculiar People:*

Women's Voices and Folk Tradition in a Pentecostal Church, Lexington, University Press of Kentucky, 1988. See also Dickson Bruce, *And They All Sang Hallelujah: Plain-Folk Camp-Meeting Religion, 1800–1845*, Knoxville, University of Tennessee Press, 1974, for the early camp-meeting tradition.

2   See Elaine J. Lawless, 'Brothers and Sisters: Pentecostals as a Folk Group,' *Western Folklore*, 43, 1983, pp. 85–104, and ' "Your Hair is Your Glory" Public and Private Symbology for Pentecostal Women,' *New York Folklore*, 12, 1986, pp. 33–49.

3   Although I have done some field research in black Pentecostal churches, most of my work has focused on white Pentecostal traditions. I can see both similarities and differences between the black and white Pentecostal traditions, yet none of these should be assumed in this article. All of the members of the churches alluded to here are white and I am suggesting no conclusions for Pentecostalism in general or for black Pentecostal traditions and beliefs.

4   My understanding of these as oral 'performances,' delivered in group-recognized and group-condoned patterns and styles and presented to a critical audience for recognition and approval, stems from Richard Bauman's development of this group consensus in tradition in his *Verbal Art as Performance*, Rowley, MA, Newbury House, 1977.

5   For a visual presentation of southern Indiana Pentecostalism set in a small-town church, see Elaine J. Lawless and Elizabeth Peterson, co-producers (1981), *Joy Unspeakable*, a video television program, Bloomington, Indiana University Radio and Television.

6   This alignment of women with the spiritual and supernatural is both beneficial and problematic to them. On the one hand, it does allow for women's free expression in the religious services; on the other hand, it works to perpetuate the dichotomy suggested by Sherry Ortner and others that women are more 'natural' than men because of childbearing and lactation. Here, the Pentecostal belief upholds a connection between natural, spiritual, and supernatural in terms of the 'spirit world' – which, of course, can be manifested in divine spirit possession of possession by evil spirits or by the devil. While not articulated, the attitude of Pentecostal males would seem to follow older Christian notions of male intellectual and *religious* superiority, while relegating women to the arena of spirits and devils. In fact, when I asked men in these congregations why more women than men went into trance, 'fell out', spoke in tongues, and evidenced the spirit, they consistently suggested that the spirit-filled experiences were rather 'sissy [feminine]', in that they were often accompanied by profusive crying, kneeling, falling on the floor, unabashed dancing, twirling, shouting, etc. They felt their role was to *administer* to the women during these spirit-filled portions of the services. See Sherry Ortner, 'Is Female to Male as Nature is to Culture', in Michelle Z. Rosaldo and Louise Lamphere (eds), *Woman, Culture and Society*, Stanford, Stanford University Press, 1974, pp. 67–89.

7   See Elaine J. Lawless, 'Shouting for the Lord: The Power of Women's Speech in the Pentecostal Service,' *Journal of American Folklore*, 96, 1983, pp. 433–57.

8   Elaine J. Lawless, *Handmaidens of the Lord; Pentecostal Women Preachers and Traditional Religion*, Philadelphia, University of Pennsylvania Press and the American Folklore Society, 1988.

9   Sandra K. D. Stahl, 'The Personal Narrative as Folklore,' *Journal of the Folklore Institute*, 14, 1977, pp. 9–30.

10 Jeff Todd Titon, 'The Life Story,' *Journal of American Folklore*, 93, 1980, pp. 176–92.

11 Joy Webster Barbre, *et al.* (eds), *Interpreting Women's Lives: Feminist Theory and Personal Narratives*, Bloomington, Indiana University Press, 1989; Bella Brodzki and Celeste Schenck (eds), *Life/Lines: Theorizing Women's Autobiography*, Ithaca, Cornell University Press, 1988; and James Olney, *Studies in Autobiography*, New York, Oxford University Press, 1988.

12 I first approached this topic in *Handmaidens of the Lord*. I need to thank the anonymous reader for this journal who pushed me to make the piece infinitely more feminist than when I first submitted it.

13 Titon, 1980, p. 290.

14 See Joseph Campbell, *Hero With a Thousand Faces*, New York, World Publishing Company, 1949, 1971 reprint.

15   Sister Anna Walters. All the names of persons, churches, and towns have been changed to protect the privacy of the persons involved in this study.

16   Carolyn G. Heilbrun, *Writing a Woman's Life*, New York, W. W. Norton and Co., 1988, p. 37.

17   Rachel Blau DuPlessis, *Writing Beyond the Ending: Narrative Strategies of Twentieth-Century Women Writers*, Bloomington, IN, Indiana University Press, 1985.

18   Patricia Meyer Spacks, *The Female Imagination*, New York, Alfred A. Knopf, 1972, p. 4.

19   My use of 'he' as a designation for God here reflects the *only* way God may be referred to in this region. Inclusive language, in reality or as an issue, simply has not become a part of their religious world view.

20   Lawless, 1988, p. 70.

21   While I have written these descriptions in past tense because they come from the recollections of women who are now generally past fifty years of age, there are many areas in both Indiana and Missouri where such revivals, complete with tents and sawdust, can still be found.

22   See Elaine J. Lawless, 'The Silencing of the Preacher Woman: The Muted Message of George Eliot's *Adam Bede*,' *Women's Studies*, 18, 1990, pp. 116–36.

23   See especially Bruce, 1974.

24   Lawless, 1988, p. 78.

25   Ibid., p. 149.

26   Ibid., pp. 76–7.

27   Ibid., p. 33.

28   Ibid., p. 82.

Part 8

EFFECTIVENESS AND EVALUATION

Introduction to Part 8

Nieman opens this section by describing the sermons of Chrysostom in Antioch of Syria in the fourth century. His preaching was frequently interrupted by applause, which he viewed with suspicion. The sermon is properly honoured when the congregation leaves the church in order to put into practice the word that they have heard. Nieman identifies the temptation for the preacher to cut short the time spent in preparation when congregational approval is easily obtained. But the point of preaching is to drive people from the church that they may serve a gospel which is inherently 'centrifugal'. Moreover, the words of the gospel intrinsically possess illocutionary and perlocutionary force: they aim to achieve a purpose and have an effect. This is no less true of scriptural narrative and parables, both of which confront the hearer with the unexpected or even the unwelcome. If Scripture decentres the hearers and leaves them 'suspended, unresolved and dissatisfied', then in the same way preaching should drive people into the world 'to complete the story' in their lives.

James R. Nieman, 'Preaching that Drives People from the Church' is from *Currents in Theology and Mission*, 20, 1993, pp. 106–15.

Eighty-two members of a Southern Baptist Church participated in the study described in the next article of the effects of preaching (P) and preaching supplemented by dialogue (PD). Five instruments were developed as measures: a knowledge test, a psuedo-behaviour test, a subjective evaluative test of the subject as a worshipper, a subjective evaluation of the preacher, and a Semantic Differential test related by subject matter to the sermons. The Semantic Differential was the only instrument which showed consistent, significant effects with a probability of the same result happening by chance of less than 5 per cent ($p < 0.05$).

Dennis L. Price, W. Robert Terry and B. Conrad Johnston, 'The Measurement of the Effect of Preaching and Preaching plus Small Group Dialogue in One Baptist Church' is from the *Journal for the Scientific Study of Religion*, 19, 1980, pp. 186–97.

The final article in this *Reader* reports on two projects which focused primarily on two questions: How does the laity understand the relationship between the words of the preacher and the Word of God; and what criteria do laity use in judging if the Word of God has been proclaimed by the preacher? Two respondent groups totalled 81 members of the Lutheran Church in America. Their results indicate that the laity closely identify the Word of God with the Bible. Sermons containing overt and explicit biblical material are judged to be a proclamation of the Word of God. The interpersonal relationship between clergy and laity was a major determining factor in judging sermons as a proclamation of the Word, frequently regardless of the actual content of sermons. Avery and Gobbel found that where there were differences between clergy and laity concerning the Bible and matters of the Faith, there was a tendency for laity to rely on some unspecified individualistic, privatistic criterion.

William O. Avery and A. Roger Gobbel, 'The Word of God and the Words of the Preacher' is from the *Review of Religious Research*, 22, 5, 1980, pp. 41–53.

27   Preaching that Drives People from the Church

James R. Nieman

Dream with me for a moment. Dream with me of a city, a great and marvellous city as only exists in dreams. Picture it bisected by a shining river like a shimmering chain bearing some rare and precious gem. See that gem itself set in a mounting of verdant hills and fertile plains. Consider the facets of that gem from every angle, a place glittering with arts, education, commerce. And among these facets, do not neglect the religious life, for there is place given here for true faithfulness. So at the very center of this shining jewel, this dream-city, imagine an immense sanctuary which is at every festival filled to overflowing. The dignity of this church is reflected in the character of its preacher: passionate, holy, beloved, one whose words are at once tender and insightful, humble and honest. And when you have dreamed this dream and pictured such a place, even then your dream will not have matched the grandeur of one city as it actually was long ago. That city was Antioch of Syria at the end of the fourth century, its church was the great octagon cathedral built by Constantine, and its preacher was John Chrysostom.

For a dozen years, Chrysostom preached every Sunday, twice a week during certain seasons, and daily during Lent. By all accounts, he was wildly successful. So crowded was the church and so enraptured were the hearers by his words that warnings were issued concerning the threat of pickpockets. The sermons which survive this period are indeed marvels of eloquence. At every turn one finds the well-crafted phrase, the enlightening analogy, the patient instruction and the passionate exhortation which characterize one of the church's greatest homilists.

One finds something else, however, something quite curious, which is hardly found in other sermons of the period: the mention of applause. Repeatedly, the scribes who recorded the sermons took great pains to recount how Chrysostom was interrupted by applause and wild cheering, sometimes as much as three times in the same homily. To be sure, the scribes were offering 'external evidence' that the preacher was just as good as his reputation allowed. But the main reason for noting the applause was to give a backdrop for recording Chrysostom's reaction to it, and his reaction was not a happy one.

Chrysostom was deeply suspicious of such public outbursts. Was not this behavior suited for the circus and the theater, not the house where the solemn mysteries of Christ were revealed? But there was more at stake here than mere decorum. Toward the end of a sermon on the closing verses of the eighth chapter of Romans, he urged his hearers to serve Christ by serving the hungry, the sick, the imprisoned in their midst, and the beauty of his words inflamed the crowd to interrupt, once again, with loud acclamation. Annoyed by the outburst, Chrysostom fired back,

> What is the good of these applauses and clamors? I demand one thing only of you, and that is the display of them in real action, the obedience of deeds. This is my praise, this your gain, this gives me more luster than a diadem. When you have left the Church then, this is the crown that you should make for me and for you, through the hand of the poor.[1]

The message is clear: preaching is honored not through applause, but through action; the gospel is served not by remaining within the church, but by leaving it.

In this essay, I want us to dream together of such proclamation, of preaching as Chrysostom imagined it. And if this dream must have a name, let us call it: Preaching that drives people from the church.

'Driving people from the church' – we already know the nightmare side of that vision. We need not detail those familiar times when our patience is strained to the limit by some sorry homiletic performance. We will not enhance the quality of *our* sermons by dwelling on the obvious flaws of those that are bad, About those preachers who, through carelessness or callousness, manage uniformly to annoy, degrade, or bore their listeners, let us say nothing more, except this: *no one sets out to preach this way!* Only a fool intends to so alienate listeners that they leave and never return. Our tendency is, in fact, just the opposite: to so please and delight our hearers that they will love the church, love our preaching, and love *us*. And therein rests the real danger.

Chrysostom's concern was with the evils implicit in good preaching that keeps 'em coming back for more. Such sermons not only corrupted the hearer, Chrysostom said, but especially endangered the preacher, who out of vanity pandered to the crowd at the expense of the message. And how subtly this danger also creeps up on us! As the pressures of parish life mount and the 'urgent' supplants what is genuinely important, we say, 'Well, it won't hurt if just *this* week I don't spend quite as much time on sermon preparation.' And lo and behold, we are absolutely right! They love us anyway! 'Good sermon', they continue to chime at the door. Week by week we learn to get by with less and less text study, prayer, and reflection. And everything works out fine so long as we just use lots of inflection, include touching illustrations, reinforce the dominant values, and wink, 'Isn't that right, Agnes?' to the congregational president. 'Just such is our case', said Chrysostom sixteen centuries ago, 'when we make it our aim to be admired, not to instruct; to delight, not prick to the heart; to be applauded and depart with praise, not to correct human manners.'[2]

And what is the point of such preaching, beyond ego gratification? I suppose we want to fill our pews and attain a critical mass of hearers who will be active, happy, and involved with life *inside* the church. We want to reinforce brand loyalty, fostering a commitment to church programs, church committees, church budgets, church events. Preaching with this end in mind is based upon a strategy of containment, trying to bring people in through the sermon and hold them there, like fireflies trapped in a mayonnaise jar, that we may bask in the light they cast upon us. But you know why fireflies flicker as they do, don't you? It's because of sex! It's so they can find one another in the dark and reproduce their kind, that they might finally be scattered like myriad jewels in the coolness of a midsummer evening. It is my plea that our preaching should have a similar aim: not sex, but *taking the lid off the jar*, driving people from the church that they may share the gospel with others.

Such preaching envisions the church as existing for the world, not simply for itself. After all, the Great Commission says, 'Go and make disciples of all *nations*', not 'Go and make disciples of all *believers*.' Behind this is the assumption that the gospel is not derivable from the culture. It is an alien word which must first be proclaimed in order that it can be heard and believed. In other words, there is something inherently outward-directed in the gospel *and* how it is preached. It is to that 'centrifugal' message I wish now to turn.

Over thirty years have passed since the Oxford philosopher, John L. Austin, inaugurated what has come to be known as speech-act theory.[3] Austin was concerned that philosophy in his day had reduced the idea of language to descriptions and reports, statements that mean exactly what they say and refer to something outside of themselves for their validity. For example, if I say 'Your hair is blonde', I am describing something we can verify by looking at the color of your hair. Surely our everyday language is more interesting than this.

Austin found the richness and variety of language manifested in another class of statements which he called 'performatives,' sentences that don't simply state facts but actually *do* something. One group of these he called 'illocutionary'. These utterances accomplish something in and through the very act of speaking. Examples include promises, bets, verdicts, and Austin's personal favorite, wedding vows. When I promise, for example, to do something for you, the validity of that promise is found in the very saying of it; a promise is something you *do* with words. Of course, you may not believe that I will carry through on my promise, but it still remains a promise, though a dubious one. This leads to a second group of performatives which Austin called 'perlocutionary'. Here, the emphasis is not on what the words do in and of themselves, but on the potential effect of so speaking. Some statements, such as warnings, invitations, and insults, intend an impact upon the hearer which may or may not come to pass. If I try to make fun of you, then the perlocutionary impact of my words is to produce shame and embarrassment, although they may also bring anger.

It's not too hard to see that Austin's work provided new insights for biblical studies. After all, the scriptures include vastly more than mere descriptions or reports. 'Let there be light' and 'Ephphatha!' are two fairly explicit illocutions, as is the whole range of covenantal language which, by its blessing and cursing, does what it says and binds two parties together. Perlocutions are also fairly easy to find. 'Follow me', 'Honor your father and your mother', and other such exhortations seek to produce the outcome to which they point. That Scripture is replete with such active language is perhaps best summarized in Jesus' one sentence Nazareth sermon on Isaiah 61: 'Today this scripture has been fulfilled in your hearing.' The illocutionary force of that sermon is that the good news, release, sight, and liberty prophesied in Isaiah, have happened in the very saying of the words. The perlocutionary force is there as well, in the doubts of Jesus' hearers concerning his origins and their ultimate efforts to throw him off a cliff.

Now, this kind of language is not especially foreign to the pastoral office. After all, we dare to say things like, 'Your sins are forgiven' in absolution, or 'The body of Christ, given for you' in distribution, fully believing that such a gracious reality is manifest in and through the words that announce it. Is preaching the gospel all that different? Maybe it is, but only through a loss of nerve on our part, a lack of confidence that declaring God's persistent and relentless love for us in Jesus Christ bears the reality it asserts. At this point we turn to gimmicks and tricks, fearing that something 'more' is needed to bring this gospel to pass. But I want to claim that to tell the gospel *is* to do it, and to hear such good news *is* to have it made active in one's life.

If the message of the gospel has such illocutionary force, it is also marked by a perlocutionary impact. In doing what it says, it leads to an outcome. When the gospel enacts peace, healing, freedom, hope, then its hearers are already being carried out toward homes, neighborhoods, and communities, local or global, where such realities will attain their fullest form. The gospel itself, then, has a kind of centrifugal direction to it. And if the gospel has this kind of dynamic trajectory, it provides the grounds for the kind of preaching I am advocating here, one that drives people from the church.

The shrewd reader will realize that I am basing the shape of the preached message upon that of the scriptural message. At that point, one might well object that the Bible contains many other utterances than the kind of performative ones I have named. And this is true. Covenants, commands, threats, promises, and all the rest are themselves embedded in a web of narrative material which, while entertaining or enlightening, doesn't really seem to *do* anything in the very saying of it.

Or does it? It might be a bit hasty to assume that the narrative framework of Scripture is a kind of documentary of biblical times into which are set clever sayings and amazing events. Such wooden and flatfooted storytelling would be profoundly dull, like the insufferable bore who doesn't see that the set-up for a joke must be at least as interesting as its punch-line if anyone is going to laugh. But good narrative relates something of special relevance to its hearers which exceeds a mere recitation of the mundane. It comes from a certain point-of-view and intends a particular outcome that will matter to someone. This is what Mary Louise Pratt has referred to as the inherent 'tellability' of narrative, the way in which it conveys something unusual, unexpected, maybe even problematic which arrests our attention and insists upon being heard.[4]

This is the very quality we find in the narratives of so much of Scripture, from the tales of Abraham and Sarah to those of Mary and Joseph, and beyond. These stories are compelling because they deal with things of substance, and what is more, they treat them in an unexpected way. If these narratives only conveyed to us a world we could already know on our own without the telling of it, they would be trite and useless. But implicit in Scripture is an unfamiliar version of reality, a different way of telling the human story that invites us into its possibilities and promises. In this regard, scriptural narrative is infused with illocutionary force: it *does* something to us by drawing us into its flow and its vision.

Of course, not all of Scripture is so open and accessible. We are well aware of the texts whose meaning is anything but clear and inviting, whose purpose seems hidden or even offensive. Many prophecies challenge our assumptions, apocalyptic seems to conceal as much as it reveals; and the cross itself may become a barrier to understanding. But my point again is that such concealment or offense is what these texts *do* to the hearer; to obscure or to alienate *is* their illocutionary force.

Jesus himself seemed to express this in Matthew 13, when he acknowledged that his parables were opaque to certain of his hearers, 'because seeing they do not see, and hearing they do not hear, nor do they understand'. This is a perfect example of what the German literary critic Wolfgang Iser refers to as 'negativity': the barriers erected in a story which call the familiar world into question. So radical is their challenge that our old ways of thinking must come to an end, requiring a new perspective from which our world can be understood and transformed.[5] Jesus' parables in Matthew 13 are 'negative' in this sense. They present God's realm as one of unexpected decisions, unforeseen growth, and undeserved rewards – a world radically different from our own. Preaching which domesticates these parables to make them utterly transparent corrupts their power to confront us and undermines their ability to *do* something.

My purpose in talking about narratives, whether they are open or closed, inviting or offensive, is not simply that they have illocutionary force, that they *do* something to the hearer, but also that they have an intended outcome as well, a perlocutionary impact. For whether a story has drawn you into a different world or rudely challenged your own, either way you have been uprooted. Just there such stories leave us: suspended, unresolved, dissatisfied. Given a new perspective, we are also given a new task: to finish the story. This is, I think, why Mark 16 ends as it does at verse 8, with the women fleeing the empty tomb in fear and silence. It is an offensive ending, and the hearer wonders, 'How can *I* bring this to some satisfactory resolution?' This same dynamic is also behind the final verse of John's Gospel, when the evangelist suggests that there are many other stories about Jesus which could be written. And again, the bearer asks, 'What would *mine* be?'

This is the activity Scripture performs on its hearers: first, to de-center us, and then, to have us complete its story in our lives. This is the biblical trajectory, and preaching based upon such a message follows the same trajectory. Its centrifugal direction is to drive people from the church and into the world, there to complete the story in the lives of those who hear it.

Up to this point, I have been describing how the message of preaching and of Scripture itself tries to engage its hearers, to grasp them and bear them outward. This means that our attention always turns from the 'what' of the proclamation to the 'to whom'. This is not an optional matter. Sermons, like animals in pet store windows, depend upon human intervention in order to be delivered from the shame of being treated like commercial products. They cry out, 'Take me home – give me a place to live!' and unless the message becomes embedded in the lives of the hearers, it will never leave the four walls of the church. The issue is: what enables hearers to be carried away by what they hear?

Most of us are somewhat familiar with the rich heritage of Black preaching in America, and one of the benefits of my having lived in Atlanta was to hear many fine practitioners of that tradition. As you well know, Black preachers are not half-hearted about their task. They are fully immersed in their message, and they bring the assembly along for the swim. Go to Antioch Baptist North, Big Bethel A.M.E. Zion, or any of a score of other Atlanta churches, and the vocal responses, the bodily movements, the whole tension of the place resonates with the sense that preacher and message and hearers are one. Now, it would be foolish and impossible for someone like me, whose very being is characterized by a kind of boundless restraint, to try to imitate such preaching. But whenever I've attended such churches, I find myself wondering: How do they do it? How do they build such solidarity?

My tentative conclusion is a musical one. Black preachers are masters at knowing the 'songs' of their listeners. Their preaching matches the tempo of the assembly and is pitched in the same key. The hearers are easily able to incorporate into their pre-existing repertoire the new melody the preacher is singing to them. Such a feat means hard work for the preacher. It requires knowing in advance the themes and variations in the lives of one's hearers, and then, just as important, not being tone-deaf to them in the proclamation.

This is what Elizabeth Schüssler-Fiorenza means when she says that preaching must attend to the experience of the *hearers* – a seemingly obvious point that is, nonetheless, generally ignored.[6] How easy it is for us to preach out of our own experience, imagining that it is everyone's instead of the socially-located, historically-situated, caste-bound one that it really is. When we universalize our experience as if it were the key signature of all our hearers, we deny both the limitations of our voice and the repertoire of our hearers. *And we need those hearers!* If the message we sing is ever to leave the confines of the church, it must be borne through the lives and voices of those who hear it, who may sing it quite differently than we would, but in ways perhaps more appropriate to the world than we might ever imagine.

Make no mistake about the ability of our hearers to detect whether we know their songs. In a thousand subtle ways we telegraph to them our respect of their experiences or lack thereof. Forty years ago, Walker Gibson, speaking of literature, made the distinction between the 'real reader' of a text, the flesh-and-blood person holding onto the book, and the 'mock reader', the one imagined by the author and signalled by various devices in the prose. We find this all the time in, say, movie reviews. Through tone of voice and vocabulary and inside jokes, the reviewer tries to build an alliance with the mock reader that whispers, 'You and I both know what trash "Batman Returns" really is and how we'd much rather be at a Fassbinder film festival.' Gibson remarked that what makes such writing good or bad in the mind of the real reader is whether or not that person wants to become the mock reader addressed by the author, to put on that mask and play that role. In the case of the movie review, it is the difference between liking the review because you aspire to be the kind of person who could enjoy films by Fassbinder (whether or not you really do), or hating it because it seems aimed at a bunch of high-brow artsy snobs.[7]

Our preaching is not immune from these issues. Our 'real hearers', the flesh-and-blood folks in the pew, are quite adept at discerning who our 'mock hearers' are, and whether or not they want to play that role. We have all heard well-meaning preachers who seem addicted to using illustrations in which, with apologies to Garrison Keillor, all the women are ditzy, all the men are heroes, and all the children are just props, every last one of 'em. Parishioners are not stupid about the subtext of such entertainment. And after most of the women and children (and, I suspect, some of the men) have left or tuned out, who will remain? Obviously, those who *like* the 'mock hearer' portrayed, who want to play that role and adopt its values, and never leave a safe church that so reinforces them.

Let us be clear about it: to project our hearers in such a way is a political act. We are deciding to form a certain kind of community, a fellowship of the like-minded committed to the gospel of the status quo, motionless and inert. But the message we are called to preach has, as I have suggested, a centrifugal trajectory that resists such totalizing closure. Just as the canon remembers a variety of stories concerning the faith, our preaching is to be sensitive to the variety of hearers who will complete those stories, each in their own way. Hearers discover in such preaching the many different roles of discipleship open to them and which of these they are able, through Christ, to adopt.

Preaching that so attends to its hearers is rooted in a particular kind of anthropology: a *rhetorical* anthropology. Rhetoric claims that people can he persuaded by words. This assumes, in turn, that what is central to human psychology is not cool, rational intellect, but the affections, the emotive aspect which words can move and transform. Luther, who himself received an extensive humanist training in rhetoric,[8] agreed that we are, at heart, hearers and bearers of words. This is true not simply because human life is swimming in a sea of language, but also because such life is called into being by a divine word.

But in accepting much of rhetorical anthropology, Luther gave it a unique twist through his doctrine of sin. If the core of our being is emotive, it is a core prone to utter corruption. In fact, our corrupt emotions cannot even see themselves as such, let alone free themselves from that tendency. What is required to move us out of this state is something from outside ourselves, a word that can reach into that corrupt core to move and transform it. That word, for Luther, was the gospel.

As preachers in Luther's tradition, these thoughts have profound implications for how we understand our hearers. Those who gather each Sunday are not rocks or boards or dense lumps of protoplasm. They are, by nature, *moveable*. What is more, they are moveable by *words*, subject to persuasion for good or for ill. The question for us becomes: which way are they going, and what word will make a difference? My contention is that proclaiming God's diverse gospel not only respects the diversity of our hearers, but also is able to set them free, get them in motion again, affect their trajectory, and drive them from the church in hope.

By introducing the topic of rhetoric, I am of course thinking about more than just our message or our hearers. I am also pointing to the role of the speaker.

Ancient handbooks on classical rhetoric recognized that different occasions implied different persuasive aims and therefore different types of speech. One of these types of speech was called 'epideictic'. The purpose of such rhetoric was to praise some person or event or, in other cases, to offer critique and blame.[9] Examples include speeches at festivals, imperial birthdays, commemorations, and the like. Early generations of Christian theologians, themselves trained in rhetoric, immediately recognized that sermons belonged to this epideictic genre.

Epideictic rhetoric has a strongly political and moral cast to it. While it doesn't attempt directly to change society, it moves more subtly to influence the virtues of its hearers. Epideictic always starts from the position that the speaker and hearers share certain basic values, and then it builds from there by lauding one figure or castigating another, until there is a unified and strengthened adherence to a particular moral outlook.[10] If I want to reinforce the virtue of selfless service, I could invoke the memory of a beloved figure who sacrificed everything for others, while scoffing at a notoriously greedy character who brought us to the edge of ruin. The basic value is made concrete, the hearers desire to share it, and my purpose is achieved. The links to Christian homiletics – and potential risks – are fairly obvious.

What is important for our purposes here is that epideictic rhetoric places special demands upon the speaker. The basic strategy of epideictic is one of *imitation*. The hearers are to imitate the figures or events extolled through the message. But what is more, they will only do so if they sense some congruity between that message and the speaker. In a significant way, the speaker, too, becomes an object of imitation, one who bears the very values being proclaimed.[11] This is why, five times over in the undisputed Pauline corpus, we hear St Paul boldly declare, 'Become imitators of me'. It's not so much that Paul was arrogant (though he may well have been) as that he recognized the epideictic nature of his message, and that his own ministry must point to the cross as surely as did his words.

What's all this got to do with preaching that drives people from the church? Just this: our hearers simply will not go where our message leads if we aren't willing to go there ourselves. What can it mean to our parishioners when we claim the centrifugal direction of the gospel, only to remain behind at the doors of the church waving, 'Have a nice trip! Be careful out there!' I guarantee you, they will grasp that message and draw the appropriate conclusions. 'Faith in the world is impossible', they will think, 'Abandon hope, all ye who venture forth.'

I do not wish to lay further burdens upon an already overburdened job. I, too, would resist the tendency of some to lay the responsibility for every ecclesial task at the feet of the clergy. I am not suggesting that we need to be models of perfection for our members – although a little virtue now and again wouldn't hurt. The issue for me is not that we try to do the impossible, but to show what is *doable* – that the faith *can* be lived in and for the world, that the gospel *can* be proclaimed in simple words and humble deeds. It is neither beyond the reach of our hearers, nor of us.

When I lived in Alaska, I sometimes traveled by small plane between remote Lutheran parishes on the Seward Peninsula. One winter as I flew between Teller and Brevig Mission, I looked down and saw the path made in the snow by dog sleds and snow machines travelling the ten miles between the two villages. And next to that path, I could see, evenly-spaced at intervals of thirty feet, six-foot long branches pounded into the ice. On a crystal clear day flying at five hundred feet, it all seemed kind of silly: why mark a trail that was so easy to spot? But of course, it's an entirely different story when you're on the ground and it's 35 below with whiteout conditions. Then those sticks are a matter of life and death. They provide a message of reassurance: 'You are not lost – someone has come this way before you, the way is passable, and your destination is just ahead.'

It seems to me that the role we have as speakers is just this straightforward and unmysterious. It is to declare through our ordinary lives that the faith is doable and the gospel can make a difference in the world, not simply in the church. And we are not the first to be given such an opportunity. Ancient hagiographies and martyrologies presented the lives of saints and martyrs as ones to be followed, not because they were people who were bigger-than-life, but precisely because they were ordinary folks whom God had made extraordinary. Did not our own models, our grandparents and parents and teachers and, yes, even pastors, offer a similar image for us? As speakers who bear God's word of mercy and grace, we must be borne away by the same centrifugal message we announce to our hearers. And who knows – as we, too, are driven from the church, we may well find our hearers out there already, far ahead of us and waiting for us to catch up.

Together in these pages, we have indulged in a little dream about preaching. It is a preaching attuned to its *message*: surprising us with something new we would not otherwise hear, knocking us off balance, propelling us into the world. It is a preaching attuned to its *hearers*: people who bear stories of their own but who are willing to be moved by a new story and complete it in their own lives. And, it is a preaching attuned to its *speakers*: those who believe that the efficacy of the gospel applies not only to the gathered, but also to themselves. Perhaps this dream has some reality to it. Maybe by attending to our message and our hearers and even ourselves, we will actually manage to drive people from the church. But then, I fear, something yet more strange may happen – *they'll be back*. Worse still, they may even *like* the preaching, answering our words with admiration and acclamation and, God forbid, even applause. I suppose there could be a worse fate.

Even old Chrysostom, with whom we began this dream long ago, had to admit that his pride swelled along with the size of the crowds. In a homily quite fittingly on the first verse of John's Gospel, he seemed downright benevolent toward those who came to hear him.

For your manner of running together, for your attentive postures, for the shoving of one another in your eagerness to get the inner places where my voice may more clearly be heard by you, for your unwillingness to retire from the press until this spiritual assembly be dissolved, for the clapping of hands, for the murmurs of applause; in a word, for all things of this kind which may be considered proofs of the fervor of your souls and of your desire to hear – on this point, it is superfluous to exhort you.

But that was not enough for Chrysostom. He concludes:

One thing, however, it is necessary for us to bid and entreat, that you continue to have the same zeal and manifest it not here only, but also when you are at home. Converse husband with wife, parent with child concerning these matters. Speak first of your own thoughts. and then ask for those of others, and in this way, all of you shall contribute to this excellent feast.[12]

Notes

1   *Homilies on Romans*, 15.

2   *Homilies on the Acts of the Apostles*, 30.

3   John L. Austin, *How to Do Things with Words*, New York, Oxford University Press, 1962.

4   Mary Louise Pratt, *Toward a Speech Act Theory of Literary Discourse*, Bloomington, IN, University of Indiana Press, 1977, p. 136.

5   Wolfgang Iser, *The Act of Reading: A Theory of Aesthetic Response*, Baltimore, Johns Hopkins University Press, 1978, pp. 225–31.

6   Elizabeth Schüssler-Fiorenza, 'Response' [to Walter J. Burghardt, SJ, 'From Study to Proclamation'], in *A New Look at Preaching,* ed. John Burke, OP, *Good News Studies*, 7 (Wilmington, DE, Michael Glazier, 1983), pp. 44–9.

7   Walker Gibson, 'Authors, Speakers, Readers, and Mock Readers', *College English*, 11, February 1950, pp. 265–9.

8   Helmar Junghans, *Der junge Luther und die Humanisten*, Göttingen, Vandenhoeck and Ruprecht, 1985. Cf. also Ulrich Nembach, *Predigt des Evangeliums: Luther als Prediger, Pädagogue, und Rhetor*, Neukirchen-Vluyn, Neukirchener Verlag, 1972.

9   Aristotle, *Rhetoric*, 1.3–14.

10 Ch. Perelman and L. Olbrechts-Tyteca, *The New Rhetoric: A Treatise on Argumentation,* trans. John Wilkinson and Purcell Weaver, Notre Dame, IN, University of Notre Dame Press, 1969, p. 50.

11 Benjamin Fiore, *The Function of Personal Examples in the Socratic and Pastoral Epistle,* Analecta Biblica 105, Rome, Biblical Institute Press, 1986, pp. 34–9.

12 *Homilies on the Gospel of John*, 3.

28   The Measurement of the Effect of Preaching and Preaching Plus Small Group Dialogue in One Baptist Church*

Dennis L. Price
W. Robert Terry
B. Conrad Johnston

Introduction

Thousands of Protestant preachers deliver sermons week after week in worship centers throughout the world. These deliveries usually constitute the central feature of a worship service. The aim of preaching, Davis (1958) states, is to win from people a response to the gospel, a response of attitude, impulse, and thought. There has been little scientific research, however, into the measureable effects of preaching on a listener.

The purpose of this research was to investigate and compare the effects of preaching, and the effects of preaching supplemented by dialogue in small groups, on a listener's knowledge, behavior, and attitudes. Many advocates of both preaching and preaching supplemented by small group dialogue maintain that these means of communication have unique characteristics when occurring in religious settings.

Preaching

The role and importance of preaching are discussed by Hall (1971), Fant (1975), Davis (1958) and Hinson (1967) among many others. Fant (1975) developed a method of sermon preparation and delivery he calls 'oral proclamation'. This method avoids delivery from written manuscripts, relying instead upon a carefully prepared sermon brief as the basis for oral proclamation. Chevis Horne (1975) emphasizes that preaching is also done by the preacher's body, voice, and signs and is not limited simply to the spoken word.

Theorizing on the dynamics of preaching often involves theology and mysticism. Horne (1975) states that a preacher becomes more than a creator of the power to persuade; he becomes a channel of power. Davis (1958) asserts that the best sermon is the very embodiment within the proclaimer of a truth brought from God. Bultmann (1948) states that the redemptive event is only present in the word of preaching, and he says that preaching is a unique kind of communication. This mysticism has been labeled 'incarnational preaching' (Horne, 1975). These concepts were endorsed by the preacher who delivered the message used in this research.

* This research was completed in partial fulfillment of the requirements for B. Conrad Johnston's doctor of ministries degree from Southeastern Baptist Theological Seminary, Wake Forest, North Carolina, under the committee chairmanship of Robert D. Dale. The support of Dr. Dale for this project is gratefully acknowledged.

255

Small group dialogue

There is a prevailing question about the importance of small group dialogue related to the sermon. Edge (1975) advocates holding small group talk-back sessions after the sermons have been presented, to maximize their effectiveness. Clemons and Hester (1974) state that such 'small groups are a calling . . . to a lifestyle change in persons and churches. . . . The group members minister to each other. . . . They facilitate change and growth.'

Drakeford (1974) defines a type of sharing group compatible with 'oral proclamation' and 'incarnational preaching' which he calls 'Experiential Bible Study'. The group shares a commitment to action. It tries to help each member decide what to do with the truths encountered in the study. The individuals in the group can confront one another with proposed changes in knowledge, behavior, and attitude, consistent with the material under study.

Methodological concerns for this study

Typically a study such as this type compares pre-test results with post-test results. The threats to the validity of such comparisons, as described by Campbell and Stanley (1963), include: the passage of time effect; pre-test treatment interaction; pre-test–post-test interaction; construct validity; and statistical conclusion validity. To evaluate some of these threats, an adaptation of Solomon's Four Group experimental design was used (Issac & Michael, 1971). In addition, attitudinal and behavioral measurements in this study used methodology previously established and evaluated: the Semantic Differential Technique for attitude measurement as investigated by Tannenbaum (in Snider & Osgood, 1969); the use of a forced choice, self-report scale describing alternative courses of action as a measure of behavior was evaluated by Belasco (1969).

One of the primary statistical problems in this research was the use of several dependent variables taken from each subject, creating a potential experiment-wise error of the alpha level (Keppel, 1973). This was accounted for by the use of multiple analysis of variance (MANOVA) followed by analyses of variance (ANOVA). The evaluation of the metric properties of the Semantic Differential scales performed by Snider and Osgood (1969) supports the legitimacy of this approach.

Method

Independent variables

There were five test instruments: the *Knowledge Test*; *Behavior Test*; *Myself as a Worshipper Evaluation*; *My Pastor Evaluation*; and the *Semantic Differential Test*. The instruments are described below.

Knowledge Test. This test included thirty multiple choice questions. Three questions were used for each of the ten doctrines. The questions asked were specific to points given in a sermon. Here is an example:

> Paul says that the Christian faith is all vain if (A) the Bible is not all true, (B) Christ was not crucified for man's sin, (C) Christ was not resurrected bodily, (D) Jesus was not the Son of God.

It was anticipated that listeners to the sermon of the Resurrection would mark 'C', but that some might select some other alternative before being provided the information given in the sermon and discussed in the related dialogue session.

Pseudo-Behavior Test. Twenty different situational scenarios with four possible behavior responses for each scenario were used. The respondents' task was to select the response which most closely conformed to the action they envisioned that they would take in real life, given that situation. The following is a sample item:

> If you decided you wished to pursue a program of personal, spiritual growth, what would you be more likely to do? (A) Study a well-recommended book on Christian growth. (B) Join a Christian personal growth group. (C) Join a group studying one of the gospels. (D) Attend church more often.

It was anticipated that preferred action would be shifted to the 'correct' response, as emphasized in one of the series sermons.

Myself as a Worshipper. This test contained ten semantic differential scales to evaluate one's self as a worshipper. This is shown in Figure 1. There were no preconceived ideas about the treatment effect on this measure.

My Pastor. This test contained fifteen semantic differential scales for evaluating the pastor. These were similar to those shown in Figure 1. There were no preconceived ideas about the effect of the treatment on this measure.

Semantic Differential Test. This test had thirty topics; three topics were associated with each doctrine (see Table 1). Each topic had thirty-nine semantic differential scales (see Figure 2). These scales were in accordance with the semantic differential factors of evaluation (the first nineteen scales in Figure 2), potency (the next twelve scales), and activity (the last eight scales) as defined in Snider and Osgood (1969). These scales provide the operational definition of 'attitudes' for this research. It was anticipated that because the theories of the dynamics of preaching, discussed earlier, emphasize 'power', 'truth brought from God', and the action of the preacher's body, voice, signs, and words, some changes in the Semantic Differential factors of potency, evaluation, and activity would occur.

These test instruments were given to 19 subjects, aged 35–58, in a small validation study. Nine of these subjects were clergymen, ten were laity. This preliminary study resulted in minor changes to the instruments or to the instructions.

FIGURE 1
MYSELF AS WORSHIPPER

Myself as Worshipper

PRODUCTIVE	:	:	:	:	:	:	UNPRODUCTIVE
EFFICIENT	:	:	:	:	:	:	INEFFICIENT
RELIABLE	:	:	:	:	:	:	UNRELIABLE
ATTENTIVE	:	:	:	:	:	:	INATTENTIVE
USEFUL	:	:	:	:	:	:	USELESS
COMPETENT	:	:	:	:	:	:	INCOMPETENT
EFFECTIVE	:	:	:	:	:	:	INEFFECTIVE
FAST	:	:	:	:	:	:	SLOW
ACTIVE	:	:	:	:	:	:	PASSIVE
SKILLFUL	:	:	:	:	:	:	BUNGLING

TABLE 1

TOPIC STATEMENTS ASSOCIATED WITH THE SEMANTIC DIFFERENTIAL

(see Figure 2)

1. My own knowledge of the Doctrine of Scripture
2. The practicality of the Bible
3. Daily Bible study

4. My own knowledge of the Doctrine of the Holy Spirit
5. Indwelling of the Holy Spirit
6. The Holy Spirit's help with your sin

7. My own knowledge of the Doctrine of the Father
8. Father
9. God the Father is knowable

10. My own knowledge of the Doctrine of Christ
11. Christ as the Word
12. Christ is good

13. My own knowledge of the Doctrine of the Church
14. Church as a covenant community
15. Laymen in the church

16. My own knowledge of the Doctrine of Man
17. Man, a part of God
18. Adam

19. My own knowledge of the Doctrine of Salvation
20. Repentance
21. Conversion

22. My own knowledge of the Doctrine of Sin
23. Sin
24. Death

25. My own knowledge of the Doctrine of Worship
26. Praise
27. Preaching

28. My own knowledge of the Doctrine of Last Things
29. Life after life
30. The sleep of death

Subjects

Eighty-two subjects, aged 18 to 75, were randomly selected from the 1200 members of Salem Baptist Church, Salem, Virginia. Both males and females were included.

The experimental design is shown in Table 2. Each subject was randomly assigned to one of six groups. A 'yes' in a column indicates that group received the conditions identified for that row. A 'no' indicates they did not. The six groups were divided by three general conditions: control (1 & 2), preaching only (3 & 4), and preaching and dialogue (5 & 6). The first group listed for each pair received the pre-tests for each instrument; the second did not.

FIGURE 2
SEMANTIC DIFFERENTIAL INSTRUMENT

(A TOPIC STATEMENT WAS PLACED HERE)

GOOD	:	:	:	:	:	:	BAD
BEAUTIFUL	:	:	:	:	:	:	UGLY
SOUR	:	:	:	:	:	:	SWEET
CLEAN	:	:	:	:	:	:	DIRTY
DISTASTEFUL	:	:	:	:	:	:	TASTY
VALUABLE	:	:	:	:	:	:	WORTHLESS
KIND	:	:	:	:	:	:	CRUEL
PLEASANT	:	:	:	:	:	:	UNPLEASANT
BITTER	:	:	:	:	:	:	SWEET
HAPPY	:	:	:	:	:	:	SAD
PROFANE	:	:	:	:	:	:	SACRED
NICE	:	:	:	:	:	:	AWFUL
FRAGRANT	:	:	:	:	:	:	FOUL
DISHONEST	:	:	:	:	:	:	HONEST
FAIR	:	:	:	:	:	:	UNFAIR
RICH	:	:	:	:	:	:	POOR
CLEAR	:	:	:	:	:	:	HAZY
STALE	:	:	:	:	:	:	FRESH
SICK	:	:	:	:	:	:	HEALTHY
LARGE	:	:	:	:	:	:	SMALL
WEAK	:	:	:	:	:	:	STRONG
LIGHT	:	:	:	:	:	:	HEAVY
THICK	:	:	:	:	:	:	THIN
HARD	:	:	:	:	:	:	SOFT
SOFT	:	:	:	:	:	:	LOUD
SHALLOW	:	:	:	:	:	:	DEEP
COWARDLY	:	:	:	:	:	:	BRAVE
BASS	:	:	:	:	:	:	TREBLE

[CONTINUED

FIGURE 2
SEMANTIC DIFFERENTIAL INSTRUMENT (CONCLUDED)

ROUGH	: : : : : :	SMOOTH
DELICATE	: : : : : :	RUGGED
WIDE	: : : : : :	NARROW
SLOW	: : : : : :	FAST
ACTIVE	: : : : : :	PASSIVE
COLD	: : : : : :	HOT
SHARP	: : : : : :	DULL
ROUNDED	: : : : : :	ANGULAR
RED	: : : : : :	GREEN
FEROCIOUS	: : : : : :	PEACEFUL
TENSE	: : : : : :	RELAXED

The control groups attended church Sunday morning but did not go into the worship service. Instead, they assembled in another building where they received a series of ten lectures on safety in the home and business, presented by a university professor. They were instructed to avoid any discussion with anyone about the morning worship services during the research project. They were also advised that their Christian service as control group members was essential to the success of the project.

The P groups attended the morning worship services during the experimental period and heard the sermons. The PD groups heard the sermons and attended the Sunday evening small group meetings to discuss the morning message. These meetings were attended only by PD group members.

All groups received post-tests for each instrument.

Analysis

The analytic procedure for each dependent variable was as follows:

1. A multiple analysis of variance (MANOVA) was performed for all group comparisons of the scores of interest.

TABLE 2
RESEARCH PARADIGM GROUPS

Condition	Group 1	Group 2	Group 3	Group 4	Group 5	Group 6
Pre-test	yes	no	yes	no	yes	no
Preaching Only	no	no	yes	yes	no	no
Preaching and Dialogue	no	no	no	no	yes	yes
Post-test	yes	yes	yes	yes	yes	yes

2. If the MANOVA was significant, individual analyses of variance were performed for each comparison.

The SAS GLM procedure (Barr, *et al.*, 1976) was used.

For example, if Groups 1 and 2 were being compared for the Semantic Differential Test results, scores from all thirty-nine scales from each group were evaluated by the SAS GLM MANOVA test criteria for the hypothesis of no overall treatment effect. If a treatment effect existed at $\alpha = .05$, or less, then the ANOVA comparisons for each scale were examined to determine where the treatment effects were located. The magnitude and direction of the significant differences ($p < .05$) were then identified by the Duncan's Range Test.

Results

Passage of time effect

The passage of time effect was evaluated for two instruments: the Knowledge Test and the Behavior Test. This was accomplished by comparing the pre-test scores for Group 1 with the post-test scores for Group 2. These instruments were thought to be the most susceptible to this contaminant, so when this effect did not occur with them, other instruments were not examined.

Pre-test – post-test interaction

If Group 1 post-test scores were higher than Group 2 post-test scores, the difference might be attributable to a pre-test – post-test interaction. This did not occur.

Pre-test – treatment interaction

If Group 3 post-test scores were higher than Group 4 post-test scores, and Group 5 higher than Group 6, then a pre-test – treatment interaction might exist. There was no evidence that this threat to validity existed.

The effect of preaching (P)

If there was a P effect, Group 3 and 4 should score significantly higher than Groups 1 and 2.

Knowledge Test. No significant differences existed in the post-test knowledge scores of Groups 1 compared with 3, or 2 with 4.

Behavior Test. No significant differences existed in the post-test knowledge scores of Groups 1 compared with 3, or 2 with 4.

Myself as a Worshipper. No significant differences were found between Groups 1 compared with 3, or 2 with 4.

My Pastor. One scale out of fifteen showed a significant difference in group 2 compared with 4 ($p = 0.034$).

Semantic Differential Test. The effect of preaching was examined by sermon topics for semantic differential scores. These results are shown in Table 3. Each set of scales were totaled for each factor, and Groups 3 and 4 scores were combined, as were Groups 1 and 2 scores. If 3 and 4 were shown greater than 1 and 2, a preaching effect might be assumed. It is evident that the sermons on the doctrines of Scripture, Salvation, Sin, Worship, and Last Things demonstrate a preaching effect for the Semantic Differential scores. The potency factor showed a preaching effect on all but two sermons. The activity factor was the least responsive to the treatment.

The effect of preaching and group dialogue (PD)

If there was a PD effect, Groups 5 and 6 should score higher than Groups 1 and 2.

Knowledge Test. A significant PD effect was shown by the scores of Group 5 compared with Group 1 ($p = 0.037$) but not Group 6 compared with Group 2 ($p = 0.11$).

Behavior Test. No significant effect.

Myself as a Worshipper. Group 5 scores showed a significant effect on 3 of the ten scales on this test when compared with Group 1 scores. Group 6 was not significantly different from Group 2.

My Pastor. Group 5 scores were not significantly different from Group 1 scores. Group 2 scores were significantly higher than Group 6 scores on 4 of the fifteen scales. (This, of course, is not in the expected direction for a treatment effect.)

Semantic Differential. This treatment effect was analysed in the same way that the P effect Semantic Differential scores were. The results are shown in Table 4 and are very similar to those contained in Table 3.

P compared with PD

If preaching complemented by small group dialogue is more effective than preaching alone, Groups 5 and 6 should score higher than Groups 3 and 4.

Knowledge Test. There was a significant difference in knowledge test scores for Group 5 compared with Group 3 ($p = 0.006$) with Group 5 scoring higher. Group 6 also scored higher than Group 4 ($p = 0.04$).

Behavior Test. There were no significant P/PD differences on this test.

Myself as a Worshipper. There were no significant P/PD differences.

TABLE 3

SEMANTIC DIFFERENTIAL GROUP RESULTS FOR PREACHING (P) EFFECTS

Sermon Topic	Semantic Differential Factor		
	Evaluation	Potency	Activity
Scripture	3&4 > 1&2	3&4 > 1&2	NS*
Father	1&2 > 3&4	3&4 > 1&2	NS
Christ	1&2 > 3&4	NS	NS
Holy Spirit	1&2 > 3&4	3&4 > 1&2	NS
Church	NS	3&4 > 1&2	NS
Man	NS	3&4 > 1&2	1&2 > M4
Salvation	3&4 > 1&2	3&4 > 1&2	NS
Sin	3&4 > 1&2	3&4 > 1&2	3&4 > 1&2
Worship	3&4 > 1&2	NS	NS
Last Things	3&4 > 1&2	3&4 > 1&2	3&4 > 1&2

*NS = not significant at the 0.05 level

TABLE 4

SEMANTIC DIFFERENTIAL GROUP RESULTS FOR PREACHING AND DIALOGUE (PD) EFFECTS

Sermon Topic	Evaluation	Semantic Differential Factor Potency	Activity
Scripture	NS*	5&6 > 1&2	NS
Father	1&2 > 5&6	5&6 > 1&2	5&6 > 1&2
Christ	1&2 > 5&6	NS	5&6 > 1&2
Holy Spirit	1&2 > 5&6	5&6 > 1&2	NS
Church	NS	5&6 > 1&2	NS
Man	5&6 > 1&2	5&6 > 1&2	NS
Salvation	5&6 > 1&2	5&6 > 1&2	NS
Sin	5&6 > 1&2	5&6 > 1&2	NS
Worship	5&6 > 1&2	5&6 > 1&2	NS
Last Things	5&6 > 1&2	5&6 > 1&2	NS

*NS = not significant at the 0.05 level

My Pastor. Both P/PD comparisons showed no significant differences except for one scale on each comparison.

Semantic Differential Test. For the evaluation factor, Group 5 scored higher than Group 3 on ten of nineteen scales. There was no significant difference between Group 6 and 4 on this factor.

For the potency factor, Group 5 scored higher than Group 3 on six of twelve scales. Three scales were not significant. (Reversals occurred on 3 scales.) Group 6 scored higher than 4 on 2 scales. The rest were not significant.

For the activity factor, Group 5 scored higher than Group 3 on three scales. One scale was not significant. Group 6 scored higher than Group 4 on 2 scales. Five scales were not significant.

Conclusions

1. An effect of P and PD treatments was indicated by the Semantic Differential Potency and Evaluative scales.
2. There was no clear evidence that the PD treatment resulted in improved behavior, or Semantic Differential scores when compared with the P treatment; there was, however, significant improvement of PD Knowledge scores compared with P.
3. The Semantic Differential Potency, Evaluative and Activity scales are useful instruments when evaluating the effects of preaching. Perhaps parts of an effective theory on the nature of preaching could be developed, using this instrument. This limited result is not a sufficient base for such a development.
4. The validity contaminants of passage of time effects, pre-test – post-test, interaction, and pre-test – treatment interaction were not evidenced in this study.

5. There was no clear evidence of treatment effects as measured by the Knowledge Test, Behavior Test, Myself as a Worshipper, and My Pastor instruments.
6. The Semantic Differential scales showed both P and PD treatment effects.

Discussion

If changes occurred in the congregation during these sermons, the instrument sensitive to the changes was the Semantic Differential. The sermons were prepared with specific knowledge and behavioral changes as objectives. Such knowledge and behavioral changes evidently did not occur compared with the control groups. However, there was a difference in knowledge between the treatment groups, with the preaching and dialogue group (PD) scoring higher than the preaching group (P). The subjects evidently did not perceive themselves as worshippers or their pastor as changing significantly during this ten sermon series.

It might be argued that the treatment effects were measured by the Semantic Differential. The Semantic Differential seems to indicate that something 'potent' and 'evaluative' resulted from both the P and the PD treatment groups. The sensitivity of the treatment effects shown by the potency factor might indicate an underlying sense of power accompanying the P and PD process for this particular preacher and congregation and, perhaps, supports the notion of 'power' as an element in preaching. The interpretation of this result becomes highly speculative.

This research raises many questions. It is the application of experimental methodology to an area of common human experience which rarely is examined. It suggests that the preaching task, which occurs in society regularly and usually has the goal of creating changes in personal knowledge and behavior, might not do so, at least in the short term. This study is limited in its generalizability. It demonstrates the Semantic Differential as a useful tool in investigating the religious phenomena of preaching.

References

Barr, Anthony J.; Goodnight, James H.; Sall, John P. and Helwig, Jane T., 1976, *A User's Guide to SAS 76*, Raleigh, SAS Institute.

Belasco, James A. (1968), *The Assessment of Change in Training and Therapy*, New York, McGraw-Hill.

Bultmann, Rudolf (1948), *Theologie des Neyen Testaments*, Tübingen, J. C. B. Mohr.

Campbell, Donald T. and Stanley, Julian C., Jr (1963), 'Experimental and Quasi-Experimental Designs for Research and Teaching', in N. L. Gage (ed.), *Handbook of Research on Teaching*, Chicago, Rand McNally.

Clemmons, William and Hester, Harvey (1974), *Growth through Groups*, Nashville, TN, Broadman.

Davis, H. Grady (1958), *Design for Preaching*, Philadelphia, Fortress.

Drakeford, John W. (1974), *Experiential Bible Study*, Nashville, TN, Broadman.

Edge, Findley (1975), *The Greening of the Church*, Grand Rapids, World Books.

Fant, Clyde E. (1975), *Preaching for Today*, New York, Harper & Row.

Hall, Thor (1971), *The Future Shape of Preaching*, Philadelphia, Fortress.

Hinson, E. Glenn (1967), *The Church: Design for Survival*, Nashville, TN, Broadman.

Horne, Chevis F. (1975), *Crisis in the Pulpit*, Grand Rapids, Baker Book House.

Isaac, Stephen and Michael, William B. (1971), *Handbook in Research and Evaluation*, San Diego, Edits.

Keppel, Geoffrey (1973), *Design and Analysis: A Researcher's Handbook*, Englewood Cliffs, NJ, Prentice-Hall.

Snider, James G. and Osgood, Charles E. (1969), *Semantic Differential Technique: A Sourcebook*, Chicago, Aldine.

29   The Word of God and the Words of the Preacher

William O. Avery and A. Roger Gobbel[1]

The Christian church has always declared that the Word of God is present in its preaching, meeting and confronting men and women in ordinary life. The declaration, however, does not answer a serious and difficult question: What is the relationship between the Word of God and the words of the preacher in the sermon? For both clergy and laity, much confusion exists concerning that relationship.

Even in the presence of the church's declaration, those who listen to sermons encounter two major problems. First, how does one know if the preacher is proclaiming the Word of God? Second, how does one discern between the preacher's opinions and idiosyncrasies and the Word of God? Certainly, part of the solution to the problems resides in a hearer's understanding of the nature of the Word of God. That understanding, whether specific or diffused, clear or cloudy, complex or simple is one criterion by which judgements on sermons are made. At the same time, hearers of sermons employ other criteria in judging if a sermon proclaims the Word of God. Some of those criteria may be unrelated to an understanding of the nature of the Word of God.

This paper reports on two projects which focused on two significant questions. First, how does the laity understand the relationship between the words of the preacher and the Word of God? Second, what criteria do laity use in judging if the Word of God has been proclaimed by the preacher? With a respondent group of laity, these questions were explored within three categories: (1) The Word of God, the Bible, and the sermon; (2) purpose and expectations of sermons; and, (3) role of the preacher's credibility.

The Christian church regards preaching as one of its necessary and essential tasks (Ebelin, 1963: 329; Hofinger, 1968:43: Lloyd-Jones, 1971:26; Ong, 1967:13f.; Steichen, 1972:6ff.). Current literature on preaching announces anew the church's declaration that in preaching, the Word of God is present. Even with different voices and varying emphases, the church 'considers the sermon a manifestation of the Word of God' (Hall, 1971:72). In the preaching of the church, God has chosen to make himself known, to reveal himself through the words of men and women (Babin, 1976:34).

A sermon ought to be judged on its faithfulness to the Bible. But the varied and contradictory understandings of the nature of the Bible make such a criterion almost useless. Much preaching starts in the Bible and remains in the Bible. It begins with a biblical text and, in varying ways, repeats the text time and time again. While some argue that such preaching is not biblical, it is 'attractive' preaching for many. It can 'identify' clearly the Word of God. It equates biblical language and imagery with the Word of God. It suggests that a sermon – the words of men and women – is to be judged as a proclamation of the Word of God by the presence of explicit biblical material and language. Much preaching equates the Word of God with the Bible and, thus, confines the Word of God to a document (Rice, 1970:1f.).

Again with different voices and varying emphases, the church declares that the intention of its preaching 'is to bring men to a meeting, into an encounter with God' (Rice, 1970:15). The church declares what preaching is and what men and women may expect of preaching. But, what do the laity expect and experience?

266

In the last decade, preaching increasingly has been viewed as an event of human communication, subject to the same influences in any human communication event. The task of preaching has been studied as an event of human communication (Abbey, 1973; Babin, 1976; Pennington, 1976; Sweazey, 1976). In various studies, significant attention has been focused on the hearers of sermons, regarding them as active participants in and 'creators' of the sermons they hear. The discussions of many communication theorists on the nature of meaning (Abbey, 1973:115f; Berlo, 1960:173ff; Faules and Alexander, 1978:8; Sereno and Bodaken, 1975:12f) direct attention to hearers as active interpreters of sermons. Meaning is the response and interpretation that a person gives to an event, experience, or word. Thus, meanings reside in persons and not in things, events, or words. The hearer of a sermon is actively engaged in giving meaning to what is heard (Howe, 1967:102).

It has long been assumed that some personal qualities of the preacher contribute to 'effective' preaching. In the past, much attention was devoted to such items as mannerisms, voice quality, dress, gestures, personal appearance, and delivery style of the preacher. Research on interpersonal communication has directed attention to a more crucial issue – source credibility, which includes both expertise and trustworthiness (Cohen, 1964:23ff; Pennington, 1976:73ff; Sereno and Bodaken, 1975:148ff). Sender credibility exerts a profound influence in the communication process. Credibility may be a quality in the sender, but it must be accepted and affirmed by the receiver. The credibility a sender has, in part, is a function of the receiver. It depends upon the relationship between sender and receiver. And on occasion the relationship may take precedence over and determine the interpretation of the communication's content.

The church has declared that in its preaching, the Word of God is present, meeting and confronting men and women in ordinary life. Yet, the church has offered few clear criteria for laity to judge if the Word of God has been proclaimed by the preacher in sermons. The most direct criterion has been 'faithfulness to the Bible'. That criterion, however, tends to equate the presence of biblical language and material with the Word of God, thus capturing the Word of God in an ancient document. Having few clear criteria for a necessary judgment, laity, it is suspected, will have difficulty discerning the purpose of sermons. They will not have a clear sense of what to expect of sermons. Yet, they listen to sermons and report that they find sermons helpful and useful. It may be that they impose their expectations on sermons, and through their own interpretive processes receive what they expect. At the same time, the most influential factor in the laity's response to sermons may be their relationship with their preachers. For many, it may be in that relationship they understand God to have met them.

Four hypotheses were considered in the two projects described here.

1. The laity do not possess a common set of criteria by which to judge sermons as proclamations of the Word of God, but the presence of explicit biblical material and language will be the most operative criterion for judging.

2. The laity do not have a commonly shared understanding of the purpose of preaching, but they have a variety of expectations and assert that sermons are helpful and useful.

3. The laity give meaning to sermons and reserve the 'right' to interpret sermons for themselves.

4. The credibility of the preacher, both expertise and trustworthiness, is given and affirmed by laity and is a determining factor in laity's response to sermons. Further, the laity's perceived relationship with the preacher takes precedence over what is said in sermons.

Method

Project I

The first project completed in Spring 1975 included 25 respondents, all members of a Lutheran (LCA) congregation in south central Pennsylvania. The respondents were selected by the writers as representative of age, gender, education, occupation, frequency of worship attendance, and participation in congregational life. The group included 13 males and 12 females. Ages ranged from 16 to 73; education from eighth grade to Ph.D. level.

Each participant completed a preliminary three-part questionnaire which elicited opinions regarding preaching in general: an evaluation of today's preaching, its vitality and weakness and contributing factors, the importance of the preacher's credibility; and the influence of preaching style. Only minimal use is made in this report of the data gathered in the three-part questionnaire.

Each respondent evaluated sermons of the same preacher on three consecutive Sundays. For each sermon, written responses were made to a series of seven open-ended questions. The questions included, among others, the following:

1.   What do you consider to be the central point of the sermon?
2.   Did you find any part of the sermon particularly helpful or exciting?
3.   Did you understand the sermon as the Word of God? Why or why not?
4.   What difference, if any, do you think the sermon will make in your behavior or opinions?
5.   In your opinion, was the sermon worth saying?

The written responses were evaluated by content analysis.

Project II

The second project, more extensive than the first but utilizing its findings, was completed in Spring, 1977. The first project identified two criteria used by laity to judge if a sermon is the Word of God: the presence of explicit biblical material and the personal qualities of the preacher. The second project explored in greater detail the laity's use of those criteria, while asking if other criteria are used. Also, laity's identification of the Bible with the Word of God, and their understanding of the relationship between the Word of God and the words of the preacher, required closer examination and clarification.

The respondents included 56 persons, members of two Lutheran (LCA) congregations in south-central Pennsylvania. The group was obtained by selecting every twelfth person on the confirmed membership roll of one congregation and every ninth person in the other. In one congregation, 71 percent of those selected participated; in the other, 72 percent. Twenty-eight persons from each congregation participated. There were 29 females and 27 males. Ages ranged from late teens to over 65 years; educational level from completion of grade school to graduate degrees. The information was obtained from a personal data sheet completed by each participant.

From an original 75 items, and with advice of an external evaluator, the writers devised a 45-item instrument which each participant completed, responding on the scale: strongly agree, agree, don't know, disagree and strongly disagree. The items were designed to focus on four issues: (1) the Word of God and its relationship to the Bible and the words of the preacher; (2) purpose and expectations of sermons; (3) humanness of the pastor; and (4) trustworthiness of the pastor.

Responses of 'strongly agree' and 'agree', as well as 'strongly disagree' and 'disagree', were considered equal. Percentages of responses for 'agree', 'disagree' and 'don't know' were calculated for questions or for clusters of questions as stated in the findings. Thus, in this discussion, we report 'trends' or 'tendencies' or 'percentages' or 'majorities'.

Findings

The Word of God, the Bible, and sermons

Project I focused on laity's understanding of the relationship between the Word of God and the sermon. To the question, 'Did you understand the sermon as the Word of God? Why or why not?' responses clustered around two foci: the Bible and the personal qualities of the preacher. There was the overwhelming tendency to identify the Word of God with the Bible. Sermons were judged to be the Word of God if explicit biblical material was present.

The following illustrate the large majority of responses. 'Yes, both main parts were taken from the Bible.' 'Yes, the message was based on the actions of Jesus in order to explain how we should act.' 'Not really, I felt that the sermon was not Bible-based.' 'Yes, but it was implied. God's Word was not read or used directly.' 'Less so than when there are more biblical quotes and passages used in sermons.'

There was the strong suggestion that the more biblical quotes and overt biblical references present, the more the sermon was judged to be the Word of God. There was a tendency toward a one-to-one correspondence between the Bible and the Word of God. Although the personal qualities of the preacher were used as a criterion by some laity, the clearest and most operative criterion was the presence of explicit biblical material.

The results of the second project, congruent with those of the first, revealed the tendency on the part of laity to identify the Word of God with the Bible. More than 80 percent of the respondents agreed that their clergy 'preaches the Bible'. A slightly higher percentage judged that their clergy 'is preaching the Word of God.' These two items, coupled with others to be discussed in a moment, indicate a close identification of the Word of God with the Bible. And as in the first project, laity judge that they have heard the Word of God when they have heard explicit biblical material and language.

Over 80 percent agreed that the minister 'is the congregation's expert in Bible and matters of faith', and that they 'expect and welcome sermons which confront me with the demands of the Gospel'. But when there are differences between them and the clergy, less than half of the respondents agreed that the 'pastor's opinion is most likely to be correct on the Bible and matters of faith.' Slightly more than one-fourth asserted that their opinions 'about things in the Bible is just as good as the pastor's'. Interestingly, 63 percent of the male respondents expected the clergy to tell them what to believe, whereas only 23 percent of the females had that expectation.

While affirming that their clergy preach the Bible, preach the Word of God, and are the congregation's expert in the Bible and matters of faith, less than half were willing to judge the clergy's opinion on the Bible and matters of faith as 'most likely correct' when there are differences. A particular dynamic appears to be at work here. Laity claim the right to make their own judgments and interpretations about the Bible and matters of faith. When there are differences, laity tend to rely on their individual, private judgments rather than the opinions of the clergy.

On what, then, is the minister an expert? It appears that the minister is regarded as an expert on the 'facts' of the Bible. But in the interpretation of what these may imply for ordinary life, the minister has no insight which the laity lack. Thus, the expertise of the clergy may be rather narrowly defined. At the same time, there is the suggestion that the narrowly defined area of expertise is identified with what the Bible is and, thus, with what the Word of God is. If this is an appropriate interpretation of the data, the Word of God is interpreted as facts and information in the Bible. Thus, the Word of God is viewed as fixed in the past.

Purpose and expectations of sermons

In Project I, a large majority of respondents expressed positive attitudes toward the preaching event, regarding it as an essential element for Christian life. However, at no point in the project did respondents specify that essentiality. At the same time, there was the clear assertion that preaching is losing its vitality today, not making an impact on individual lives or on the life of the world. There was no articulated description of what 'vitality' and 'impact' might entail.

Participants tended to blame themselves for the weakness of preaching. They suggested a lack of 'something' in their listening, a lack which weakens the impact of preaching on their lives. Yet, not one respondent attempted to identify that lack. They blamed themselves and not the preacher. Are laity so convinced that sermons are supposed to be helpful that they are willing to blame themselves when helpfulness is not experienced?

There was a pervasive lack of clarity and consistency concerning the purpose of the preaching task. Some respondents indicated that they expected 'very little' to happen to them as a result of preaching. Others, in rather general ways, hoped that the preaching event would enable them 'to be a better Christian' or 'to be more patient' or 'to love my neighbor more'. It appears that some undefined behavior change might be expected as a result of hearing sermons. Still, the respondents did not listen to preaching with the expectation that sermons would have clear and definable effects in their lives.

In the second project a cluster of items focused upon parishioners' expectations of sermons. More than 75 percent responded that the 'hearing of sermons' was essential to their Christian growth. Though the particular item was cast in broad terms, the response denoted a positive attitude toward preaching. Further, the laity did expect that sermons would have some effect upon their lives, even if the expectations were ill-defined.

As instrument items gave greater specificity to expectations, responses became mixed and revealed few shared expectations. Approximately 60 percent regarded the sermon as 'a primary source of comfort'. Slightly more than 44 percent agreed that sermons should make persons feel guilty for wrongdoings. But at the same time, only 10 percent agreed that 'more judgment' should be announced in sermons. Only 66 percent agreed with the statement, 'A major function of sermons is to proclaim God's love and acceptance of the sinner, the rejected, even liars and murderers.' Finally, 55 percent agreed that sermons should be spiritually satisfying rather than intellectually stimulating.

In still another direction, 88 percent disagreed that, 'A minister's sermons should stick to the Bible and only the Bible, and not discuss such matters as solutions for poverty, political issues and social problems.' In the presence of such a broad statement, laity did not wish to restrict the content of sermons. But as greater specificity was given to the range of content and subject matter, responses became more diffuse.

Slightly more than 77 percent agreed that they 'expect and welcome' sermons which confront them with the demands of the Gospel. Approximately 55 percent wanted the clergy to preach 'openly and freely' on such subjects as 'draft resisters, war, capital punishment, public education, sex and behavior of public officials'. Only 42 percent wanted the clergy to confront them with the 'political implications' of the Gospel. While asserting, on the one hand, that the clergy should not be restricted concerning subject matter for sermons, the respondents tended, on the other hand, to be restrictive as they expressed their 'wants' and 'expectations'.

The credibility of the preacher

In both projects, the laity's perceptions of the personal qualities of the preacher were critical criteria for the judgments they made concerning sermons. In the first project, one respondent wrote, 'My inclination, of course, is to assume that this good man is preaching the "Word of God". I know he sincerely endeavors to do so. However, I feel it would be presumptuous of me to judge whether or not in fact he does.' This respondent, illustrative of others, indicated no clear understanding of the nature of the Word of God. However, regarding the preacher as a good and sincere person, he simply assumed that the Word of God was being proclaimed.

Another respondent declared, 'I understand that the sermon was the word of the pastor but that his word was based upon education, contemplation and prayer; therefore the message is "God blessed".' The sermon remained the word of the minister. But, in some unexplained manner through some activity, quality, or characteristic of the preacher, the message – not the words – was 'God blessed'. In many responses, the personal qualities of the preacher were identified as criteria for judgments relative to sermons.

In Project II, one set of items focused directly on the pastor and his sermons. The laity affirmed that: the pastor's sermons were 'spiritually satisfying' (70 percent); his sermons 'challenge my thinking' (77 percent); the pastor in sermons 'shares with me what he believes' (93 percent); his sermons 'speak concretely and directly to the real issues of my life' (72 percent); and the faith and hope expressed in sermons 'are of great help to me in daily life' (75 percent). But responses to another item may call into question all those affirmations. Only 25 percent agreed that 'On such issues as social concerns, social action and politics, I agree with my pastor.' Slightly more than 50 percent responded 'don't know'.

Such data prompt several questions. Do the laity give careful attention to the content of sermons? Do they judge that such matters as 'social concerns, social action and politics' are outside of and unrelated to the Bible and, thus, the Word of God? Are such matters regarded as outside of the preacher's expertise and, thus, his discussions of such matters ignored? If 93 percent affirm that their pastor shares with them what he believes how can more than 50 percent assert that they 'don't know' if they agree on such issues as social concerns, social action and politics?

One explanation might be that the pastor has not discussed these issues in sermons. But what also may be at work here is the assertion that '"who" says what is just as important as "what" is said.' Perhaps the content of the pastor's interpersonal relationships with the laity is regarded more highly than the content of the sermon. Moreover, it is possible that the content and nature of those relationships is regarded by the laity as the content of the Gospel.

Clergy frequently assume the laity put them 'on a pedestal' demanding moral perfection and denying them their humanness in the sense of *simul iustus et peccator*. The results of the project clearly indicate that the vast majority of respondents did not impose the expectation of perfection on the clergy. Over 90 percent disagreed with the statement, 'If the pastor truly believes the good news, nothing will bother or upset him.' Well over 80 percent expected and accepted expressions of anger by the clergy. Only 34 percent agreed that '*How* my pastor lives his life is more important to me than *what* he says in a sermon.' There was not a demand for total congruency between *what* the clergy say and *how* they live out their lives.

However, the laity did not take a laissez-faire attitude toward the life-style of the clergy. The degree of incongruency between 'preaching' and 'practice' which would be tolerated was not explored in the project. More than 60 percent expressed the opinion that it is difficult to believe the minister if he does not 'attempt to practice what he preaches'. While not demanding congruency between 'speaking' and 'doing', the respondents expected 'attempts' at achieving congruency.

More critical than the issues of perfection and attempted congruency were the attitudes laity have toward their clergy. The nature and quality of emotional relationships between laity and clergy and laity's perceptions of how clergy regard them appeared to be the most influential factors in determining 'how' parishioners listen to sermons and what they listen to. Further, these two factors appeared to be critical criteria for judging if the Word of God has been proclaimed.

Where that relationship was positive and when laity perceived that the preacher had genuine concern for them (i.e., displaying openness and warmth, exercising and dealing kindly and seriously with their opinions), hearers assumed the Word of God was being preached. The assumption was made even though the Word of God was primarily identified with the Bible, and even though there was lack of agreement concerning the purpose of a sermon.

Almost 83 percent of respondents disagreed with the statement, 'In a minister's sermon, theological expertise and intellectual soundness are more important than warmth, friendliness or kindness.' Clearly, interpersonal relationships were more critical elements than theological expertise and intellectual soundness.

A series of items focused on the laity's perceptions of relationships with their pastor. Almost 95 percent agreed their pastor displays warmth, care and respect for others. Over 77 percent agreed that 'my minister listens carefully to me when I talk with him'. The same percentage stated they could count on their pastor 'to deal kindly and understandingly with my opinions and ways of doing things'. Over 80 percent felt they faced some difficulty or trouble, they could talk easily with the pastor, 'confidently expecting understanding and kindness from him'. Where there are differences between clergy and laity, 90 percent of respondents did 'not doubt [the pastor's] sincerity and commitment'. With the statement, 'When my pastor preaches, I feel he is not concerned with me, but only his own ideas', 86 percent disagreed. And 96 percent disagreed that 'My pastor tries to force his opinions upon the congregation, acting as if he has all the answers.'

Clearly, a large majority of respondents in the project trusted their clergy. They could count on the clergy to deal with them in consistent ways, with understanding and empathy. They expected consistent behavior on the part of their clergy toward them. There was certainty concerning relationships which have positive dimensions. Two questions emerge from these data. First, does the positive relationship function as the primary criterion in judging if the preacher proclaims the Word of God? Second, is the interpersonal relationship the 'where' or 'location' in which the Word of God meets them?

Within the project there were respondents who expressed negative relationships with their clergy. These same respondents tended to doubt that their clergy 'preach the Bible' and 'preach the Word of God'. Also, they did not regard the minister as the 'congregation's expert in Bible and matters of faith'. Further, they asserted that their opinion 'about things in the Bible is just as good as the pastor's'. They were not willing that the preacher discuss a wide range of subject matter and tended not to regard the 'hearing of sermons' as essential to their Christian growth. The perceived negative quality of clergy-laity relationships appears to have been a significant influence determining negative responses.

Conclusions

The projects reported here explored the laity's criteria for determining if the Word of God has been proclaimed in a sermon, and the relationship between the Word of God, the Bible, and the words of the preacher. Recognizing the limitations of the projects, we identify some implications and offer some conclusions.

Identification of the Word of God with the Bible

The laity identified the Bible with the Word of God and, thus, the Word of God as the Bible. Sermons which contained biblical material and language were judged to be the proclamation of the Word of God. The amount of biblical material present determined the extent to which a sermon was perceived as the Word of God. Further, the data suggest a tendency to identify the Word of God with the facts and the information of the Bible.

By implication, these data suggest that the Word of God is primarily restricted to the ancient past. With such a restricted definition, the laity have an extremely limited understanding of the Word of God as dynamic, living, ever breaking into ordinary life in new and exciting ways. One does not expect such from that which is static, belonging primarily to the past.

The need to which the projects point is neither the gathering of more facts and information from the Bible, nor the amassing of more communication skills. Rather, there is need for greater clarity concerning 'what' is to be communicated in the church's preaching. There is the need for both laity and clergy to explore in greater depth the nature and authority of the Bible and to appropriate a more dynamic understanding of the Word of God.

Expertise of the preacher

There was general agreement that the minister is the congregation's expert in the Bible and matters of faith. But the parameters of that expertise were highly restricted in the same direction that the Word of God was identified with the Bible. 'Preaching the Word of God' was defined by the presence of biblical material. The expertise of the preacher appeared to be limited to facts and information in the Bible and the contents of the Faith.

While the preacher was afforded broad freedom to discuss a wide range of subjects in sermons, the laity did not expect any particular insights or understandings about those subjects from the minister simply because of his function as proclaimer of the Word of God. The lack of such expectations may result from the tendency to restrict the Word of God to the ancient past – to the Bible. Less than half the respondents agreed that in differing *opinions* on the Bible, the minister's position is most likely to be correct. The task of the minister as proclaimer of the Word of God is understood by the laity in narrow, restrictive terms.

If the preaching task of the church is to have greater impact, the laity must come to a fuller understanding of the preacher's role. The laity need assistance in viewing the minister as not dealing merely with interesting items from the ancient past, but as one who speaks the Word of God in this day, a word that is as alive and active in this day even as it was in the ancient past.

Purpose of the sermon

Attitudes toward preaching and sermons generally were very positive. The 'hearing of sermons' was judged by a high percentage to be essential to Christian growth. In a general way, the laity had some expectations of sermons. But, in specific terms, the expectations were rather diffused and tended to focus on individual and private needs. The most commonly shared expectation was that of comfort. For many a major function of sermons was to help give clues to 'coping with life'. Frequent emphasis was on behavior.

Perhaps because of a restricted understanding of the Word of God, and the narrow area of clergy expertise, the laity may lack an understanding of what a sermon is and what its purpose is. Thus, the laity would have some difficulty in determining what they should listen for. Assuming the sermons should be helpful to them in some way, the laity tend to view the purpose of sermons in highly individualistic and personal dimensions. The results of these projects strongly suggest that renewed emphasis needs to be given to the argument that preaching is not merely the task of individual ministers, but is the task of the church, for the church.

Who interprets for whom?

Obviously, the task of the preacher is a task of interpretation. The ability of a particular minister to engage in and accomplish that task, or the quality and adequacy of a particular interpretation, is not an issue in this paper. In the second project, there was a high level of agreement on three items: (1) the minister was judged as the congregation's expert on the Bible and matters of faith; (2) laity asserted that their clergy proclaim the Word of God in sermons; and (3) laity expected to be confronted by the Word of God in the preacher's sermon. Nevertheless, both projects indicate clearly that the laity did not necessarily regard the minister's 'speaking' of the Word of God as normative nor binding for them.

Clearly, while the laity assert that the preacher must be free to speak on any issue, they do not permit the preacher to impose his interpretation on them. They do not permit the preacher to do their own personal interpretation. They reserve for themselves the 'right' to determine if the Word of God has been spoken. By some ill-defined criteria, they determine the presence of the Word. Thus, the laity are involved in their own interpretive task, and their interpretations often take precedence over those of the preacher. The laity are active interpreters of the preaching event and the significance of that event for their lives.

The findings raise some serious concerns regarding the nature and task of preaching, and certainly challenge any view of preaching as a 'hurling of the Word of God'. If the laity are active interpreters, we should regard the preaching event as an invitation which calls the laity to share in the task of interpretation. Thus, the sermon, in a major sense, is a model describing the preacher's understanding of the presence of the Word of God and inviting another to consider and explore the Word of God in new ways.

Pastor–laity interpersonal relationships

Both projects provide evidence that the laity's attitudes toward their minister determine the way in which they listen to sermons. Moreover, there is the strong suggestion that those attitudes are dominant in determining if the Word of God has been spoken in a sermon. In determining the presence of the Word of God, relationships between the minister and the laity appear to take precedence over what is said in a sermon.

Laity do not demand moral perfection of their clergy, but they do seek attempted consistency between words and action. Yet, these are not crucial items for the laity. Rather, they are far more sensitive to, and influenced by, the personal relationships they have with the pastor. When the laity perceive kindness and understanding in their minister, and that the minister has concern for them expressing openness, warmth, and empathy, they consider seriously interpretations of the Gospel which may be at variance with their own understandings. When that relationship is positive, the laity are most prone to say that their minister is 'preaching the Word of God'; they are likely to assert that the Word of God has been spoken with almost no reference to the content of a particular sermon. Where that relationship is perceived as negative, the laity quickly dismiss sermons which express understandings contrary to their own. That negative relationship becomes the occasion for doubting the presence of the Word of God in a minister's preaching without reference to the content of particular sermons.

If these findings concerning relationships are confirmed in future research, they will indicate that the relationship between laity and clergy is a dominant factor in the interpretive task of the laity. For most laity, understanding of the Word of God may be synonymous with their relationship with their pastors. The pastor's biblical and doctrinal expertise, his intellectual astuteness and competency, and the content of the sermon do not appear to be the criteria by which laity judge the presence of God in preaching.

These projects identified several areas which are marked by general confusion and disagreement which dull and negate the church's preaching. A doctrine of the nature and authority of the Bible and a theology of preaching are crucial to the church's task. But the simple announcement of these will not alter or change how persons interpret this task of the church. The laity need to be invited to a new and serious exploration of the nature of the Word of God and the Bible which can lead to a new understanding and appreciation of the church's task of preaching.

Notes

1   This article is based on the findings in *The Word of God and the Words of Men* by William O. Avery, the final project for the Doctor of Ministry degree, with A. Roger Gobbel as project director. The complete document is located in the Abdel Ross Wentz Library, Lutheran Theological Seminary, Gettysburg, Pennsylvania 17325.

References

Abbey, Merrill R. (1973), *Communication in Pulpit and Parish*, Philadelphia, Westminster.

Babin, David E. (1976), *Week In – Week Out*, New York, Seabury.

Berlo, David K. (1960), *The Process of Communication*, New York, Holt, Rinehart and Winston.

Cohen, Arthur R. (1964), *Attitude Change and Social Influence*, New York, Basic Books.

Ebeling, Gerhard (1963), *Word and Faith,* translated by James W. Leitch, Philadelphia, Fortress.

Faules, Don F. and Alexander, Dennis C. (1978), *Communication and Social Behavior: A Symbolic Interaction Perspective,* Menlo Park, Addison-Wesley Publishing Co.

Hall, Thor (1971), *The Future Shape of Preaching*, Philadelphia, Fortress.

Holfinger, Johannes (1968), *The Good News and Its Proclamation,* South Bend, IN, University of Notre Dame Press.

Howe, Reuel L. (1967), *Partners in Preaching*, New York, Seabury.

Lloyd-Jones, D. Martyn (1971), *Preaching and Preachers,* London, Hodder & Stoughton.

Ong, Walter J. (1967), *The Presence of the Word,* New Haven, CT, Yale University Press.

Pennington, Chester (1976), *God Has a Communication Problem,* New York, Hawthorn.

Rice, Charles (1970), *Interpretation and Imagination*, Philadelphia, Fortress.

Sereno, Kenneth K. and Bodaken, Edward M. (1975), *Trans-Per Understanding Human Communication,* Boston, Houghton-Mifflin.

Steichen, Alan J. (1972), 'Bultman's Theology of Preaching', *Preaching Today*, 6, 5 (September–October).

Sweazey, George E. (1976), *Preaching the Good News*, Englewood Cliffs, Prentice-Hall.

Acknowledgements

The publisher and editors would like to acknowledge the following permissions to reproduce copyright material. All possible attempts have been made to contact copyright holders and to acknowledge their copyright correctly. We are grateful to:

Reformed Liturgy and Music, for T. G. Long, 'The distance we have traveled: changing trends in preaching', 17, 11–15, 1983, and for D. G. Buttrick, 'A sketchbook: preaching and worship', 16, 33–37, 1982, and 'On preaching a parable: the problem of homiletic method', 17, 16–22, 1983; *Theology Today*, for W. Brueggemann, 'Preaching as reimagination', 52, 3, 313–329, 1995, and for E. Farley, 'Preaching the Bible and preaching the gospel', 51, 1, 90–103, 1994 (© *Theology Today*: reprinted with permission); *Interpretation*, for T. G. Long, 'The use of Scripture in contemporary preaching', 44, 4, 341–352, 1990, and for H. H. Mitchell, 'African-American preaching: the future of a rich tradition, 51, 4, 371–383 (© *Interpretation*: reprinted with permission); J. Mitchell and *Anvil*, for J. Mitchell, 'Preaching in pictures', revised and updated version of 'Preaching in an audio-visual culture', *Anvil*, 14, 4, 262–272, 1997; *Anvil*, for D. Day, 'Preaching the epistles', 14, 4, 273–282, 1997; *Journal for Preachers* (Columbia Theological Seminary, PO Box 520, Decatur, GA 30031, USA), for R. L. Eslinger, 'Story and image in sermon illustration', 9, 2, 19–23, 1986, for W. Brueggeman, 'An imaginative "or"', 23, 3, 3–17, 2000, and for R. Lischer, 'Martin Luther King, Jr's preaching as a resource for preachers', 23, 3, 18–22, 2000; *Rural Theology*, for L. J. Francis, 'Psychological type and biblical hermeneutics: SIFT method of preaching', 1, 1, 13–23, 2003 (© *Rural Theology*; reprinted with permission); *Review and Expositor*, for F. B. Craddock, 'From exegesis to sermon: 1 Corinthians 12:4–6', 80, 417–425, 1983; *Reformed Review*, for T. G. Long, 'Pawn to king four: sermon introduction and communicational design', 40, 1, 1986; *Evangel* and P. K. Stevenson, for P. K. Stevenson, 'Preaching and narrative', 17, 2, 43–48, 1999 (© P. K. Stevenson, published by Paternoster Periodicals, Carlisle); *Lexington Theological Quarterly*, for D. E. Stevenson, 'Eleven ways of preaching a non-sermon', 10, 19–28, 1975, and for J. Killinger, 'Preaching and silence', 19, 91–101, 1984; T. H. Troeger and *Worship*, for T. H. Troeger, 'Emerging new standards in the evaluation of effective preaching', 64, 4, 290–307, 1990; *Word and World*, for R. Lischer, 'Imagining a sermon', 5, 279–286, 1985, and for A. C. Reuter, 'Ethics in the pulpit', VIII, 2, 173–178, 1988; *Journal of the College of Preachers*, for D. Day, 'The Lenten preacher, 29–38, January 1999 (an abbreviated version of this article appears in S. I. Wright *et al.* (eds), *A Preacher's Companion*, Oxford, BRF, 2004); the College of Preachers, for J. A. Melloh, 'Homily or eulogy? The dilemmas of funeral preaching', *College of Preachers Fellowship Paper*, 45–50, 1998; *Journal of Women and Religion*, for V. Purvis-Smith, 'Gender and the aesthetic of preaching', 11, 74–83, 1992; *Journal of Feminist Studies*, for E. J. Lawless, 'Rescripting their lives and narratives: spiritual life stories of pentecostal women preachers', 7, 53–71, 1991; *Currents in Theology and Mission*, for J. R. Nieman, 'Preaching that drives people from the church', 20, 106–115, 1993; *Journal for the Scientific Study of Religion*, for D. L. Price, W. R. Terry and B. C. Johnston, 'The measurement of the effect of preaching and preaching plus small group dialogue in one Baptist church', 19, 186–197, 1980; *Review of Religious Research*, for W. O. Avery and A. R. Gobbel, 'The Word of God and the words of the preacher', 22, 5, 41–53, 1980 (© Religious Research Association, Inc. All rights reserved).

Index of Subjects

Index of Names

285